CONTINGENCY AND SOLIDARITY: LABOR AND ACTION IN ENGLISH COMPOSITION

PERSPECTIVES ON WRITING
Series Editors, Susan H. McLeod and Rich Rice

The Perspectives on Writing series addresses writing studies in a broad sense. Consistent with the wide ranging approaches characteristic of teaching and scholarship in writing across the curriculum, the series presents works that take divergent perspectives on working as a writer, teaching writing, administering writing programs, and studying writing in its various forms.

The WAC Clearinghouse, Colorado State University Open Press, and University Press of Colorado are collaborating so that these books will be widely available through free digital distribution and low-cost print editions. The publishers and the Series editors are committed to the principle that knowledge should freely circulate. We see the opportunities that new technologies have for further democratizing knowledge. And we see that to share the power of writing is to share the means for all to articulate their needs, interest, and learning into the great experiment of literacy.

Recent Books in the Series

Barbara J. D'Angelo, Sandra Jamieson, Barry Maid, and Janice R. Walker (Eds.), *Information Literacy: Research and Collaboration across Disciplines* (2017)

Justin Everett and Cristina Hanganu-Bresch (Eds.), *A Minefield of Dreams: Triumphs and Travails of Independent Writing Programs* (2016)

Chris M. Anson and Jessie L. Moore (Eds.), *Critical Transitions: Writing and the Questions of Transfer* (2016)

Joanne Addison and Sharon James McGee, *Writing and School Reform: Writing Instruction in the Age of Common Core and Standardized Testing* (2016)

Lisa Emerson, *The Forgotten Tribe: Scientists as Writers* (2016)

Jacob S. Blumner and Pamela B. Childers, *WAC Partnerships Between Secondary and Postsecondary Institutions* (2015)

Nathan Shepley, *Placing the History of College Writing: Stories from the Incomplete Archive* (2015)

Asao B. Inoue, *Antiracist Writing Assessment Ecologies: An Approach to Teaching and Assessing Writing for a Socially Just Future* (2015)

Theresa Lillis, Kathy Harrington, Mary R. Lea, and Sally Mitchell (Eds.), *Working with Academic Literacies: Case Studies Towards Transformative Practice* (2015)

Beth L. Hewett and Kevin Eric DePew (Eds.), *Foundational Practices of Online Writing Instruction* (2015)

CONTINGENCY, EXPLOITATION, AND SOLIDARITY: LABOR AND ACTION IN ENGLISH COMPOSITION

Edited by Seth Kahn, William B. Lalicker, and Amy Lynch-Biniek

The WAC Clearinghouse
wac.colostate.edu
Fort Collins, Colorado

University Press of Colorado
upcolorado.com
Boulder, Colorado

The WAC Clearinghouse, Fort Collins, Colorado 80523-1040

University Press of Colorado, Boulder, Colorado 80303

Printed in the United States of America

Library of Congress Cataloging-in-Publication Data

Names: Kahn, Seth, editor. | Lalicker, William B., editor. | Lynch-Biniek, Amy, editor.
Title: Contingency, exploitation, and solidarity : labor and action in English composition / edited by Seth Kahn, William B. Lalicker, and Amy Lynch-Biniek.
Other titles: Perspectives on writing (Fort Collins, Colo.)
Description: Fort Collins, Colorado : The WAC Clearinghouse ; Boulder, Colorado : University Press of Colorado, [2017] | Series: Perspectives on writing | Includes bibliographical references and index.
Identifiers: LCCN 2017034926| ISBN 9781607327653 (pbk.) | ISBN 9781607327660 (ebook)
Subjects: LCSH: College teachers, Part-time—United States. | English language—Rhetoric—Study and teaching (Higher)—United States. | Universities and colleges—United States—Faculty.
Classification: LCC LB2331.72 .C66 2017 | DDC 808/.0420711—dc23
LC record available at https://lccn.loc.gov/2017034926

Copyeditor: Don Donahue
Designer: Mike Palmquist
Series Editors: Susan H. McLeod and Rich Rice

This book is printed on acid-free paper.

The WAC Clearinghouse supports teachers of writing across the disciplines. Hosted by Colorado State University, and supported by the Colorado State Univeristy Open Press, it brings together scholarly journals and book series as well as resources for teachers who use writing in their courses. This book is available in digital formats for free download at wac.colostate.edu.

Founded in 1965, the University Press of Colorado is a nonprofit cooperative publishing enterprise supported, in part, by Adams State University, Colorado State University, Fort Lewis College, Metropolitan State University of Denver, Regis University, University of Colorado, University of Northern Colorado, Utah State University, and Western State Colorado University. For more information, visit upcolorado.com.

CONTENTS

ACKNOWLEDGMENTS

A project that has been four years in the making has had many sounding-boards, advisors, and well-wishers. We'd like to acknowledge first retired West Chester University colleague and our continuing friend, Karen Fitts, who not only was a full partner in the 2012 Watson Conference roundtable session that started the conversation guiding this book, but has been a progressive voice for justice for all in the workplace for every moment of her long career. Susan McLeod, Mike Palmquist, and Rich Rice of WAC Clearinghouse provided support for our aims from the very start, and then encouragement, smart advice, and organized guidance at every step of our work. Eileen Schell's early agreement and enthusiasm for the project, and her agreement to write the foreword, lent the book the strong voice of a premier scholar and advocate on the subject of contingent labor. Among the many scholars whose counsel moved the project forward, we would like to thank Debra Frank Dew, with whom we had many discussions that helped us sharpen the book's focus; and Jeff Sommers, who connected us to a community of two-year college faculty whose expertise added vital voices to our considerations of contingent labor justice. We also thank our many supportive colleagues at Kutztown University and West Chester University, so many of whom have engaged us with perspectives that contribute to our scholarly understanding. We would also like to thank members of the various groups in which we have agitated, collaborated, and struggled together in various permutations over the last several years: the CCCC Labor Caucus; the CCCC Committee on Part-time, Adjunct, and Contingent Labor; and the group of teacher-scholar-activists who composed and have organized around the Indianapolis Resolution.

Seth would like to thank a great many members of the adjunct activist community for helping me find a place in the movement, and for helping me earn the trust of other activists: Maria Maisto, Sue Doe, Natalie Dorfeld, Robin Sowards, Joe Fruscione, Mary Grace Gainer, Gordon Haber, Bri Bolin, Kat Jacobsen, Joe Berry, Anne Weigard, Judy Olsen, Karen Lentz Madison, Robert Craig Baum, Lee Kottner, T. L. Mack, Bob Samuels, Debra Leigh Scott, Jessica Lawless, David Wilder, and many, many more. I would also like to thank leaders of our professional organizations for their willingness to take up issues of labor equity, particular Susan Miller Cochran, Rita Malenczyk, Malea Powell, Howard Tinberg, and Linda Adler-Kassner. And thanks to my wife Ann for her support and patience, and also for her near-perfect sense of when to make me talk about my work and when not to, when to challenge my thinking and when to let me have my way.

Bill would like to thank an early mentor, Sharon Crowley, whose unerring voice for the most important values in our profession showed the way to connect teaching and living; and those in the long-ago Wyoming Conference and Wyoming Resolution community she helped to bring together, particularly Connie Hale, Jim McDonald, and Susan Wyche. I also thank my wife, Melanie Kisthardt, a great professor and a trustworthy conversant on matters of the teaching life and life in general.

Amy would like to thank her father, Jim Lynch, a teacher and labor organizer who instilled in her the importance of solidarity and social justice. Thanks to Kevin Mahoney, rabble-rouser, Raging Chicken, colleague and friend, who taught me much through example. I owe much to Mark Pitely, who has read every word I've ever written. Most especially, I'm thankful for my husband, Matthew Biniek, whose patience, perspective, and support make so much possible.

THE NEW FACULTY MAJORITY IN WRITING PROGRAMS: ORGANIZING FOR CHANGE

Eileen E. Schell

Syracuse University

This volume, in concert with a growing body of labor scholarship, strives to help readers make the tight connection between teachers' working conditions and students' learning conditions. As co-editors Seth Kahn, William B. Lalicker, and Amy Lynch-Biniek contend, the way we treat writing teachers as a class translates into the quality of writing education we can provide for our students. Their co-edited volume is "less about envisioning a utopia toward which we strive—particularly because we don't all agree on what that utopia looks like—and more about taking concrete steps to fight both exploitation of adjunct faculty and the denigration of composition studies as a worthy field of study" (Introduction). This is a goal that volume contributors commit to wholeheartedly across the varied sections and chapters.

As this collection documents, the economic conditions of higher education have shifted over the past thirty plus years due to increasingly neoliberal, corporatized, and privatized models of higher education. In turn, this neoliberal model of higher education guides the budgeting and prioritizing of academic goals and labor practices. As instructional budgets have been slashed and federal and state funding for higher education has diminished, colleges and universities, to save monies and maximize work-force flexibility, have intensified their hiring of faculty off the tenure track, including adjunct, part-time, and full-time, non-tenure track positions, with some of these faculty members teaching entirely online instead of on brick and mortar campuses. The Coalition on the Academic Workforce, an interdisciplinary group studying and addressing labor conditions in higher education, found that of the "nearly 1.8 million faculty members and instructors who made up the 2009 instructional work-force in degree-granting two- and four-year institutions of higher education in the United States, more than 1.3 million (75.5%) were employed in contingent positions off the tenure track, either as part-time or adjunct faculty members, full-time non-tenure-track faculty members, or graduate student teaching assistants" (Coalition on the Academic Workforce 1), according to data drawn from the United States Department of Education's 2009 Fall Staff Survey. As this volume affirms, contingent faculty members are particularly prevalent in required, lower-division courses like writing, math, languages, and the introductory social sciences. Writing programs and required writing courses have long been sites that are staffed by large numbers of contingent faculty and teaching assistants.

Contingent positions, once represented as a temporary measure to cover teaching shortages in the 1970s (see Abel), have now become a long-term labor strategy: a way for universities and colleges to avoid the provision of health benefits, shrug off responsibilities for pensions and/or retirement benefits, undercut shared governance and the tenure system, and create the greatest possible flexibility in the academic work force. Indeed, the conditions of many contingent faculty members bear a striking resemblance to that of workers at Walmart and other corporations that make heavy use of part-time employees and who also make sure their female employees do not rise into higher-level positions as managers.

While the term "contingent" describes positions in which faculty members teach on short-term contracts with low pay and little or no job security, inadequate office space, and challenging curricular and professional conditions, the idea of contingency fails to capture the true complexity of positions located off the tenure track. Across higher education, contingent faculty members have become the "new faculty majority" as Kahn, Lalicker, and Lynch-Biniek argue, and many, along with tenure-track faculty allies, have worked tirelessly to transform their professional conditions through alliance-building and resolute collective action (Introduction). These chapters, authored by tenure-line and non-tenure-line faculty alike, address strategies to improve teaching and learning conditions with respect to compensation, contracts, benefits, professional conditions, and shared governance processes. The contributors do not emphasize a "one-size-fits-all" model for change; rather, they demonstrate how strategies for organizing and reform arise in response to specific local, political, historical, and economic conditions.

INSTITUTIONAL CASES

More specifically, the co-editors and the contributors focus on the idea of "institutional realities and cases," what they refer to as "multiple, creative, constructive responses that can both enact labor justice and champion the disciplinary energies of all members of our collegial community" (Introduction). The tone across the volume consistently cuts against what Kahn, Lalicker, and Lynch-Biniek refer to as the "three more common registers of discourse on contingency—hollow (but certainly well-intentioned) exhortations; dramatic (and not unjustifiably so) depictions of abusive exploitation; or a combined anger and despair" (Introduction). What the co-editors and volume contributors offer instead are discourses of resolute change, problem-posing, problem-solving, and institutional and department/program-level change, all finely attuned to the tensions, challenges, positionalities, and rhetorical registers of institutional reform and transformation.

The movement toward drawing upon institutional cases to document labor reform and transformation is a well-instantiated and long-standing one in the labor scholarship in our field—a move that Linda Robertson, Sharon Crowley, and Frank Lentricchia along with others involved in the Wyoming Resolution called for in the late eighties and one modeled earlier in M. Elizabeth Wallace's 1984 edited collection *Part-time Academic Employment in the Humanities*. It is also the approach that Patricia Lambert Stock and I largely adopted in our 2001 co-edited collection *Moving a Mountain: Transforming the Working Conditions of Contingent Faculty in Composition Studies and Higher Education*. The institutional case, informed by the larger discourses of organizing and scholarly work on labor and higher education, thus can become a space from which to analyze, assess, and dissect local reform and organizing strategies.

Many of the chapters in this volume explore the successes and possibilities as well as the potential limitations and unexpected outcomes of local reform. As chapters by Mark McBeth and Tim McCormack, Richard Colby and Rebekah Schultz Colby and others demonstrate, departments and programs across the country have created non-tenure-track faculty positions that offer reasonable salaries correlated to recommended national standards, multi-year renewable contracts, opportunities for professional development, and other structures needed to support professionalization. Even with these improvements, the authors and co-authors across this volume document the challenges that accompany local reform: the challenge of new academic leaders implementing labor structures and assessment measures without consultation; budgetary crises that affect the most vulnerable instructors and students; tenure-track faculty members who are out of touch with non-tenure-track faculty's needs and concerns; and a lack of shared governance practices. In the midst of necessary and needed reforms to improve pay, benefits, professional conditions, and participation in shared governance, the authors have a healthy and clear-eyed understanding of what they are up against in both implementing and sustaining reforms. For instance, Carol Lind and Joan Mullin's chapter considers "a course release award process" whereby non-tenure track faculty (NTTF) are offered a semester away from teaching in order to pursue intellectual development and/or new course development. This system, while it has boosted morale among NTTs and resulted in improved courses, is subject to changing administrative conditions, since NTTs "live with the possibility that those in control—in a department in which they have limited voice—might decide at any time that it is not a good use of departmental resources" (Chapter 1).

Other contributors explore similar themes and questions of how to improve labor conditions and departmental culture in the midst of competing claims about how time and resources should be spent. Institutional memory and dynamics of institutional change must be considered when assessing the strengths or weaknesses of specific reforms. As Rolf Norgaard asks in his chapter: "What happens when gains are made, then risk being undone?" (Chapter 9).

ORGANIZING STRATEGIES

Beyond creating specific change with respect to compensation, contracts, benefits, and professional conditions, the chapters in this volume also assess varied organizing strategies in academic departments, programs, and across university campuses, including building alliances with tenure-track faculty members and enacting strategies for improving shared governance. Chris Blankenship and Justin M. Jory argue that NTTF (non-tenure-track faculty) must work toward creating an "organized public within the department that is dedicated to improving NTT conditions" and to "addressing the socio-cultural tensions among TT [tenure-track] and NTT faculty" (Chapter 10). Through exploring how contingent faculty can use specific genres such as departmental reviews and institutional surveys for advocacy purposes, they analyze how NTTF can advocate for themselves, but also how non-tenure-track faculty can make tenure-track faculty aware of the need to advocate for their non-tenure-track colleagues and the impact that contingent issues can have on departments. The uneven effects of contingency, though, raise these questions: Who can advocate for faculty working off the tenure track? What must their tenured and tenure-track allies keep in mind as they participate in such advocacy efforts?

The question of who can speak in concert with and advocate for non-tenure track faculty is raised and addressed thoughtfully by Seth Kahn, who offers important caveats to keep in mind about being a tenured/tenure-track ally and activist. Indeed, throughout the volume, readers will see examples of tenure-track and contingent faculty working together to advocate for labor justice (see Wootten and Moomau, for instance). Solidarity can be created, in part, through tenure-track and non-tenure track faculty working in concert with one another to change working conditions. However, working conditions are tied to complex emotional states and life narratives that must be acknowledged as well—the anger, disappointment, frustration, fear, anxiety, timidity (see Wootten and Moomau) and other emotions that both galvanize and halt action. The chapter by Desirée Holter, Amanda Martin, and Jeffrey Klausman comes to terms, in a frank and open fashion, with the hard emotions associated with precarity and underemployment: increasing disappointment, disillusionment, and disaffection when adjunct faculty seek out and participate in professional opportunities that cannot result in long-term job security.

One point of solidarity, among many that Maria Maisto, Sue Doe, and Janelle Adsit underscore, though, is the potential of uniting faculty of all ranks around the "fraying fantasy" of "secure academic employment." In doing so they argue that we can

> underscore that the "adjunct activist" agenda has the best
> interests of all faculty in mind. While we know that contin-
> gency is not evenly distributed in academe, it is nonetheless
> the case that contingency affects us all. The idea that tenure
> means security is rapidly being exposed as anachronistic,
> if not mythical. This reality should translate into a united
> cause—contingency as an issue that involves the faculty at
> large. (Chapter 14)

And it is the idea of pursuing a "united cause" that percolates across chapters, with some authors exploring unionization and collectivization (see Layden and Donhardt, Lalicker and Lynch-Biniek, Heifferon and Nardo among others) while others seek department-level changes by committee or group. Lalicker and Lynch-Biniek argue in their essay that the way toward labor justice is through supporting "a culture of equal sharing" (Chapter 6). Inspired by union activist Joe Berry, they argue that "we have to act like unions even when we're not legally organized in unions."

THE LOCATIONS OF WRITING

This collection also gives us cause to consider where a writing program and its contingent faculty might be located institutionally and professionally. How does a university or college's institutional mission and status influence the labor structures and delivery of writing instruction? What are the institutional spaces allotted to writing programs and those who teach in them? How are writing centers, writing across the curriculum programs, online programs, independent writing programs outside of English departments, and English departments spaces for the work of writing instruction and writing-oriented scholarship, spaces that may marginalize and make our labor invisible, and yet also spaces we can appropriate for organizing to improve labor conditions? Moreover, what do those spaces say about the politics of labor on our campuses?

Michelle LaFrance and Anicca Cox offer a fascinating look at how material spaces in writing programs—in the form of architecture, office space, class-rooms, hallways, and other locations—"are the material manifestations of our institutional discourses" (Chapter 18). LaFrance and Cox ask readers to consider how spaces of marginalization and invisibility can be spaces to launch both con-crete resistance and the resistance of critical consciousness, arguing that "[i]n Composition, we have long known that our marginalization as a field also allows us to imagine a different form of resistance—this most often takes the form of a critical consciousness shared by many members of the field."

Michael Murphy succinctly brings that critical consciousness to bear on the problem of automation in writing instruction: the rise of tutoring and writing assessment provided by educational software and remote tutoring/paper grad-ing services. He argues that in our advocacy efforts we must account for ways that "writing and reading aren't language processing. Both require *a transaction between human minds*—even in solitary texts, when writers struggle to articulate and refine ideas for themselves, or in most machine code, since most applications are of course written to be experienced ultimately by human users" (Chapter 5). While he argues for ways to address the complexity of what we do as writ-ing teachers to stave off the so-called easy labor and money-saving solutions offered by automated/online assessment and tutoring services, he also argues for addressing how we understand and promote the scholarship and intellec-tual work that teaching-intensive faculty can provide. Through describing and assessing the potential of a certificate program for community college faculty, he asks readers to consider what it means to make places in our field to value and promote the knowledge-making of "both scholar-teachers and teacher-rhetors."

QUESTION POSING: BODIES AND BUDGETS

As I read through this volume several times over roughly a year-long period, I found that the rich institutional cases, organizing strategies, and insights pro-vided by each chapter raised as many questions as they answered, and that is a strength throughout the volume. I found myself wondering about and wanting to know more about how contingency is tied to the intersectional identities of contingent faculty and the "vulnerable student" bodies that Kahn, Lalicker, and Lynch-Biniek reference. How is contingency tied to the bodies of workers and students that are marked as non-normative and different? In a globalized econ-omy, white women, women of color, and men of color, working class men and women (see Dew), people living with disabilities, and queer and trans people are often treated as an exploitable and expendable workforce; how does higher education mirror that exploitation?

Contingent Faculty Bodies

We know that multiple studies show a clear connection between gender and contingency, which is an undercurrent throughout these articles (see Fels; Maisto et al.). In the NCES data from 2009, "[o]f part-time faculty respondents who provided information about their gender, 61.9 percent were women, as compared with 51.6 percent in the National Center for Education Statistics (NCES) 2009 Fall Staff Survey (Table 2)" (7). Moreover, the Modern Language Association (MLA) report *Education in the Balance: A Report on the Academic Workforce in English*, which drew on data from the National Survey of Postsecondary Faculty, found that in English studies, women continue to represent more than 60 percent of the faculty in non-tenure-track positions, both full- and part-time" (4-5). In her chapter, Dawn Fels, reminds us that writing center directors are predominantly female, citing two sources (Healy et al.) that place the rate at an estimated 73 to 74 percent (Chapter 8).

As I argued in *Gypsy Academics: Gender, Contingent Labor, and Writing Instruction*, women are often thought to "choose" contingent work for the flexibility it affords. In fact, many institutions feel it is acceptable to hire large numbers of women at the contingent ranks because it is still assumed that they have male partners who are supporting them financially, a dubious claim in a society where half of all marriages end in divorce and where many adult women are single. Women are also thought to find contingent work to be more flexible than full-time work when they have young children to raise, even as the conditions and costs of that flexibility in the long run may remain underexplored: the so-called on and off ramps of part-time work for women and the long-term costs to their overall financial health and retirement savings. It is also still the case that women are thought to be particularly good at delivering the kind of care work associated with teaching writing or providing language instruction: painstakingly poring over drafts and making comments, tutoring and administering writing centers and writing programs, holding one-on-one conferences, offering informal advising and support for students struggling with writing and with adjusting to the higher education environment, especially first-generation college students, students of color, international students, and women students. Writing instructors and non-tenure-track administrators thus often occupy a locus of "care work," as pointed out in several essays in this volume.

Along with considerations of gender, we need to think through questions of race, age, ability, and sexuality as we consider who is contingent in our field.

For instance, Tressie McMillan Cottom argues in *Slate*, being "contingent" is a hardly new phenomenon for black faculty members in higher education. She cites the AAUP report that shows that the proportion of African American faculty members in non-tenure-track positions is 15.2 percent whereas whites are 9.6 percent, to a difference of 50 percent. She also cites a 2009 article from the *Journal of Blacks in Higher Education* that if current rates of hiring and promotion of black Ph.D.s remained steady, it would take over 150 years for African American faculty to reach proportional numbers with the larger societal population of African Americans: "If you leave out the high proportion of black Ph.D.s working in historically black colleges and universities, black full-time faculty in the U.S. barely clears 4 percent." McMillan Cottom points out that professional organizations addressing labor conditions have been late to addressing the adjunctification and ghettoization of black faculty, especially when we consider that black students and faculty have been involved in "protesting the ghettofication of black scholars in adjunct roles for almost 20 years," citing actions such as the one in 1968 where "black students took over an administration building at Columbia; among their demands was a call for more tenured black faculty."

Thus, we need to make sure that histories of anti-racist struggle and solidarity are included in our analyses of the contingent labor movement: the stories of black faculty who were hired as tenure-track, but denied tenure, and shuffled into non-tenure track roles; the stories of women of color working off the tenure-track who have dealt with structural harassment, disrespect, and questions about their competency (see also Gabriella Gutiérrez y Muhs Yolanda Flores Niemann, Carmen G. González, Angela P. Harris). Accounting for the material bodies of contingent workers and histories of discrimination and struggle will make our organizing work richer and more accountable to historic patterns of discrimination and exclusion and also reveal ways that organizing strategies can break down if questions of white privilege and bodily difference are not addressed.

STUDENT BODIES

As we consider the identities, bodies, and histories of discrimination that specific contingent faculty have faced, we also need to consider how to include the bodies and perspectives of students in the struggle for labor justice in higher education. Kahn, Lalicker, and Lynch-Biniek mention vulnerable students in the introduction to this volume, and it is clear that our students are increasingly contingent workers and contingent students as well. Many of our students are saddled with student loan debt that they will not be able to repay for many years if at all; many are working one or more part-time positions while taking classes, taking online courses to fit in a degree around family life and working life, often unable to complete their degrees in a timely fashion because the classes they want have been cut or because they don't have access to faculty who can advise or mentor them through their degree programs.

Recognizing that contingency is often a common denominator between teachers and students, international movements like Campus Equity Week have historically encouraged contingent faculty and tenure-track allies to include their students, both graduate and undergraduate, in their advocacy efforts. Across the country and on my own campus, students, both graduate and undergraduate, have rallied with contingent faculty, have assisted with and have spoken at teach-ins about how contingency impacts their teachers and them. On some campuses, students have walked out of classrooms on National Adjunct Walkout Day to protest and organize around contingent labor issues. Thus, how we locate students in narratives of labor transformation and reform is also significant—how they can be agents of change in this fight for labor justice in higher education since teachers' working conditions affect them directly.

BODIES OF ADMINISTRATIVE LEADERSHIP AND BUDGETS

In addition, leaders of higher education must be addressed in the movement to organize against contingency. Department culture matters a great deal with respect to addressing labor conditions, but we have to look at the leaders above the departmental level and hold them accountable for the situation of contingency and the undercutting of instructional budgets. Our organizing efforts must include targeted interactions and questions posed to deans, provosts, vice presidents, chief financial officers, boards of trustees, university chancellors, presidents, state-level higher education boards and committees, state legislators, and others with respect to the decisions they make about the allocation of university budgets. Where does the money go that students and their parents put into higher education through tuition monies? What about the money taxpayers put into public higher education through their taxes? How are university budgets being configured, and what transparency is there about the money being allocated toward instruction and faculty positions of all ranks? Why are instructional budgets so flat or diminishing even as the leaders of colleges and universities authorize university budgets to be spent on a growing array of administrative positions? And what about the university and college expenditures for real estate, gleaming new buildings and recreational centers, special non-academic programs and endeavors, sports teams, and lavish salaries for coaches and upper-level administrators? Where is the accountability for diminishing instructional budgets in the face of these expenditures? These questions must be at the heart of our organizing strategies for they address the larger economic decisions behind higher education funding.

In recent years, scholars, national organizations and groups like the Delta Cost Project have begun to examine how universities are allocating and spending their precious budgetary resources, especially with respect to the rising costs of administration. As political science professor Benjamin Ginsberg summarizes in his seminal *Washington Monthly* article "The Administrators Ate My Tuition," in "1975, colleges employed one administrator for every eighty-four students and one professional staffer—admissions officers, information technology specialists, and the like—for every fifty students"; by 2005, the administrator to student ratio went to "one administrator for every sixty-eight students" and one professional staffer "for every twenty-one students" (2011).

This is a significant boost in the number of non-instructional staff in higher education, yet numbers vary based on institutional type. Drawing on two decades of data from the U.S. Department of Education's Integrated Postsecondary Education database, Donna Desrochers and Rita Kirshstein, writing for the Delta Cost Project,[1] find that public institutions experienced slow growth in hiring in the first decade of 2000 compared to their hiring trends in the 1990s because the "recent expansion in new positions largely mirrored rising enrollments as the Millennial Generation entered college" (2). Public research universities and community colleges saw decreases in the hiring of staff, with "sixteen fewer staff per 1,000 full-time equivalent (FTE) students compared with 2000, while the number of staff per student at public master's and bachelor's colleges remained unchanged" (2). Private colleges, however, were a different matter and experienced significant hiring increases: "Private institutions employed, on average, fifteen to twenty-six additional workers per 1,000 FTE students between 2000 and 2012. And even during the Great Recession, many public and private colleges kept hiring in response to the uptick in new students" (3), even as they reduced or flat-lined instructional budgets (2).

As Desrochers and Kirshstein indicate, professional staff positions, such as business analysts, human resources personnel, and admissions staffers, "grew twice as fast as executive and managerial positions at public non-research institutions between 2000 and 2012, and outpaced enrollment growth" (3). This trend, in particular, demonstrates that colleges and universities are directing their dollars toward "noninstructional student services, not just business support" (3). The report indicates that across all institutional types, the "wage and

---

1   The Delta Cost Project draws on data connected to employment changes and patterns, administrative costs, and the recession's impact on higher education staffing (IPEDS) (1–2). They also address how these patterns affect "total compensation, institutional spending patterns, and ultimately tuitions" (1).

salary expenditures for student services (per FTE staff) were the fastest growing salary expense in many types of institutions between 2002 and 2012" (3). As these numbers rose, the faculty and staff per administrator ratio dropped "by roughly 40 percent in most types of four-year colleges and universities between 1990 and 2012, and now averages 2.5 or fewer faculty and staff per administrator" (3). Faculty salaries have largely stayed flat for almost a decade; however, "additional savings from shifting to part-time instructors have not been enough to offset the costs associated with continued hiring and rising benefits expenditures" (4). The report concludes that these changes "represent long-standing trends" (13), and that the hiring and support of administrative positions have taken precedence over instructional positions, something that many of us have noted in our workplaces. In our arguments about contingency, how can we connect administrative costs to contingency and the rising tide of student debt? These questions and more must be at the forefront of our efforts to organize against contingency, for they address the core questions of value behind higher education budgets.

CONCLUSION

Finally, this volume underscores that we are at a significant juncture in higher education and that we must take action to achieve a more just workplace. If we want to preserve the instructional base of university education and student learning and create more just workplaces, we must act now to ensure productive working conditions and learning conditions for all involved in higher education. This volume will take us farther down the road toward meeting that goal.

WORKS CITED

Abel, Emily K. *Terminal Degrees: The Job Crisis in Higher Education*. Praeger, 1984.

Coalition of the Academic Workforce. "A Portrait of Part-Time Faculty Members: A Summary of Findings on Part-Time Faculty Respondents to the Coalition on the Academic Workforce, Survey of Contingent Faculty Members and Instructors," June 2012, www.academicworkforce.org/CAW_portrait_2012.pdf.

Desrochers, Donna, and Rita Kirshstein. "Labor Intensive or Labor Expensive? Changing Staffing and Compensation Patterns in Higher Education." *Delta Cost Project at American Institutes for Research*, Feb. 2014, www.deltacostproject.org/sites/default /files/products/DeltaCostAIR_Staffing_Brief_2_3_14.pdf.

Ginsberg, Benjamin. "Administrators Ate My Tuition." *Washington Monthly*, Sept./Oct. 2011, www.washingtonmonthly.com/magazine/septoct-2011/administrators-ate -my-tuition/.

Gutiérrez y Muhs, Gabriella, et al., editors. *Presumed Incompetent: The Intersections of Race and Class for Women in Academia*. Utah State UP, 2012.

Modern Language Association and Association of Departments of English. "Education in the Balance: A Report on the Academic Workforce in English." *A Report of the 2007 ADE Ad Hoc Committee on Staffing*, 10 Dec. 2008, pp. 1–55, www.mla.org /Resources/Research/Surveys-Reports-and-Other-Documents/Staffing-Salaries-and -Other-Professional-Issues/Education-in-the-Balance-A-Report-on-the-Academic -Workforce-in-English.

McMillan Cottom, Tressie. "The New Old Labor Crisis." *Slate,* 24 Jan. 2014, www .slate.com/articles/life/counter_narrative/2014/01/adjunct_crisis_in_higher_ed_an _all_too_familiar_story_for_black_faculty.html.

Robertson, Linda R., et al. "The Wyoming Conference Resolution Opposing Unfair Salaries and Working Conditions for Post-Secondary Teachers of Writing." *College English,* vol. 49, no. 3, 1987, pp. 274–80.

Schell, Eileen E. *Gypsy Academics and Mother-teachers: Gender, Contingent Labor, and Writing Instruction*. Heinemann-Boynton/Cook, 1997.

Schell, Eileen E., and Patricia Lambert Stock, editors. *Moving a Mountain: Transforming the Role of Contingent Faculty in Composition Studies and Higher Education*. NCTE, 2001.

Wallace, M. Elizabeth, editor. *Part-Time Academic Employment in the Humanities*. Modern Language Association, 1984.

CONTINGENCY, EXPLOITATION, AND SOLIDARITY: LABOR AND ACTION IN ENGLISH COMPOSITION

PATHS TOWARD SOLIDARITY

Seth Kahn
West Chester University

William B. Lalicker
West Chester University

Amy Lynch-Biniek
Kutztown University

When Richard Rorty juxtaposed the terms *contingency, irony, and solidarity* in the title of his 1989 book, he wasn't talking about labor conditions in twenty-first century university English departments or writing programs, but we wish he had been. He got the contingency and irony parts right. Solidarity is much harder to come by.

At the 2012 Watson Conference on Rhetoric and Composition, Seth, Bill, Amy, and our friend and colleague Karen Fitts conducted a roundtable session called "Taming the Intractable, Finding Justice for All in Composition's Labor Relations." The session emerged from a complicated labor situation in the university system where we work. Our collective bargaining agreement includes a contract provision that allows departments to convert long-term, full-time adjunct faculty into tenure-track status by majority vote of the tenured/tenure-track faculty and subsequent approval of the administration. Instead of offering the shining beacon of hope that we thought might be an answer to contingent faculty exploitation, our respective departments, on two separate campuses, debated the wisdom of these conversions, revealing some festering resentments and some disagreements among generally like-minded people about the best courses of action for addressing contingent faculty exploitation wisely. Even the four of us, committed to labor reform and social justice, found we had differences.

Obviously conversions are not the only, or even the best, solution to adjunct labor exploitation; no single policy solution is best for every contingent faculty member or every department. As Maria Maisto (contributor to the collection) contends regularly, what contingent faculty want most is simply to be compensated fairly for whatever work they do. Those who want to teach an occasional course for supplementary income or for fun deserve the same equity as those who teach full-time with a long-term stake in the profession. Contingent faculty are contingent for many reasons, sometimes willingly and sometimes not, and in survey after survey they reveal a wide variety of ambitions in terms of employment security and status. Some want full-time work; some don't. Some ideally would like tenure-track appointments; some not. And so on.

In the last few years, the data describing contingent labor conditions and contingent faculty perceptions have developed significantly. Since 2010, survey results have come forth from the Coalition on the Academic Workforce; the Delphi Project; the Modern Language Association; the Adjunct Project; and the New Faculty Majority, all of which are largely mutually reinforcing. We've been documenting the exploitative conditions of adjunct faculty for a long time, and while trends and specifics matter, continued surveying and data-collecting all too often preclude movement towards equitable treatment in the name of ignorance. We *know*. We know *enough*, anyway, and as the New Faculty Majority and the Adjunct Project, among other efforts, have shown, it's possible to make concrete progress based on what we know *right now*. When the *Chronicle of Higher Education* announced that it would house and support the continued work of the Adjunct Project early in 2013, prominent adjunct-equity activist "[Margaret] Hanzimanolis, who holds a Ph.D. in English, [said] the ability to see the 'big-picture terrain' about pay on the Adjunct Project site will make it easier for adjuncts to maximize their own pay" (qtd. in June and Newman), and founder Josh Boldt contends:

> When I first made the spreadsheet, I had one intention: that people who were thinking about getting a job somewhere could look and see what the job paid. . . . The ability to compare institutions allows adjuncts to make choices about where to work based on pay and others' reviews. In the past adjuncts essentially had no power to do something like that . . . but now they do. (qtd. in June and Newman)

Likewise, we've seen increasing calls for contingent faculty equity (or at least humaneness) in our professional discourse: former MLA president Michael Berube's "From the President" blog, on which he devoted significant space to articulating what he sees as minimally acceptable compensation and working conditions; a series of research reports from the Campaign for the Future of Higher Education laying out specifics about the harm that inequitable treatment does to our students and our institutions (see, for example, "Who Is Professor 'Staff' and How Can This Person Teach So Many Classes?"); and organizing efforts like the New Faculty Majority, the Congress on Contingent and Adjunct Labor (COCAL), PrecariCorps, and Adjunct Action.

Contingent faculty exploitation has even begun to see coverage from non-academic press outlets, where the plight of temporary faculty is often connected to the plight of other temporary workers. Writers are noting that increased college tuition and expenses aren't winding up in the pockets of faculty. The 2013 death of Margaret Mary Vojtko, a long-time adjunct professor at Duquesne University who died destitute from health problems that she might have addressed with insurance benefits, underscored this point, and was covered by the mainstream press in outlets including *The Huffington Post*, National Public Radio and *USA Today*. In January of 2014, the *New York Times* finally considered the scope of labor problems in higher education in "Crowded Out of the Ivory Tower, Adjuncts See a Life Less Lofty." Even the popular lifestyle magazine *Elle* has addressed contingency, in December 2014's "Hypereducated and on Welfare."

Organized action is on the rise, too. A petition to David Weil at the Department of Labor, co-authored by a group of loosely connected adjunct activists (including Seth), and calling for government investigations into wage-theft, teaching load reduction and other unethical/illegal labor practices, garnered nearly 10,000 signatures in summer/fall 2014. An anonymous adjunct used social media to plan National Adjunct Walkout Day in February 2015, encouraging a nationwide work-stoppage to demonstrate the overwhelming reliance of higher education on contingent workers. The MLA Democracy Campaign nearly elected a slate of adjuncts to executive positions, and succeeded in raising the discourse and the stakes around that organization's treatment of contingent members. At CCCC in 2015, members of the Labor Caucus shared and opened for public comment and revision a draft of the Indianapolis Resolution, a reworking of the Wyoming Resolution, calling for our professional organizations to revise and redouble their efforts in working for adjunct equity; in April 2016, the CCCC membership approved a motion calling on the leadership to enact three major provisions of the resolution. Also in April 2016, CCCC published a new Statement on Working Conditions for Non-Tenure-Track Writing Faculty. The groundswell is growing.

Claire Goldstene writes in *Dissent* (and it's worth quoting at length because it was one of the first times this much important information appeared in a non-academic source):

> Most teachers in higher education across the country lack
> long-term job stability. Presently, close to 70 percent of all
> faculty appointments in degree-granting institutions are off
> the tenure track, a number that includes over one million
> people. The label "contingent academic labor" encompasses
> an array of arrangements, among them adjuncts paid on a

per-course basis, one- or multi-year contract faculty, visiting professors, and post-docs. In general, these positions are characterized by low pay, no-to-little job security, and, frequently, no health or retirement benefits. According to the Adjunct Project, the national average remuneration for adjuncts is $2,987 for a 15-week, three-credit course, usually with a high student enrollment, and some teachers are paid as little as $1,000 per class. Currently, nearly 34,000 Ph.D. recipients receive food stamps to supplement their earnings. In an effort to cobble together a living, many adjuncts teach at multiple institutions, taking on a course load of six or more classes per semester and spending significant time traveling among campuses. Most recently, numerous university systems have reduced the number of courses adjuncts can teach in a single year to avoid the thirty-hour per week threshold established by the 2010 Affordable Care Act that would trigger access to employer healthcare benefits. (n.p.)

Among the contingent-faculty-activist community, there is clear frustration over looming implications for employment possibilities resulting from the Affordable Care Act: we're seeing institutions limit teaching loads in order to get out of the provision requiring them to offer healthcare to employees who average thirty hours per week. We are alarmed by routine dismissals of contingent faculty whose work clearly should be covered by any meaningful definition of academic freedom (á la James Kilgore at the University of Illinois). We are angered by races to the bottom, typified by an administrative proposal, during a recent round of negotiations with the faculty union, that we slash our adjunct faculty pay by 35 percent because they are paying over "market value."

As Seth argued in a presentation at the 2013 CCCC, and which we believe is just as true (if not more so) a few years later, there are success stories, and they are newsworthy; at the same time, frustration and the sense of intractability are unsurprising ("Refracting"). Our response to these conditions, therefore, is twofold. First, this book clarifies and specifies the means and effects of exploitation across institutional contexts. We recognize that the discourses around contingency tend toward one of three sorts: hollow (but certainly well-intentioned) exhortations; dramatic (often justifiably so) depictions of abusive exploitation; or a combined anger and despair. Each of those discourses is important and has its place, but obviously they have not worked in any curative sense. Second, then, this collection addresses the situation by highlighting alternatives to the hollow and horrific, to the anger and despair; we compile and present efforts that have led concretely and effectively toward improved adjunct faculty working conditions. In the years we've been thinking about labor issues, and more recently contingent labor issues in the field, we have in fact seen a shift towards more proactive stances against poor labor practices. This shift increasingly includes faculty across ranks; administrators willing to be ethical in their treatment of faculty; and, in short, anybody willing to make common cause to fight exploitation.

To call ourselves *hopeful* is perhaps imprecise. *Resolute* is better. Our project is less about envisioning a utopia toward which we strive—particularly because we don't all agree on what that utopia looks like—and more about taking concrete steps to fight both exploitation of contingent faculty and the denigration of composition studies as a worthy field of study. Those two goals are intimately related, of course. It's no accident: departments that exploit contingent faculty the worst are almost always the ones that respect the intellectual value of composition the least. The department in which Bill and Seth work seemed to have established a healthy relationship between the literature and composition faculty, until the dispute over adjunct faculty hiring and conversion to tenure-track status exposed unhealed wounds, which our chapters will elaborate.

Not everybody in the book holds our twin goals of fighting both adjunct exploitation and the denigration of composition studies to be equally important; in fact, many chapters don't even try to address both goals. We do, however, expect that the interplay between them will be evident throughout; and to highlight it further, in the next section we will provide a series of *threads* to tie together arguments among chapters, providing readers alternative ways to navigate through the text according to their needs and interests.

A note on terminology: Names matter. And many names exist for non-tenure-track faculty, including lecturer, adjunct, temporary faculty, contingent faculty, and visiting professor. As editors, we didn't want to force a particular nomenclature on the contributors to this collection, as the social, economic, professional, and political associations with each term are often local and contextual. Further, we sometimes use these terms interchangeably, when in fact many may see each as distinct. Our intention is neither to insult non-tenure-track faculty, nor to impress our own associations with the terms upon readers. We should call faculty what they wish to be called, yet we can't anticipate the preferences of every reader. Therefore, the authors in this collection simply used their preferred or local terminology because that terminology itself may help identify local conditions and contexts. Rather than being interpreted as inconsistent, we hope readers will see in it our recognition of the wide array of differences.

SUMMARY OF CONTENTS

The chapters raise a complex array of issues, ideas, strategies, tactics, and cautions, often within the same pieces. For those working with the complete book, we have arranged the chapters so that similar emphases or locations are near each other. We begin with Carol Lind and Joan Mullin's "Silent Subversion, Quiet Competence, and Patient Persistence," in which they describe efforts to create a NTT course reassignment award, framing it as "a story of subversion, competence and persistence, and a commitment to ethical action." In "Despair is Not a Strategy," Barbara Heifferon and Anna K. Nardo recount how the tenured faculty at LSU advocated for secure positions and improved compensation for their contingent colleagues by forming alliances with an activist group on their campus, even in the face of budget crises and threats of termination. Mark McBeth and Tim McCormack offer "An Apologia and a Way Forward: In Defense of the Lecturer Line in Writing Programs." They propose that it acts as "a workable resolution that lies between necessary accommodation and affirmative writing program labor practices." In "Real Faculty But Not: The Full-Time, Non-Tenure-Track Position as Contingent Labor," Richard Colby and Rebekah Schultz Colby, full-time non-tenure-track faculty themselves, contend that such positions dis-incentivize scholarship on teaching and recommend strategies for continuing to support it.

In "Head to Head with edX," Michael Murphy explores the changing identity of adjunct composition faculty in the age of the MOOC, juxtaposing the mechanizing and casualizing of academic labor with a Sophistic approach as a possibility for expanded professional development that improves NTT faculty's work as writing instructors and their labor situation. Considering professionalism and credentialing from a different direction, Amy Lynch-Biniek and William B. Lalicker describe in "Contingency, Solidarity, and Community Building: Principles for Converting Contingent to Tenure Track" the differing ways their two English departments within the same state system respond to a contractual policy that allows for the conversion of temporary faculty to the tenure track, and induce from those experiences a set of principles that help departments to build both equitable labor conditions and programmatic soundness. Dani Neir-Weber's "The Other Invisible Hand: Adjunct Labor and Economies of the Writing Center" turns the lens of professional development towards her contingent writing center staff, focusing especially on the ways TT faculty attitudes were challenged as she fought for professional development funding for her staff. In "The Risks of Contingent Writing Center Directorships," Dawn Fels takes on the problems not only of contingent writing center staff, but of the larger trend towards making directorships precarious, a growing trend that may harm both "quality and integrity" of these units.

The next two chapters, Rolf Norgaard's "The Uncertain Future of Past Success: Memory, Narrative, and the Dynamics of Institutional Change" and Chris Blankenship and Justin M. Jory's "Non-Tenure-Track Activism: Genre Appropriation in Program Reporting" take up two parallel sets of issues in very different ways: involving contingent faculty in shared governance, and protecting against backsliding after initial successes. Jacob Babb and Courtney Adams Wooten, in "Traveling on the Assessment Loop: The Role of Contingent Labor in Program Development," offer contingent faculty participation and responsibility in program assessment as another route into enhanced professional status and recognition.

Chapters Twelve through Fifteen address both the importance and complexities of what we refer to as "self-advocacy" (but might also be called *internal organizing within contingent ranks*). In "Adjuncts Foster Change: Improving Adjunct Working Conditions by Forming an Associate Faculty Coalition (AFC)," Tracy Donhardt and Sarah Layden narrate the process by which they organized in an environment where unionizing is legally and politically difficult; along the way, they also highlight the importance of what may seem like incremental wins. Lacey Wootton and Glenn Moomau's "Building Our Own Bridges: A Case-Study in Contingent Faculty Self-Advocacy" describes how lasting change was achieved at American University by emphasizing "faculty reputation, alliances with tenure-line faculty, and participation in unit and university governance." From a less local and more theoretical/historical perspective, Maria Maisto, Sue Doe, and Janelle Adsit, in "What Works and What Counts: Valuing the Affective in Non-Tenure-Track Advocacy," ask us to reflect on the meanings of "action" and "activism," arguing for the important role of affect in any lasting change. In "Hitting the Wall: Identity and Engagement at a Two-Year College," Desirée Holter, Amanda Martin, and Jeff Klausman caution activists to remember that even well-intentioned changes in employment status can negatively affect adjunct faculty's personal and professional identities, and to proceed with care.

The final three chapters take on very different questions and problems that connect ethics, individual/collective agency, and institutional spaces. Seth Kahn's "The Problem of Speaking for Adjuncts" proposes "strategies for avoiding colonization of contingent faculty, offering non-contingent faculty ways of understanding contingent faculty advocacy beyond pity and paternalistic good will." Allison Laubach Wright, in "The Rhetoric of Excellence and the Erasure of Graduate Labor," considers graduate students' labor-identity, rejecting the conventional model of graduate assistants as mere "apprentices." Finally, Michelle LaFrance and Anicca Cox juxtapose stories from the 2003 University of Massachusetts Dartmouth contingent faculty strike with photos documenting adjunct work spaces, presenting "a story of possibility, collaboration, and resistance. . . ."

Because we expect many readers to be downloading individual chapters rather than reading the entire book in order, we opted out of *sections* that inevitably tried and failed to categorize these multifaceted arguments, and decided instead to articulate *threads* that we believe connect arguments across chapters. Readers will find in each chapter a note just below the by-line that tags the threads, connecting it to other chapters so you can find other helpful resources, positions, and responses.

Thread 1: Self advocacy. Chapters in this thread feature contingent faculty-led efforts on their own behalf. The stories they tell present mixed levels of success and help establish contingent-faculty driven frameworks for collaborating with tenure-track and/or tenured (TT/T) faculty.

Layden/Donhardt; Wootton/Moomau; Blankenship/Jory; Maisto/Doe/Adsit

Thread 2: Organizing within and across ranks. These chapters describe linkages across faculty (and in some cases even managerial) ranks or status; taken together, they present allies with both options for advocacy or alliance-building and a sense of the ethical considerations of doing so.

Lind/Mullin; Kahn; Maisto/Doe/Adsit; Blankenship/Jory; Colby/Colby; Holter/Martin/Klausmann; Wootton/Moomau; McBeth/McCormick; Heifferon/Nardo; Nier-Weber; Norgaard

Thread 3: Professionalizing and Developing in Complex Contexts. These chapters respond in various ways to the problem of un/under-professionalized or non-specialized writing faculty and their access to professionalizing opportunities (conference attendance, research support, job security, access to position conversions, further graduate education/training).

Murphy; Blankenship/Jory; Colby/Colby; Babb/Adams-Wooten; Holter/Martin/Klausmann; LaFrance/Cox; Laubach-Wright; McBeth/McCormick; Lynch-Biniek/Lalicker

Thread 4: Local Changes to Workload, Pay, and Material Conditions. These chapters focus on the most concrete changes in the most specific, local settings—individual campuses/programs.

Lynch-Biniek/Lalicker; Wright; Fels; Neir-Weber; Norgaard; LaFrance/Cox; Murphy; McBeth/McCormick; Heifferon/Nardo

Thread 5. Protecting Gains, Telling Cautionary Tales. In these chapters, contributors acknowledge the often-provisional nature of success and the complexities, even risks, of engaging in the struggle for equity.

Lind/Mullin; Heifferon/Nardo; Blankenship/Jory; Norgaard; Holter/Martin/Klausmann; Fels; Laubach-Wright

This collection, then, seeks to address contingency, exploitation, and solidarity in activist terms deriving from institutional realities and cases. The resulting conversation illustrates the present crisis, but ultimately focuses on multiple, creative, constructive responses that can both enact labor justice and champion the disciplinary energies of all members of our collegial community.

WORKS CITED

Goldstene, Claire. "The Emergent Academic Proletariat and Its Shortchanged Students." *Dissent,* 13 Aug. 2013, www.dissentmagazine.org/online_articles/the-emergent-academic-proletariat-and-its-shortchanged-students.

June, Audrey Williams, and Jonah Newman. "Adjunct Project Reveals Wide Range in Pay." *The Chronicle of Higher Education,* 4 Jan. 2013, www.chronicle.com/article/Adjunct-Project-Shows-Wide/136439/.

Kahn, Seth. "Reflecting Disciplinarity through the Lens of Contingency." Presentation at the Conference on College Composition and Communication, Las Vegas, NV, Mar. 2013.

Quart, Alissa. "Hypereducated and on Welfare." *Elle,* 2 Dec. 2014, www.elle.com/culture/career-politics/a19838/debt-and-hypereducated-poor/.

Rorty, Richard. *Contingency, Irony, and Solidarity.* Cambridge UP, 1989.

Street, Steve, et al. "Who is Professor 'Staff,' and How Can This Person Teach So Many Classes?" *Center for the Future of Higher Education Policy,* Aug. 2012, www.futureofhighered.org/policy-report-2/.

Swarns, Rachel L. "Crowded out of the Ivory Tower, Adjuncts See a Life Less Lofty." *The New York Times,* 19 Jan. 2014, www.nytimes.com/2014/01/20/nyregion/crowded-out-of-ivory-tower-adjuncts-see-a-life-less-lofty.html?_r=0.

CHAPTER 1

SILENT SUBVERSION, QUIET COMPETENCE, AND PATIENT PERSISTENCE

Carol Lind

Illinois State University

Joan Mullin

University of North Carolina Charlotte

Threads: Organizing Within and Across Ranks; Protecting Gains, Telling Cautionary Tales[1]

Contingent faculty often have the same experience and research curiosities as their tenure-track counterparts, but rarely have the same opportunities to continue their professional growth. Reduced workloads, access to travel funds, and other internal resources are seldom available to non-tenure-track (NTT) faculty, even those with terminal degrees: contracts usually specify their primary responsibility as teaching, and workloads leave little time for extensive scholarly pursuits. While tenure-track (TT) faculty can seek reassignments and resources by claiming the necessity of continued research, NTTs often cannot, even though they would agree with Judy Olson, chair of the NEA's Contingent Faculty Caucus, that

> [p]articipating in scholarship makes us better teachers, traveling makes us better teachers, reading and taking classes make us better. We cannot help students understand how to participate in academic conversations unless we participate ourselves. College teachers who only teach can become drained of their creative and intellectual nutrients without a source of replenishment. All students deserve to have teachers who have their own creative wells to draw from. (44)

---

1   The threads are meant to guide you to other chapters in the collection that speak to related issues. Sometimes the chapters that we've threaded together agree or extend each other; at other times they contest or complicate each other. For a complete list of the threads, see the Introduction.

Olson continues to reason that "well over half of all the faculty members students now encounter in their classes are off the tenure track and generally not eligible for sabbatical leaves. Students deserve to have teachers who have access to all the resources that we know make people better teachers, regardless of tenure status" (44). The authors of this chapter were part of an effort that began to address this need to create a research opportunity for contingent faculty within what has been a traditionally resistant academic culture. This narration traces the development of an NTT "reassignment award," perhaps not as rich a sabbatical as it should be, but a step towards practicing the equity about which English department tenure line faculty often try to teach their own students. Here, we outline a one-semester course release, the fears that had to be overcome in the process of integrating it into academic culture, the negotiation of departmental politics that occurred, and the affective and professional effects that resulted from its success. Collaboratively written by the then-chair of the department and an NTT, it is also a story of silent subversion, quiet competence, and patient persistence, pointing not only to the difficulties of achieving equity in the academy, but also to the need for mutual trust and a mutual commitment to ethical action. We begin with our narrative and then, drawing upon some of the recent commentary on contingent academic labor, we ask that all academic workers reconsider the stakes that necessitate supportive collaboration, recognition, and rewards, stakes that affect our collective efforts to teach, research, serve and model the democratic practices we teach. We suggest here that to enact policies of fair treatment, all faculty need to face histories, attitudes, and fears that arise from their prior experiences.

CAUTIOUS STEPS AND AGENCY

Out of seventy faculty and staff in the department described here, there were thirty-eight TT, a handful of adjuncts, eighty teaching assistants and nine full-time NTTs. After teaching 4/4 loads for ten consecutive semesters in the institution, NTTs earn "status" and are scheduled for courses before non-status NTTs and adjuncts. Several of the NTTs referred to at the time had "status" and others were on their way to earning it, so they were a fairly long-term and committed working group. The planning for a course reassignment program took place in the fall of 2010 after a meeting between the department chair (Joan) and the NTT faculty working in the English department. Joan had recently become chair of the department, and this meeting was one of many that she held with different groups of faculty and staff in an effort to get a feel for the needs and concerns of those working within the department. There was no way for the NTTs at the meeting to know Joan's own history as a marginalized academic, or of her previous advocacy for contingent faculty; and, sitting there with the group, Joan could already see the distrust leveled at her as chair—with good reason.

Within her first weeks as chair, Joan had heard TT faculty in one breath praise some NTTs in the room for their well-regarded teaching, and then follow it with a criticism of their abilities as academics in the next, with implied—or direct, pointed—comments: *NTTs don't understand what it is like to research and teach; some are home grown* [said as a negative]*; they cannot serve on search committees, even when the search is for one of their direct supervisors, because they have no real stake in the department.* Pleasant and collegial in public, several faculty had already approached Joan in private about limiting NTTs' current voting rights on general matters affecting the whole unit; about reducing the number of NTTs hired (perhaps by increasing graduate student teaching assistantships); and about creating a protocol for determining which courses could only be taught by TT faculty, full time NTTs with status, and graduate students. While TT faculty agreed many of the contingent faculty could expertly teach not only first year writing, but writing and literature courses, and had done so successfully, there was also an expressed fear that continuing to do so meant TT faculty would be giving up their control over the curriculum. While this latter fear was only that—a fear—it was often tied to the idea that giving privileges/equity to NTTs meant TTs would lose more of their own autonomy and control over curriculum.

It would be unfair to characterize all of the thirty-eight TT negatively, or to even characterize many of those who made these comments as overtly malicious, since issues of academic privilege, especially in humanities departments, often cause faculty to feel their usefulness, status and resources attacked on every side. While there was also a good deal of camaraderie among TT and NTT and an understanding among the TT that NTTs' loads allowed the TT to teach more graduate and upper division courses, historical feelings that NTTs could not be considered equal intellectual partners prevailed, often tacitly.

Given this context, one that simmers under collegiality, it is not surprising that at Joan's first meeting with them, NTTs stated that they would feel more valued if assigned courses based not only on departmental needs, but upon their own experience, training and/or publications. They noted that over half have terminal degrees (M.F.A. and Ph.D.), are published, read in their fields, and participate in faculty development. They could redesign the writing and general education literature courses that they regularly teach as much as they managed, but they wanted the time to further research even these areas, to incorporate new material, and to improve their theoretical and pedagogical knowledge. As they spoke about their desires and possibilities, it became apparent that every NTT seated around the table had an idea for a radical redesign of an existing course, but had no time to create, let alone an opportunity to implement, such a reimagined course. Lecturers lamented that they were being more often pigeonholed into the most rudimentary teaching assignments, often teaching the same four courses every semester. The department sometimes struggled to offer enough advanced courses across its nine sub-disciplines to its seven hundred majors, and when the schedule was really pressed, select NTTs did teach advanced courses, often either those NTTs married to TT faculty, or one or two home grown former graduate students. Overall, however, lecturers were not regularly assigned to teach courses other than general education requirements, since the unstated belief was that the graduate and upper division curriculum belongs to TT faculty; NTTs were equipped for and hired to teach "service courses."

Joan agreed that given NTTs' current workloads, it was difficult to pursue their own professional development. She asked whether a course release award process could be created for them, whereby they would apply for a semester's "reassignment" in order to do research and course development; "reassignment" was institution-speak for release time and would parallel the term given to TT course releases. The response was positive of course; the meeting broke up, and then the chair did something that none of the NTTs really expected her to do—she followed up on the idea by asking them to come up with an award plan that she would then submit to the Advisory Council for approval. The surprise was not based upon Joan's personal credibility; the NTTs knew very little about her, but they did have a great deal of experience with well-spoken chairs and TTs in the past, particularly with those in power positions within the English department. They had met at different times with several candidates applying for departmental administrative positions. Each and every one of these expressed their genuine intention to work closely with the NTTs in order to better integrate them into the rich and varied work of the department. Once hired, however, those "intentions" were forgotten as quickly as promises made during a heated political campaign. Because of this, the NTTs had (and still have) a healthy skepticism toward such promises.

Since the NTTs are a small community within the department, they are a very close-knit group, working together almost daily to address issues within classes, the department, and the university at large. Many are involved members in the NTT union on campus, helping make great strides in some areas, and refining the union rules (such as they are). What may be visible, but less acknowledged, is their active participation on departmental and college committees, as allowed, or their mentoring of first year students who come to know them and turn to NTTs as mentors. In each of these roles, they demonstrate their commitment to students and colleagues and believe they help promote a more collegial workplace for all faculty, be they tenured, tenure-track, or NTT.

Nonetheless, there was a great deal of discussion concerning Joan's invitation in the "NTT hallway," a spur off the main floor office areas, where most NTT offices are located. Certainly, there was astonishment that someone in authority had actually followed-up on the meeting, but there were several other reactions as well: happiness; a new sense of purpose; curiosity; and—it must be said—a good deal of skepticism and suspicion.

The first question Joan's proposal produced was, "Why?" Why would she offer us this boon? What motives could she possibly have in doing so? It was suggested by one of the members that she might be doing it in order to get NTT support within a department that is rife with intrigue and infighting. However, since NTT support really doesn't mean much more than the proverbial hill of beans, that motive seemed unlikely. Torn between their own desires to be in the community as equals and by their consciousness of their treatment over the years, NTTs also feared being caught in their own siege mentality; so while they wanted to support one another, they also knew they suspected the motives of anyone who was not part of their NTT community.

For that reason, the thesis that gained the most traction was more conspiracy theory than anything else: perhaps Joan was putting this program into place in an effort to divide the lecturers, to put them into competition with one another as they vied for the coveted award.

This seemed most likely since each person had ideas about redesigning a course, and there would only be one course reassignment per semester. Would choosing to prioritize one course proposal over another put the lecturers at odds with one another and make them easier to control? It seemed that all the NTTs harbored that fear to some degree, and were at least a little suspicious about the proposal. It was such a great opportunity, however, that they felt the risks would be worth going forward: what more did they have to lose? So, working together, the NTTs drafted the course release proposal in September of 2010:

> We propose that a course release should be awarded each
> semester in order to enable an NTT to develop or redesign a
> course in his/her area of expertise, to be taught within the next
> calendar year as part of the NTT's regular teaching assignment
> load. This course release would be used to plan course readings
> and content, explore new modes of delivery, and to develop
> assignments and assessment tools. It would be a rotating
> opportunity for NTT faculty modeled, in part, upon the
> research sabbatical offered to tenured and tenure-track faculty.
> This course release would be used to redesign a course already
> on the books, not to develop new curriculum.

The chair's first response to the NTTs' proposal was a strong recommendation that the name of the program be changed to "course reassignment" rather than "course release." This was common institutional language for a course reduction, and maintaining that language would avoid possible backlash from TT faculty, who might object to the department granting the NTTs a release from any of their standard four-four commitment (as compared to TT's three-two, two-two, two-one, or one-one). Any course release contractually granted to an NTT might also mean a faculty member would have to pick up an additional class, should it be needed. A "reassignment" signaled that the NTT was doing work for the department. This proved a prescient rename, for one member of the Advisory Council did approach the chair before the award was approved at a meeting, asking whether the department could "afford" a course release: "What if we need someone to teach a course at the last minute?" Assured that such occasions were rare, the TT member replied, "Oh, so if there were an emergency, the NTT could just delay her award until the next semester." (Chairs' noncommittal comments to such replies are an art form.)

The next step was to create a group that would oversee the selection process. It was decided that the committee would be made up of the department chair, the associate chair, the director of the writing program, and one NTT. These selections were not made randomly, but were intended to create a committee that would be TT heavy, yet, at least with the current administrators in those positions, would be comprised of people known to be respectful of the process and respectful of those submitting applications. The members appointed to the committee would also make sense to TT faculty administratively, since the chair was the direct supervisor of the NTTs, and the associate chair was in charge of course assignments; and, since it was assumed that many of the proposals would concern courses within the writing program, the director of writing could also best evaluate the contribution of proposals to the program. Carol was selected by the NTTs to be their first representative on the committee, with the understanding that thereafter each award recipient would rotate onto the selection committee, and then off as the next took his or her place.

Though the NTTs felt it was vital to have an active role in the selection, implementation, and evaluation of the reassignment award, that decision was met with some apprehension within their community. Certainly, they were happy to be part of the decision-making process and preferred that idea over having only tenured faculty members evaluating proposals, but there was still a great deal of concern that choosing one proposal over another might cause a rift within the group. Carol assured them that she would make her work on the committee as transparent as possible and would see that the decision represented the NTTs' best interests as individuals and as a group. The fact is, though, that she approached the committee work with a good deal of trepidation of her own, concerned that any disgruntlement over who received the assignment might be aimed at her. Carol had a good relationship with her colleagues, which is why they chose her to represent them, but she didn't want to jeopardize that camaraderie for the sake of this program. Fortunately, when she expressed her concerns to the NTTs, they assured Carol that they trusted her to make an impartial decision and to represent their best interests. With that assurance, a fellow NTT and Carol designed the call for proposals and, after receiving committee approval, sent out the initial email to their peers (see Appendix A).

Of course, not everyone submitted a proposal that first go-round. Some weren't ready to submit a proposal at that time and others preferred to sit back and see how the program went before throwing their hats in the ring. Since Carol served on the committee, she didn't submit a proposal during that first call, but two other NTTs did. One proposal, submitted by Anne Norton, was for a redesign of English 145.13—Composition II for Business and Government. In it, Anne noted that the current course was in serious need of revamping.

This course has always had close ties to the College of Business, which has some relatively firm expectations for what its students will have learned and accomplished, and the writing skills that they will carry on into the "real world" of their business careers. While it allows for a certain amount of academic freedom for the English instructors who teach it, it is not a course to be blindly kicked around just for the purpose of playing with pedagogical theories of composition.

For the last few years, there has been little to no direct collaboration between the English Department Writing Program and the College of Business to make certain that 145.13 stays current with the college's needs and expectations. For the proposed re-design, it was *crucial* to reinstitute that collaboration.

Anne realized that the department's business writing courses had become stale over the years, employing business writing models that were out of date and far removed from the current reality. She would use her reassignment to reevaluate the course material through meetings with the university's department of business and with local business leaders.

The second proposal came from Elizabeth Hatmaker, who proposed a redesign of a course in Interdisciplinary Studies—IDS 121.47: Film and the Artist, a general education course she often taught for the department. In her proposal, Elizabeth outlined her work in the course and the challenges that she faced teaching a class in which some students were technologically advanced, while others were much less so. She had very clear ideas of what she'd like to do with the time that a course reassignment would afford her:

It is my hope to use this course release opportunity to learn digital technologies such as MovieMaker, Photoshop, and Audacity. I also hope to shoot some film footage with which I hope to illustrate to students in class how basic editing practices work. I hope to use these technologies not necessarily to teach filmmaking per se, but to engage students in the practice of editing so that they might develop more sophisticated skills interpreting films.

Having had some time to examine both proposals, the committee shared their opinions with each other via email and ultimately came to the decision to approve Anne's proposal, based upon departmental needs. Although Elizabeth had submitted a strong proposal, the committee felt that Anne's redesign of her writing class would be more beneficial to the work of the department. (Elizabeth did resubmit her proposal a couple of semesters later and was approved for the course reassignment at that time.) The committee contacted Joan, who sent the congratulatory email to Anne.

Anne's reassignment was in the spring semester of 2011, and she taught her redesigned course in the fall of 2012. The information she gleaned from working within the Business College was layered into a redesign of that course, and tangentially contributed to the composition curriculum.

Since Anne was granted the first reassignment, she became the NTT representative on the committee charged with overseeing the program, and helped make the decision about who would receive the next reassignment, which would take place in the fall semester. Because Carol was no longer the NTT representative on the committee, she decided that this would be a good time to submit her own proposal to redesign an existing face-to-face general education course (English 110: British Literature and Its Contexts) into one that could be taught completely online. The university, the college, and the department were all desirous of offering more online courses in the summer, so this redesign would prove beneficial not only to them, but to Carol's pedagogical interests, as well. (Not to mention the students who could take a general education course wherever they happened to be during the summer semester.) In order to redesign the course, Carol needed to learn how to deliver information and evaluate performance in an online setting—a time consuming task if she were teaching three other courses, but an impossibility if she were teaching four.

Without the course reassignment, Carol would have never had the time or opportunity to do such a radical redesign of that class. In fact, she would probably not even be teaching anything but the same course in first year writing every semester. Carol feels deeply indebted to those in the department who gave her the opportunity to teach a course that never fails to delight her, as does her 2010–11 University Teaching Award. Such delight and recognition should be any university instructor's just reward within academic systems that claim to value teaching. The opportunity for NTTs to pursue their passions, and the personal benefits that accrue as a result, contribute to their own sets of personal and professional growth, but the program has generated several important curricular contributions for the department, including:

- A redesign of a "Grammar for Writers" course that had stagnated over several years of neglect;
- The creation of new course material for a text and context course that will focus on labor history and working class issues; and
- A face-to-face course in the English education program redesigned to be taught online.

The process itself hasn't changed much since the program's inception. The only major change is that proposals are accepted in the spring for the following fall and spring semesters; that way, the submission process only needs to occur once a year, rather than every semester.

UNPACKING THE PROBLEMS

Finally, there is the silence that always seems to go along with the work that NTTs do within departments. The call for proposals states,

> Following the semester of teaching, the faculty member
> would submit an outcomes statement (two page maximum)
> to the Chair of the Department that will document the pro-
> cess of the course and reflect on successes and revisions to the
> course based on assessments such as student comments and
> peer review.

This aspect of the program has never been completed by any of the NTTs who have been granted course reassignments. Such a statement has not been requested, which appears to imply a lack of respect (and curiosity) about the work the NTTs are doing within their classrooms and this program. And to some extent that is true. Even in Joan's mind, the program was not part of the culture of the department, so it was left to the NTTs to remind the chair that the annual call should be sent; the committee should meet; the decision should be made. The problem, though, is not as simple as a lack of respect, but perhaps backhanded respect: the NTTs are the most reliable to perform the usual and expected work assigned, the least (publicly) complaining, and therefore, the easiest to overlook. Speaking on behalf of contingent labor, Angela Billa notes:

> Our institutions value [contingent labor] mostly in the utilitarian role we play: we fill the holes, we quiet the masses, we deal with the charge to fix the problems that underprepared high school graduates bring to college. We are the mechanics in the assembly line, plugging in little parts. (387)

Since NTTs do mind their own work and do not demand the attention that TT faculty and students do—since NTTs know their jobs and realize that their course assignments (and possibly their careers) are at risk if they speak out—a vicious cycle continues; they often don't remind others of obligations and promises.

If we combine the facts of contingent academic labor conditions made clear by statistical data and anecdotal evidence (like that of Schell and of Vincent Tirelli) with theories about how the human mind shapes an identity, we can begin to see that the isolation and exile of contingent faculty common across the disciplines and across institution types creates a body of faculty who are likely to see themselves as outsiders and outcasts, taking on and expressing all of the psychological traits thereof (Jacobe 380–81).

Jacobe's observation of isolation and exile could sadly apply to any number of campus communities; that is, it could apply unless there is a persistent commitment on the part of all faculty to bring about real change. Although the NTTs in our department were aware of the risk of victim mentality, and Joan and other TT track faculty sought to reassure them, that assurance could easily have been read as patronizing protection and could have fed the perceived and actual academic bullying of contingent faculty. In "Workplace Bullying in Higher Education," Lester names treatment of and "exclusion of contingent faculty" as "behaviors [that] are constant and continuous and show a pattern of abuse that causes psychological harm to the victim" (ix). Lester pulls together the work of other experts, noting that such conditions prevail in academe and nurture too many TTs' "big egos, an individualistic ethic, and tolerance for behaviors not accepted elsewhere" (1).

Rank and privilege, with the accompanying hierarchy, exclusion and abuse, continue to trump democratization and collegiality, even as that privilege is fast disappearing through the "emergence of the modern research university as a fundamental site of struggle over the corporatization and privatization of knowledge" (Gilbert 34). Gilbert's critique is pertinent here, for he calls for a new strategy for preventing corporatization, one that depends on the creation of a public sphere. Essential to our point, he notes:

The landscape of intellectual work in the age of the corporate casualized university is increasingly defined by a dangerous hierarchy in which tenure and job security are reserved for a select few and non-tenured, casual workers conduct a disproportionate amount of the instruction. (37)

That the fight for status, the exclusion of contingent faculty, and negative and bullying behaviors are too often engaged in by the very faculty teaching Marxism or social justice demonstrates the double standard that exists within tenure-track faculty. Those fighting social justice through their scholarship and classrooms don't always recognize as injustice the position of lecturers in their own departments. One of these TT faculty members made an appointment with Joan to explain why NTTs should not have even a marginal vote in the department. Her logic? If we keep hiring NTTs, their votes and voice may outnumber that of tenured faculty. She insisted that NTTs don't understand the academy like TTs do. This may be true in some ways given the differing contractual work of each group; but in the process of privileging TTs, this woman excluded the rights and perspectives of the NTT group whose labor enables the TTs to teach fewer classes and engage in research. Another TT advocate for feminist issues assured the female NTTs that if they voted for her for Advisory, a body that made decisions for the department, she would continue to advocate for their rights and privileges. She was later overheard by an NTT telling another tenured feminist faculty member that "over [her] dead body would those NTTs get any more power in this department." She wanted to be on Advisory to stop the "encroachment" of NTTs.

As Gilbert rightly notes, movements to rectify such inequities in the academy do not usually come from TT faculty, but rather from recently organized graduate students who understand that change will only come "alongside other workers and as part of broader publics . . . [through] an academic community built in collaboration with democratic concerns and constituencies" (44). There are, however, tenure-track faculty willing to join forces. In the case outlined here, while there were several TT supporters of the reassignment award, they proceeded very carefully: assuming that a conversation about the conditions that existed in our department would be doomed and, in turn, doom the proposal, the TT administrative awards committee members strategized how to downplay the reassignment proposal as it proceeded through the department. This was especially important since at that time TT faculty were also demanding course releases to serve as departmental library liaison, or for volunteering to advise students, or "because I research a lot and publish." Asking to give the "workhorses of the department" a course release required cautious diplomacy because of these faculty requests, and because TT faculty attempting to foster this award at best risked their standing with their TT peers, and at worst feared at least one member in the department might file a faculty grievance against them. As it turned out, the proposal passed through the department without an overt whimper. There were covert personal consequences that accrued to TT members, and the grumblings continued about NTT voices in the department, as did the suggestions to remove what little voting rights they had and the plans to replace NTT lines with graduate students.

TO BE CONTINUED . . .

Beyond the NTT community, this award program has not, to date, significantly impacted the culture of the department. Yet in the case we describe here, the agency taken by the NTTs has continued. Had they and supporting faculty not persisted, the obligations and promises could have easily been forgotten, and prior fears reasserted themselves. With the NTTs' encouragement, Carol did propose the creation of an online class, and was granted a course redesign award. She also gave a professional development talk about designing online courses in April of 2014. It was well attended, and since then she has had several TT attendees ask her for advice on designing and maintaining their own online courses. Her redesigned course is now regularly scheduled, enrolls quickly, and is seen as an asset to the department curriculum. This example of NTT recognition and collaboration represents the kind of work that needs to happen in the academy, a breaking of barriers that demonstrates, rather than just theorizes, that issues of social justice and equity are what we practice in our own backyards. Gilbert concludes that to save higher education, TTs have to realize that "[t]he mode of being of the new intellectual can no longer consist in eloquence, which is an exterior and momentary mover of feelings and passions, but in active participation in practical life, as constructor, organizer, 'permanent persuader' and not just a simple orator" (44). We have to work collectively, enacting equity among ourselves instead of merely speaking about equity—while fighting together to maintain fair distribution of resources. We can't call this one project an unqualified success in shifting attitudes, but we do see it as a success: it continues.

The reassignment award also continues to be important to NTTs, to their morale, and to their continued growth as teachers; and yet they live with the possibility that those in control—in a department in which they have limited voice—might decide at any time that it is not a good use of departmental resources. A recent change in administration has unfortunately created a somewhat chilly climate for contingent faculty. In spite of this setback, the NTTs continue to listen to each other, pat themselves on the back, and walk into the classroom just a little more excited, a little more prepared, and a lot more creative than they would have been had there been no follow-up on that original meeting. Quiet though they may be in public, word of their enthusiasm and of their teaching accomplishments does ripple through all the hallways. There is a sense that the course reassignment award benefits the university, the NTTs, their students, and the department members as a whole, although the latter do not always acknowledge the exciting, innovative work going on in that little NTT hallway at the corner of the building. They should, though, because as the course reassignment program continues, the NTT competency is more noticeable; the subversion is a little less silent, and the patience of this hard-working group of educators—although often tried—persists.

WORKS CITED

Billa, Angela, et al. "Forum on Identity." *Contingent Faculty*, special issue of *College English*, vol. 73, no. 4, 2011, pp. 379–95.

Gilbert, Daniel A. "The Generation of Public Intellectuals: Corporate Universities, Graduate Employees and the Academic Labor Movement." *Labor Studies Journal*, vol. 38, no. 32, 2013, pp. 32–46, www.citeseerx.ist.psu.edu/viewdoc/download ?doi=10.1.1.825.3768&rep=rep1&type=pdf.

Lester, Jaime. *Workplace Bullying in Higher Education*. Routledge, 2012.

Olson, Judy. "Sabbaticals: Why Not for Adjunct Faculty Too?" *NEA Higher Education Advocate*, vol. 29, no. 2, 2012, p. 44.

Palmquist, Mike (chair), et al. "Statement on the Status and Working Conditions of Contingent Faculty." *Contingent Faculty*, special issue of *College English*, vol. 73, no. 4, 2011, pp. 356–59.

APPENDIX A

CALL: NTT COURSE DESIGN PROPOSAL

Proposals are being solicited from NTT faculty interested in developing or redesigning a 100 or 200 level course in his/her area of expertise. The redesign should address an existing English or Interdisciplinary Studies course currently listed in the ISU catalog. The applicant chosen would use one-course reassigned time to plan course readings and content, explore new modes of delivery, and to develop assignments and assessment tools.

At the end of the semester for which the reassignment is given, the selected applicant will submit a copy of the course syllabus and reading list to the Proposal Committee, noting in brief, the reasons for the changes that have been made (one page maximum). Consistent with curricular needs, during the next academic year, the department would schedule this faculty member to teach the redeveloped course. Following the semester of teaching, the faculty member would submit an outcomes statement (two page maximum) to the chair of the department that will document the process of the course and reflect on successes and revisions to the course based on assessments such as student comments and peer review.

Applicant Criteria: All Department of English status NTTs or full time probationary NTT faculty who have completed six semesters of instruction.

Application Materials: Applicants should complete the attached form and a current cv.

Application process: Applications are due, electronically, to [the Administrative Assistant] by 4:30 p.m. November 19, 2010.

Proposals will be reviewed by the appointed NTT representative, the chair of the Undergraduate Committee, and a faculty representative of the Writing Committee, who will make a recommendation to the Department Chair. Applicants will be notified by December 3, 2010.

CHAPTER 2

DESPAIR IS NOT A STRATEGY

Anna K. Nardo and Barbara Heifferon

Louisiana State University

Threads: Organizing Within and Across Ranks; Local Changes to
Workload, Pay, and Working Conditions; Protecting Gains, Telling
Cautionary Tales

The meaning of the term *contingency* depends on your position within a university system. When full-time, non-tenure-track faculty members regularly serve on important departmental and university committees, when they enjoy appropriate voting rights and take on administrative positions within and beyond their departments, and when they regularly win university awards and teach the curriculum's foundational courses for thirty years—they are, by no means, "contingent labor." Nevertheless, this is how instructors have been classified at Louisiana State University. Although they have always officially held one-year contracts, the continuing employment of instructors who passed a rigorous review was never questioned . . . until recently. In the following essay, we will outline

- The stable and functional, if imperfect, employment conditions of instructors in the LSU English department up until 2003;
- The upper administration's backlash against the department's system; and
- On-going efforts to counter this backlash, to create a more equitable system of job security, to improve working conditions, and to lobby for better wages.

We tell this story from two perspectives: that of a former department chair who came to LSU in 1975, and that of a writing program administrator (WPA) who faced the aftermath of the backlash when she came to LSU in 2010. We have joined forces to tell our story and to oppose the university's treatment of instructors as "contingent labor" because despair is not a strategy.[1]

---

1   In order to counter the "rhetoric of despair" that accepts unjust university structures of employment as inevitable, Seth Kahn proposes activism based on an ecological model of systems. Marc Bousquet also argues against despair, but he doubts that low-level managers, like WPAs and department chairs, can effect meaningful change: "Composition as Management Science" (157–85).

HISTORY

From the early 1970s to 2003, the LSU English department cultivated a cadre of well-trained, experienced, full-time, non-tenure-track Instructors. They were the core teachers in both the writing and the general education literature programs; they served on important departmental and university committees; they had full benefits; and they regularly won prestigious teaching awards. Some who had taken on administrative tasks were promoted into the tenure track.

During this thirty-year period, LSU made a concerted effort, first, to achieve the Carnegie Foundation's "Research I" (now changed to "Comprehensive/ Doctoral") designation and, second, to reach "Tier I" status in the *U.S. News & World Report* annual rankings.[2] These efforts did not affect research professors alone; universities are giant webs and, when one filament is touched, all the other parts of the web vibrate. Whereas prior to this effort to raise the university's research profile, professors of English had taught three courses per semester, including composition and general education literature courses, in the late 1970s professorial teaching loads were reduced to two courses per semester. These changes had a double effect: Because of the reduced professorial teaching load, professors (especially new hires) developed active research agendas, and the prestige of the graduate programs advanced substantially.

Differential work expectations for professors (two units of teaching/two units of research) and instructors (four units of teaching) created the kind of two-tiered faculty structure that is common in large universities throughout the U.S.[3] Professorial labor was needed to staff graduate seminars and courses for English majors. Almost no professors have taught in the composition program for years. Thus instructors and graduate students took over the major responsibility for teaching the skills of reading, writing and research that are fundamental to undergraduate education.

Another change during these years had unexpected consequences for the instructor rank. Prior to the effort to elevate LSU's standing in high-profile rankings of universities, the English department had to wage war every semester to keep class size in writing courses at acceptable levels. In the late 1990s, however, the upper administration decided that one way to impress the rankers, who awarded points to institutions whose undergraduates were enrolled in at least one small class among their total schedule of courses, was to allow no more than nineteen students in sections of first-year writing. Of course, the department

---

2   Frank Donoghue critiques the quest for higher rankings in the *U.S. News and World Report* list of best colleges: "Prestige and Prestige Envy" (111–37).

3   David Bartholomae analyzes the problems that a two-tiered teaching and research faculty creates.

rejoiced that instructors, who teach three sections of writing and one section of introductory literature (capped at forty) every semester, would be able to give students the individual attention required for effective instruction in writing. But the new cap also required the English department to hire many more instructors. The cadre of instructors swelled to exceed the size of the professorial ranks—more than seventy instructors, fewer than fifty professors.

Through all these changes, the LSU English department continued to recognize the vital contribution of instructors. If not all the professorial faculty, at least the departmental administrators have always known that the power the English department wields within the larger university depends not only on the publication record of its productive professors, but also on the size of the writing program and the high standard of instructor teaching. During these years, however, a division existed between the English department's recognition of instructors and the official employment status of instructors as contingent labor hired annually.

Unlike large metropolitan centers like New York City or Los Angeles, Baton Rouge, Louisiana does not have a large pool of M.A.s or Ph.D.s looking for work. So even if the LSU English department had tried, it could never have depended on adjunct labor to staff the writing program, the common practice in many universities across the country. Except for last-minute appointments and a few instructors who, for personal reasons, preferred permanent part-time status, all English instructors are full-time employees. Strong leadership in the writing program, supported by the professorial faculty of the English department, has always insisted on hiring full-time instructors, who must participate in a graded series of extensive teaching reviews: normative evaluations in the first and third year, and a summative evaluation in the sixth year. Instructors who passed the rigorous sixth-year review were awarded the departmentally designated rank of "Career Instructor," which insured their continuous employment so long as there were writing courses to teach. This is the stable, functional, if imperfect, system[4] that the English department was able to sustain through the period of LSU's evolution toward "Comprehensive/Doctoral" and "Tier I" status.

University policy, however, still required that instructors be hired on one-year contracts, which must be "continued" every year. Some of these award-winning instructors—who serve as rectors for residential colleges, as writing program administrators, as leaders in service-learning courses, etc.—have taught at LSU for thirty or more years. Nevertheless, the university still classified them as contingent labor. Every year they were "continued," the official term for "re-hired," and they could be "released," the official term for "fired," with one-year's notice (for those instructors who had worked at LSU for three years or more). At the

---

4   Marc Bousquet emphasizes that the turn toward hiring full-time non-tenure-track teachers, although not as abusive as the dependence on adjuncts, is neither new nor ideal (170–72).

turn of the millennium, the English department led an effort to develop a professional career path with appropriate job security for instructors. With the support of the mathematics department, we crafted a proposal to bring university employment procedures in line with departmental recognition of the value of instructor labor. The proposal would have created three-year rolling contracts for all instructors who had passed their sixth-year review. Although the proposal had the support of the Faculty Senate, the upper administration flatly rejected it. Deans of powerful colleges insisted that they needed the freedom to "release" instructors, regardless of years and quality of service—which is precisely what they did in 2003 (making hollow promises to create more tenure-track lines) and in 2008 (insisting that budget cuts demanded harsh measures).[5]

Although the English department failed in its effort to convert accepted practice (indefinitely "continuing" instructors with demonstrated records of excellence) into contractual employment security (three-year rolling contracts), no changes disrupted long-standing departmental practice until 2003. This year marks the university backlash against the English department system of regular reviews and promotion to "Career Instructor"—a backlash impelled by a change in administrative philosophy. In search of higher rankings, a stronger research profile, and more grant dollars, LSU hired a series of upper administrators to create and implement a "Flagship Agenda." But instead of dedicating the time and resources required to implement the agenda's lofty goals for research, education, and community engagement, these administrators announced initiatives, stayed a few years, then moved on to higher paying positions elsewhere.[6] One of these initiatives, imposed in 2003, was devastating. It required the English department to "release" forty-five (out of a total of seventy-two) or 62.5 percent of the instructors, with the promise of new professorial budget lines, plus stipends for additional graduate students.

What impelled this backlash against long-standing instructor employment practices? Whereas one set of upper administrators had sought to advance LSU in the rankings by creating small sections for teaching writing, a new set of upper administrators, alarmed at the size of the instructor rank, sought to advance LSU's status by converting instructor budget lines to professorial budget lines. With no regard for the exigencies of staffing a writing curriculum that included hundreds of sections of basic composition courses, as well as courses in

---

5   Cary Nelson exposes administrators' insistence on the need for "flexibility" as code for the plan to maintain a pool of cheap laborers who can be hired and fired at will as staffing needs change (3–5).

6   Bousquet discusses the proliferation of university administrators since the 1990s, their theories of "continuous reinvention" for improving efficiency, and their frequent moves for career advancement: "The Faculty Organize, but Management Enjoys Solidarity" (90–124).

business and technical communication, the upper administration insisted that resources be reallocated as part of the new "Flagship Agenda." Soon, however, this set of upper administrators made advantageous career moves: their promises for a much larger professoriate in the English department were never kept, and the department was left with about half of its cadre of instructors, devastated morale, and the task of rethinking how to teach its writing courses.[7]

In order to cope with the fallout from the "releases" (negotiated down from forty-five to thirty-five), the English department decided to do what it could within its power. We formalized our system of regular reviews and instructor ranks into a document, "Instructors: Rights, Responsibilities, Evaluation, and Review," adopted by the entire faculty in 2007. Our goal was to:

- Base departmental procedures on best practices advocated by the Conference on College Composition and Communication and the Modern Language Association;
- Restate our procedures in the language of the LSU policy statement that governs hiring, review, and promotion of non-tenured faculty;
- Demonstrate the solidarity of the full English department (including all professors) with instructor policy; and
- Prepare a base for continuing to lobby for appropriate job security for Instructors.

In addition to defining the review and promotion procedures, the document opens with a preface explaining the responsibilities and rights of instructors.

> Instructors are crucial to the continuity and enhancement of undergraduate instruction in English. They serve as the primary teachers of record for university writing courses, and they teach general education and specialized courses at the 2000 and 3000 level. Thus they constitute a professional cadre of teachers—indeed, the core faculty responsible for writing and introductory literature and language courses. They serve on almost every departmental standing committee (e.g., the Executive Committee) and on many university committees (e.g., Faculty Senate). In addition, they help administer programs both in our department (e.g., Associate Director of University Writing) and in external units (e.g., Rector of Residential College Programs).

---

7   Much has been written about the development of the American corporate university and its deleterious effects on teaching. For a study that focuses on the link between corporatization and the "casualization" of labor, see Johnson, Kavanagh, and Mattson, editors.

In keeping with their role in departmental decisions, this document outlines instructors' voting rights and committee memberships.

Voting rights:

Instructors will have votes in the following areas:

- Undergraduate curriculum decisions, excluding 4000-level courses.
- Election for a departmental chair. See Election Procedures administered by the Executive Committee.
- Instructor review. The voting faculty on instructor reviews will include instructors who have passed their sixth year review (or who held the internal departmental rank of Instructor III in 10/2003).
- Election for the Instructor Personnel Committee.
- Committee memberships:
- All departmental standing committees (such as Undergraduate Studies, Community Relations, Readers & Writers, etc.), with the exception of committees governing the graduate program and professorial appointment, review, tenure, and promotion.
- Appropriate university standing committees and governing bodies, such as the [College of Humanities and Social Sciences] Senate and the Faculty Senate.
- Instructor Review Panels. Review panels will include instructors who have passed their sixth year review (or who held the internal departmental rank of Instructor III in 10/2003).

This preface serves as both a reminder to all English department faculty members, and an explanation to the wider university community of how crucial instructor labor is to the mission of LSU.

Refusing to surrender to the administrative backlash of 2003, the English department, with the full support of the dean of the College of Humanities and Social Sciences, then petitioned the upper administration to adopt procedures for awarding three-year "rolling" contracts to instructors who pass their sixth-year review. Not only are these procedures congruent with the university policy statement governing non-tenure-track faculty and with the by-laws of the LSU System Board of Supervisors, but also they have a precedent in multi-year contracts awarded to non-tenure-track faculty in one of the university's research centers.

Unfortunately, our petition coincided with the economic downturn of 2008, exacerbated in Louisiana by the repeal of a state income tax. Fueled by conservative ideology and political ambition, a deliberate campaign to contract all state services, including education, has had devastating effects at LSU. At one point, LSU was told to prepare for a *thirty percent* budget cut. A new team of administrators, all of whom have since left LSU, responded to the budget crisis by issuing "release" letters to all instructors university-wide—regardless of years of service or number of teaching awards. Eventually, fourteen foreign language instructors were "released" (read "fired"), and programs in Japanese, Russian, German, etc., were terminated.

Meanwhile, our "revenue neutral" petition for three-year rolling contracts for instructors languished on the desks of three successive provosts. (The cycle of career administrators, who stay for a year or two, then leave, is now complemented by a cycle of interim administrators, who serve for a year or two, then step down.) Because regular university channels were blocked, we moved forward on two fronts: within the department, we implemented strategies for improving instructor morale; outside the department, we formed a faculty activist organization, LSUnited. The following will address both of these fronts.

IMPROVING INSTRUCTOR MORALE

When the new WPA arrived, she met a much-bruised group of teachers. Wary instructors, fearing the worst after the 2003–2005 releases, had now been sent "termination letters." A number of instructors had resigned; others were visibly angry and discouraged. New strategies needed to be designed and put into place as soon as possible in order to begin to turn morale around. The strategies included:

1. Implementing bottom-up input, rather than top-down leadership;
2. Respecting instructor curriculum design;
3. Streamlining a labor-intensive assessment process;
4. Providing instructors with clear goals, consistent implementation, and open communication; and
5. Advocating for instructors through labor organizing and activism.

IMPLEMENTING GRASSROOTS LEADERSHIP

The opportunities to change the culture of discouragement within the writing program and develop more positive and less despairing rhetoric were legion.

Most new WPAs know that effecting genuine program change requires patient listening and observing first, before suggesting changes or even soliciting input. Unfortunately, shortly after arriving, the new WPA learned that a new and more rigorous curriculum would be demanded of the first-year writing course if it were to pass a new assessment review. The present course had been based more on personal writing, and the assessment committee made clear it would not pass in its current form. This was the first opportunity to employ the grassroots approach as a strategy to gain instructor trust, although the message from the review committee had been delivered via a top-down approach. The new WPA convened a new first-year writing course committee that also included a rhetoric and composition professor and a graduate student, but most members were instructors and an instructor chaired the committee. After gathering input from their colleagues and holding several well-attended instructor meetings, the committee came up with a rigorous and exciting first-year writing course. Rather than the WPA taking ownership of the excellent instructor work, the committee itself led the meeting to roll out their new curriculum, answer questions, and explain in detail how the new curriculum might be taught. They brought in examples of papers and assignments. Once the main thrust of the new course had been agreed on (analytical writing), the administration of the writing program developed a course website, gathered materials from instructors, and served as facilitators and web designers in support of the committee and the many instructors who enthusiastically embraced the work of their colleagues. In addition, one holdover assignment from the previous curriculum, which was the only assignment that was researched, analytical and not personal, was expanded and retained as the assessment paper. The strategy here was to avoid changing everything and to give instructors time to develop the other new paper assignments. Although the original mandate had come from the upper administration, the new WPA had asked the instructors to take charge of the implementation of the mandate.

HONORING CURRICULUM DEVELOPED BY INSTRUCTORS

In response to the devastating 2003–2005 instructor layoff, the English department had moved the second required writing course to the sophomore year. The thinking was that sophomores have chosen their majors and thus have a disciplinary focus to write about. Furthermore, there are fewer sophomores than freshmen; thus fewer instructors would be needed to teach the new curriculum. When the new WPA arrived, she was charged to "gel" this relatively new course, which was taught by veteran instructors, new hires, and graduate students: the course lacked a clear identity. Again pursuing a grassroots strategy, she called for all syllabi for this second-year course and analyzed them. This review revealed that the second required course was in some ways very traditional and argument based. After this discovery, the WPA called another instructor meeting, also well attended. The WPA led a discussion of the argument-based structure evident in syllabi submitted by faculty, articulated this genre and its historical underpinnings, and then asked if faculty wanted to continue what seemed to be a broad-based consensus of what that course should teach. Instructors were enthusiastic, partly because, in spite of the need to change the curriculum for the first writing course to meet the review committee's criteria, the second course could still be taught as it had been in the last few years. Because research had been an element insisted on by the review committee, instructors agreed to add more research to the assigned papers. Otherwise, the main aspects of the course had been developed by individual faculty over time, and the fact that the new WPA was valuing previous practice was important and served to boost morale.

Streamlining Assessment

When the new WPA arrived, the current method of assessment was a vexed issue for the instructors. It required all instructors to spend several intense days grading/ranking all the end-of-semester papers, which were written within an electronic interface. Instructors resisted and resented such a labor-intensive assessment, especially since the additional work was not compensated. In response, the WPA suggested other statistically valid and reliable options for assessment.

Instructors were especially encouraged by the prospect of using random sampling and combining it with a rotation of about one-fourth to one-third of the faculty for each semester assessment. This option also insured that instructors would not have to give up valuable grading time at the end of the semester. To achieve a high level of confidence in the results (95%), it would be necessary to randomly sample four papers from each section; this method resulted in a reduction of the number of hours instructors had to devote to assessment. Instead, teachers gained more time for grading and served on the assessment on rotation. Instructors were ecstatic over the new assessment.

This streamlining, along with the validation of the second-year course, seemed to relieve some of the tension in the program. However, the termination letters still hung over the instructors' heads and no one could convince them that, because of their importance in the university, their jobs were safe. Everyone had either experienced or heard about the 2003–2005 "releases." What would prevent layoffs from decimating their ranks again?

Advocacating Within University Channels

Clearly, the only real solution to the threat of the termination letters would be to have them rescinded. Any lip service toward job security and advocacy could, at best, be seen as the WPA's naiveté and, at worst, increase the cynicism and frustration toward all things and people administrative. More than one instructor had resigned or made plans to retire as soon as possible because of the letters. The dean of the college also addressed the issue and pledged support. At times, the lip service only seemed to increase the anger. The termination letters had been issued to insure maximum legal flexibility in releasing staff during a period of brutal budget cuts. The chances that a new WPA would be able to have them rescinded were nil. Early in that first semester, though, a couple of opportunities for addressing the situation presented themselves.

One such opportunity was a meeting with the interim provost, the dean of the college, the department chair, the WPA, and a handful of instructors teaching in the department's English as a second language program (ESL). The WPA had requested an opportunity to re-introduce the three-year rolling contract petition to this interim provost. In part because of repeated administrative turnovers, this petition had sat on the desks of provosts and interim provosts, although the English department chairs kept resubmitting it. During the meeting, the WPA presented a chart illustrating the large proportion of writing classes taught by instructors. In response, the provost said (off the record and not in writing) that English instructors were too important to be "released." In order to try to ameliorate instructor anxiety, the new WPA communicated to instructors, in small groups and one-on-one, that there had been verbal reassurance at "high levels" of their continuing employment.

At this vulnerable moment, it was important that the WPA advocate for job stability and fair treatment of instructors to the upper administration, but also it was crucial that the WPA communicate that commitment to the instructors themselves. This kind of communication helped build confidence in the brand new WPA, assured instructors that the problem of job security had not been forgotten, and stifled rumors.

A new challenge to job security came early in that same first semester of the new WPA. A senior administrator in the Department of Mathematics attempted to convince the WPA that it was in the students' best interest to turn all required writing courses over to a computerized grading and commenting system, thereby eliminating the need for all but one instructor. The administrator boasted of his having been able to do just that in basic mathematics courses. It was difficult for a new WPA to confront such strong persuasive efforts, while the dean and chair had either not been briefed on the purpose of the meeting or had just failed to warn the WPA. Since the mathematician did not know the realities of teaching writing, the WPA carefully explained the differences between the programs. Meanwhile the dean's body language revealed his support. Again, the WPA communicated to instructors these advocacy efforts and the dean's apparent support, and teaching all sections of required writing courses with one instructor has not surfaced again.

After a year and a half of receiving termination letters that were renewed each semester, instructors were finally returned to one-year contracts in 2011, and morale improved . . . somewhat. Nevertheless, the 2003–2005 "release" of thirty-five instructors, followed by the termination letters of 2010–2011, had made it abundantly clear that the upper administration considered instructors contingent labor, regardless of years of service and demonstrated excellence in teaching. More than one instructor, even some of the best, announced that they were less inclined to perform departmental service or participate in professional development activities, given their low salaries, the university's failure to award raises for five years, and the lack of job security. New strategies were needed to address the issues of salary and job security.

ADVOCACATING BEYOND UNIVERSITY CHANNELS

In 2010, based on a recommendation from a Faculty Senate exploratory committee, a faculty group began to organize a local chapter of the Louisiana Association of Educators (LAE), an affiliate of the NEA. The former chair, the WPA, a few other English professors and instructors saw this effort as a way to address both the salary and contract issues. Although the organizing efforts seemed rather disorganized, a number of English department faculty members signed union cards and began paying dues to the local chapter. Their hope was expressed in the chapter name, "LSUnited." But convincing fellow faculty members, especially instructors, to become card-carrying, dues-paying members of a union proved very difficult.[8] The annual dues were very high: over $500/year for professors making salaries in the $60–100,000 range, and only slightly less for instructors who made around $30,000 per year. During the first two years of organizing efforts, most members joined primarily because the union gave LSU faculty access to a paid lobbyist. Any meaningful change in funding for the university would require legislative action, and the Louisiana legislature had imposed massive budget cuts on higher education during the economic downturn. Indeed, these budget cuts were the cause of the instructor termination

---

8   Michael Berubé, Stanley Aronowitz, and Marc Bousuet detail the challenges of organizing unions of university teachers—whether graduate teaching assistants, adjuncts, full-time non-tenure-track instructors, or tenure-track professors.

letters. What LAE could provide during this period of vulnerability was a voice for public education in the legislative process.

Nevertheless, high dues impeded recruitment, and repeated requests to LAE and NEA for organizing assistance were ignored or denied. All NEA's resources were focused on union-busting efforts in states like Wisconsin, and LAE was busy fighting its own battles to protect the K-12 teachers threatened by legislation to reduce pensions, to award state funding to private academies, and to impose arbitrary teacher performance reviews. It soon became apparent that the interests of LAE and university faculty were not always congruent, and that LSU faculty did not yet have the political will to unionize. So LSUnited disaffiliated from the union, and redefined itself as a faculty advocacy group.

Although disaffiliation might have appeared to be a step backwards, it had the opposite effect. It allowed the active members of LSUnited to concentrate on what mattered most to members: securing faculty raises after five dry years, protecting and improving retirement benefits, and lobbying for appropriate job security for instructors. LSUnited also found a forum for bringing these issues to the attention of not only the university's upper administration, but also the governing board of the entire LSU system and the public. Monthly LSU System Board of Supervisors meetings include a period for public comment during which representatives from the local press are present. Using these public comment periods as a platform, LSUnited mounted a consistent campaign of speakers before the Board of Supervisors: activists from LSUnited; award-winning "Distinguished Research Masters" and chaired professors; veteran instructors; and young professors who had decided to take jobs elsewhere. Month after month, these speakers shocked board members with their frank, but always professional, testimony. Local press began to publish sound bites from speakers' prepared remarks, and word spread among the faculty that someone was speaking publicly about salaries and appropriate job security. Board members themselves seemed embarrassed, assuring the speakers at the end of every public comment period, "Please don't think you are being ignored. We hear what you are saying and we're sympathetic." Such comments, of course, allowed LSUnited to return at the next meeting with demands for actions to match sympathetic words.

At his first LSU Board meeting, the new incoming chancellor and system president heard these testimonials. In his first open meeting with faculty, he alluded to our concerns. Then, in his first weeks on the job as chancellor and system president, he announced 4 percent raises. What role LSUnited's campaign of lobbying the board played in securing the long overdue raises is indeterminable, but the faculty certainly saw and appreciated that LSUnited was speaking for them. Likewise, there were hopeful signs that LSUnited's persistent lobbying convinced the provost to consider the petition, submitted four years earlier, for three-year rolling contracts for instructors. At a Faculty Senate meeting in the fall of 2013, the provost stated, "I don't see any reason why we can't get this done this year." Soon thereafter, the Office of Human Resource Management convened discussions with selected instructors.

Finally in 2014, the university adopted a new instructor policy that included first and third-year reviews, three-year contracts awarded to instructors who pass a rigorous sixth-year review, and the new rank of "Senior Instructor" (with a step-raise) awarded to instructors who have served continuously for twelve years. The next year, all instructors received salary adjustments based on merit and years of service. Although the new policy does not include "three-year rolling contracts," and although the raises are insufficient to compensate for years of neglect, we count these gains as a modest victory. Our writing program survived the backlash against its previous system of instructor employment, review, and promotion, and it has now added a modicum of appropriate job security to that imperfect but workable system.

There is, of course, more work to be done: recent letters announcing the instructor raises state that, in addition to annual performance reviews and student evaluations, raises will be contingent on "your rate of student success as measured by the percentage of students receiving a D, F, or withdrawing from your course." The upper administration is now focused on student retention (on which tuition dollars depend), and, yet again, vulnerable instructor labor has become the site of a wrong-headed response to a perceived crisis.

CONCLUSION

Our story demonstrates that despair is not a strategy—even though strategies must change over time as obstacle after obstacle surfaces. For many years, LSU had a stable cohort of respected instructors with a measure of job security. Despite repeated attempts to dismantle this functional system of instructor review and employment, the WPA and the department chair, with the support of the entire English department, have projected a firm belief in the value of instructor expertise and advocated publicly for fair compensation and appropriate job security. Respect and advocacy have helped restore morale, returned stability to the core writing faculty, and made substantial progress toward concrete improvements in employment conditions.

WORKS CITED

Aronowitz, Stanley. "Academic Unionism and the Future of Higher Education." *Will Teach for Food: Academic Labor in Crisis*, edited by Cary Nelson, U of Minnesota P, 1997, pp. 181–215.

Bartholomae, David. "Teaching On and Off the Tenure Track: Highlights from the ADE Survey of Staffing Patterns in English." *Pedagogy*, vol. 11, no. 1, 2011, pp. 7–32.

Bérubé, Michael. "The Blessed of the Earth." *Will Teach for Food: Academic Labor in Crisis*, edited by Cary Nelson, U of Minnesota P, 1997, pp. 153–78.

Bousquet, Marc. *How the University Works: Higher Education and the Low-Wage Nation*. NYU P, 2007.

Donaghue, Frank. *The Last Professors: The Corporate University and the Fate of the Humanities*. Fordham UP, 2008.

Johnson, Benjamin, et al., editors. *Steal This University: The Rise of the Corporate University and the Academic Labor Movement*. Routledge, 2003.

Kahn, Seth. "Ecology of Sustainable Labor Equity in Writing Programs." Council for Writing Program Administrators Conference, Boise, Idaho, 17 July 2015. Plenary Address.

Nelson, Cary. "Between Crisis and Opportunity: The Future of the Academic Workforce." *Will Teach for Food: Academic Labor in Crisis*, edited by Cary Nelson, U of Minnesota P, 1997, pp. 3–31.

CHAPTER 3

AN APOLOGIA AND A WAY FORWARD: IN DEFENSE OF THE LECTURER LINE IN WRITING PROGRAMS

Mark McBeth

City University of New York

Tim McCormack

John Jay College

Threads: Organizing Within and Across Ranks; Professionalizing and Developing in Complex Contexts; Local Changes to Workload, Pay, and Working Conditions

> To pursue educational reform is thus to work in an impure space, where intractable material conditions always threaten to expose rhetorics of change as delusional or deliberately deceptive; it is also to insist that bureaucracies don't simply impede change; they are the social instruments that make change possible.
>
> – Richard Miller, As If Learning Mattered: Reforming Higher Education

To date, the critical (and criticizing) discourse of contingent labor in writing programs has thoroughly charted the exploitation of part-time instructors, and the curricular and programmatic consequences such hiring practices have on reformed approaches to writing (Aronowitz; Bradley; Bousquet et al.; McMahon & Greene). Additional research indicates that reliance upon adjunct faculty has a direct impact on student learning, retention, and achievement (Baldwin). While part-time faculty provide a diverse and talented group of expert practitioners, their tenuous and marginalized positions in the university prevent them from a fully-integrated commitment to program development and ongoing instructional improvement. Adjunct faculty juggle differing curricular criteria from the varying programs where they teach, rarely receive pay for hours other than "teaching time," and often are not around long enough to fully invest in their departments because enrollment-dependent employment is unpredictable. While the research cited above analyzes adjunct labor in numerous disciplinary departments, part-time teaching causes extra collateral damage in first-year writing where incoming freshmen first learn new literacy expectations of the university, and where doing poorly can spell doom for their future college careers.

Meanwhile, largely relying upon these disempowered and underpaid contingent instructors, writing program administrators (WPAs) face persistent injunctions from upper-level administrators to improve student writing outcomes. Though WPAs may value adjunct instructors for their versatility and innovation, the university system for which the WPA administers treats these teachers as dispensable—an institutional inconsistency that places both the disenfranchised adjunct faculty and the compromised administrator in an awkward relationship of codependency and confrontation. As the semester-by-semester hiring wheel turns, writing program administrators grapple daily with the debilitating consequences of contingent labor practices and their resulting impact on writing program success, for which they are held responsible. Elizabeth Wardle laments the dependence on transient part-time faculty and its relationship to writing program performance in "Intractable Writing Program Problems." She states:

> This set of problems can be paralyzing, preventing composition courses and programs from moving forward and acting on the knowledge of our field in both their curricula and their employment practices. How can we act on the knowledge of our field in our composition curricula, particularly when that knowledge suggests multiple paths forward, and when so many of those actually in composition classrooms are not necessarily familiar with any of it? How can we work against entrenched labor practices and material conditions in order to make changes?

While scholars have exposed the financial and political forces that enable the ill treatment of educational laborers, and while they have detailed the limiting instructional outcomes for such labor practices, too often the solutions offered are limited to calls for complete labor revolutions or line-in-the-sand workplace uprisings. However, since the adjunct labor challenge impacts everything that WPAs must achieve, the irresolute question of how to untangle the relationship of part-time faculty exploitation and the goals of writing program administrators cannot wait for a moment of complete academic labor upheaval. Instead, we would argue, the reliance on part-time faculty in writing programs has caused such systemic breakdowns that the "winds of change" have already begun to blow (Hairston 76).

In this chapter we explain our local labor situation at a mid-sized, public, urban college-writing program, where part-time faculty taught more than 95 percent of the first-year writing courses. We analyze how creating and implementing a new curriculum provided an opportunity for reform in the hiring practices of writing faculty that concurrently improved the working conditions of part-time faculty and enabled a wider-ranging cohort of full-time faculty in our program. Miller asserts that "all teaching occurs within the context of a deeply entrenched bureaucratic system that exercises any number of material constraints on what must take place in the classroom, on who and what may be allowed in that space, and on how those entities and materials may interact" (19). Within this constraint-driven decision making, the WPA's goals cannot simply resist bureaucratic imperatives, but must alternatively re-envision judicious solutions to them, even if not legibly revolutionary. Exceeding a pessimistic critique of labor issues that induces only inertia, this apologia of administrative policy-making details how WPAs can enable hiring practices that take into account the often conflicted objectives of the institution, the labor union, the writing program, the full-time/adjunct faculty, and the writing student. Our workable resolution to writing program labor contingency sits somewhere between purposeful accommodation and a building block for imagining a progressive (and progressing) future for writing program labor practices.

REDESIGNING A WRITING PROGRAM

In 2002, for the first time in more than a decade, John Jay College of Criminal Justice/CUNY hired a Ph.D. in composition/rhetoric as a full-time, tenure-track faculty member to direct the writing program. In that role the English department asked him to upend a thirty-year-old composition curriculum, based in belletristic essay/writing-for-literature, and replace it with curricular and programmatic structures that represented the best new practices in the field. In just a few years, he designed a portfolio-driven, inquiry-based, and writing across the curriculum (WAC)-focused writing program grounded in the *WPA Outcomes Statement* and later reinforced by the *Framework for Success in Post-Secondary Writing*. Using scaffolded assignments, reflective writing, and a rhetorical focus, this curricular design engages students in deep revision as they compose for diverse audiences in diverse contexts. The three-course sequence (basic writing and two semesters of composition) offers a coherent and consistent curriculum, what we have come to call an equal opportunity writing curriculum—a common composing experience for all students, regardless of section, semester, or instructor.

The then lone-wolf WPA navigated the new curriculum through varying committees of department, college, and university governance, and in 2006 the

College Curriculum Committee and College Council both voted this theoretically-framed, post-secondary writing curriculum into institutional existence. Once approved, the WPA completed faculty training for the more than eighty-five part-time writing faculty, but with limited resources he slowly realized that curriculum change does not occur through institutional fiat, and that national organizations' guiding resolutions for curriculum design had not yet adequately articulated how to overcome a major curricular revision barrier: contingent labor.

During curricular conversion, adjunct faculty had little motivation to alter their already established course designs, and with only two hours per semester of paid part-time faculty development time in the union contract, we had no way to leverage instructor buy-in for the curricular changes. Prior to the curriculum restructuring, the lack of ongoing faculty development had not posed much of a quandary because faculty designed their individual courses to meet loosely articulated departmental guidelines, and no assessment process existed. In comparison, however, the new curriculum demanded that faculty learn new ways to teach writing, and required more consistency and cohesion across sections. In "Redefining Composition, Managing Change, and the Role of the WPA," Geoffrey Chase asserts that a writing program must, in fact, have programmatic "internal coherence," resting upon four components:

1. common goals, specific and detailed enough to be meaningful and useful;
2. common assignments;
3. standard methods for evaluation and assessment across multiple sections; and
4. a commitment to examining and discussing these shared features openly.

He later asserts that internal coherence is the area "over which we have the most control, and it is the facet of administration most directly linked to the training we receive as graduate students and junior faculty" (245). However, designing a coherent curriculum only accomplishes the first of Chase's stated components, leaving 2, 3, and 4 unrealized. Without funding for part-time faculty, a WPA is unable to introduce the new curriculum standards, develop common curricular assignments, assess the new curriculum's outcomes, nor collaboratively share faculty insights; thus, a new curriculum on paper does not convert to a new curriculum in action.

While most of our dedicated adjunct faculty saw how our new curriculum advanced students' college literacy and were willing to try it out, their implementation depended on a mixture of workload generosity and their particular expertise in understanding and translating the guidelines into course materials. From their perspective, once again, the institution (including the WPA) wanted to improve the writing program by asking for more work and expertise, while maintaining the same low pay and low institutional status. Meanwhile, the WPA-boss had to decide between curricular innovation and contingent exploitation: an administrative stalemate.

At this problematic juncture for the John Jay Writing Program, the upper administration of the college agreed to hire four tenure-track composition/rhetoric faculty over a three-year cycle. Each new comp/rhet Ph.D. hire brought their particular beneficial talents to the new curriculum (i.e., basic writing, rhetoric, and applied linguistics), and all of them contributed to faculty development, program assessment, and co-curricular initiatives. However, these tenure-track hires did not solve our curricular coherence problems because new faculty needed to negotiate their "publish-or-perish" imperatives, as well as contribute to a variety of literacy-based initiatives at the college, which inevitably pulled them away from teaching in the first-year writing program. Even with combined course loads of these freshly hired full-time composition faculty (each teaching seven courses per year), eighty percent of composition courses were still taught by part-time faculty. To achieve the full benefits of the new curriculum design, the program needed to devise a divergent type of teaching staff; cautiously, we approached our department with the idea of full-time lecturers. With historically-based, well-reasoned rationales, the faculty opposed the plan, fearing that lecturers would create a "two-tier" system of "lesser-status" instructors. Weighing our colleagues' disinclinations alongside curricular advantages, we began a research process to change their minds.

THE NATIONAL AND LOCAL CONTEXT

In 1986 the AAUP released a report, "On Full-Time Non-Tenure-Track Appointments"[1] that warned against "the scope and extent of the problem" of FTNTT positions, and concluded that these "tenure-ineligible full-time faculty

---

1   In "Why Hire Non-Tenure Track Faculty?" Cross and Goldenberg (2002) further elaborated upon the institutional controls of these positions:

> Whereas the appointment of tenure-track faculty is always closely monitored by university administrations, non-tenure-track appointments are usually governed by decentralized decision-making that is almost invisible at the university level . . . leading to collective decisions that may be wholly inconsistent with overall university priorities. These two factors—growing numbers and lack of awareness—create a context within which the nature of the professoriate can change in ways directly contradictory to the educational preferences of university leaders. (27)

Their critique of such hiring conditions underscored the ad hoc nature that often defines FT-NTT faculty positions, not only creating brutal working conditions for faculty, but often mitigating the learning goals of the program in favor of an easy fix for increasing full-time faculty to student ratios.

appointments are without merit and that, for the sake of higher education . . . the abuse of these appointments should be stopped" (92). A somewhat softened position appeared in the *NEA 2008 Almanac of Higher Education* where Rhoades and Maitland examined the "best practices" and guidelines for institutions to hire FTNTT faculty: they suggested explicit parameters of employment, such as "defined dates and process for appointment, renewal, or termination; evaluations, with explicit criteria; equitable salaries; [and] equitable benefits" (72). Unfortunately, the explosion in hiring of FTNTT faculty in the last decade has often occurred without addressing these best practices.

At CUNY the lecturer title had existed for many years and, per status quo, our university followed less-than-fair norms for lecturer lines, such as high teaching loads (five to four per annum), hiring descriptions that did not match job expectations, underestimated status in departments, ill-defined service responsibilities, and restrictive "gen-ed"-only teaching assignments. In its own contradictory way, our union had long argued against the "devaluing of tenure" by hiring lecturer lines, while simultaneously championing the need for more stable, better rewarded adjunct faculty positions. Serendipitously, in 2008, the union tried to solve this inconsistency by creating "conversion lines" where colleges could approve full time, non-tenure-track lines, as long as long-time adjunct faculty filled the positions. In a 2010 PSC (Professional Staff Congress, a CUNY union)/CUNY update on "Adjunct Rights and Benefits," a section sub-titled "Full-time Lecturer Positions" further articulated this position:

> . . . 100 new full-time lecturer positions were created, for
> which the hiring pool will be restricted to experienced CUNY
> adjuncts. To be eligible to apply, you must have taught in the
> department in which the position is offered or have taught a
> related course in a different department of the same college
> for 8 of the 10 most recent semesters (excluding summers),
> and in 7 of those 10 semesters, you must have taught at least
> 6 classroom hours including the semester in which the search
> is conducted. As with regular full-time lines, specific hiring
> criteria are established by each department.

While this circuitously-articulated hiring statement emphasizes the amount (and frequency) of time that an eligible adjunct professor had to work within a department, it leaves the pedagogical qualifications (and job description) to the department's discretion. In this union proposal, we recognized an open invitation to define the hiring practices and job descriptions for FTNTT faculty. With a carefully proposed articulation of the FTNTT position, we could increase the full-time faculty-to-student ratios under the conditions of the CUNY contract and still prevent the same-policy-as-usual exploitations of faculty. While some in our department considered non-tenure-track faculty a risky compromise, writing program faculty saw this strategic organizational move as an opportunity that we could control: by further defining the hiring process, job description and faculty status of FTNTT lecturers, we could turn perceived accommodation into a progressive solution.

Seizing this kairotic administrative moment,[2] we drafted a proposal to not only hire the two lines "requested" from upper administration but, additionally, to hire eight programmatically-assigned lecturers. We realized, somewhat intuitively, that the stakeholders (i.e., the writing program, the department, the college administration, the union, and the university's central offices) could all achieve their seemingly disparate goals, and with added full-time faculty for our new curriculum, we would make an immediate and dramatic impact on student learning. Despite our university's misguided history in hiring FTNTT positions as well as our own discipline's complicity in the contingent labor problem (see Anderson & Cara-Fals; Jacoby), we strove to re-envision how lecturers could contribute to our programmatic initiatives, while also enhancing their status, livelihood, and career track.

DEFINING A LOCAL LECTURER POSITION

Taking into consideration the skeptical views about FTNNT positions, and our own goals to have long-term, invested FT faculty, we immediately rejected the following models of lectureships:

1. The "turnover lecturer model," where a department hires lecturer faculty for a few years and then returns them to the contingent labor pool. This post-doc model cannot offer the writing program the invested stability to enhance a new curriculum;
2. The "teaching only model," where lecturer faculty members teach courses but don't participate in faculty life. As a mere "doubling down" on the current adjunct faculty practice, this position benefits adjunct faculty by paying minimally more and increasing stability, but ultimately minimizes the influence these talented faculty could contribute to a writing program;
3. The "graduate student model of lectureships," where graduate students teach in a writing program while they earn advanced degrees. Though graduate programs may benefit by offering their students paid learn-as-you-go placements, and graduate students gain teaching experience,

---

2   See Wardle's description of kairotic administrative moments.

inevitably such positions exploit emerging members of our profession during the vulnerable graduate school career moment. In addition, their degree-related workload prevents them from programmatic service, and they only stay until their degree's completion, so this model doesn't foster continuing writing program development;

4. The "freshman-composition-only model," where lecturers teach only in the composition sequence while ignoring their other areas of expertise (i.e., creative writing, professional writing, digital rhetoric, etc.). In this case, lectureships become mono-modal, second-tier teaching positions, under-utilizing FT faculty capabilities for developing a vertically-driven writing program.

After rejecting these models, we reviewed related scholarship in the field, interviewed our adjunct and full-time faculty colleagues, and sought advice from our union to formulate a freshly-conceived lecturership. We then drafted a single-spaced, eight-page proposal to hire ten lecturer lines over the next five years. Along with a statement of need and a general job description, we included detailed sections on the following:

- hiring processes of lecturers;
- lecturers' contributions to faculty life in the department and the college;
- personnel evaluations for promotion of lecturers;
- pedagogical and administrative challenges of lecturers; and
- detailed timelines of these positions' implementation and contractual advancement.

From the very beginning of our proposal process, we aimed for affirmative conditions that could benefit not only the writing program and the college but also most importantly our lecturers and their students. We made sure to define lecturer lines as positions of not just need but expertise:

> The addition of ten lecturers would provide curricular, programmatic, and staffing stability for the John Jay Writing Program. Lecturers could enhance the teaching in the core composition classes, provide energy and expertise for the existing literacy initiatives at the college, and create new literacy programs for our students.

In other words, these positions reach well beyond the teaching work-horse models described above and, instead, look to create faculty lines that professionalized these teaching career tracks.

To ensure the success of these positions, our proposal delineated the specific requirements that the college would need to guarantee:

- Lecturers hold full-time positions within the English department, with the potential of a Certificate of Continued Employment [hereafter, CCE] in their fifth year, as provided by the union contract;
- Lecturers earn one course of reassigned time in their first year to take a teaching practicum seminar;
- Lecturers have a constructive and progressive agenda of service to the writing program, the department, and the college;
- Lecturers will go through faculty review and promotion processes of annual review by the chair and submission of a Form C; however, these evaluations will focus only on teaching and service;
- Lecturers are assessed by the P&B committee based on their teaching observations, their student evaluations, their pedagogical and curricular contributions, and their service to the writing program, department, or college;
- Lecturers are eligible for promotional steps to associate and full lecturer (discussed more fully below);
- Lecturers may apply for sabbaticals after attaining the CCE and 6 years of full-time service;
- Lecturers have departmental voting rights, office space, and travel funds in the same way that tenure-track faculty do;
- Lecturers are eligible for the same reassigned time as tenure-track faculty, based on service contributions to the writing program, the department, or the college;
- Lecturers can apply for fellowships, grants, and other non-teaching opportunities and have access to reassigned time for college or departmental service in the same manner as full-time faculty.

By listing specific work criteria and explicit benefits, we defined the positions as equal to tenure-track positions; lecturers would have additional teaching and service contributions in place of the scholarship and publishing responsibilities of TT faculty. By outlining lecturers' equal access to the benefits and opportunities of full-time faculty, we also circumvented concerns of our tenure-track colleagues who worried about a two-caste full-time professoriate.

We took great pains to identify the potential pitfalls in creating a writing program staffed with lecturer lines, and to preemptively offer solutions before bureaucratic controls interceded. For example, in the proposal we discuss the issue of teaching "burnout" and subsequently, the need for promotional steps in these positions:

- With a teaching load of 4/4, mostly in the composition sequence, there is the potential for lecturers in the Writing Program to be unable to handle the crush of students (close to one hundred students per semester). In a program that requires individual student conferences for each student and thorough feedback on students' written work there is a potential for lecturers to be overwhelmed. In addition, this teaching load over a number of semesters may lead to "burnout" of these faculty colleagues. The following steps will be taken to reduce the potential for "burnout" and to maintain the quality of their teaching: lecturers should consider teaching one of their courses over the winter intersession; lecturers should be eligible for reassigned time; lecturers should teach one course per year outside the writing sequence; lecturers should be given preferential scheduling.
- *Three-step Lectureships.* Promotional steps for lecturers are not part of our current CUNY-PSC contract. They are, however, crucial to our vision of this position. Steps will provide incentive for lecturers to continue growing and contributing professionally even after they receive their CCE [Certificate of Continuous Employment]; steps will further increase the comparability of lecturer and faculty lines; and steps will reinforce to lecturers that these positions are as close as possible to the equivalent of tenured professorial lines.

By forthrightly acknowledging the potential problems, we gained support from both our departmental colleagues and our upper administration. Union contractual limitations precluded certain possibilities of our proposal, such as how lecturers could divide their course load over a fiscal year (aka, not being allowed to spread their course load over the summer session if they wished).[3] Our early recognition of locally-contextualized obstacles kept us vigilant about these challenges and led us to make other workload accommodations in their stead.

To further allay the perception that there is a two-tier faculty, and as a means to insure a competitive hiring process, we asked applicants to meet rigorous candidacy requirements equal to our tenure-track hires. Each applicant submitted a philosophy of teaching, a course syllabus they had taught, and a prospective course they could teach, as well as examples of their teaching practice. All candidates completed a qualifying interview, and a full-day campus visit. For lecturer candidates, the job talk consisted of a "curriculum" presentation where they tackled a literacy issue and how they addressed it in their teaching. All members of the English department—both comp/rhet and literature faculty

---

3   In fact, the provision to have "three step lectureships" was not allowed by the union contract, but we have continued to argue for it in each succeeding contract, with the college's support.

alike—attended these presentations and then weighed in on the quality of the candidates. In the process of hiring lecturers, departmental faculty understood the valuable contributions that these candidates could bring to pedagogical, curricular, and administrative functions of the writing program, even if they didn't increase our research agenda.

Not only did we explicitly define lecturer lines to our institutional stakeholders, but we reciprocally disclosed the parameters to the candidates throughout the hiring process. Without this transparency, a candidate could enter a job for all the wrong reasons, or later, be surprised by the specific workload of lecturer lines. We also forewarned candidates that these were not temporary, postdoctoral-style positions, nor stepping stones to tenure-track positions based in publishable scholarship. Quite frankly, applicants who stated a strong interest in purposefully pursuing scholarship did not make it to our interview list. We intended to hire people who placed teaching and curriculum-related service at the center of their careers. While some candidates held terminal doctoral degrees, the majority of the best applicants had M.A.s or M.F.A.s in a writing-related discipline.

The other stakeholders in this hiring process—our own longstanding and talented adjunct faculty—had an advantage when applying. Our faculty had helped us implement our new curriculum, knew our student body well, and brought a range of expertise in legal, business, and digital writing. Through a job ad that sounded familiar and reassuring to them, we encouraged these "natural candidates" to apply, and those who did out-performed the national candidates.[4] Though the hiring committee consisted of mostly non-writing faculty, who did not know our adjunct writing faculty well, seven of the nine lecturer positions we have currently filled went to long-time adjunct faculty from our department ranks.

THE BENEFITS

Once hired, new lecturers earned one course of reassigned time in their first semester to participate in a practicum course that covered both current theories and praxis in the field of composition and rhetoric, and that analyzed how those perspectives related to the curriculum at John Jay. As a result of our comprehensive hiring practices, these selected colleagues had formidable teaching capabilities, but we wanted to ensure that they had composition-rhetoric theory to undergird their veteran teaching practices. Most importantly, their practicum work solidified and added another level of coherence to the writing program

---

4   Surprisingly, some of our best adjunct faculty did not apply; they divulged to us that a full-time commitment did not interest them because of conflicting artistic pursuits, reminding us that not all adjunct faculty seek full-time academic employment.

because, as a programmatic group, we could discuss issues from a collective foundation of knowledge. This theoretical initiation into the John Jay program didn't end all disagreements about how to approach the classroom. (We didn't serve a comp/rhet Kool-Aid during the practicum.) It did, however, create a community of practice and set the tone for open discussion about our writing program goals, pedagogical approaches, and future plans.

Participating in the practicum also allowed the writing program director to learn the strengths of each newly hired lecturer, thus acting as a means to career mentorship and program placement. After their first year, each lecturer, with the informed advice of the director, could choose a service contribution to the writing program. In this service they would learn the ropes of the program and, subsequently, would assume more responsibilities which would earn reassigned time. This process would define their service to the department, add to their accumulating vitae, and provide validation for their Certificate of Continuous Employment. Currently, we have a lecturer working in our writing across the curriculum program, another helping to direct first-year writing, another overseeing the writing minors in Journalism/Fiction writing, and yet another acting as a coordinator of testing and curriculum for our small number of Basic Writing students. Another lecturer (who holds a J.D.) has redesigned our legal writing courses, and our most recent hire works with our full-time ESL faculty to redesign the curriculum for English-language learners. Four of the nine lecturers have a semester's worth of reassigned time for these projects, reducing their course load to 4-3. Perhaps more importantly, the expertise of our lecturers has enriched out writing program, solidifying their roles in the department and the college.

Beyond the investment in writing program initiatives, these lecturer lines have increased the number of first-year writing courses taught by full-time faculty: the percentage of courses taught by part time faculty has dropped from a high of ninety-nine percent in spring of 2007 to seventy percent in the current semester. With the full integration of our last two lecturer hires, we should reach a 50/50 split. As we had predicted, lecturer faculty enable our robust assessment practice, contribute to faculty development and mentoring for adjunct faculty, and provide veteran faculty for placement into special programs like Learning Communities. Perhaps most importantly, lecturer faculty advance our new curriculum through their semester-by-semester experiences teaching the courses and providing new innovations. If the original designer of this curriculum and the subsequent director previously espoused the theory-rich and research-based foundation of the college's writing curriculum (which often fell on deaf ears and glazed eyes), these highly gifted and informed practitioners perpetuate curricular development by constantly showing and evolving the curriculum to its next stage.

MOVING ON: A VISION FOR THE FUTURE OF FULL-TIME NON-TENURED FACULTY

In the MLA report "Education in the Balance: A Report on the Academic Workforce in English," the committee vacillates between two contradictory ideas about NTTFT positions:

> the concept of a non-tenure-track faculty is an illegitimate exercise of institutional authority; it is, and it ought to be, contested by whatever means available. . . . On the other hand . . . a multi-tiered system has been in place across the entire one-hundred-year-plus history of English departments and is likely to be for the foreseeable future. . . . We hope our report can newly inform the discussion of the academic labor market and assist efforts to bring respect and equity to all who are teaching on our campuses. (15)

In this vacillation, we see the mistake of manufacturing a binary labor division between fully-employed, happy tenure-track faculty and underemployed, unhappy, part-time faculty. At John Jay College, if we had retained this either-or vision, we would not have gained the qualified writing program faculty that we can boast today, and those faculty would have remained on the low-status spinning wheel of "adjunctland." WPAs must interrogate the context (or predicament) of their programmatic staffing; analyze their institutional contexts and budgetary constraints, and institutional mission goals; and seize upon administrative moments where change is possible, to proactively address the too-often-undiscussed status quo. As Richard Miller has advised:

> If one is genuinely interested in improving both the working conditions of writing teachers and the quality of instruction undergraduates receive, it's important to ask where the money will come from to support such improvements. It's also important to know who is in a position to make the decisions that will actually bring about such changes. Who are the stakeholders? Who are the agents of change? Who are the allies that matter? Who can help with the problems that exist right here, right now? ("Opinion" 369)

At John Jay College, we heeded fair labor practices to hire full-time lecturers and fulfilled the "right here, right now" needs of our urban, public institution and its students. We listened to a wide-range of stakeholders whose valid input nuanced and strengthened our decision-making about NTTFT faculty, to eliminate their legitimate concerns.

After years of sitting on the borderlands of the academy as adjuncts, our current lecturers are fully "matriculated," active department colleagues. One reported that she finally has found an academic home; another finally published the novel she had penned for years; a third went on a health leave for a semester, relieved that he did not lose the salary and job benefits he gained as a lecturer. Our lecturer lines are not perfect by any means, but in terms of incrementally "fairer and fairer" employment practice, we now have a point of departure upon which to improve.[5] It would serve all involved to re-envision the types of instructional positions we can create in our local institutions and, as a result, attempt to create equal opportunity writing programs that offer an equitable handshake to students, instructors, faculty members and, yes, even administrators (at least the intellectual bureaucrats who strive to support pedagogically-sound programming). While we should never end our scrutiny and resistance to oppressive labor practices, we also can't sit idly year-after-year, waiting for wholesale revolution that never arrives. After all, our writing students who march along with us need the benefit of revisionary writing programs to develop their own voices of resistance.

WORKS CITED

American Association of University Professors. "On Full-Time Non-Tenure-Track Appointments." *Committee on Academic Freedom and Tenure (Committee A)*, 19 June 1986, aaupatnyit.org/nontenure.pdf.

Anderson, Lynn E., and John Carta-Falsa. "Factors That Make Faculty and Student Relationships Effective." *College Teaching*, vol. 50, no. 4, 2002, pp. 134–38.

Aronowitz, Stanley. *The Knowledge Factory: Dismantling the Corporate University and Creating True Higher Learning*. Beacon Press, 2000.

Baldwin, Roger G., and Matthew R. Wawrzynski. "Contingent Faculty as Teachers: What We Know; What We Need to Know." *American Behavioral Scientist*, vol. 55, no. 11, 2011, pp. 1485–509, researchgate.net/publication/254074400_Contingent _Faculty_as_Teachers_What_We_Know_What_We_Need_to_Know.

Benjamin, Ernst. "How Over-Reliance On Contingent Appointments Diminishes Faculty Involvement in Student Learning." *Peer Review*, vol. 5, no. 1, 2002, p. 4.

---

5   As Steve Street suggests in *Academe*, we need to move past this full-time/part-time divide to understand that we already have a professoriate that has a multiplicity of tiers: adjunct faculty (recently hired one course), adjunct faculty (long time/more than one course), graduate teaching fellows, faculty emeritus who still teach, tenure-track faculty, tenured faculty, emeritus faculty who do not teach, faculty chairs, lecturers, instructors, and teaching assistants. All faculty positions would benefit from the explicitly defined and carefully guarded job descriptions we have delineated for our lecturer lines.

Education Source, aacu.org/publications-research/periodicals/how-over-reliance -contingent-appointments-diminishes-faculty.

Bousquet, Mark et al., editors. *Tenured Bosses and Disposable Teachers: Writing Instruction in the Managed University.* Southern Illinois UP, 2004.

Bradley, Gwendolyn. "Contingent Faculty and the New Academic Labor System." *Academe,* vol. 90, no. 1, 2004, pp. 28–31.

Chase, Geoffrey. "Redefining Composition, Managing Change, and the Role of the WPA." *The Longman Source for Writing Program Administration,* edited by Irene Ward and William J. Carpenter, Pearson, 2008, pp. 243–51.

Cross, John G., and Edie N. Goldenberg. "Why Hire Non-Tenure-Track Faculty?" *Peer Review,* vol. 5, no. 1, 2002, tomprof.stanford.edu/posting/463.

Hairston, Maxine. "The Winds of Change: Thomas Kuhn and the Revolution in the Teaching of Writing." *College Composition and Communication,* vol. 33, no. 1, 1982, pp. 76–88.

Jacoby, Daniel. "Effect of Part Time Faculty Employment on Community College Graduation Rates." *The Journal of Higher Education,* vol. 77, no. 6, 2006, pp. 1081–103.

McMahon, Deirdre, and Ann Green. "Gender, Contingent Labor and Writing Studies." *Academe,* vol. 94, no. 6, 2008, pp. 16–19.

Miller, Richard E. *As If Learning Mattered: Reforming Higher Education.* Cornell UP, 1998.

———. "Opinion: Our Future Donors," *College English,* vol. 66, no. 4, 2004, pp. 365–79.

Modern Language Association. "Education in the Balance: A Report on the Academic Workforce in English." Report of the 2007 ADE Ad Hoc Committee on Staffing, 10 Dec. 2008, mla.org/content/download/3255/81374/workforce_rpt03.pdf.

PSC-CUNY. "Adjunct Rights and Benefits." 7 June 2010, psc-cuny.org/members /adjunct-rights-and-benefits.

Rhoades, Gary, and Christine Maitland. "Bargaining for Full-Time, Non-Tenure Track Faculty: Best Practices." *The NEA 2008 Almanac of Higher Education,* 2008, pp. 67–73.

Street, Steve. "Don't Pit Tenure Against Contingent Faculty Rights." *Academe,* vol. 94, no. 3, 2008, pp. 35–37, jstor.org/stable/40253634.

Thompson, Karen. "Contingent Faculty and Student Learning: Welcome to The Strativersity." *New Directions for Higher Education,* no. 123, 2003, pp. 41–47, researchgate.net/publication/229599066_Contingent_Faculty_and_Student _Learning_Welcome_to_the_Strativersity.

Wardle, Elizabeth. "Intractable Writing Program Problems, *Kairos,* and Writing about Writing: A Profile of the University of Central Florida's First-Year Composition Program." *Composition Forum,* vol. 27, 2013, compositionforum.com/issue/27/ucf .php.

CHAPTER 4

REAL FACULTY BUT NOT: THE FULL-TIME, NON-TENURE-TRACK POSITION AS CONTINGENT LABOR

Richard Colby and Rebekah Shultz Colby

University of Denver

Threads: Organizing Within and Across Ranks; Professionalizing and Developing in Complex Contexts

Composition has long been familiar with the exploitation of adjunct labor. The labor-intensive cost of teaching the undergraduate population of first-year writing has often meant a "piecemeal" (Ritter 388) approach to teaching: the majority of courses are often taught by part-time adjuncts hired at the last minute to ensure that all the sections are staffed. As a result, part-time faculty make up about 60 percent of faculty in English departments within four-year institutions and 80 percent of English faculty in two-year colleges (Laurence, "Demography" 252). Numerous *Forum: Issues about Part-time and Contingent Faculty* articles have recounted the abuses of adjunct labor: wages that are at or are only slightly above minimum wage, which force instructors to teach at several different institutions, while often juggling over four courses a term (Griggs A4). For example, in a 2008 *Forum*, Evelyn Beck stated that her institution only paid $1,100 for a three-credit-hour writing course (A1). Even the most recent report from the Coalition on the Academic Workforce found a median of $2,700 per course (12). Within the 2013 AAUP Annual Report on the Status of the Profession, John Curtis and Saranna Thornton reveal that there was little or no wage adjustment for inflation reported for jobs that fall under contingent labor, and only 18.8 percent of respondents reported receiving any pay raises (9). Teaching at many different institutions means that, for adjuncts, the paper load is often crushing and isn't made any easier by the fact that many adjuncts receive minimal, if any, teaching support other than a prescribed syllabus or textbook (Heller A8; Behm A7). Not to mention that many adjuncts do not receive medical benefits or any type of sick leave (Beck A1).

Despite these well-documented abuses of adjunct labor within composition, the numbers of adjuncts teaching within higher education are only increasing and show no sign of stopping. The 2008 MLA report "Education in the Balance" indicated a clear trend that "increases in student enrollments are being accommodated by increases in the non-tenure-track faculty" (3). The most recent AAUP report shows that contingent labor accounts for the largest increase in employment within higher education, making up 75 percent of the workforce, while tenure-track professors only make up 25 percent (Curtis and Thornton 5).

There are several ways that departments and programs have responded to exploitation of adjunct labor. Specifically, the MLA "Education in the Balance" report makes six recommendations for improving working conditions and the education of students by adjunct labor, which were reiterated again in 2011's "Professional Employment Practices for Non-Tenure-Track Faculty Members." These recommendations include such changes as: offering long-term contracts and benefits, integration into departments, teaching and research resources, mentoring and professional development, and annual review.

Writing and composition programs such as those at Duke, Stanford, and the University of Denver have responded to the realities of increased contingent labor within higher education by enacting the MLA recommendations through adding or shifting faculty to fixed contracts or full-time, non-tenure-track positions (FTNTT). The growth in these positions has outpaced part-time and full-time positions. The 2008 MLA report shows that while tenure-track faculty employment has increased 5 percent between 1995 and 2005, FTNTT positions have shown a 40 percent increase and adjunct faculty a 38 percent increase during that same time (21), which the AAUP reports is also true across departments. As indicated by the MLA data, even though the total percentage of FTNTT faculty in English departments (22.2%) is lower than adjunct (39.5%) and tenure-track (TT) faculty (38.3%), many programs and departments are increasingly acknowledging at least a few of the recommendations proposed by the MLA by adding more FTNTT positions with acceptable pay and benefits, as well as reviews of teaching and resources.

However, these new FTNTT positions carry with them a number of potential problems.

In 1986, the AAUP addressed the then relatively new trend of replacing tenure-track lines or hiring new lines with FTNTT. They write in "On Full-Time Non-Tenure-Track Appointments" that "these non-tenure-track appointments do considerable damage both to principles of academic freedom and tenure and to the quality of our academic institutions—not to mention the adverse consequences for the individuals serving in such appointments" (85).

The adverse consequences they warn of are inferior status and exclusion from shared governance, "the erosion of the quality" of education (89), faculty anxiety, and a brain drain as the best and brightest graduates turn to private industry rather than higher education. They have since written reports in 2006 and 2010 further supporting this position. In our experiences in talking to faculty in such positions and in our FTNTT positions at the University of Denver, these consequences are not widespread. Many FTNTT positions provide faculty opportunities to sit on faculty senates, participate in advising students, direct programs, or share in the governance of the writing programs to which they belong, and, most importantly, to provide comparable if not better instruction to students than TT faculty. As for whether graduates turn increasingly to work outside universities, the most recent MLA data indicate that this is just a fact that we cannot do much about, except for adding more TT positions since there are more Ph.D.s awarded than there are positions, TT or FTNTT, available (Laurence "Our PhD Employment"). Although in some circumstances these adverse consequences are realized, there is little doubt that shifting part-time, piecemeal faculty into FTNTT positions can improve the lives of the majority of faculty teaching writing and the education of their students, at least if these positions replace part-time, adjunct positions.

The MLA recommendations in "Education in the Balance" focus on benefits to faculty; but what of the effect of these changes on composition-rhetoric as a discipline? We do not believe the adverse consequences to individuals from these FTNTT positions is widespread, but we contend that the overall effect of these positions on composition as a field is the erosion of the gains from and application of research in this field. Simply put, for research within composition to continue, research and the teaching of first-year writing need to go hand in hand. Those who actually teach first-year writing should also be doing research within it because, as teachers, they know firsthand the problems and issues involved within first-year writing that need further research. However, as we detail later, because these positions often fail to incentivize scholarship for FTNTT faculty, the increase in FTNTT positions could lead to fewer first-year writing teachers actually conducting pedagogical research that could improve writing, rhetoric, and its teaching.

As two of the nineteen founding faculty of the University of Denver Writing Program who are all FTNTT, we detail some advantages to the FTNTT position and outline some of the significant disadvantages such as the lack of job security and the lack of incentives to publish research. Finally, we offer program administrators and faculty recommendations for protecting both the research interests of first-year writing and the continued professionalization of those engaged in this research.

THE ADVANTAGES OF THE FTNTT POSITION

In 2006, the University of Denver, a private university of about 11,600 students, inaugurated a writing program that would serve as both the home of first-year writing courses and a campus resource on writing. The program was put under the directorship of Douglas Hesse, who holds tenure within the English department, but the writing program itself is free-standing, employing twenty-five FTNTT faculty members and a FTNTT writing center director as of this writing. The positions were originally offered with nine-month, yearly renewable contracts. Consequently, we are guaranteed employment for a year, but contract renewal is still contingent upon program needs and the university's budget.

The University of Denver FTNTT positions manifest the MLA recommendations in a number of positive ways. First of all, these positions can provide faculty with oftentimes more manageable teaching loads, which lead to higher quality teaching. For instance, within our program, we have a 0/3/3 teaching load. We teach three classes of fifteen students each in the winter and spring quarters. During the fall quarter, faculty can devote their time to programmatic research, writing center work, or may teach a first-year seminar based on a research interest. The decreased teaching loads mean that teachers can give more individualized attention to student writing. It also means that teachers have the time to innovate teaching pedagogy. As a result, faculty in our program teach a diverse array of first-year writing courses. Some focus on genre theory and ask students to investigate the writing of their majors; others focus on service learning, even earning special recognition from our campus's Center for Community Engagement & Service Learning. We ourselves have created a course that uses the computer game *World of Warcraft* as a space for research and writing across the curriculum.

In order to help us continue to innovate pedagogy and pursue other research interests, we have ample research and travel funds. We receive $1,000 a year for conference expenses; and for large conferences in rhetoric and composition like the Conference on College Composition and Communication (CCCC), 80 percent of expenses are paid for those who are not presenting. In addition, we receive $500 each year for professional development, which can go toward any research costs such as books or paying research participants.

We also have a hand in the self-governance and curriculum development of our Writing Program, even though self-governance is not absolute within our program structure; that is to say, our director is solely responsible for communicating with the provost about our program. However, the founding faculty of our Writing Program (who are, again, all FTNTT) collaboratively developed our curriculum, including the course goals and objectives. Every year, all program faculty contribute to reviewing and revising these course goals and objectives, and the director often operates as a colleague in these conversations rather than arbiter. When our Writing Program was founded, faculty who were interested in writing assessment formed a committee that developed an annual assessment of student writing, which includes a portfolio and a reflective cover letter. Our assessment process is also reviewed annually by the entire program faculty, and faculty can be involved in the assessment process each year. Most importantly, a steering committee of four elected FTNTT faculty help the director make larger administrative decisions which impact the Writing Program. However, the steering committee's role is largely advisory, as the director still makes all final decisions.

Last but not least, we enjoy health and retirement benefits and decent pay. We receive full medical coverage, dental coverage, and paid twelve-week maternity leave. We also enjoy a salary close to the national median yearly income for FTNTT positions that the AAUP reports: $47,500 (Curtis and Thornton 10). Finally, in the past, we have received small pay raises each year, which are determined annually by merit review. However, because of the slowed economy, these pay raises have largely ceased across our university for tenured and non-tenured faculty alike, and we have no idea if they will continue in the future.

THE DISADVANTAGES OF THE FTNTT POSITION AND THE FUTURE OF COMPOSITION

We have indicated a number of advantages of our positions for the faculty who teach in them. For some faculty, moving off the tenure track into these positions may provide increased quality of life with ample time to focus on teaching or individual interests such as writing, or time to raise families, without the pressures of publishing and acquiring tenure. For those who have worked as adjuncts, the FTNTT position can offer security of employment, benefits, a living wage, and time to develop professionally and pedagogically. Furthermore, as an academic couple with newly minted Ph.D.s, we counted ourselves lucky to have found positions where one or both of us did not have to commute for hours to work as adjuncts at multiple institutions.

Yet, these FTNTT positions are not without problems.

A problem with many FTNTT positions, ours in particular, is that we are still very much contingent labor. Our director reports solely to the provost; while our director has control over our Writing Program budget, an FTNTT position does not carry the longer-term budgetary status of a tenure-track line and thus has minimal job security, as the provost is ultimately responsible for securing our FTNTT positions and can add or cut positions as demanded by university or budgetary needs. While we trust that our current director is savvy enough to secure our positions with the provost even in tough economic times, we still worry about what would happen to our positions if another director were to replace our current one. In actuality, even though we only receive yearly contracts, so far all faculty have been renewed. However, the added job security of a tenure-track line is still needed during insecure economic times or a replacement of the director. We say this knowing full well that even TT positions are susceptible to financial realities, and some universities have lost entire departments or fired tenured faculty because of budget cuts—yet tenured faculty still have greater protection in these circumstances, as demonstrated by many examples where non-tenure-track (NTT) faculty positions are not renewed, while TT faculty positions are saved, reinstated, or reassigned (see Etchison; Schmidt).

Furthermore, even if our FTNTT positions remain secure and faculty are rehired from year to year, many FTNTT positions are not tiered in the same way the tenured positions are, so that pay increases that come with promotion from assistant to associate professor, for example, are largely absent in FTNTT positions, including our own. This also means that pay increases within FTNTT lecture positions are often based solely on the Writing Program director's discretion. Consequently, if there is not a transparent set of recommendations in place for awarding merit-based pay raises, raises may seem arbitrary.

However, we contend that the most noteworthy problem with FTNTT positions is that they can negatively impact both the amount and quality of scholarship conducted within the field of composition as a whole. Continued pedagogical scholarship within first-year writing is important to good teaching. It is essential that we maintain our practice as writers and researchers. As teachers of first-year writing, we are uniquely positioned to understand its problems, both with composing and teaching, and can thus address these problems by conducting research about both composing and pedagogy. Additionally, this continued scholarship makes us more innovative and reflective teachers.

Unfortunately, FTNTT positions have the potential to separate faculty into tenure-track researchers, on the one hand, and non-tenure-track teachers on the other, as these latter positions often do not offer significant enough incentives to research and publish in the field. Without tenure and publishing requirements, as onerous and stressful as they might appear, or even department or program expectations to research, there is no obligation and little incentive to do such work. If, increasingly, more writing faculty are placed in situations where they are expected only to teach, the motivations to research their teaching, students' writing, or the application and functions of writing beyond the classroom become less important. This separation of researching and teaching also draws so-called "research" faculty away from what we do in our discipline: teaching students about writing. If "research" faculty are not teaching writing, then they are not as well positioned to study writing or the teaching of writing. They will not be aware of issues or problems that come up when teaching writing that could then generate research questions for further study. In this way, this separation could potentially de-emphasize scholarship on writing pedagogy, creating an arbitrary binary between teaching and research and relegating teaching to merely service—a service which, within this separation, becomes mindless, as teaching then becomes separated from the knowledge construction of research. Ultimately, a lack of pedagogical research hurts composition as a field because it relegates any teaching of writing to being divorced from the knowledge construction of theory building and, as Brad Hammer writes, "further reinforce[es] the utility structure and non-disciplinary nature of writing instruction" (A4).

We understand there are some potential problems in this argument that without tenure there is little motivation for those in FTNTT positions to publish. Tenure or extrinsic rewards are, in fact, not the only motivations to publish. And we are not contending that this is the case. However, the data here is varied, and none exists that we are aware of in composition specifically. Two studies looking at motivations to publish have found that tenure and promotion are powerful incentives for scholarship. A study on increases in international submissions to the journal *Science* found that "[c]areer incentives are positively correlated not only with submissions but also with publications, which suggests that they encourage faculty to submit their best work" (Franzoni et al. 703). When considering additional motivation factors in a study of faculty, Flora F. Tien found that "after controlling for the impact of demographic, educational, and institutional variables, the multivariate analyses show that faculty publish articles both to gain promotion and to satisfy their intellectual curiosity" (744). We are aware that full professors, those who have, in theory, attained the highest promotional rank, continue to publish as well. Intellectual curiosity does play a significant role in publishing productivity, especially for tenured faculty, as some studies have shown that full professors produce the most scholarship (Tien and Blackburn 17). However, Hesli and Lee explain this phenomenon with selection theory: "only the most productive faculty members are promoted, eliminating low producers before they reach higher ranks and thus creating a situation in which higher ranking faculty produce more" (395). Although intellectual curiosity is a powerful intrinsic motivator for those who have decided to devote their lives to a field of study, there exist still the extrinsic rewards of promotion and tenure that cannot be overlooked.

In fact, the importance of extrinsic motivation to publish is evident within our program of twenty-five faculty, in which only about half of the faculty consistently work to publish in rhetoric and composition, despite having decreased teaching loads and ample time to do so. Moreover, the faculty who do publish are not solidifying their positions within our university as securely as they would if they could receive tenure. While faculty might be compensated for publishing with a positive merit review, in our program this is not guaranteed, as merit review is judged more on teaching and service, with scholarship comprising only 10 percent of the review. For these reasons, those who do such research, while surely satisfying their intellectual curiosity, are most likely also doing so for the potential of a TT job at another university. After all, tenure confers a type of status. It matters as a measure of prestige. It matters to the university bylaws about mentoring, serving on dissertations, having a voice on certain types of committees, and promotion. And, as we saw in 2004, it matters for political office when some questioned Barack Obama's claim that he was a professor even though he was not on the tenure track (Sweet).

Even more problematic though, changes in the economy at large and within academe suggest that universities will continue the trend of not increasing tenure-track (TT) lines while increasing FTNTT positions, all with the expectation that universities can expect more for less, enacting more and more of what Kelly Ritter characterizes as a "pay for product status" (388). That is, without the possibility of a TT job, if all that is left is intellectual curiosity, universities can still expect some scholarship from those faculty still interested in pursuing their intellectual curiosity and a high level of teaching from most faculty, while paying them significantly less and denying them security of employment or academic freedom. The quality of labor still remains fairly high but it becomes cheaper and conveniently disposable. The AAUP writes that while FTNTT positions superficially resemble those of "junior faculty," but with "fixed term appointments, limited participation in the full range of faculty work, and insufficient support from their institutions, these full-time non-tenure-track colleagues constitute a second tier of the academic labor structure" (Curtis and Thornton 15), while part-time adjuncts become even more marginalized.

Before offering recommendations for programs and faculty interested in maintaining the importance of research in FTNTT positions, we want to acknowledge an apparent contradiction. While we believe that the FTNTT position can be improved, our intention is not to encourage faculty to stay in them. As we have established, the move to increase contingent labor is a strategic decision made by many universities. These FTNTT positions are not postdocs, an intermediary position for faculty as they look for tenure-track jobs elsewhere. Most postdoc positions, in fact, encourage research. However, with the exception of Duke's writing program where faculty are expected to publish and are only given three-year contracts with the expectation that they will then move on to TT (or other FTNTT) jobs, many FTNTT positions in composition are teaching positions, and as such, can bewitch faculty into spending all of their time teaching. Although there is something to be said for experience in teaching, there is also the potential for burnout and intellectual stagnation if these positions offer no other opportunities (Mamiseishvili and Rosser 122). In addition, a well-committed faculty with a consistent roster can wield considerable power, even if they are NTT, but if there is high turnover or a lack of consistency, such solidarity and agency can be diminished.

RECOMMENDATIONS

To ameliorate these problems with FTNTT positions, we propose several recommendations. Foremost among them, to support composition as a discipline, we propose that such positions should offer promotion with merit pay and designate a minimal (10 to 20 percent) expectation of research in order to merit these incentives. Within our program, research is worth ten percent of our annual merit review. This research expectation does make an impact on merit pay (in addition to improvements in teaching and faculty development), but with only about half of faculty seeking publication, the results are mixed, so we believe that research should be valued more highly. Faculty are encouraged to do scholarship; however, if faculty are serious about pursuing scholarship, with no tenure-track status, there is little left but intellectual curiosity and the potential to be exploited at lower pay than TT faculty if scholarship is only valued at ten percent for merit review. For administrators who see composition purely as a service in teaching, research expectations in these positions might be the most difficult to negotiate. After all, our roles are still seen by many as readers of student texts, *cancellare* of errors. We do not mean to paint all administrators in such a negative light because, after all, a desire to improve education of students rather than only gather research monies is an enviable goal, but we also must fight for our continued status as a discipline whose interest is in improving student education through our own scholarship.

Second, there should be at least some security of employment with multiyear contracts of at least three years, but preferably five years, based on comprehensive and transparent review. Such modest, multi-year contracts allow the faculty who work in such positions to feel secure and therefore to experiment with teaching or engage in multi-year research projects at their universities, while also offering a compromise to TT faculty who might be wary that their own positions or the position of faculty in general are weakened by FTNTT positions that offer the same security as TT contracts.

At our university, the faculty senate, on which two of our program faculty serve, proposed and enacted a shift to multiyear contracts for non-tenure-track

(NTT) faculty across the university. Our current annual instructor review for contract renewal is transparent, and it goes well beyond only student evaluations, two criteria established in the 2011 MLA "Professional Employment Practices for Non-Tenure-Track Faculty Members" guidelines. Such a faculty review for contract renewal, annually or multi-year, consists of multiple ways of reviewing teaching: student evaluations, teaching observations, a portfolio with course syllabi, assignments and other teaching materials, student papers that showcase written comments, and a teaching reflection.

Mentoring is also imperative. As in our Writing Program, the Writing Program director should meet with the faculty member to review his or her teaching but also offer advice and feedback as a mentor in areas where the faculty member either seemed to be experiencing difficulty in teaching, or indicated in his or her reflection a request for feedback. Thus, this teaching review would be more in line with a teaching review for tenure-track faculty, with pedagogical mentoring in place as needed, as Janet Ruth Heller suggests. We would also like to see such reviews cover the faculty member's scholarly contributions. Although only vaguely suggested in the MLA Guidelines, encouragement, recognition, or even feedback and mentoring of scholarly endeavors can be a small but positive incentive.

These FTNTT positions should allow faculty the possibility to apply for research grants and at least partial sabbaticals, as the 2011 MLA guidelines suggest. Our own program provides a healthy professional development and travel fund, and our university provides opportunities for NTT faculty to apply for additional research money. We recommend programs provide not only such professional development funds but also additional travel or research grants or awards based on scholarship on a competitive basis as an incentive to do additional research. Furthermore, faculty and program directors or administrators should negotiate with the university so that faculty in these programs are eligible for university research grants when they are offered. We are lucky that all of these funding opportunities are available to us in our program and at our university, but even in cases at other universities with strict policies that prevent funding for NTT faculty or highly competitive circumstances, directors or administrators who happen to be tenure-track might apply for such grants as co-researchers with FTNTT faculty members.

Incentivizing talented faculty to stay fulfilled in FTNTT positions leads to the last recommendation. Although we agree with the MLA "Professional Employment Practices for Non-Tenure-Track Faculty Members" that, when possible, FTNTT faculty should be eligible for TT lines as they open up within their home institutions, we understand that these can be rare instances. So, we recommend that FTNTT positions should be open for at least some form of tenure. Some universities have instituted alternative types of tenure including the University of California system that offers lecturers "security of employment" after a number of years, and other state universities that leverage collective bargaining agreements through unions (AAUP "Tenure and Teaching"). In our program, teaching gets top priority, comprising 60 percent of our annual merit review. This focus on teaching does seem to lead to innovative teaching which is cutting edge in our field, and hence continues to energize our program. However, receiving at least a type of teaching tenure would ensure that faculty continued to focus their efforts on taking chances in their teaching since there would be a mechanism in place that rewarded teaching innovation. More importantly, teaching tenure would add an extra mechanism by which faculty would be rewarded for any scholarly research on teaching, thereby ensuring that our teaching remained cutting edge. It would also ensure that teachers of first-year writing continued to pursue research on writing and the teaching of writing. Teaching tenure would also create at least some additional status and greater job security than three or five year contracts alone. Criteria for such teaching tenure could be modeled after programs that want to maintain a teaching focus but provide additional rewards for extraordinary research or service. For example, when St. John's University converted its FTNTT positions to tenure-track lines, they instituted promotion criteria that "require that faculty, in addition to documenting successful teaching, document accomplishments in two of these three areas: publishing, conference presentations, and service" (AAUP "Tenure and Teaching"). Such criteria continue to emphasize teaching but provide an incentive to write and research. With this recommendation, we also want to acknowledge that converting positions can create problems of shifting faculty who may have specifically sought out a particular program or department based on one set of expectations. Establishing early on in a new program's development options for promotion and status is our primary point here.

CONCLUSION

The FTNTT position is, in many of the ways we have covered, a positive response to the exploitation of adjunct, part-time faculty; however, such positions are still contingent labor, often reliant on a director or administrator and strategic decisions from upper-level university administrations. That said, we do see the FTNTT position as a viable track for many faculty with concerns about the workload of a tenure-track position or with other interests that more demanding positions might preclude. But we want to stress that the FTNTT positions should also provide opportunities for scholarship and research not only as a means of improving faculty's teaching but also in enriching understanding of writing and pedagogy for faculty at large. Furthermore, research opportunities, incentives, and support in these positions will provide a type of professional development for faculty who might want to seek tenure-track jobs later in their careers.

These FTNTT positions are often enacted with many good intentions, most noble of which is a desire for a committed teaching faculty who are adequately compensated and supported. But we also want to contend that as representatives of the discipline of composition, a field that still is so often considered merely service, we are in fact scholars of practice with research agendas that improve our teaching and understanding of writing and rhetoric. And even though the 2008 MLA report shows much greater increases in percentages of faculty off the tenure track, tenure-track positions still exist and are valued—in "The 2013 Insider Higher Ed Survey of College and University Chief Academic Officers" (CAOs), 70 percent of CAOs "strongly agree or agree that tenure remains important and viable at their institution" (Gallup 17). The conflict here is that in that same survey, 64 percent of CAOs stated they favored "a system of long-term contracts over the existing tenure system" (Gallup 19). If FTNTT positions continue as a strategic trend with long-term contracts replacing tenure, we should push to also maintain a place for research even as we recognize that doing so holds the possibility that administrations might see ways to exploit such faculty by paying them less but benefiting the university the same as the tenure-track faculty.

WORKS CITED

AAUP. "Tenure and Teaching-Intensive Appointments." *Bulletin of the AAUP*, vol. 96, 2010, www.aaup.org/article/tenure-and-teaching-intensive-appointments#.WC5qF MkXvkY.

American Association of University Professors. "On Full-Time Non-Tenure-Track Appointments." Committee on Academic Freedom and Tenure (Committee A), 19 June 1986, aaupatnyit.org/nontenure.pdf.

Beck, Evelyn. "From the Editor: What is a Fair Wage?" *Forum: Issues about Part-Time and Contingent Faculty*, vol. 12, no. 1, 2008, pp. A1–A3.

Behm, Nicholas. "A Brief Comparison of Teaching Assistantship and Adjunct Faculty Positions." *Forum: Issues about Part-Time and Contingent Faculty*, vol. 12, no. 1, 2008, pp. A5–A8.

Coalition on the Academic Workforce. "A Portrait of Part-Time Faculty Members: A Summary of Findings on Part-Time Faculty Respondents to the Coalition on the Academic Workforce Survey of Contingent Faculty Members and Instructors," 2012, www.academicworkforce.org/CAW_portrait_2012.pdf.

Curtis, John, and Saranna Thornton. "The Annual Report on the Economic Status of the Profession 2012–2013," *Academe*, vol. 99, no. 2, 2013, pp. 4–19.

Etchison, Haley. "Philosophy Department Would Be Saved in Revised Plan." *The Rebel Yell*, vol. 7, 2011, unlvrebelyell.com/philosophy-department-would-be-saved-in -revised-plan/.

Franzoni, Chiara, et al. "Changing Incentives to Publish." *Science,* vol. 333, 2011, pp. 702–3.

Grigs, Claudine. "Off the Tenure Track: The Tenuous Act of Adjuncting." *Forum: Issues about Part-Time and Contingent Faculty*, vol. 12, no. 1, 2008, pp. A3–A5.

Hammer, Brad. "The 'Service' of Contingency: Outsiderness and the Commodification of Teaching." *Forum: Issues about Part-Time and Contingent Faculty*, vol. 16, no. 1, 2012, pp. A3–A7.

Heller, Janet Ruth. "Contingent Faculty and the Evaluation Process." *Forum: Issues about Part-Time and Contingent Faculty*, vol. 16, no. 1, 2012, pp. A8–A12.

Hesli, Vicki L., and Jae Mook Lee. "Faculty Research Productivity: Why Do Some of Our Colleagues Publish More than Others?" *PS: Political Science & Politics*, vol. 44, no. 02, 2011, pp. 393–408.

Jaschik, Scott, and Doug Lederman, editors. "The 2013 Inside Higher Ed Survey of College and University Chief Academic Officers." *Inside Higher Ed*, 2013, www .insidehighered.com/news/survey/skepticism-about-tenure-moocs-and-presidency -survey-provosts.

Laurence, David. "Demography of the Faculty: A Statistical Portrait of English and Foreign Languages." *Profession*, vol. 22, 2009, pp. 245–66.

Laurence, David. "Our PhD Employment Problem, Part I." *The Trend: The Blog of the MLA Office of Research*, vol. 26, 2014, mlaresearch.commons.mla.org/2014/02/26 /our-phd-employment-problem/.

Mamiseishvili, Ketevan, and Vicki J. Rosser. "Examining the Relationship Between Faculty Productivity and Job Satisfaction." *Journal of the Professorate*, vol. 5, no. 2, 2010, pp. 100–132.

MLA Committee on Contingent Labor in the Profession. "Professional Employment Practices for Non-Tenure-Track Faculty Members: Recommendations and Evaluative Questions," 2011, apps.mla.org/pdf/clip_stmt_final_may11.pdf.

Modern Language Association. "Education in the Balance: A Report on the Academic Workforce in English." Report of the 2007 ADE Ad Hoc Committee on Staffing, 10 Dec. 2008, mla.org/content/download/3255/81374/workforce_rpt03 .pdf.

Ritter, Kelly. "'Ladies Who Don't Know Us Correct Our Papers': Postwar Lay Reader Programs and Twenty-First Century Contingent Labor in First-Year Writing." *College Composition and Communication*, vol. 63, no. 3, 2012, pp. 387–419.

Schmidt, Peter. "Arbitrator Orders Florida State U. to Rescind Layoffs of Tenured Faculty Members." *The Chronicle of Higher Education*, vol. 5, 2010, chronicle.com /article/Arbitrator-Orders-Florida/125296/.

Sweet, Lynn. "Sweet Column Reprise. Obama's Book: What's Real, What's Not." *Chicago Sun Times*, 8 Aug. 2004, p. 32, beldar.blogs.com/beldarblog/2008/03/Prof _Obama.htm.

Tien, Flora F. "To What Degree Does the Desire for Promotion Motivate Faculty to Perform Research? Testing the Expectancy Theory." *Research in Higher Education*, vol. 41, no. 6, 2000, pp. 723–52.

Tien, Flora F., and Robert T. Blackburn. "Faculty Rank System, Research Motivation, and Faculty Research Productivity: Measure Refinement and Theory Testing." *Journal of Higher Education*, vol. 67, no. 1, 1996, pp. 2–22.

CHAPTER 5

HEAD TO HEAD WITH EDX?: TOWARD A NEW RHETORIC FOR ACADEMIC LABOR

Michael Murphy

State University of New York at Oswego

Threads: Professionalizing and Developing in Complex Contexts; Local Changes to Workload, Pay, and Working Conditions

In a recent meeting with the directors of individual programs inside the English department I work in, I discovered something I found striking: even though it would clearly make institutional life easier for each of us, we all shared the same instinctive disinclination to simplify learning outcomes in our programs, as assessment experts had been counseling us to do for some time. Give yourself manageable, measurable hoops to jump through—set your bar low and clear—and things will be fine, we'd been advised. Of course, the most fundamental reason for our shared unease with this advice isn't hard to understand: what sort of intellectual wants to caricature and minimize what he or she has spent a lifetime enriching with complication? Who likes playing dumb? But my suspicion is that there was more going on here, too—that in the back of our minds, my colleagues and I also shared an instinct to be wary about simplifying learning outcomes for something closer to *tactical* reasons. In cynical moments, I told my colleagues—unsure whether I was joking exactly or not, I think—assessment seemed to me a plot to so simplify our work that it could all eventually be pretty much outsourced anyway. The more measurable and concrete our learning outcomes—the more we talk down what we do so we can make reporting on it simpler—the more those outcomes can be plausibly met in course delivery platforms that make use of contract graders in Bangalore (June) or automated reading software for MOOCs (Markoff). None of us by any means felt any tangible threat. No one inside the institution had ever asked us to adopt a standardized exam for assessment purposes or even develop universal syllabi for commonly taught courses. But I think we all recognized intuitively that notions of education that ignore the complexity of ideas and the learning process make well-prepared, reflective teachers entirely dispensable: *If that's really all you're doing, what do we need you for, anyway?*

During the years when I was a two-campus adjunct, struggling to make a manageable life for myself without abandoning work that I loved, I used to joke that if it didn't pay much, at least my job was secure: nobody, I was sure, was ever going to read all those papers as well as I would for less money. I suspect at least for now that's still largely true. But it occurs to me that the pressures around the academic labor market have shifted appreciably in the last ten years, especially around the expansion of online learning, and that the same dynamic my tenure-track colleagues and I sensed in assessment at the program level also exerts itself powerfully on the struggle for improving working conditions for adjuncts: *If edX and Smarthinking can do it passably, why would administrators pay instructors any more than they do now?* This shift, I argue, gives new urgency to what should feel like very familiar arguments in composition and rhetoric for publicly acknowledging the complexity of our work in the classroom. James Berlin insisted for years that teaching bad composition courses based on impoverished and discredited notions of rhetoric gave literary studies a conveniently toothless alter-ego through which to demonstrate its own apparent rigor and seriousness, thus keeping composition-rhetoric in its place disciplinarily. Now it's clear that the more significant and insidious institutional function of popular assumptions about "bonehead English"—which is of course constantly under pressure to declare especially obvious, clearly measurable, universally agreeable learning objectives—is to keep writing teachers in their place. Which is to say poorly paid, disenfranchised, and unsupported for professional development.

As was clear to any viewer of Barbara Wolf's groundbreaking 1997 documentary *Degrees of Shame*, the first wave of contingent faculty activists in the late 1990s found understandable rhetorical power in their comparison of contingent faculty to migrant farm workers. Though of course neither the film nor the larger discourse around fairness of employment issues have proved substantially more successful in actually improving working conditions than the Edward R. Murrow film *Degrees of Shame* invokes, the terms of the argument that needed to be made in 1997 seemed clear enough. It was indeed difficult for any reasonable person to look at the swelling ranks of part-timers, who'd in many cases been working for years on short-term contracts without health or retirement benefits, representation in governance, or meaningful assurances of academic freedom, and not feel outrage. And it was equally difficult for anyone who'd worked in the field not to recognize that the best of those instructors had cultivated a significant practical expertise—often greatly exceeding that of whichever out-of-field tenure-track colleagues wound up teaching first-year writing—that was worth far more than instructors were paid. What more need contingent faculty advocates do than point this all out? What could serve higher education better than to do the right thing with their employees, which would at the same time cultivate a stable faculty of increasingly skilled teachers and improve instruction? But technological changes in the last three or four years have begun to broaden and diversify the market for academic labor in ways that have complicated the rhetorical situation and multiplied the arguments necessary to work toward improved working conditions for contingent faculty: even if robo-professors and off-site stand-ins never replace a single instructor, their simple availability will give colleges and universities yet another disincentive to get around finally to improving working conditions for contingent faculty.

Indeed, those teaching off the tenure track in the age of automated reading software, outsourced grading services, and MOOCs may well identify more with John Henry than with Tom Joad.

The good news, of course, is that while rock-drilling machines seem ultimately to have worked, readings offered by either machines or those urged to read like them don't and can't. Or at least they can't if we insist on defining the task in a way that acknowledges the complexity of what real readers—and thus dedicated faculty-mentors—do. While we can't hope to show that we can read papers faster or cheaper than machines or grading services, we need more than ever to show that what matters is that we read them *far better*. As such, this chapter will explore the strategic and rhetorical importance of cultivating a discourse about teaching writing that makes both its labor-intensive nature and its considerable complexities clear. We have little chance of improving the material conditions of writing teachers unless we insist emphatically on the real, demonstrated complexity and urgency of their work.

FROM TOM JOAD TO JOHN HENRY: MOOCS, AUTOMATION, AND OUTSOURCING

American higher education is almost certainly evolving faster and undergoing greater changes right now than it has in decades, at least since the GI Bill, and these changes revolve clearly around the expansion of for-profit providers. *College Inc.*, Public Broadcasting's much-viewed 2010 examination of the University of Phoenix and other for-profits, documents this expansion insightfully, estimating that by 2009 for-profit colleges and universities enrolled 10 percent of all U.S. post-secondary students, receiving about a fourth of federal student aid and accounting for a stunning *44 percent of student loan defaults* (Frontline). Of course, the expansion of corporate enterprise in higher education has been most conspicuous at the level of degree-granting institutions, with slickly conceived marketing plans designed to cast for-profits—despite extraordinarily high tuition rates—as the defenders of a forgotten educational underclass (as in the famous *I am a Phoenix* ad campaign) and to legitimate them with the trappings of traditional colleges and universities (consider University of Phoenix Stadium, the naming rights to which cost $154 million, which hosts the Fiesta Bowl as well as the NFL's Cardinals, and which doubtless helps reinforce the misimpression for many that Phoenix's online courses are an extension of face-to-face instruction offered on a central physical campus. But this expansion has been at least as prolific at the level of niche-oriented academic service providers, whose function is far less visible to the average U.S. education consumer. Though the landscape of such providers will almost certainly have moved on by the time this chapter is published, at its writing some of the more striking of these ventures include learning outcomes management firms like EduMetry, eLumen, and TracDat, which compile student responses to assessment instruments indexed to departmental learning outcomes; VirtualTA, a division of learning assessment firm EduMetry that outsources the grading of student writing to readers mainly in India, Singapore, and Malaysia (June); Smarthinking and TutorVista, both acquired by Pearson in 2010, which offer online tutoring services to colleges and universities that find setting up their own student support services too expensive or too complicated; Smarthinking's subsidiary, StraighterLine, which under the motto "the shortest distance between you and your degree" offers open enrollment Gen Ed courses for $99 a month; Professor Direct, the new division of StraighterLine that takes the downward pressure of competition in the academic labor market to new extremes, inviting faculty *to set their own tuition rates*, calculating for themselves the personal and marketplace break-even points for taking on yet one more student ($149 . . . $119 . . . $99?); and of course, the MOOC providers Coursera, Udacity, and EdX, which have famously created the possibility of truly mass instruction online, enrolling thousands or tens of thousands of students in a single course tuition-free, an arrangement made tenable as a for-credit enterprise largely by the promise to create automated reading and grading software.

Of course, higher education is increasingly suffused with corporate involvement at every level, even in quarters traditionally imagined steadfastly not-for-profit. Educational Testing Services and the College Board, which many argue look more and more like for-profit corporations over the last twenty years or so, are often cited as examples. Created in 1947 as the test administration arm of the College Board—and technically still a nonprofit foundation—ETS now sells prep books for its own exams, chief among them the ubiquitous SAT, pays its CEO nearly three-quarters of a million dollars in salary (Americans for Educational Testing Reform, "Scorecard"), and in 2007 acquired Prometric, a test development and delivery provider once owned by Sylvan Learning, for $435 million from Thomson Corp. (Cho), running it since then as a for-profit subsidiary. The closely allied College Board, founded in 1900 to democratize higher education by creating exams that would fairly assess students' abilities and thus de-emphasize the importance of elite Eastern prep schools in the college admissions process—and still registered like ETS with the federal government as a 501(c)(3) charitable organization—reported gross 2009 profits of $53 million, or 8.6 percent of revenues, and paid its president $1.3 million the same year (Americans for Educational Testing Reform, "President"). And of course, the largest education corporations are more and more deeply involved in the articulation of policy and curricula all the time: Pearson, purveyor of textbooks, teaching materials, teacher assessment programs, and most anything else public education consumes, is also, notoriously, the principle developer and administrator of the highly controversial Common Core Standards—making $500 million of its annual $9 billion profits from its five-year Common Core testing contract with the State of Texas alone (Figueroa). Indeed, the creeping influence of the for-profits is well documented: building on his long, eloquent worries about "the reduction of writing to job skills" (10), Doug Hesse's "Who Speaks for Writing?" tells the powerful story of NCTE and MLA's fruitless attempts to intervene in the production of the Common Core Standards—and by extension to have a seat generally at what's become the increasingly corporate table of literacy education. The counsel of faculty in Writing Studies, Hesse concludes, was "missing in the development stages, sought during the end game and pretty much after the fact, then ignored" (11).

But more narrowly defined educational course and service providers like VirtualTA and StraighterLine fly generally under the radar of public attention, much less visibly than ETS, Pearson, or the University of Phoenix. No one who applies to the University of Houston School of Law necessarily knows that his or her work might well be outsourced for reading to VirtualTA, and no one at Colorado State has likely been alerted in the university's glossy literature that his or her peers might earn credit for classes through StraighterLine.

Indeed, no one entering my own institution five years ago would have known, either, that the tutoring services it offered in writing were to be administered for the academic year by Smarthinking, an administrative decision made quickly over the preceding summer without faculty consultation in response to long-felt pressure to reform the campus writing center. Faculty groups were invited in the fall to participate in the evaluation of the service, set up as a pilot, and what my department's College Writing Committee found after submitting some of our own students' papers for tutoring actually exceeded our worst suspicions. To our ears, responses to student work sounded clearly canned, pasted largely or wholly from standing language the company or individual online tutors had developed. The advice offered was disablingly commonsensical and over-general, full of inane clichés and reductive acronyms to represent the "proper" features of an academic essay. And "e-structors," as Smarthinking calls its tutors, almost never connected the advice they offered to details from the student text at hand: they seemed to have read the text only as closely as they needed to in order to make a reasonable guess at which canned lecture to give tutees (thesis, organization, complete sentences). Having worked in writing centers before, committee members initially found the thirty minutes Smarthinking charged for working with each student astonishingly low for a process that they assumed must necessarily involve evaluating the student's written description of the sort of help they needed, reading the student's text itself, deciding what needed to be done with it, considering how to present that advice to the student, and composing an effective written response—a process of course complicated by the fact that most "e-structors" would be unable to have back-and-forth exchanges with students or read facial expressions. And wouldn't Smarthinking want to claim as much time as it could in any case? But after reading their responses, we understood: for Smarthinking, reading papers was indeed a fast and dirty business. Thirty minutes *was* sufficient, perhaps *more* than they needed. In fact, though we know nothing about the remuneration of Smarthinking tutors, the responses we read made committee members—all longtime two-campus adjuncts who knew all about the pressure to produce rushed, superficial readings of student work and what it takes to resist it—feel certain that e-structors must be paid not by the hour but by the *piece*. And we guessed that many were actually written in less than thirty minutes. It was, we remarked with irony, precisely the sort of superficial feedback we struggle so hard to discourage students from giving to peers in course workshops, and we worried, further, that it would not only offer students bad advice but also that it would model such advice powerfully for them. It was hard not to worry by extension, moreover, that whatever signals it gave to students about appropriate levels of response from teachers might ultimately be communicated to instructors as well (both new instructors without well-developed habits of response as well as veteran instructors who were experienced but staggered by overwork). Normalizing Smarthinking's expectations about what it means to read and respond to a draft, we felt sure, could do nothing good for the larger culture of writing on campus.

I want to be careful not to suggest here that the attention to cost-effectiveness of any of these services—or even their for-profit nature—should indict or disqualify them. Indeed, I have myself pointed out in the past that the rhetoric of cost-effectiveness can at times be invoked to great effect on behalf of contingent faculty in part-time roles—and I still take this to be true. But our committee's worries about Smarthinking speak directly to what's most troubling about the recent expansion of for-profit providers in education. What's really insidious about all these services—outsourced tutoring, grading software, commercially conceived MOOCs—is their target: the intellectual intimacy between students and teachers, which their success depends directly on devaluing. In the clichéd discourse of retail, warmly embraced on most provider websites, teachers are essentially middle men to be cut out. Indeed, the profitability of each of these services depends squarely on *a diminished capacity for student-teacher interaction*. The shortest distance between students and their degrees, as StraighterLine imagines it, is clearly one uncluttered with the messiness—and expense—of real teachers.

At an academic integrity conference I attended about ten years ago, keynote speaker Gary Pavela talked about being deeply affected on a tour of the Vatican by the tradition of mentorship depicted in Raphael's *The School of Athens*, at the very center of which appear Plato and his student Aristotle, strolling forward together but with eyes locked, as if engrossed in some eternal dialogue.[1] Pavela

---

1   It seems to me too interesting an index of the embeddedness of the for-profit spirit in higher education to ignore that this detail from Raphael's famous fresco now forms the centerpiece of the academicintegrityseminar.com home page set up by Pavela, noted Academic Integrity researcher Don McCabe, and research economist DeForest McDuff, who provide online seminars on academic integrity—at $100 per student—to the colleges and universities who contract with them. The website explains:

> Plato and Aristotle were properly depicted by Raphael in his wonderful
> "School of Athens" as former teacher and student who developed a lifelong
> friendship in the pursuit of truth. That spirit—friendship, intellectual curiosity, and dialogue about how a good and worthy life might be defined—
> forms the core of our work.

Clearly, the academic integrity movement has not inherited Socrates' distaste for accepting compensation in exchange for wisdom.

took this as an inspiring symbol of a sacrosanct commitment educators make to students and their disciplines: real education is about authentic, disinterested exchanges between mentors and mentees around ideas both care about deeply. This part of the presentation seemed to me undeniable, and still does: if we give students less than this, then of course we get what we ask for with respect to rates of student dishonesty. But it occurred to me then—as a faculty member at a public university where keeping class sizes small was a continual struggle—that the material circumstances surrounding instruction had everything to do with the possibilities for cultivating this sort of intimacy, which obviously can't be sustained in classes with enrollments numbering in three figures.[2] This dynamic seems much clearer now, though, a decade later, in the context of the sort of educational outsourcing I have begun to describe: How does one maintain a platonic intimacy with a student whose work is evaluated for its conformity to a standardized rubric by a contract grader 8,000 miles away?

If it's increasingly the popular perception that education no longer requires this sort of close work between teachers and students—that it can be done in a lecture hall with clickers or from home behind a laptop, asynchronously and at your convenience—it has much to do with the sort of exchange we've come to imagine that learning constitutes. After a number of years in which it seemed critiqued to the point of final irrelevance, the notion of education as the transmission of content—and instrumental content, at that—is experienced for more and more people as a largely unchallenged norm. A well-meaning and good-willed middle-class acquaintance, not herself a college graduate, recently asked me if I really needed to bother actually attending the graduate seminar I was rushing off to. She wasn't joking or commiserating with me about a busy schedule. I'd already given students the readings, which she assumed must contain what they needed to know, and they were smart enough to have made their way into a graduate course—what could there be to talk about? Maybe some of the students had somehow not obtained the text? The knowledge had already been transmitted, she figured—so maybe I needed to be there to give them an exam?

---

2   It's instructive here to consider the infamous 2001 cheating scandal at the University of Virginia, a campus well-known for its long-established Honor Code, administered and adjudicated by a student-run Honor Committee. The incident resulted in the suspension of forty-five undergraduates, and the University was widely lauded as a courageous defender of intellectual integrity and upholder of academic principle. Much less often reported, however, is that the 145 students charged with plagiarism were enrolled in an introductory physics course that routinely seated between 300 and 500 students (Trex)—and that the cheating was only discovered after a disgruntled student who'd received a bad grade for honest work reported the widespread practice to the course professor, who'd been unable to read student work even closely enough to recognize that a significant percentage of his students' papers were in fact "virtual replicas" of others submitted across five semesters (Schemo).

If arguing for worklife improvements for non-tenure-track faculty teaching writing means arguing for the importance and complexity of their work—and I think it does now more than ever—then these arguments depend fundamentally on distinguishing the teaching of writing clearly from this sort of simple positivist transmission. We need to insist that writing—and by extension the exchanges between writing teachers and their students—are about the construction and not the transfer of knowledge. This is an idea that will seem familiar enough, certainly, to most teachers of writing—and would have even before Paolo Freire began to talk about "the banking concept of education" forty-five years ago—but it is increasingly foreign to our students and to those outside academia.

Of course, this larger project begins with mounting a calculated and principled resistance to the ongoing inducement to reduce our work to easily quantifiable goals: we need ourselves to acknowledge the complexity of our own work. Whenever we mechanize any aspect of our practice for the sake of convenience (relying on exams or exam scores for placement) or accept without protest an administrative charge that ignores the messy reality of how writing actually works (developing a generic rubric for the evaluation of writing across campus—even if it never gets used), we run a calculated risk. But resisting the transmission model of learning and its underlying positivism also means working against the increasing cultural authority of technology, equated by many with science. We need to demonstrate what Haswell and Wilson's *Human Readers Petition* insists powerfully: that there are some things technology can't do. Convincing people of this is not as easy as it sounds, I think, and it will get more difficult as reading software gets more sophisticated.[3] And by all means we need to embrace technological tools, which many have pointed out are daily reinventing what we mean by "writing." But in the end, writing and reading aren't language processing. Both require *a transaction between human minds*—even in solitary texts, when writers struggle to articulate and refine ideas for themselves, or in most machine code, since most applications are of course written to be experienced ultimately by human users. The still unreleased software that EdX keeps promising its users reportedly works by emulating the readings of its MOOC instructors, so that after reading seventy or eighty papers closely, the same standards can be applied to thousands. But no matter how refined, variable, and sophisticated, autopilot is still autopilot. An algorithm can never serve as what Paolo Freire would have

---

3   Indeed, I worry that we've become complacent in our humanist dismissals of artificial intelligence: it's a reassuring half-lie—whistling in the dark, even—when we tell our students that grammar check doesn't work. Aren't we all pretty sure deep-down that it can and at some point will? And I don't just mean more consistent structural analyses of sentences and more qualified judgments about error: I don't see why applications can't do web scans to make informed assessments about usage and register, pass judgment on style and other rhetorical choices—perhaps even assess novelty.

called a "co-inquirer." As Ann Harrington and Charles Moran pointed out over a decade ago, writing meant to be processed by an application rather than a human mind *isn't* writing. And it doesn't get "read," either. This is the battle we need to fight in order to convince people that machines will always be an inferior replacement for human mentors—and that those mentors are well worth what they cost.

This is a daunting prospect, certainly, and forecasts for the future of the humanities are notoriously gloomy. But I think that we have reason for a level of optimism, or at least that there exists a greater recognition of the complexity of our work in certain quarters than we sometimes assume. When my department last year succeeded in bringing our central administration to the table to renegotiate instructors' salaries, we were all quite astonished and heartened to find that they readily agreed to consider funding a roughly *sixty-five* percent *raise* for our part-time faculty. We never argued hard for this—we didn't need to. Eventually, the department balked in the interests of collectivity when it discovered that this figure wouldn't be extended to other academic units on campus, which administrators deemed prohibitively expensive. So the matter went back to the union, and the administration responded to a proposal of the same figure we discussed with them by essentially spreading across the campus as a whole what they'd planned on spending to raise adjunct salaries in the English department—which of course resulted in a very nominal raise in the end. These disappointing results aside, I take the administration's willingness to negotiate with us—and not with part-time colleagues in other departments—as an indication of its recognition of the complexity and labor-intensive nature of teaching writing, and it seems to me a heartening sign. It's worth noting, too, that students themselves seem increasingly disenchanted with online courses, and reports are that they are likewise disinclined to enroll in MOOCs even when they bear credit (Weiner)—an indication that they too recognize something of the complexity of authentic teaching and learning. The growing backlash against the Common Core standards and excessive testing, what's more, create great synergy with the arguments we might make against automation in higher education. And it's very significant that these arguments stand for the first time in years, if ever, to unite and not divide constituencies in academic labor—unlike arguments for improving the working conditions of part-time faculty, which many in the professoriate have long regarded as against their interests and as potentially damaging to tenure as an institution. My own best guess, for what it's worth, is that eventually the University of Phoenix and Coursera may well go away on their own under the pressure of woeful student placement and loan default rates on one hand and simple student disinterest and disengagement on the other. But of course, both have done and can continue to do significant damage to public expectations about learning and the role of teachers before then—and almost certainly the teacherless dynamic in higher education will find new forms afterward. This is not a fight likely to end anytime soon, then, but it's also not one we're necessarily destined to lose.

OWNING ONE'S EXPERTISE: INSTRUCTORS AND PROFESSIONAL DEVELOPMENT

Of course, it's often observed that the greatest source of damage to the public image of first-year writing teachers is the staffing practices of college writing programs themselves, which have long been notorious for hiring faculty with minimal experience and preparation only days before courses are scheduled to begin as new sections are opened or other faculty resign at the last minute.[4] The reasons for these practices aren't hard to recognize: it's understandably difficult to find and retain qualified faculty to teach for a fraction of what the colleges that employ them hope their graduates will earn in their own starting positions. In this way, underfunding the field becomes its own tautological justification, at once both cause and effect. This is why one of Hesse's prescriptions for empowering Composition and Rhetoric in the larger culture rightly speaks so directly to professional development:

> . . . let's expect all writing teachers to know the field's history, research, practices, and contestations and be able to justify their teaching within that knowledge. Historically, the dismissive treatment of writing and its teachers may have blunted this expectation. (21)

Indeed, insisting on the complexity of teaching first-year writing depends on cultivating a faculty who appreciate that complexity and are able to develop courses that bespeak it.

In the spring of 2012, I was approached by the Writing Program director at a local two-year college, Malkiel Choseed at Onondaga Community College, about exactly this problem. He was troubled by how little the faculty teaching in his program—both contingent and tenure-track—knew about fundamental issues in composition studies, and after trying with mixed success to set up a departmental reading group, he was looking for new ways to incent busy instructors to do some structured reading and thinking in the field. How might it complicate and enrich the course designs or classroom practices of

---

4   See "Who is Professor 'Staff' and How Can This Person Teach So Many Classes?", a report of The Center for the Future of Higher Education, for a systematic review and discussion of these practices.

instructors, he wondered, if they knew about David Bartholomae's critique of surface correctness, what Kathleen Blake Yancey had to say about digital literacy, or Rebecca Moore Howard's work on plagiarism and intellectual property? And typically, his program hired from a labor pool—essentially the same one as ours—in which an awareness of this work was quite unusual. His idea was to offer graduate credits for a course in composition theory, which his administration indicated a willingness to pay for. The financial commitment was slow to be finalized—indeed, funding wasn't made official until the course was in its third week—but as we worked out the administrative details, we discovered that we were peculiarly situated to make this arrangement work. By a little-used provision of the large state university system that housed both the community college and my own campus, we could offer the course for a discounted rate, reducing the already reasonable graduate tuition by almost a third to around $850, as long as it was paid by the institution and not the individual (an arrangement which would make it qualify as a "contract course").[5] This meant that the college could offer faculty members a three-credit graduate course for a little less than the price of attendance at most national conferences—a very compelling professional development experience for administrators making public claims about their commitment to writing. What's more, the faculty union on the state system's four-year campuses (different from the two-year campus' union) had a program for tuition remission that would allow faculty on those campuses to take the course entirely without charge to their institutions. This meant that within a driving radius of an hour or so, we could draw faculty who might be in a position to take the course for free from roughly ten two-year and four four-year institutions, including my own.

This realization in turn led to more serious discussion of a prospect we'd both considered in our earliest talks: expanding the number of courses we might offer in order to develop a certificate, which we thought would have special appeal for contingent faculty. The experience of participants in the spring 2013 course, eager for more work in composition theory, confirmed our suspicions about this appeal, and it's our hope at this point that we might ultimately be able to offer a four-course certificate in teaching first-year writing. Given the current limits of my department, this certificate would have to depend in large part on visiting faculty, likely including WPAs on two or three local campuses. But faculty members from a comp-rhet doctoral program nearby—a couple of whom expressed some interest in the chance to work with local teachers of writing in order to

---

5   Sadly, as this chapter goes to publication, I've been informed by administrators on my campus that this crucial provision is no longer in place. If we can offer a discounted tuition, we'll need to fund it differently, and if we aren't able to find alternative funding, this arrangement will be less attractive to the community colleges we've been working with.

improve practice on a regional basis—provide another potential resource for this program. For those faculty, already teaching graduate courses, the commitment might be relatively simple—another one-night-a-week section of whatever they were teaching in a given semester on a rotating basis once every two years or so. This would mean that contingent faculty would have a chance not only to read work by—but to meet and work with—some of the leading scholars in the field nationally, an understandably exciting prospect.

Ultimately, we imagine, it's conceivable that a program like this could in the future have a transformative effect on a whole regional market for teachers of first-year writing. How powerful would it be in negotiations over salary and appointments if the expectation was not only that teaching first-year writing required some significant level of training but also that most teachers in the labor pool indeed had that training?

Of course, I want to be clear that this is all still in the earliest stages of specu-lative planning, more a vision and a hope at this point than anything else. And even if everything went exactly right, we recognize that like all attempts to address labor problems in the field, this program too would be a compromise. In the best of all possible worlds, faculty teaching writing everywhere would have not four courses but Ph.D.s in composition-rhetoric. They wouldn't need to do graduate work on a night-school basis after long days of teaching (and likely before long nights of grading) but would have a true grad school experience with the funding that allowed them proper space to read and think imaginatively. And we wouldn't depend on the good will of talented research faculty to, in effect, accept a course overload at the same rate we pay part-time faculty teaching first-year writing (a new form of labor exploitation, undeniably, even while it says something admira-ble about the faculty members willing to take on this work).

Still, as compromises go, this strikes me as a good one—probably for all involved, in fact. For one thing, it's an opportunity to complicate and enrich instruction in the region substantially. I asked participants in the pilot section not to write conventional graduate papers for the course but to prepare some-thing that would use course readings and ideas to inform some aspect of their professional lives—for example, articulating a new approach to using peer revi-sion, revising a departmental plagiarism policy, or developing a writing across the curriculum workshop for colleagues in different disciplines. Among the projects participants chose to pursue were one piece of conventional scholarly writing—a conference paper that was in fact submitted to and included in early versions of this volume—but also a new course unit on digital literacy centered on student work with digital stories, an overhauled modes course intended to challenge departmental prescriptions emphasizing formal approaches to teach-ing first-year writing, and the organization of a regional conference. Both the students enrolled in first-year writing courses and the programs they take them in will be better off for this work, I think.

Our greatest hope for this sort of a certificate, though, is that it will improve the job prospects of the contingent faculty involved. Faculty on tenure-track search committees at community colleges tell me that they find any documented coursework in composition very compelling: they say they want more than anything else to hire good colleagues who can help them solve pedagogical and curricular problems and that, though most of them have trained in literature, their main pedagogical and curricular project is *always* teaching writing. I know that having taken a course or two in composition theory has played an important role in the employment success of a number of graduate students from our M.A. program now on tenure lines at community colleges. I believe a certificate would have a similar effect. More importantly, though, I think a certificate program would make it easier to argue for significant worklife improvements for contingent faculty on their present campuses. Understanding all the arguments against them—and recognizing that they too are a compromise—I've argued on my own campus for a very long time that we need to establish senior instructor positions with full-time loads, significantly better pay, expanded roles, and enhanced job security, and as the prospect of such positions finally materializes slowly, it occurs to me that campus administrators would see a certificate like the one I've described as a meaningful qualifying credential. And I think they should.

But this same dynamic works on a larger scale as well, I think. How might it affect work in the field—and how colleges and universities were willing to fund it—if the rest of the world saw college-level writing and rhetoric teachers as expert practitioners with a demonstrated grasp of a tangibly shared set of texts and ideas who spoke a common disciplinary language? This, of course, is not the only front on which to fight the teacherless dynamic in higher education. Some, like Eileen Schell, have pointed out the continued importance of organizing in response to the globalizing of the academic labor market online, for example, arguing for the cultivation of "open source" unions (Schell). But whether writing teachers are organized as bargaining units or not, I believe that cultivating this sort of a professional identity for teachers of writing is a key part of getting colleges and universities to invest in teachers—and not in machines and outsourcing.

A TALE OF TWO VISIONS: REEMPLOYING THE SOPHISTS

Much celebrated in the last twenty-five years by composition theorists for epistemological reasons—but generally ignored as a labor model—the ancient Greek Sophists have something important to tell us about actually achieving this sort of identity, I think. Of course, the Sophists, who have never had very good press, make an unlikely model of professional ethos. They were the notorious whipping boys for Socrates in Plato's dialogues, where they were depicted as shifty, opportunistic double-talkers, providing a convenient foil for sober, disinterested Platonic rationalism. And the Sophistic tradition is invoked most in the common pejorative "sophistry," a word recognizable through most of the history of western Europe (from Medieval Latin to Old French to Middle and Modern English, according to the O.E.D.) as a byword for specious reasoning. Sharon Crowley argued passionately in "A Plea for the Revival of Sophistry," however, that this was a misrepresentation seized upon by science and rationalist philosophy in order to discourage public deliberation about debatable ideas, which would be resolved instead by experts with special power to ascertain truth. In actuality, according to rhetoricians like Crowley and Susan Jarrett in the late 1980s and early 1990s, the Sophists were principled relativists who'd anticipated much contemporary philosophy and rhetorical theory by recognizing the constructed nature of knowledge and the inherent interestedness of all positions and perspectives—and who were for that reason committed not to self-interest and deception, as Plato's readers generally imagined, but to democracy and inclusion. As what some called "New Sophist" scholarship had it in the 1990s, the Sophists were the enlightened and unfairly maligned antidote to pompous Platonic idealism, giving the lie to self-congratulatory patrician assumptions about philosophy and truth.

But it's clear, too, that Socrates and Plato objected to the Sophists as much out of a distaste with their life's work—which took them slumming in the earliest markets for rhetoric and rhetoricians—as out of any objection to their teachings. Protagoras and Gorgias were not noblemen expounding on the steps of the Academy in studied disinterest, but itinerant teachers and advisors—the very first professional writers and language consultants in some sense—who, much to the outrage of Socrates, accepted money for their efforts as both teachers and rhetoricians. They didn't just talk about the way language created knowledge in social contexts from a disembodied distance but participated in the process, intervening in public arguments and teaching others how to do the same. And they embraced their embeddedness in that process.

I can think of little that should put us more in mind of the army of contingent faculty in composition and rhetoric than this description of the Sophists. If Protagoras were alive today, he'd almost certainly be a two-campus part-timer who blogged on the side and edited copy when he needed extra cash. And it's hard for me not to connect their tenure-track critics to the disapproving patrician nobles dispensing wisdom about writing from above, but recoiling in distaste with the willingness of "comp droids" to sell out "serious" intellectual work by participating in the production and dissemination of real text on the ground—

supplementing their incomes by writing grants, blogs, articles for alumni magazines, or anything else they find alternately interesting or profitable. Defenders of the professorial tradition against the continuing encroachment of academia's *real* great unwashed—not student "outlanders," as Patricia Bizzell once put it, that is, but the growing instructorate who meet them in first-year writing courses—share more here with Plato and Socrates than they like to think.

It's hard for me not to think of this side of the Sophists when I think about the best of my non-tenure-track colleagues: Carol, the romance novelist who gave students the most layered, insightful, tangible advice about editors and audiences I've ever heard; Steve, the performance poet who lionized Ginsberg, quit teaching for a year to help write the Massachusetts state budget as Communications Director for the State Senate Ways and Means Committee, and ran a classroom with all the energy and engagement of a good poetry slam; or Henry, the accomplished fiddle player and sometime writer of folk songs who taught professional writing but made a significant part of his living as a freelance editor and the co-author of a psychopharmacology textbook.

In "Teaching On and Off the Tenure Track," a careful reflection on the 2008 report of the committee he led for the MLA's Association of Departments of English (Modern Langauge Association) on staffing trends, David Bartholomae addresses the issue of striking a balance between teaching and research in the field as a matter of making sure the two dimensions of academic work don't pull irretrievably apart. For Bartholomae, this means that teaching-intensive faculty need to maintain a connection to scholarship in the field, even if they don't see research as their primary interest, but also (and much to his credit, I think) that research faculty teach regularly at the lower division—not so beginning undergraduates can learn from them, but so they can learn from the undergraduates. Bartholomae writes:

> It is not simply the case that the curriculum needs to be in touch with current research; it is not simply that students can profit by contact with leading researchers; it is that current research needs to be informed by the issues raised in lower division courses, issues having to do with ordinary language, with reading and writing as practices broadly distributed. English, as a field of study, is impoverished when it loses touch with the lower division. (19)

I agree entirely. But it also occurs to me that in rhetoric, scholarship is not the only form of significant intellectual work that faculty can bring to their classrooms. Many part-time faculty have experiences as practicing rhetors that inform their teaching in very meaningful ways. So while research and teaching need to be conversant, *I think the range of possibilities for "research" in composition and rhetoric also define different legitimate professional identities in the field*—if not separate faculty tracks, then at least different emphases. If our faculties don't look like the faculties in philosophy, maybe that's appropriate. I worry that the field runs the risk of losing a very important dimension of its real disciplinary expertise if we don't make places for both scholar-teachers and teacher-rhetors.

How's this related to my own vision for the future of contingent faculty? I'd love to see teaching faculty in my own program on 4/4 loads, one section of which each semester included work across campus as liaisons to faculty and students in various colleges, roles I'd institutionalize as fellows in our writing across the curriculum program. Their appointments would be contingent on some significant level of graduate work in composition-rhetoric—perhaps enrollment in the certificate program I've described—and, on nine-month contracts, they would also be required in the summer to have significant experiences as practicing rhetors that they might bring to their teaching. The choice of what to write would be up to them—music and arts reviews, technical documents, local journalism, political materials, ad copy, grants, organizational documents for local nonprofits, or more than likely, some combination of different sorts of writing—but they would include this work in portfolios for review just as faculty in traditional professorial lines include scholarship in tenure, promotion, and merit reviews. Like Protagoras, Gorgias, and the rest, they'd doubtless develop expertise in specific sorts of writing, and this expertise would speak to the disciplinary constituencies they served on campus. How helpful would it be to our School of Business if they had a writing fellow who spent summers writing up studies on publicly held corporations for accounting agencies or helping prepare a guide for human resources managers on the Affordable Care Act? What if a fellow in the School of Education developed multi-media textbooks, a fellow in the social sciences worked as a media consultant for local political campaigns, a fellow in the natural sciences wrote NSF grants, or a fellow in the humanities worked for Literacy Volunteers or wrote arts journalism for an alternative weekly?

Imagining the roles for these faculty is an important project, since teaching-intensive positions clearly aren't going away, as Bartholomae's ADE study points out. Even the American Association of University Professors (AAUP), long reluctant to endorse the expansion of teaching-intensive positions on the grounds that they contributed to the erosion of tenure-track privilege, now formally recognizes them and calls for their tenurability (AAUP). And the most vociferous former critics of full-time lectureships now either work in or in fact direct programs that employ them. The reason for this isn't hard to identify. My worry is that if it's not some form of this vision of the field that defines its future—one that acknowledges the developed expertise of non-professorial faculty and cultivates their often significant skills as writers in given genres and socio-rhetorical contexts—then it's likely some version of Smarthinking and Coursera's.

WORKS CITED

American Association of University Professors. "Tenure and Teaching-Intensive Appointments." *AAUP Publications and Reports,* 2009/2014, aaup.org/report/tenure -and-teaching-intensive-appointments.

Americans for Educational Testing Reform. "Scorecard: ETS." *Americans for Educational Testing Reform,* 2012, aetr.org/the-facts/ets/.

Americans for Educational Testing Reform. "College Board Leader Paid More than Harvard's." *Americans for Educational Testing Reform,* 25 Aug. 2011, aetr.org/2011 /08/college-board-leader-paid-more-than-harvards/.

Bartholomae, David. "Teaching on and off the Tenure Track: Highlights from the ADE Survey of Staffing Patterns in English." *Pedagogy,* vol. 11, no. 1, 2011, pp. 7–32.

Berlin, James. *Rhetoric and Reality: Writing Instruction in American Colleges, 1900–1985.* Southern Illinois UP, 1987.

Cho, Hanah. "ETS Buys Prometric." *Baltimore Sun,* 3 July 2007, articles.baltimoresun .com/2007-07-03/business/0707030146_1_prometric-testing-and-assessment -assessment-services.

Crowley, Sharon. "A Plea for the Revival of Sophistry." *Rhetoric Review,* vol. 7, no. 2, 1988, pp. 318–34.

Figueroa, Alyssa. "8 Things You Should Know About Corporations Like Pearson that Make Huge Profits from Standardized Tests." *AlterNet,* 6 Aug. 2013, alternet.org /education/corporations-profit-standardized-tests.

Freire, Paulo. *Pedagogy of the Oppressed.* 30th anniversary ed. Continuum, 2000.

Godley, Amanda, and Jennifer Seibel Trainor. "Embracing the Logic of the Marketplace: New Rhetorics for the Old Problem of Labor in Composition." *Tenured Bosses and Disposable Teachers: Writing Instruction in the Managed University,* edited by Marc Bousquet et al., Southern Illinois UP, 2004, pp. 171–185.

Haswell, Richard, and Maja Wilson. "Human Readers: Professionals against Machine Scoring of Student Essays in High-Stakes Assessment." *Human Readers,* 12 Mar. 2013, humanreaders.org/petition/.

Hesse, Douglas. "Who Speaks for Writing?" *Who Speaks for Writing?,* edited by Jennifer Rich and Ethna Lay, New York: Peter Lang, 2012, pp. 9–22.

Hutchings, Pat. "The New Guys in Assessment Town." *Change,* May–June 2009, changemag.org/May-June%202009/full-assessment-town.html.

Jarrett, Susan. *Rereading the Sophists: Classical Rhetoric Reconfigured.* Southern llinois UP, 1998.

June, Audrey Williams. "Some Papers are Uploaded to Bangalore to be Graded." *Chronicle of Higher Education,* 4 Apr. 2010, chronicle.com/article/Outsourced -Grading-Comes-to/64954/.

Markoff, John. "Essay Grading Software Offers Professors a Break," *New York Times*, 4 Apr. 2013, nytimes.com/2013/04/05/science/new-test-for-computers-grading -essays-at-college-level.html.

Murphy, Michael. "New Faculty for a New University: Toward a Full-Time Teaching -Intensive Faculty Track in Composition." *College Composition and Communication,* vol. 52, no. 1, 2000, pp. 14–42.

Schemo, Diana Jean. "U. of Virginia Hit by Scandal over Cheating," *New York Times*, 10 May 2001, nytimes.com/2001/05/10/us/u-of-virginia-hit-by-scandal-over -cheating.html.

Street, Steve, et al. "Who Is Professor 'Staff' and How Can this Person Teach so Many Classes?" *Center for the Future of Higher Education Report #2, Inside Higher Ed*, 23 Aug. 2012, insidehighered.com/sites/default/server_files/files/profstaff(2).pdf.

Trex, Ethan. "Seven College Cheating Scandals." *Wall Street Journal*, 15 May, 2009, wsj.com/articles/SB124216746702112585.

Weiner, Jon. "Inside the Coursera Hype Machine." *The Nation*, 23 Sept. 2013, thenation .com/article/inside-coursera-hype-machine/.

Wolf, Barbara. "Degrees of Shame," 1997, vimeo.com/37920244.

CHAPTER 6

CONTINGENCY, SOLIDARITY, AND COMMUNITY BUILDING: PRINCIPLES FOR CONVERTING CONTINGENT TO TENURE TRACK

William B. Lalicker
West Chester University

Amy Lynch-Biniek
Kutztown University

Threads: Professionalizing and Developing in Complex Contexts; Local Changes to Workload, Pay, and Material Conditions

In the fourteen-campus Pennsylvania State System of Higher Education (PASSHE), the Association of Pennsylvania State College and University Faculty (APSCUF) has worked towards labor justice for contingent faculty by establishing principles that can empower adjuncts, enact inclusion and fairness for them as members of our academic communities, and provide contingents fair access to the tenure track. While a variety of labor problems persist, APSCUF has done much to improve the working conditions of non-tenure-track faculty, including in the collective bargaining agreement (CBA) "the right to the grievance procedure, sick days, personal days, and health and welfare benefits" (APSCUF) for all contingent teachers.

A key provision of the CBA (the "11G" clause, named for its section of the document) mandates that each department develop a procedure for voting on the conversion of temporary faculty to the tenure track. Additionally, this policy is intended to protect and value the contributions of non-tenure-track faculty, providing a path to more stable employment, while encouraging campuses to pay greater attention to their uses of contingent teaching.

The official PASSHE contract term for contingent faculty is "temporary," even though many such colleagues serve for years, even decades. The conversion clause reads as follows:

G. 1. Effective with the Fall 1999 semester and each fall semester thereafter, a full-time, temporary FACULTY MEMBER, who has worked at a University for five (5) full, consecutive academic years in the same department, shall be placed in tenure-track status, if recommended by the majority of the regular department FACULTY in accordance with the procedure developed by that department FACULTY. Such FACULTY shall complete the tenure procedure as provided in Article 15. This Section shall not apply to FACULTY MEMBERS whose salaries are funded by a grant.

2. Time spent in a temporary or regular full-time position at the UNIVERSITY may be counted toward the required probationary period in accordance with Article 15, Section B. 22. (APSCUF)

Our differing departmental cultures—the Kutztown University English department where Amy is a tenured associate professor and the West Chester University English department where Bill is a tenured full professor—produced differing policies in the application of 11G and revealed differing pitfalls and advantages of specific approaches to achieving contingent faculty justice through conversion to the tenure track.

Our department cultures differ in several ways that create variations concerning contingency—and highlighting, in some cases, the need to achieve collegial community as a contributor to, if not a prerequisite for, individual workers' justice.

The Kutztown University (KU) department is moderately sized (thirty-one tenureable faculty, seven temporary) and is formally divided into two faculty groups according to major: English, including both the literature and the composition and rhetoric faculty; and Professional Writing. The West Chester University (WCU) department is very large, including seventy tenureable faculty, ten temporary, and no formal disciplinary units, with all faculty simply categorized by rank or tenureability. In addition to majors in professional writing and English, the latter spanning both literature and rhetoric, KU's program includes a minor in literature, a concentration in cultural and media studies, and an M.A. also combining literary and rhetorical study. Most KU faculty teach some general education composition, and temporary faculty are not limited to teaching general education courses. WCU's program, on the other hand, includes minors in many areas of English studies, but a major in which students choose a literatures track or a writings track, and separate M.A. concentrations in literature; or in writing, teaching, and criticism; or in creative writing. All WCU English faculty teach some general education literature or composition, but contingents (with the exception of one creative writer and occasionally part-time faculty who help supervise student teachers in our Secondary Education program) mostly teach only composition or business writing.

We are able, though, despite the differences of department cultures, to identify a clear set of principles that can make contingent faculty conversion to the tenure track a successful way to achieve inclusion and fairness in our workplaces, at the same time that we strengthen our composition communities. Below, we offer nine such principles and, where possible, note how our experiences at KU and WCU elucidate the benefits or challenges of applying them.

PRINCIPLE 1

Departments should advertise for, and hire, real compositionists for composition-teaching jobs, not Jacks- and Jills-of-all-trades. We wouldn't hire a literature instructor who's only studied, or loved, composition, would we? Then why do we, too often, advertise for generic "English M.A.s," when the literature-centric default mode of many graduate programs means we'll be hiring literary specialists without much interest or experience in composition? Among the recommendations the Conference on College Composition and Communication provides for teacher preparation and continuing development is "to study research and other scholarly work in the humanistic discipline of the teaching of writing" ("CCCC Position Statement"). CCCC, in a context wherein faculty have a variety of English Studies backgrounds, acknowledges the vital role that disciplinary study plays in good teaching. Unless the size and faculty makeup of your department requires a cadre of true generalists, hire people not for their willingness to teach any class tossed at them, but for their expertise in a single area for which the department has a regular, long-term need.

Especially in departments with strong salary, benefits, or working conditions for contingent faculty, the attractiveness of the positions in a perennially tight job market should allow a department to advertise nationally (at least through listservs—a low- or no-cost approach) and draw on strong composition graduate programs rather than advertising for anyone available. If your institution is in a populous, multi-university region with a large number of degree holders in the job market, you should be able to find compositionists, not generalist English instructors. We should advertise for specialties, and mentor toward conversion in those specialties. This not only assures that faculty are more comfortable in their teaching assignments, but also makes contention over expertise less likely when professors are considered for conversion.

For example, at both of our institutions, temporary faculty with degrees in literature, hired to teach composition-heavy schedules, have been considered for conversion into tenure-track positions in composition; the current process of applying 11G in WCU's English department virtually requires that any contingent faculty converted to the tenure track be defined as, and assessed for tenure as, specialists in whatever they've taught the most. Therefore, at WCU, most adjuncts (except for one creative writer who was assigned to teach many creative writing courses) are, supposedly, prepared for the tenure track (including advanced and graduate writing studies teaching) as scholarly composition specialists. Tenured and tenure-track composition professors are at times divided over how to handle these situations. On the one hand, the pedagogical knowledge that comes with years of teaching composition, regardless of one's degree, should be respected and recognized. At the same time, what Stephen M. North calls the "lore" acquired by teaching composition (23–33), though it may be valuable and workable, is not necessarily sufficient, especially in departments (like both KU and WCU) where compositionists must bring a theorized and historicized understanding of the field to a Cultural and Media Studies (KU) or Writing, Teaching & Criticism graduate program (WCU). We also must recognize, of course, that expertise comes not only from a degree program, but from what happens after one graduates. Indeed, many of the most widely-known and respected composition scholars hold degrees in literature, having found the field or had a scholarly epiphany only after completing the Ph.D. We should further acknowledge the hypocrisy of hiring individuals to teach writing—often for many, many years—yet telling them, when conversion becomes a possibility, that they are not qualified to do so (Lynch-Biniek).

We also recognize that regularly converting professors with other specialties into composition lines may underscore the already hierarchical structure of English departments in which literature is often privileged over writing. That is, literature degrees are often seen as sufficient qualification to teach writing, but a composition degree does not qualify one to teach literature. Further, given that temporary lines dominate in composition, national searches for tenure-track positions might become the domain of literature. Working in a system that already often treats composition as an also-ran, compositionists may resent any departmental practice that further reifies the composition-slighting, pedagogy-disdaining departmental hierarchy. Altering our practice at the point of hire may, at least to some degree, indicate an equal valuation of teaching and scholarship, and a mutual respect for literature and composition within English Studies.

Of course, departments may not always have the time to search exclusively with expertise in mind. Exceptions exist, as in hiring faculty to cover sabbatical or emergency leaves or immediately after a retirement. Therefore, if we do hire or convert faculty to positions outside of their degreed specialties, it should be with the expectation that they will receive mentorship and do scholarship in the area for which they are hired. (We'll comment more on mentorship and on support for adjunct scholarship later.) Further, the provision of better mentoring and scholarly support for contingent faculty does not address the overall adjunctification of higher education and adjuncts' potentially precarious employment stability or second-class salary and benefits.

PRINCIPLE 2

Hire contingent faculty with as much care and attention to their long-term collegial and scholarly roles as you demonstrate towards regular tenure-track faculty. Though contingent hiring may not have the funding for some rituals of national searches, many of the on-campus activities that identify the best tenure-track faculty can be applied to contingent faculty. Hire early (not last-minute); discuss scholarly interests; include a teaching demonstration and meetings with prospective colleagues; get student input.

At KU and at WCU alike, we are still challenged to hire early; often administrators do not release temporary lines until late in the spring. Changing the culture of hiring, then, requires lobbying and likely even bargaining for reform beyond the departmental level. Nevertheless, at KU we have otherwise made the temporary faculty hiring process parallel that of the tenure track. While it has not been easy, requiring more work from hiring committees and additional financial expense for a budget-strapped department, it has also allowed us to find faculty for whom we are a good fit, and vice-versa.

PRINCIPLE 3

New faculty should all be made directly aware of a conversion clause and any departmental policies guiding it. In the PASSHE context, new temporary faculty could ideally be advised that the 11G clause amounts to a "ten-year tenure track" for those who seek it. The job advertisement could even allude to the convertibility of the position from contingent to tenure-track, for suitably interested candidates.

At the same time, temporary faculty should be told at hire whether or not the department sees them as potential permanent faculty. For example, an adjunct might be hired at the last moment to fill an unforeseen need and not be ideally suited for the position. In such circumstances, the job should be clearly framed as a single-year position with the option for renewal. Such honesty avoids the unethical practice of keeping temporary faculty in limbo, unaware if conversion is indeed an option the department will offer; and it keeps departments from treating the first-year composition courses, which contingent faculty most often teach, as unworthy of the same attention to staffing as upper-level courses.

PRINCIPLE 4

Make sure all current or longstanding contingent faculty are credited for doing satisfactory service according to the real requirements under which they were hired—"grandparent" them into qualification when any new requirements for conversion are established by the department or the administration. As we have noted, there's a hypocrisy in some of the conditions and assumptions we traditionally bring to contingent hiring: we hire you to teach composition, potentially for decades; we then deny that you have any professional qualifications worthy of permanent scholarly employment. It is vital that, as we adopt new conditions and assumptions, no matter how necessary, we acknowledge contingents' good-faith service and adherence to the standards we set in the past. Grandparenting contingent faculty into any new tenurability conversion system is plain fairness. Moreover, it allows us to acknowledge the value of professional development completed in composition while in contingent positions. Similarly, our regular tenure-track hiring ought to give preference points to applicants we know. Too often, contingent status is treated as a mark of unsuitability for the tenure track—as if it's better to hire new instructors with little experience, about whom we know little beyond a carefully crafted dossier, rather than the contingent down the hall whose teaching and scholarly opinions we've known for years, and whose service has been endorsed by repeated rehiring for years.

PRINCIPLE 5

Maximize contingent faculty access to the complete collegial life of the department: meetings, policy discussions, social events, scholarly discussions, committee service and funding for professional development. But don't require such participation where it is not at least indirectly rewarded or evaluated. Where contracts do not forbid contingent faculty from voting, include them in the governance process. Remember that informed participation requires context: the more we include all faculty in our departmental culture, the better they can contribute. When adjunct colleagues are included in professional discussions, they can bring their experience and insight to bear accordingly. In the PASSHE system, temporary faculty's participation in departmental culture varies greatly from campus to campus, and even from department to department.

At Kutztown University, the English department took years to normalize the involvement of temporary faculty in meetings and committees, and the result, we believe, is not only a richer department, but one in which contingent faculty want to work. At the same time, the right to vote is occasionally contentious, as in instances when some constituencies fear being out-voted. We need to be vigilant in safeguarding the participation of all of our colleagues. As Coordinator of Composition at Kutztown, Amy is also very aware of the power dynamic at work when she asks temporary faculty to join committees or attend events. She encourages contingent faculty to serve on perhaps a single committee in their first year, and only if they feel the work will benefit their conversion or job search. Even so, she grapples with the truth that, in a tenuous employment position, they may take on more work than they feel is practical, despite reassurances. Having been an adjunct herself once, she doesn't blame them. No easy solutions exist, beyond good communication and monitoring for abuse. At KU, contingent faculty in English now have long been empowered in the membership of the department, which has made questions of conversion to tenure track easier. KU's tenured faculty have worked more closely with their contingent colleagues; contingent faculty have regularly had voices in policy discussions.

West Chester University's Department of English is now working to change a culture in which contingent faculty were not expected to participate in—or, by some tenure-track colleagues, were specifically denied access to—departmental life beyond their own classrooms. The changes are occurring both because of a change in the department leadership—the current chair favors inclusion and has previously been a union liaison to contingent faculty—and because the 11G conversion process has alerted tenurable faculty to the imperative of knowing their contingent colleagues more fully. At WCU, Bill's view is that, possibly because of the sheer size of the department (largest department of any kind in the fourteen-campus state system), whole-department communication and exchange is extremely difficult. Tenured faculty, not just contingent faculty, have complained about being outsiders to decisions made in committees; the problem was serious enough that a dean convened a task force with an outside mediator to attempt to improve communication in early 2014. Committee service is enacted at a distance from central departmental discussions; and this structural challenge pushes contingent faculty further to the margins. In Bill's past service as writing program administrator for the department's first year composition program, he found it very difficult to bring tenurable and contingent faculty together for program policy discussions: tenurable faculty seldom wanted to contribute to composition policies; contingent faculty, sometimes "freeway flying" among campuses in metropolitan Philadelphia, had little time—and earned no service recognition—for policy meetings. The leadership of WCU's English department has, until recently, not invited contingents to department meetings, and has previously excluded contingent faculty from almost all committees. A new set of department bylaws, as well as a consciousness of the value of service as a guideline for suitability for conversion, encourages more committee service and collegial engagement for contingents in future.

PRINCIPLE 6

Evaluate contingent faculty for their whole set of academic talents, just as you evaluate tenure-track faculty: for teaching, but also for collegial service and scholarship. Conversions in the Kutztown University English department were largely possible because we had an official record of teaching, scholarship, and service to discuss for each contingent faculty. Having worked side by side with tenure-track faculty on committees and extracurricular assignments, these professors became less easily reducible to a name and a schedule, the anonymous person in the bullpen office taking up the mantle of "Professor Staff" (Street et al.) this semester. At West Chester University, the conversion process and individual conversion qualifications are highly problematic because of the lack of any regular assessment of scholarship or service. Indeed, WCU English effectively forbids most temporary service by not inviting temporary faculty onto most committees. WCU English uses the same annual performance review forms for tenurable and for contingent faculty, but the electronic document provided for contingents, in its sections for comment on "Scholarly Activity" and "Service," is pre-completed with the letters "NA" in the blank spaces. Contingent faculty deserve access to evaluation in the same categories, with the same standards of expectations and rigor, as tenure-track faculty. Evaluations should never be pro forma.

As noted, though, we should not require service or scholarship unless it's recognized and rewarded—that is, we should require it only for adjuncts seeking options for tenurability or promotion. It is problematic to expect further work from contingent faculty who may already be over-burdened by first-year composition schedules that come with a significant paper-grading load, especially if they are working out of their specialty or have no interest in conversion.

PRINCIPLE 7

Encourage contingent faculty to embrace the agency of self-identification by academic field and by career-track preference. Potential temporary faculty should have the right to choose whether to take on the service and scholarship challenges that would lead, potentially, to conversion to the tenure track. Does the instructor just want to teach a class or two as a sideline to her main priorities in work life? Or is she focused on a full-time academic career that might develop more completely as options become available, as mentoring is offered, as great work is valued? A "one-size-fits-all" job description for contingent faculty demeans the individuals, and the variety of talents and areas of expertise and life goals, of our contingent colleagues. In PASSHE, the "Statement of Expectations" carries legal weight: annual performance reviews, and thus re-hiring, or tenure and promotion, are made with reference to expectations achieved or not achieved. When all Statements of Expectations for contingent faculty are the same—declaring all to be compositionists, or all to be limited to teaching a slate of courses that may not be appropriate to the available faculty expertise—we are doing a disservice to faculty and student alike.

PRINCIPLE 8

Mentoring is a basic element of collegial initiation and a powerful tool for professional growth, and thus should be available to all faculty, tenure-track and contingent equally. Mentoring of all faculty is crucial, especially when professors are hired to teach out of their degreed specialty or when they are not familiar with the culture of academic scholarship—or the culture of a particular department. If we hold contingent faculty to meet standards of teaching, scholarship, and service, as we do tenure-track faculty, then we should offer contingents the same support. Indeed, in its own "Statement of Principles and Standards for the Postsecondary Teaching of Writing," CCCC insists upon the need for all composition faculty to "have access to scholarly literature and be given opportunities for continuing professional development" in the field. We will note, below, other ways universities can do this, but here we argue that mentoring is both a right and a responsibility for creating and sustaining a collegial community. Mentoring applies to service, scholarship, and teaching alike; since it contributes to faculty performance, it is an essential ingredient in providing well-informed and effective pedagogy to our students. Part of the regular mentoring process that each faculty member deserves, contingent or conventional tenure-track, should be guidance toward tenurability, including conversion-position strength.

PRINCIPLE 9

Support contingent faculty for whom the tenure track means embracing composition as not just a teaching assignment, but as a scholarly endeavor. Be generous not only with mentoring, but also with financial support for additional academic coursework, conference presentations and opportunities for publication of every kind. Such support means that traditional tenure-track faculty may have to sacrifice their usually exclusive proportion of available funding and institutional support for scholarship, and must share available resources. But given the common historical inequity with which contingent faculty have been provided salary and benefits and fair material conditions—even as contingent faculty work is often structured in order to free tenurable faculty to publish, earn salary raises, and become promoted—it's high time to institute a culture of equal sharing in the departmental community.

CONCLUSION

For any of these recommendations to work, administrative buy-in is required. Deans and provosts must be willing to support the policies and costs that result in fair practices. Advocates need actively to work for reform not only on the departmental level, but throughout the institutional administration and system. This is not an easy task, but allies are sometimes easier to find outside a Department of English than within the department. Deans and provosts and granting units often see the value of building a faculty that is better at teaching writing—a faculty that brings research-based savvy to produce assessable products of written communication and distinctive ways of connecting writing and thinking. We, as experts in composition and rhetoric, are well equipped to bring our arguments for a strong, permanent, justly-inclusive, collegial community of writing specialists into the tenure track to build better composition programs for the benefit of our student writers.

While we chose these principles in respect to their application to our specific contexts, adoption of them beyond the PASSHE system might bend the curve toward justice for adjuncts even where union-supported conversion to tenure track isn't an apparent option. In *Reclaiming the Ivory Tower*, contingent-faculty activist Joe Berry contends that we have to act like unions even when we're not legally organized in unions; likewise, departments can create conditions in which contingent faculty are obvious candidates for secure positions by treating them as likely candidates for those positions from the beginning. Our CBA mandates some version of that process, but nothing precludes any department from developing one on its own. Justice is the journey before it is the arrival.

WORKS CITED

Berry, Joe. Reclaiming the Ivory Tower: Organizing Adjuncts to Change Higher Education. Monthly Review Press, 2005.

Conference on College Composition and Communication. "CCCC Position Statement on the Preparation and Professional Development of Teachers of Writing."
NCTE, 2015, ncte.org/cccc/resources/positions/statementonprep.

———. "Statement of Principles and Standards for the Postsecondary Teaching of
Writing." NCTE, 2015, ncte.org/cccc/resources/positions/postsecondarywriting.

Lynch-Biniek, Amy. "You're Perfect for the Job . . . for Now." Paper presented at the
Thomas R. Watson Conference, University of Louisville, Oct. 2012.

North, Stephen M. *The Making of Knowledge in Composition: Portrait of an Emerging
Field*. Boynton/Cook, 1987.

Street, Steve, et al. "Who is 'Professor Staff' and How Can This Person Teach So Many
Classes?" *Center for the Future of Higher Education,* Aug. 2012, futureofhighered.
org/policy-report-2/.

CHAPTER 7

THE OTHER INVISIBLE HAND: ADJUNCT LABOR AND ECONOMIES OF THE WRITING CENTER

Dani Nier-Weber

SUNY Sullivan Community College

Threads: Local Changes to Workload, Pay, and Working Conditions; Organizing Within and Across Ranks

I recently watched an awareness test on *YouTube,* a short clip that asks viewers to accurately count the total number of passes by the team in white during a fast-moving basketball scrimmage. At the end of the clip, I found that I'd counted the number of passes correctly—thirteen—but I'd missed the fact that a giant bear had moonwalked across the court, mid-game. The clip ends with a warning, "It's easy to miss something you're not looking for" (dothetest), then cautions viewers to watch for cyclists. Like most of us, presumably, I didn't see what I was not paying attention to. In *Peripheral Visions for Writing Centers* (2013), Jackie Grutsch McKinney calls for those of us working and researching in the field of writing centers to challenge our own deeply held assumptions—to interrogate what she calls the "grand narrative" of writing centers in order to see what we might otherwise miss.

At the intersection between writing centers and contingent faculty, adjunct labor has been particularly invisible. A great deal of the current literature centers squarely around "peer" tutoring, which refers primarily to undergraduate and, to a lesser extent, graduate tutors in the writing center. A search of contingent faculty and writing centers reveals a fundamental confusion even in key search terms; "professional" staff sometimes seems to refer to adjunct (composition) instructors who serve part of their day in the writing center, and sometimes to professional tutors hired solely to work in the writing center but who do not work as instructors (at least not at the same institution), and thus arguably can be counted as another kind of contingent faculty. The labor of tutors in the writing center who are not student "peers" or graduate students, but who perform similar kinds of—contingent—work, has been little articulated or examined; as yet, the classifications and their distinctions remain unclear and ill-defined. Thus far, little corresponding discussion exists about the particular challenges, ethics, and economics of labor conditions faced by composition adjuncts and other professionals for whom writing center work comprises part, most, or all of the job.

The telling of alternative narratives of writing center labor provides greater space for, as McKinney puts it, "multiple interpretations, thick descriptions, and even dissonance" (34) as we investigate and document what is going on in writing centers. All too often, undergraduate "peer tutoring" is so central to descriptions of writing center work that other realities, whether occurring on the periphery or perhaps increasingly at the center, often go largely unnoticed and un-narrated. Contingent faculty are among the "people and events normally excluded" (McKinney 12) from the dominant conversation; they remain, in many ways, the unsung and invisible hand—the moonwalking bear—of writing center work.

According to McKinney, the largely unchallenged "grand narrative" of writing centers goes like this: *writing centers are comfortable, iconoclastic places where all students go to get one-on-one tutoring on their writing* (6). McKinney deconstructs multiple aspects of this narrative, taking it apart piece by piece as she challenges 1) metaphors of "home" and "family" that underlie descriptions of writing centers as cozy and comfortable, 2) narratives of the writing center as both a part of and outside the mainstream academic world, i.e., as "outsiders on the inside" (37), and 3) depictions of the peer tutor as iconoclastic maverick. Further, McKinney investigates, among other things, the physical and metaphorical spaces in which writing center work takes place as well as the idea that "all students" benefit from that work. Beyond our usual narratives, in other words, where is the moonwalking bear?

In my experience in three university writing centers, first as assistant director during my graduate studies, then as interim director, then permanent director at a third institution, the centers, like the institutions in which they were housed, spanned a variety of expectations, material conditions, and student and consultant demographics. Two of the universities were relatively small and located in rural, isolated areas. Both largely served first-generation populations of lower socio-economic status, including non-traditional students seeking to create for themselves new opportunities after regional industries and other venues for local employment had diminished or vanished altogether.

The consultants who staffed each center reflected a diversity of characteristics as well. The writing center where I received my training as assistant director was housed in a large, suburban university and staffed by a cohort of undergraduate and graduate peer consultants, while the second center used only undergraduates, many of whom I inherited and some of whom I hired and trained during my stint as visiting director. In *Peripheral Visions,* McKinney describes the stereotypical peer tutor as

> someone who went to a college but was not part of the college—someone who doesn't know the name of the football team's quarterback—own a hoodie or bumper sticker with the school logo, but one who is on a first-name basis with the reference librarian, runs the student Greenpeace chapter, and whose best friend is the town's record shop owner. (35)

The peer tutors I supervised spanned broad differences in styles, approaches, and personality types, from Maria, who had five siblings and who treated student clients like she was their bossy older sister, to Jeff and Kate, a young married couple who—when they weren't playing (or writing about) video games—spent their days in my office giving eagle-eyed reports of every transgression their fellow tutors committed in the center. Following McKinney's resistance to stereotypical assumptions, I could not have identified the common denominator in tutor identity as, say, maverick, activist, or subversive; at the centers in which I worked, consultant identities seemed to cover too broad a spectrum to make any such claims.

At the behest of the administration at my third institution, however, the brand new Writing Center was staffed exclusively with faculty consultants[1]: Elizabeth, Michaela, Glen, and me. (Other adjuncts—Karen, Jenny, Cara, and Whitney—would join us over the course of the next two years as schedules allowed/demanded). In part the decision to staff the Writing Center with faculty was due to a problematic history with peer writing tutors, who had needed more training and supervision than another support service had been able to provide them prior to my arrival. Most of these faculty consultants were adjunct composition instructors whose teaching load was partly shifted to hours in the Writing Center. Unlike the programs at my two previous institutions, composition at this university was almost exclusively taught by contingent faculty. In this model, providing ten hours per week in the center of one-on-one consulting and occasional other, related tasks was equivalent to teaching one three-credit composition class. During the first two years a number of adjuncts, including Elizabeth, Cara, and Jenny, along with Glen, a full-time, non-tenure stream

---

1   I use the term "faculty consultants" to denote full-time instructors or contingent, part-time composition faculty who also tutor in the writing center—a designation my writing center faculty chose for themselves.

assistant professor who had been re-assigned to ten writing center hours a week, served as part-time faculty writing consultants.

Elizabeth, Cara, and Jenny did not really fit the image of "maverick" or "subversive" tutor. All three had obtained master's degrees in English from the same local private university and had worked in that university's writing center as graduate students before being hired as adjuncts at our current institution. Each was assigned between five and fifteen hours per week in the Writing Center while also teaching part-time. Course loads, classes, and writing center hours changed each semester, depending on the needs of the composition and English programs. In fact, the Writing Center would ultimately serve as a "fallback" option for several part- and full-time faculty in both programs whenever classes didn't fill. Although as director I placed a high emphasis on non-directive, globally-focused consulting practices, I did notice a common characteristic in the approaches Elizabeth, Cara, and Jenny used in both teaching and tutoring sessions, one that coincided with the feedback and assignments students were bringing into the Writing Center from across the composition program: namely, a strong focus on the improvement of lower order errors and numerous formulaic "tips" for sentence, paragraph, and thesis structures. This was closer to what I would call a traditional approach (without negative judgment) than had been the focus of my own education and training. On the whole, however, I had to acknowledge that this approach seemed to fit well with my new institution's emphasis on "rigor" and on improving bad—error-filled as well as incoherent—student writing.

I also had to acknowledge that, while I deeply believed in the Writing Center's mission to build a campus-wide cohort of expert student writers and tutors, the overall performance of the new Writing Center with its group of faculty consultants was nothing short of excellent. Not only was the atmosphere as comfortable, fun, and collegial as any writing center I had ever worked in, despite an immediate, high demand from students that did not let up all semester, but we soon received tangible, outside affirmation for the work we were doing as well. After that first semester, the registrar—the "numbers guy" on campus—announced at a composition meeting that retention among freshmen who had visited the Writing Center had increased by up to approximately 30 percent. The professionalism and skill among the full-time and contingent instructors who staffed the Writing Center, in other words, was nothing short of stellar, and we had the results to prove it.

~~~

Our brand new Writing Center began in an 8' × 9' outer office space that barely held three small tables with two chairs each, which we divided from the adjacent hallway using two tall bookshelves. All of us were either adjunct instructors (Elizabeth and Michaela) or full-time non-tenure stream faculty (Glen and myself) who also taught in the composition program. Glen, who was supporting a family, routinely taught additional overload courses, while Elizabeth and Michaela carried a load of three classes, or thirty hours per week, in addition to putting in between five and seven and a half hours in the Writing Center. Rapid success and high demand—students and faculty alike, it seemed, had long hungered for help with writing on campus—quickly compelled us to add ten more hours of tutoring, split between two more adjuncts, Karen and Jenny, who both were also already teaching three classes. The following semester Karen, who also worked part time as a copy editor at the local paper and cared for two aging parents, opted out of writing center consulting due to sheer overwhelment. A year later we hired Cara, fresh out of graduate school, as an additional adjunct. Like the others who worked part-time in the Writing Center, Cara devoted between thirty-five and thirty-seven and a half hours per week to the university, spread between the Writing Center and composition, and like every other adjunct with that schedule, also worked a second job in retail—invariably Friday nights, it seemed—to make ends meet. And like many of our adjuncts, Cara also commuted between thirty and forty-five minutes to the university, one way.

Scheduling adjuncts to teach thirty-seven and a half hours a week, I was told, was "pushing it" because the university still officially counted this as "part time" labor. At our institution, adjuncts were paid roughly $2,000 per ten-hour per week section, or the same amount for the corresponding ten hours in the Writing Center (pay was slightly higher for adjuncts with Ph.D.s, which only Michaela had). According to the university faculty and staff newspaper, pay on our regional campus throughout the ranks was lower than the national average for similarly ranked positions. Happily, our institution offered adjuncts access to health benefits if they committed to teaching at least one three-credit class during both the fall and spring semesters of one academic year. As far as I am aware, nearly all the adjuncts availed themselves of the opportunity to obtain health insurance.

Interestingly, I discovered later, health benefits would not extend to a part-time consultant hired to work only in the Writing Center but not as an adjunct instructor. Part-time consulting was apparently considered a staff, not an instructional, position, and health benefits did not extend to part-time staff. This brought home the reality that, although lip service is often given to the idea that writing center work is, in fact, instruction as opposed to primarily a remedial or support service, there seems to be little awareness outside the discipline of what that actually means.

Another side effect of the part-time status of adjunct faculty at the university became clear when one of our composition instructors applied for a mortgage over the summer. Although he had been teaching classes at this university, and at least one other institution, for over ten years and was scheduled to teach composition that coming fall, because he was not "officially" employed over the summer the university would not verify his employment. His mortgage application was denied. He eventually straightened it out, but the consequences of residing in that liminal contingent space—employed yet not employed—created stress and hassle for him and his family that, as I saw it, seemed unnecessary and unwarranted.

The dominant narrative about the adjuncts on our campus, as mostly young graduate students who would soon move on, did not, in fact, reflect the material reality of the lives of most of the adjuncts who actually worked there. In the prevailing view of at least certain members of the administration, who made decisions about hours hired, pay offered, and positions created, adjuncts were continually depicted in scheduling and other conversations as a temporary, part-time, and transient labor force. While Elizabeth, for one, had indeed applied that first year to several doctoral programs around the state—and with her gift for multi-modal composition, I believed, could eventually create for herself a fine career in that specialty—the reigning narrative did not accurately describe the situation most of our adjuncts found themselves in. In part because we were a rural institution, many of our faculty as well as our students were extraordinarily place-bound. One of our adjuncts had been teaching at the university for seventeen years, while Karen had been there for eleven (and vividly recalled the last raise she had received, $50 seven years previously). Almost every adjunct who was a long-time employee of the university was there because of family; they wanted to live with or near parents, aging or otherwise, with husbands who had permanent, local jobs, or they had grown up in the area and did not want to leave. Although one adjunct, Jenny, eventually took a full-time job at a local private high school that paid little better than the adjunct job she left, and Cara eventually found a similar adjunct position closer to home, many if not most of the others would likely have freely chosen to remain at the university long-term if the university had offered them a "real" job—that is, a position that enabled them to adequately support themselves and view their own work as part of a legitimate, long-term career. Most of them remained in any case. Clearly, the justification for low paying jobs based on a narrative of temporariness and transience worked to perpetuate the very impermanence that characterized these contingent yet professional lives, not to mention negatively impacting the material realities of those lives.

As a new director who had previously worked mainly with peer tutors, I only slowly became aware of the extent to which the university failed to view adjuncts as full-fledged contributors to the professional culture on campus. Notably, the university prided itself publicly as an institution that focused above all on teaching excellence, which I assumed included professional development for all our instructors. I focused on professional development in the Writing Center from the beginning. At our first meeting of the year, consultants chose topics for monthly workshops to help address whatever issues arose. We read theory, literature, and research, prepared for discussion, and shared materials, questions, and ideas.

At my previous institutions, I had helped peer tutors write proposals to two regional writing center and peer tutoring conferences, so when the opportunity arose for our faculty writing center consultants to submit a proposal to the International Writing Center Association Collaborative, I did not hesitate to suggest we give it a try. As much as an exercise in professional development and collaborative writing as for any other reason, the consultants and I researched, brainstormed, and then collaboratively wrote the proposal. Every participant contributed something valuable, even Michaela, who stated she would not be able to afford to go if the proposal were accepted. We were so encouraged by our success that we submitted a similar proposal—a workshop that would solicit different feedback from each audience and allow us to gather interesting data about writing center cultures across the country—to the regional writing center conference as well.

To our delight, first the national and then the regional proposal were both accepted. We then set about trying to find funding, including applying for the travel grants and scholarships offered through the organizations that had sponsored both conferences. My gratification at our success, however, was short-lived. In a rare visit to the Writing Center, my supervisor told me that I had put the university under duress to fund adjunct attendance at the conferences, and that this was problematic. On that, and on at least three subsequent occasions, I was admonished not to apply to conferences again (as a group, I assumed), and if we did, to only apply to local conferences, and then only if we had obtained prior permission.

Although I had not intended to put pressure on the university, and I never approached the administration to request financial support, I realized I had unwittingly created a situation where at least some administrators felt they would "look bad" if they did not offer any funding. Graciously, the university found funding to partially support the adjuncts' attendance at the national conference, albeit on the condition that the adjuncts present "what they learned" to my supervisor upon their return. I was also clearly told that there were to be no expectations of future funding and that I could not use funds I had carefully set aside in my budget to pay for conference fees on the assumption that attendance was more valuable for us than, say, purchasing Writing Center T-shirts (fortunately, this ban was later lifted). In the end, only one (other than Michaela) was unable to attend the conference due to financial constraints. Beyond the faculty development grant I regularly applied for and received (with or without travel companions), the total cost to the university from all sources for two adjuncts to attend the national conference and three to attend the regional conference was under $1000, plus the regular $250 allotment I would have spent on my own travel in any case, which paid for all lodging and gas at the regional writing center conference.

Rhetorically, adjuncts were cast both as transitory and as representatives of the university, at least insofar as their inability to fulfill an obligation might reflect badly on the institution, but also implicitly as second-class and of course, once again, contingent. I began to see fault lines that had previously been invisible to me, the hierarchies and divisions of the campus culture—another moonwalking bear. I had naively assumed that working toward a common goal, i.e., improving instruction through professional development, would take precedence over other, less pressing (at least to me, if wrongly) considerations such as the "appropriateness" of funding professional development for adjuncts. I became much more careful about making such assumptions, including assumptions about the positionality of adjunct faculty and the legitimacy of their professional development outside of internal Writing Center meetings.

Further, it was also stressed repeatedly in composition meetings that providing contingent faculty with financial or professional support might engender resentment on the part of full-time tenured or tenure-track faculty. This view—which cast professional development and scholarly engagement as a zero-sum game, with clear winners and losers—was communicated so clearly that, after one meeting at which the director of composition reiterated the point, Cara (the youngest member of the group) stood up and exclaimed with obvious bewilderment, "I had no idea the faculty resented us so much!" I question that narrative; I am not sure whether this view was generally shared across the campus, or perhaps stemmed from one or two lone, if influential, voices in the division, in which case it would be unfair to paint the majority of faculty with that broad (and ugly) brush. The effect, however, was the same. Contingent faculty's lesser—less important—status came through loud and clear to all. I became more aware as well that whenever I was silent in the face of exploitative or unfair practices, I was essentially providing tacit approval for exactly those sorts of conditions.

The following year, I will note, Elizabeth and others were still regularly referring to various ideas, strategies, and pedagogical approaches we had encountered at both conferences. Although I had blundered into a victory, perhaps a fleeting one, I did notice two things. First, a conversation opened up on the campus, at least in various discursive pockets, about possible sources of funding for professional development for adjuncts, and that conversation has yet to be concluded. And second, the dividends of our small success permanently altered our own internal professional conversations within the Writing Center, and very much for the better. They are still paying off.

~~~

At a recent workshop given by Beth Carroll, Writing Center director from Appalachian State University, Carroll called the quiet research adjuncts do in their fields, unrecognized and unrewarded, the "Don't Ask, Don't Tell" of academia—yet another aspect of adjunct life that remains invisible. The hunger of at least some academics in adjunct positions, like Elizabeth and Michaela, to freely participate in "the" academic culture, to be counted as fully legitimate members of the community, often somehow remains invisible, unacknowledged, and at worst, unimportant. Particularly striking, especially for writing centers and composition instructors, is that on the other hand the conversation about needing better instruction, better writing, better student writers, is ongoing and loudly vocal across the disciplines—and across the country. Jeffrey Zorn's August 28, 2013 article, "English Compositionism as Fraud and Failure," is only one recent example in a long string of scathing laments about how "Johnny can't write" (and it's all composition's fault). (And why doesn't the writing center fix it?)

If teaching composition is so important, however, then why aren't we investing institutional support in faculty development? Why aren't we at least recognizing the longstanding, if fluid, commitments that actually do exist on both sides? Why don't we—who are academics—interrogate and resist the dominant narratives of transience that help not only create, but perpetuate, systems of impermanence and exploitation? Why do we continue to marginalize exactly those laborers in the trenches who perform some of our most crucial work? Such dominant narratives are particularly bewildering in light of adjunct work that takes place on the front lines of retention, not to mention the contributions adjuncts make that support the existing, at times aristocratic, culture. In our division, for example, adjuncts taught a great number of Friday classes, thus relieving tenured faculty from pressure by the administration to balance course loads and meet complicated scheduling needs across the entire work week. Yet adjunct contributions to favored faculty scheduling went unacknowledged at division meetings whenever scheduling was discussed.

The recognition, along with alternative understandings, of adjunct work, however, goes beyond mere calls to address the flaws in an increasingly exploitative system out of altruistic or lofty ethical motives. Beyond the grand writing center narratives identified by McKinney, I had begun to see an even bigger moonwalking bear—a different common denominator among consultants that applied across the entire spectrum of writing center staff, but perhaps particularly to the faculty adjuncts with whom I was working. Key to writing center labor was the desire and ability to build positive, nurturing relationships; in fact, I began to see the consultants, each in their own individual way, as often driven by a *compelling desire to help others*. As much as writing centers attracted mavericks, nerds, and iconoclasts, they also attracted people who wanted to contribute, be of service, and make a difference.[2]

I would add, then, to the grand narrative of writing center work the core characteristic of *relational*. Born of the impulse on the part of consultants, directors, and very often student-clients as well, to build positive relationships, whether for the next thirty or fifty minutes, over the course of the semester, or even beyond, relationship is the beating heart of the writing center. I see this core characteristic as both empowering writing centers and contributing to their (ongoing?) marginalization as contingency encroaches into even this hospitable space. Further, this impulse toward relationship is at least as descriptive of contingent faculty consultants as it is of undergraduate peer tutors. One might, in fact, argue that

> adjuncts are drawn to Writing Centers because Writing Centers—by design—*should* be congenial spaces to work in for people who want to feel connectedness in a way that conventional classroom assignments may deny them as adjuncts. That is, it IS different for them than for peer tutors or grad students on TA assignments, or what have you. They ARE closer to the stereotypical iconoclastic writing center consultant than the average peer tutor is, at least in that very substantive way. (Kahn)

In other words, one key value that attracts students, staff, and faculty to the writing center may be the desire to serve others, because that—relationally, cooperatively, collaboratively—is at the center of our mission.

Further, I suggest that this desire is not merely an attitude of wanting to provide help, support, and service, but can be defined more broadly as directly centered in a (feminist) ethic of care that defines *caring* as both a value and a practice. In *The Ethics of Care: Personal, Political, and Global*, Virginia Held characterizes an ethic of care as a focus on relationships between inter-reliant actors rather than on the individual autonomy and independence that defines

---

2   According to writer Ariel Schwartz and others, this is also a key characteristic of our current generation of students.

a self-interested capitalist society. Relationships are not primarily seen as occurring between rational agents of equal power, but as occurring between people who are "relational and interdependent, morally and epistemologically" (14), and who may, at various stages of life, experience actual dependency as well. Caring, in other words, includes services—such as the interested and informed audience the writing center offers—that receiving parties could not necessarily provide for themselves. Further, traits such as "sympathy, empathy, sensitivity, and responsiveness" (10), which Held identifies as core to the ethics of care, correspond seamlessly to core components of writing center work; in both arenas, the "values of trust, solidarity, mutual concern, empathetic responsiveness have priority . . . relationships are cultivated, needs are responded to, and sensitivity is demonstrated" (Held 15–16). The success of any writing center session is defined by cooperation and collaboration as well as the consultant's ability to do a close reading—of the text, the student, the assignment, the situation, the moment—i.e., an ability that requires, among other skills, masterful utilization of the sets of traits listed above.

Admittedly, depicting the labor of adjunct consultants as caring may play into the stereotype of the service work of writing centers as "feminized" (and perhaps "femininized"?), i.e., as "mothering" in the sense of the overarching nurturing family metaphor that frames writing centers—and arguably the field of composition. As Held also acknowledges, constructing work as "feminine" contributes to the exploitation of those—typically women and minority groups—who "perform much of the paid but ill-paid work of caring" (Held 16). Necessarily, in the eyes of traditional institutional assumptions that privilege "research and group instruction, not service and individualized instruction" (Ianetta et al. 16), such service work is also regarded as subordinate or lesser and is generally less rewarded in academia (and certainly elsewhere). In general, as Ianetta et al. note, research by Balester and McDonald shows that directors of writing centers in comparison to writing program administrators are "less likely to be in tenure track positions, to be granted faculty status, and to be Composition specialists" (21). Similarly, as Joan Tronto and others have pointed out, altogether "caring activities are devalued, underpaid, and disproportionately occupied by the relatively powerless in society (31)" (qtd. in Held 18). The generally lower status of writing centers and writing center directors is representative of the lower status with which service work, and exponentially adjunct labor, are institutionally regarded.

The central importance, nonetheless, of the relational nature of writing center work to consultants and students can routinely be seen, for example, in the results of end-of-session and end-of-semester surveys collected by many writing centers. At the institution where I served as assistant writing center director, the total number of positive responses that year to the question of overall satisfaction with their writing center experience was 98 percent, of which 637 responses, or 71 percent, were very satisfied and 238, or 27 percent of overall responses, were satisfied. Similarly, in exit survey results at the institution where I served as visiting director, 234 responders, or also 98 percent, deemed the writing center's services helpful, while only six responders, roughly 2 percent, found us not helpful (including one, perhaps inevitable, "hell no").

Comments on all three centers at which I have worked expressed student appreciation in multiple ways: "Thank you Maria! I appreciate the time and patients [sic] you provided in helping me write an abstract. Words can not [sic] adequately express my feelings to what we accomplished today. You are a blessing! Thanks! Thanks! Thank you!" "Elizabeth did an excellent job. She was very patient, helpful, and friendly. I would highly recommend the Writing Center to current . . . students. Thank you for providing such a wonderful service for students." "I think that the Writing Center is the most helpful place that anyone could get help from for essays." "Cool stuff happens in my head when i'm here." "Raises for all tutors!" "The Writing Center is my new best friend!" And my favorite: "He was very helpful, suggestive, and nice." Across the board, complaints centered almost exclusively around a lack of sufficient time for sessions or the occasional crowdedness of the space.

The central, relational nature of writing center work thus supports two core goals: 1) to build human capital, that is, to increase human knowledge and skills, and 2) to build social capital, that is, to create the relationships that support and sustain goal #1, above. Presenting at a regional conference in 2009, writing center consultant Philip Call explained it this way: "These social networks between people and the norms of reciprocity that arise from them are known as 'social capital' . . . they constitute another convergence point between philanthropy and writing centers." These are not merely "touchy-feely," feel-good positives; as seen in the retention results mentioned above, they support "actual relations that are 'trusting, considerate, and caring'" (Held 12), which in turn support learning. Relationships, research has repeatedly shown, are crucial in creating the "communities of inquiry" that help students to "assume responsibility to actively construct and confirm meaning" (Swan et al. 4) and to communicate purposefully in an atmosphere of trust. Our students recognize this; professor of psychology Christy Price asserts that millenials "seem to care more about who we are and how we interact with them, than they care about what we know . . . [and they] highly value positive interactions with their professors" (4). As Dewey and many others have recognized, social networks and nurturing learning communities are necessary to student success.

The idea of writing center labor as a reciprocal, relational resource—as "giving," caring work—applies especially to contingent faculty who bring additional expertise to the table. Occasionally, in my observation, contingent faculty will err on the side of drawing too few boundaries, going a few too many extra miles and offering more of their time and energy than has been or can reasonably be asked of them. While it is crucial for directors to be aware of this tendency, and to protect individual adjunct faculty from over-volunteering their time and effort, as a group writing center workers are a rich, abundant source of human and social capital. It is also important to note that writing instructors have chosen a giving and relational profession, even though it often pays little and offers little prestige. Composition adjuncts and writing center faculty consultants form, in fact, a caring and infinitely renewable resource that will arguably remain abundant—and important—as long as there are universities, students, faculty, staff, and writing centers.

~~~

According to the Writing Center Research Project (WCRP) at the University of Arkansas Little Rock, the number of contingent faculty (as well as that of other demographics) working in writing centers has been steadily increasing over the last decade. For example, the WCRP reports the total percentage of undergraduate tutors at a variety of institutions who responded to the survey, including two-year and four-year, public and private universities, as follows: 72.5 percent in AY 2001–2002, 81 percent in AY 2003–2004, 77 percent in AY 2005–2006, and 79 percent in AY 2007–2008. These numbers show an increase of just under 10 percent overall for the seven year period for peer tutors in writing centers. Over the same period, however, the percentage of graduate student tutors increased nearly 35 percent, from 15 percent in AY 2001–2002 to 49 percent in AY 2007–2008; the percentage of faculty tutors saw more than a 20 percent increase, from 7.5 to 30 percent over the same period; and the percentage of professional staff serving as consultants increased by more than 25 percentage points, from 4 to 30 percent, during that time (see Fig. 1) (McKinney, "Re: Thanks").

Table 7.1 Changes in demographics of writing center consultants

	2001–2002	2007–2008	% Increase
Undergraduate tutors	75.2%	79%	approx. 10%
Graduate student tutors	15%	49%	approx. 35%
Faculty tutors	7.5%	30%	over 20%
Professional staff consultants	4%	30%	over 25%

Clearly, the work of writing centers is being distributed differently over the spectrum of academic workers than the literature has reflected up to now. In part, these shifts in the distribution of labor may perhaps be due to an attempt, as I believe was true of my third institution, to "professionalize" writing centers and to ensure a certain assumed level of consistent, quality support. On the other hand, however, the increasing use of adjunct faculty, with all the attendant conditions and pressures, is at the same time serving to increasingly "casualize" the work of the writing center, as faculty who work there are barred from accessing the same opportunities for professionalization and advancement as faculty in other disciplines—or, conversely, as they are relegated to the same diminished professional space as adjuncts in composition and other fields.

If composition is the step-child of the disciplines, and writing centers are perhaps the step-child of composition, the adjuncts who work in writing centers are the step-children locked away in the closet under the stairs. Questions remain, for me, about institutional goals and priorities as well as the underlying reasons for enforcing strict hierarchies of position, privilege, and place—especially, it would seem, when it does not best serve the greater good, or the students, of the institution. Writing centers are, however, and possibly have been from the beginning, at the forefront of alternative—and yes, iconoclastic—practices, modeling non-hierarchical, egalitarian approaches to serving, supporting, building relationships with, and learning alongside and along with, each other. Writing centers have always worked to increase the human and social capital upon which we all ultimately depend. Such giving work is of great value, whether or not it is currently institutionally *valued*. The writing center, in other words, may be exactly where many adjuncts who crave affirming and effective relationships want to be, even as this space, too, is perhaps increasingly characterized by practices and policies that ensure their marginalization. To paraphrase McKinney's description of the stereotypical peer tutor, adjunct faculty "work at the college but are not part of the college" (35).

The giving work that writing centers exemplify also draws upon the sustainable and renewable resource of human relationships. This labor maps a different way to *make things work* than older models based on hierarchy, scarcity, competition, vast inequalities, and the zero-sum games—destructive ill-distribution of resources, the dominance of individual egos to the detriment of entire communities—that increasingly plague our human economies. In the end, students need to learn to write—and write well. Workers need to earn respect and respect each other. As a species, we need to find sustainable ways of nurturing each other and the planet. Our students have plenty to say, but they need to learn how to say it in ways that allow them to be heard. That is where we—compositionists, adjuncts, writing center workers—come in.

As do feminist ethics of care, this way of seeing "offers suggestions for the radical transformation of society" (Held 12) based on definitions of caring as "ethically important . . . express[ing] ethically significant ways in which we matter to each other, transforming interpersonal relatedness into something beyond ontological necessity or brute survival" (Bowden qtd. in Held 33). This of course may also suggest radically different, expanded models for honoring adjunct labor. In "Iceberg Economies and Shadow Selves: Further Adventures in the Territories of Hope," author Rebecca Solnit describes the effects of a "brutal" economic system that "ensures that hungry and homeless people will be plentiful amid plenty" (n.p.). She also posits, however, a "shadow system" (n.p.) that already exists, outside of the dominant narrative. The shadow system provides food, support, shelter, "and a thousand other forms of practical solidarity, as well as emotional support" (n.p.) for those who have been unable to claw their way to the top—or even to a comfortable middle—in the existing hierarchies of recognition, support, and security, but who labor on all the same. The shadow system Solnit envisions could well describe the world created and inhabited by largely invisible adjunct labor:

> Think of the acts of those . . .who do more, and do it more
> passionately, than they are paid to do; think of the armies of
> the unpaid who are at "work" counterbalancing and cleaning
> up after the invisible hand and making every effort to loosen its
> grip on our collective throat . . . Capitalism is only kept going
> by this army of anti-capitalists, who constantly exert their pow-
> ers to clean up after it, and at least partially compensate for its
> destructiveness. Behind the system we all know, in other words,
> is a shadow system of kindness, the other invisible hand. (n.p.)

Adjunct labor, then, may now be not only the other "invisible hand" of the university but increasingly the invisible dancing bear of the writing center as well. According to Solnit, the work of that invisible hand, in conjunction with the work of the rest of us—the giving hands, the open hands, writing large on the walls of writing centers, composition programs, and across the university—does not yet "know itself or its own power" (n.p.) But it should, says Solnit. "We all should" (n.p.). That narrative reconfigures, re-narrates, and re-envisions service, adjunct labor, not as lesser or inferior, but as one of the driving forces behind a working, caring world.

Surely that, too, is one story we can tell.

WORKS CITED

Call, Philip. "Exploring the Writing Center's Convergence with Social Capital." Converging at the Vanishing Point, East Central Writing Center Association, Conference, Lansing, MI, Apr. 2010.

"Consultant Levels." *The Writing Centers Research Project.* University of Louisville, 2004. 5 Oct. 2013. coldfusion.louisville.edu/webs/as/wcrp/reports/report_consul tant_level_type.cfm.

Davis, Kevin. "Life Outside the Boundary: History and Direction in the Writing Center." *Writing Lab Newsletter,* vol. 20, no. 2, 1995, pp. 5–7, wlnjournal.org/archives /v20/20-2.pdf.

Held, Virginia. *The Ethics of Care: Personal, Political, and Global.* Oxford UP, 2006.

Ianetta, Melissa, et al. "Polylog: Are Writing Center Directors Writing Program Administrators?" *Composition Studies,* vol. 34, no. 2, 2006, pp. 11–42.

McKinney, Jackie Grutsch. *Peripheral Visions.* Utah State UP, 2013.

———. "Re: Thanks." Received by Dani Nier-Weber, 9 Apr. 2013.

Price, Christy. "Why Don't My Students Think I'm Groovy?: The New R's for Engaging Millennial Learners." *Millennial Traits and Teaching,* Ed. Thomas A. Lifvendahl, 2009, 5 Oct. 2013, www.drtomlifvendahl.com/Millennial%20Characturistics.pdf.

Schwartz, Ariel. "Millennials Genuinely Think They Can Change The World and Their Communities." *fastcoexist.com. Fast Company,* 27 Jun 2013, www.fastcoexist.com /1682348/millennials-genuinely-think-they-can-change-the- world-and-their -communities.

Solnit, Rebecca. "Iceberg Economies and Shadow Selves: Further Adventures in the Territories of Hope." *Tomdispatch.com.* Tomdispatch.com, 22, Dec. 2010, www. tomdispatch.com/post/175335/tomgram%3A_rebecca_solnit,_a_shadow _government_of_kindness.

Swan, Karen, et al. "A Constructivist Approach to Online Learning: The Community of Inquiry Framework." *Information Technology and Constructivism in Higher Education: Progressive Learning Frameworks,* edited by Carla R. Payne, IGI Global, 2009, pp. 43–57.

Transport for London. "Test Your Awareness: Do the Test." 10 Mar. 2008, www .youtube.com/watch?v=Ahg6qcgoay4.

Zorn, Jeffrey. "English Compositionism as Fraud and Failure" *Academic Questions,* vol. 26, no. 3, nas.org/articles/english_compositionism_as_fraud_and_failure.

CHAPTER 8

THE RISKS OF CONTINGENT WRITING CENTER DIRECTORSHIPS

Dawn Fels

University of Pittsburgh

Threads: Local Changes to Workload, Pay, and Working Conditions; Protecting Gains, Telling Cautionary Tales

INTRODUCTION

Writing centers' role in contingent labor concerns dates back to 1909. Lerner's research traces the first mention of "rhetorical laboratory" to 1894, when the benefits of laboratory methods of teaching were first recognized in early composition classrooms. Those methods, characterized by the one-to-one writing conference, grew in popularity as student populations grew in number and diversity. And with that growth came a labor crisis. In 1909, according to Lerner, the Modern Language Association (MLA) and National Council of Teachers of English (NCTE) commissioned Hopkins to "detail and quantify the burden under which high school and college English teachers suffered" (26). Apparently, they suffered a lot. Lerner shares Hopkins' findings:

> The result was that "instructors wear out, suffer from indigestion and nervous exhaustion, lose their efficiency, impair their eyesight, become the prey of shattered nerves, break down and find their way to the hospital or cemetery because of 'killing' work in English Composition." (27)

Hopkins reported similar results a decade later. The English professoriate certainly wasn't going to be very effective if its membership was greatly reduced by exhaustion or worse.

Enter contingent faculty to save (literally) the professoriate from having to teach a) too many students, and b) too many unprepared students. These contingent faculty taught basic and remedial composition courses or ran writing clinics. They became tools to relieve the "real" classroom teachers of their underprepared students—those students whose first language was not English, whose family income placed them lower—much lower—on the socio-economic ladder than students who belonged in college and were worthy of professors' attention. The contingent faculty and clinic approach were to cure students who arrived ill-prepared for college, to get those students out of the classroom and out of the way, or, as Lerner describes, "out of sight and out of mind" (32). The writing center field has fought against this remedial reputation ever since, not only because of the subtractive light it casts upon diverse students' abilities but also because it devalues the work of writing center workers and the role they play in students' academic success.

Though some writing center directors who've been around long enough will argue that the writing center field's fight for institutional credibility has improved throughout its history, there is new evidence to cause concern. Today, 71 percent of writing center directors hold non-tenure-track positions (Isaacs and Knight 48). When other things are equal, these directors enjoy relative job security, collegiality, adequate resources, administrative support, and autonomy. In the midst of a depressed economy and cuts to federal and state funding for higher education, though, anything can happen. I wanted to write this chapter to alert readers to the risks of contingency. I especially hope to reach those who have yet to identify with the contingent crowd and those who claim to be labor activists but "abuse the contingency of their contingent faculty to solve other problems" (Kahn). My aim is to offer a set of realities to those who say that things aren't so bad. Well, things are never that bad until they are.

This chapter offers readers a glimpse into the interconnected risks of contingent writing center directorships: the programmatic, the professional, and the personal. Writing center directors' contingency affects the programs they develop and administer, the decisions they can make, the institutional support they receive, their membership in local and national communities of practice, and the academic freedom and autonomy they need to direct their program as they professionally see fit. Contingency affects writing center directors' access to professional development opportunities: sabbaticals, conference travel and attendance, research and scholarship, leadership positions both on- and off-campus. Contingency also threatens directors' financial security and, consequently, theirs and their family's health and well-being. My hope is that, once aware of these risks, readers will work with others to create more sustainable, equitable writing center positions and programs.

WHAT IS A CONTINGENT WRITING CENTER DIRECTOR?

When I proposed this chapter, I planned to describe the risks of contingent, non-tenure-track (NTT) writing center directorships by sharing contingent directors' stories about the programmatic, professional, and personal risks associated with the precarity of their positions. I surveyed new and veteran writing center directors—tenured, tenure-line, and non-tenure line. I asked for the good, the bad, and the ugly about their positions. Then one by one, the NTT directors I hoped to spotlight either left or lost their jobs. This did not surprise me. Attrition and dismissals are by-products of contingency. Most of those who moved on did so because they found better pay, working conditions, and longer contracts. At least one, whose two-year contract was up, found herself having to reapply for her job, despite having built a thriving writing center program. Those who lost their jobs were fired for reasons that had nothing to do with their performance. Some were given notice and the chance to say goodbye to their tutors. Others were escorted off campus before they could even clean out their desks. These directors all had pristine performance evaluations. Some even had new contracts. None had union protection.

Then as the 2014 academic year got underway, posts to WCENTER, the main listserv for writing center directors, revealed a startling trend. Tenured and tenure-line (TT) writing center directors described events that led to the loss of their centers. One described feeling forced to resign as director of a thriving, model center that she created two decades ago. That announcement elicited responses from other directors, NTT and TT alike, who shared similar "traumatic," "devastating," and "shocking" experiences. Among those who lost their centers were icons in the writing center and composition fields. As the discussion ensued, questions arose about the value of longevity and continuity in program development, contracts, academic freedom, performance evaluation, advancement. Also raised were questions about the effects on teaching and learning and students' and tutors' rights to success. As was the case for the TT and NTT directors who lost their positions, once they resigned, someone higher up the food chain with absolutely no knowledge of the theoretical, pedagogical, and administrative trends germane to writing centers appointed an ill-qualified person to take over, leading to additional questions about the value of qualified writing center directors.

But then a different kind of question emerged. Questions like: What did I do to let this happen? What should I have done differently? How did I not notice what was happening? What should I have done earlier to prevent this? With whom should I have connected who might have become an ally? Why did I trust the decision-makers? How can I now come to a better understanding of what motivated the decision-makers to do what they did? Troubling and telling questions, those. Troubling because they place the director in the position of blaming themselves for what happened to them.

One of the greatest risks of contingency is the failure of writing center directors and their colleagues to see how vulnerable they are. The American Association of University Professors (AAUP) describes contingent faculty as those who work off the tenure-line in full or part-time positions and, as such, "serve in insecure, unsupported positions with little job security and few protections for academic freedom" (AAUP para. 1). It is worth repeating that 71 percent of writing center directors hold contingent positions (Isaacs and Knight 48). That means that over two-thirds of current directors, like other contingent faculty, are at far greater risk for losing their jobs or a portion of their jobs than tenure line directors. While that statistic should alarm us, Isaacs and Knight's research points to others that should, as well. Rather than rely on self-reported information from writing center directors, Isaacs and Knight chose their study participants. They then used writing centers' websites and other documents to evaluate how "writing centers represent themselves to their stakeholders" (43). They compared writing center director positions to those held by other writing program administrators (WPA). Their findings are relevant to my discussion for two reasons. First, writing centers are writing programs, and on some campuses, directors direct not only the writing center but other writing programs, such as WAC and FYC, programs often headed by a TT faculty member. Second, in their sample of 101 schools, Isaacs and Knight found that 92 offered first-year writing programs, 79 percent of which were run by a WPA. Interestingly, of those WPAs, only 47 percent held tenure-track positions. Only 47 percent.

Isaacs and Knight also looked for trends related to the gender of the writing center director and makeup of the writing center staff. Of the writing center directors whose gender Isaacs and Knight could identify from center websites, 73 percent were female, a finding they point to as "remarkably similar to Healy's 1995 finding that 74 percent of the writing center leaders were female" (49). With regard to writing centers' tutoring staff, Isaacs and Knight found that 81 percent of centers were staffed by undergraduate and graduate students. "Thus," they wrote, "we saw students as major forces in writing center work at the four-year university, a trend readers might applaud as a sign of a capable student body or deplore as a sign of the low professional status of writing tutors" (49). Isaacs and Knight's study begins to describe the perfect conditions for the exploitation of NTT writing center directors: a field that has historically relied on self-reported information that falls short of describing reality; a field in which other writing program directors' tenure status falls short of a majority; a field dominated by women; a field staffed by students.

CONTINGENCY AND EFFICIENCY

Recessionary rebounds and administrators' calls to do more with less have led to trends that affect the job security of writing center directors. One is the move to turn once tenurable writing center director positions into contingent positions. At one institution, the director's position was split into two contingent positions upon the director's retirement; one portion of the job went to a part-time adjunct. In two other cases, tenured writing center directors lost their centers when oversight for them was moved to administrators with no composition or writing center experience. In yet another case, a contingent director was fired and replaced by someone else within the department who had no experience, publications, or research in the writing center field but who had already been on the university's payroll. In the past, these moves might have been blamed on administrators' misunderstanding of what writing center directors do and why it's necessary to have someone at the helm with expertise in composition pedagogy and writing center praxis: a "real" writing center director. But misunderstanding was not the reason for these changes. Nor, frankly, was the contingent status of the director, made evident by the tenured directors' experiences. In all of these cases, economic efficiency was the motivating factor—the need to save on salaries. When economic efficiencies must be gained, it is easier to cut a contingent director and either not replace them or replace them with another employee who is already on the payroll. Tenured directors are harder to fire. In fact, in the cases where tenured directors lost their centers, they still retained a portion of their jobs, but direction of their centers fell to less expensive, less experienced contingent labor.

THE BENEFITS OF TT STATUS AND THE HARMS OF CONTINGENCY

The topic of whether a writing center director's position should be TT or NTT comes up every so often on WCENTER. The overwhelming number of respondents to a recent query noted the benefits to directors who hold a TT position. James Mischler referred to the issue of program "permanence," noting how "a director with a full-time faculty budget line seems to provide more stability to the writing center program than an admin. [sic] staff member line that can be eliminated at the first sign of budget trouble" ("tenure track"). In the same discussion, Neal Lerner described how his tenured status afforded him opportunities to advance and serve in ways that NTT directors don't always get to: ". . . on graduate studies committee, undergraduate studies committee, tenure-review committee within the department . . ., and Faculty Senate, all positions that ask for a fairly broad institutional view. . . ." Nick Carbone, a former writing center director, acknowledged how directors "fulfill the three obligations expected of most faculty: research, teaching, and service." He went on to note that writing center directors strengthen the college's commitment to its students and faculty, helping to improve retention and student success, in palpable and measurable ways. [They] sit on key university committees—QEP, assessment, placement—where their expertise in writing and teaching of writing, student outreach and tutoring, tutor and faculty professional development, make them essential to their institutions' missions. . . . Because they are central to an institution's life and mission, [writing center directors] foster the intellectual development of students and colleagues, and deserve the recognition, support, responsibilities, and privileges that come with being tenure-track faculty members. ("tenure track")

While there are those who argue that contingency isn't as bad as some people make it out to be, Mischler, Lerner, and Carbone all point to reasons why writing center director positions should be tenurable. Mischler raises an important point about what contingency says about program permanence. And while some institutions may invite or expect NTT directors to engage in the work that Lerner and Carbone describe, not all reward or compensate them for it. In fact, contracts and performance evaluations may actually state that engaging in these activities will not affect future decisions about employment, compensation, or promotion.

PROFESSIONAL IDENTITY AND CONTINGENCY

Why do NTT directors work as hard as they do, then, if contingency poses so many risks? Professional identity motivates many to engage in activities they know will not result in added job security, salary, or recognition. Working hard is simply what writing center directors do. It's part of their ethos and service to students. It's part of who they are and want to become as professionals in the composition and writing center fields. In her article "Professional Identity in a Contingent-Labor Profession: Expertise, Autonomy, Community in Composition Teaching," Penrose describes three dimensions of professionalism:

Researchers in sociology, education, history, rhetoric, sociolinguistics, and other fields have posited a number of interacting factors constituting membership in a profession. Synthesizing across a range of studies . . . three primary dimensions emerge: . . . 1) a specialized and dynamic knowledge base or body of expertise, 2) a distinctive array of rights and privileges accorded to members, and 3) an internal social structure based on shared goals and values. (112)

Penrose notes that ongoing professional development is one mark of a "true professional." She further acknowledges how a "community's distinctive language or terminology represents a lens through which members 'view reality in a professionally relevant way,'" which then "influences what members do or do not notice or attend to in the world around them" (113). Contingent writing center directors work as hard as they do because they believe they are a part of the We of the field, their institution, and their department. And they often are. Those connections empower them to do work they know matters. They know it matters because they're told it does—directly by colleagues in the field, by their supervisors, or by others in their department. They know it matters because students tell them it does, and because students say it does when they complete exit surveys. Feedback can empower. It can lead contingent directors to work even harder, especially when the feedback is good. But it can also blind them to the threats of contingency.

Losing a job deals a devastating blow to one's professional identity. Penrose describes what happens "when there is a mismatch between faculty members' own sense of expertise and what the profession seems to value":

> At the extremes, faculty members may question their identity as professionals and wonder if they belong, or they may question the legitimacy or coherence of the profession and choose not to belong. . . . [T]hose who have confidence in their own professional knowledge and also respect the program they're working in . . . may find that the two are not in sync and therefore see themselves as teaching outside their profession. Under any of these scenarios the faculty member is distanced from the professional community and unlikely to see him- or herself as contributing to it, making it difficult to sustain an image of oneself as expert. (114)

Penrose's arguments describe the sentiments of the writing center directors I know who lost their jobs for reasons that had nothing to do with their job performance. With few exceptions, those directors continue long after their dismissal to stay connected to their professional communities. They attend and present at conferences. They serve professional organizations. They mentor junior faculty and future writing center directors. They continue with their research and publications. But not having a writing center to lead makes a tremendous difference. Doing all that work doesn't feel as significant as it once did because, without a center to lead, there are no students to serve. And students are always at the center of the work that writing center directors do.

Penrose's discussion of professionalism is especially helpful in understanding the risks of contingent writing center directorships. The two-tiered system of academia creates the internal structure of a department or institution that prevents NTT directors' access to the same rights and privileges enjoyed by their TT colleagues. That system influences the internal structure of a department or institution that then prevents development of shared goals and values. This creates an inequitable environment where, under the most dire circumstances (say, budget cuts), someone or something has to lose. Penrose argues that "as academic professions seek to protect their autonomy in the face of shrinking university budgets, increasing public oversight, corporate sponsorship and other influences, the mechanisms of professionalization *within* the field of composition may be interpreted as an attempt by some members to restrict the autonomy of other members" (116).

These restrictions carry over into the rules of interaction that govern groups of colleagues and lay the foundation for a two-tiered system within a department or writing program, a system that affects contingent writing center directors. In fact, on some campuses, the writing center program is not considered a writing program in the way that FYC, WAC/WID, or ESL programs are. And within the composition and writing center fields, little attention has been paid until recently to the risks of contingent directorships, though plenty of work has been done on some campuses to make director's positions more secure (see Brady and Singh-Corcoran). What we do have are anecdotes offered by contingent writing center directors, often after they lose their jobs. Those anecdotes relate to inequities in shared governance, professionalism, collegiality, and continuity. They relate to inequities made apparent by who works year-round; who can teach what; who gets paid for teaching additional courses; whose conference travel is funded; and who has support to propose new programs. They extend to whose books are included in the department display; who gets invited to events, even the informal happy hour or holiday party; whose research matters; whose presence matters at department meetings, candidate receptions, and campus events. They even include who gets introduced to the dean or the provost or the president—at the interview stage, after being hired, or ever. As Penrose concludes, "How one views oneself is powerfully influenced by local circumstance, including the physical setting and institutional context and the structural relations these symbolize" (119). If we want to change the risks that contingent writing center directors face, we need to change the structural and systemic conditions that create the inequitable and exploitative conditions under which many say they work.

PERSONAL RISKS OF CONTINGENCY

Losing a job is traumatic. In a depressed job market, especially when relocation isn't an option, a dismissal could mark the end of a writing center director's career. Losing a job places directors and their dependents in danger of losing their homes, their health insurance, their cash savings, their retirement. Losing a job causes further risks. Belle and Bullock co-authored a policy statement on "The Psychological Consequences of Unemployment" for The Society for the Psychological Study of Social Issues (SPSSI), a division of the American Psychological Association (APA). In the statement, they cite several studies that point to the psychological effects of unemployment.

> Job loss is associated with elevated rates of mental and physical health problems, increases in mortality rates, and detrimental changes in family relationships and in the psychological well-being of spouses and children. Compared to stably employed workers, those who have lost their jobs have significantly poorer mental health, lower life satisfaction, less marital or family satisfaction, and poorer subjective physical health (McKee-Ryan, Song, Wanberg & Kinicki, 2005). A meta-analysis by Paul and Moser (2009) reinforces these findings—unemployment was associated with depression, anxiety, psychosomatic symptoms, low subjective well-being, and poor self-esteem. (para. 5)

The authors go on to note that these effects are especially hard on unemployed single mothers, African-Americans, Latinos/Latinas, and those with fewer family resources.

Losing a job also means days of completing applications for resources that barely keep an individual and their dependent family members' heads above the rising waters of poverty. The process of applying for those resources is time-consuming, long, frustrating, and adds to the trauma of job loss. And then, despite qualifying for aid, one might find that there isn't any available. In 2014, state and federal lawmakers made drastic cuts to programs on which the unemployed rely. One was the federal government's Emergency Unemployment Compensation (EUC). According to the U.S. Department of Labor's website, EUC, federally-funded extension of benefits to those whose state benefits expired, ended on January 1, 2014. Though news outlets reported the Senate's vote to extend those emergency benefits, the Labor Department's website currently indicates that extensions are still unavailable. Medicaid was also affected by federal and state lawmakers' decisions. In 2013, the Obama administration recommended that Medicaid "be opened up to anyone who earns up to 133 percent of the federal poverty level, which [was] $15,282 for a single person" (Young para. 3). However, states could decide whether to adopt this expansion, and not all have. Drastic cuts also greatly reduced the Supplemental Nutrition Assistance Program (SNAP), a/k/a food stamps. Dean and Rosenbaum of the Center on Budget and Policy Priorities described how a projected $5 billion cut to the program in 2014 would affect over 47 million individuals and their families, including 22 million children, who already received SNAP benefits (4).

Those of us in academia don't think about how these cuts might affect us until they do. Right now, 71 percent of our colleagues walk a fine line between having a job and experiencing the hardships that come with unemployment. Once someone higher up the food chain decides to eliminate or drastically change a director's position, very little can be done to save it, and nothing we say matters will. Stellar evaluations will not matter. Award-winning publications or research will not matter. Letters of support from students or leaders from the composition and writing center fields will not matter. Distinguished achievements on or off-campus will not matter. Service will not matter. Improvements made to writing center services will not matter. Contributions to student achievement and retention will not matter. Contracts will not matter. Nothing will matter but what administration decides. That, too, is the nature of precarity.

CONCLUSION

We should all be alarmed by the contingency of an entire field, but we don't seem to be. Instead, we hum along until a writing center director posts to WPA or WCENTER or Facebook the devastating news that they've lost their job or been forced to resign, or their position has been eliminated, or their contract expired, or their center moved under the supervision of someone less qualified, if at all, to run it. We rarely see posts by those who have simply been fired without warning, escorted off campus, only to come back weeks later, under the cover of darkness and when no one else is around, to retrieve their personal belongings from their offices. But they exist, too. And we never hear from tutors who are, perhaps, the lowest paid and most exploited worker in the composition and writing center fields today.

Despite all of the information available about writing centers' importance to student success, directors remain vulnerable to conditions that have nothing to do with their job performance. And that affects writing center labor. When administrators see writing center directors as little more than administrative assistants, recessionary pressures place directors and their tutors at further risk. At risk for losing their jobs in an already depressed job market. At risk for working well beyond contractual expectations. At risk for relying on a contract that, ultimately, will not protect them. At risk for wage theft. At risk for exploitation. At risk for having their professional expertise and academic freedoms devalued. At risk for disenfranchisement. At risk for personal hardship.

Having been an IWCA member since 2001, and having served on its Executive Board and various committees for a number of years, I am familiar with the expertise, energy, and commitment that writing center directors display in a variety of fields charged with the task of educating students, fields that include rhetoric and composition, linguistics, TESOL, K-12 education, educational policy, and assessment. Look to any of those related fields, and you'll find someone who either got their start or made their career in a writing center. Look at the list of books, articles, and chapters published by writing center directors, and you'll see work—award-winning work—on a range of topics. These books don't just sit on the shelves of writing centers for directors and tutors to peruse during downtime. They are used in tutor training, and more and more often, they're being used outside centers in undergraduate and graduate classes taught by writing center directors or other faculty. They're used by students outside of writing centers for their own research projects. Or they're adopted by schools and community groups who want to create community-based literacy programs. In particular, what we know about student writers, writing pedagogy, and writing assessment would be greatly reduced without the research that comes out of the writing center field.

Perspective changes with hardship—or by becoming aware of others' hardships. Right now, too many fail to see the risks associated with contingent writing center directorships—even their own. This is especially true of those who work in programs that have yet to examine the risks and build structural protections for contingent writing center directors. In 2013, Brady and Singh-Corcoran described their work at West Virginia University to create a non-tenure line writing center director position that was "stable, central, well-integrated, and secure" (73). More institutions should follow their lead. Our professional organizations can also do more to enact the protection each calls for in their statements on the working conditions of contingent faculty, or to create a statement if one doesn't exist. Currently, research is underway in the writing center field to raise awareness of the risks of contingency to both directors and tutors, another contingent workforce, whom Isaacs and Knight identified as staffing 81 percent of the centers they studied (49). Those with any influence at all over the hiring of writing center directors should use the model Brady and Singh-Corcoran describe to develop contracts. Those applying for contingent writing center directorships should carefully review their contracts before accepting any offer. Among the details to look for are explicit expectations for attendance, performance, evaluation, promotion, course releases, service, research, publication, and professional development. Report lines also need to be clear, as well as what will happen to the writing center director's position if new administrators are hired. Those who apply for contingent directorships should also reach out to mentors in the writing center field to get a sense of how the contractual expectations match the work they'll do and to get advice on negotiable points.

Unlike other writing programs, writing centers serve all students. They serve faculty and staff, too. Many writing center directors and their tutors also serve area K-12 students and teachers. Writing center directors conduct award-winning and otherwise significant research that benefits literacy educators and their students around the world. They advise and otherwise support undergraduate and graduate students' research. Their relationships with other professors' students keep those students in college and move them toward degree completion. Writing center directors serve in leadership positions in regional and national organizations, including but not limited to NCTE, CCCC, TYCA, IWCA, and the CWPA. And if those acts of engagement are not enough, we have research, scholarship, and national surveys that show the benefit of writing center visits to every student population one can imagine. The composition and writing center fields have a responsibility to the 71 percent. When we lose valued directors, we all lose.

WORKS CITED

American Association of University Professors (AAUP). "Contingent Faculty Positions." *AAUP*, 2014, aaup.org/issues/contingency.

Belle, Deborah, and Heather E. Bullock. "The Psychological Consequences of Unemployment." *SPSSI*, 2010, spssi.org/index.cfm?fuseaction=page.viewpage&pageid=1457.

Brady, Laura, and Nathalie Singh-Corcoran. "Non-Tenure-Track Faculty as Administrators: Planning and Evaluation." *ADE Bulletin*, vol. 152, 2013, pp. 71–81.

Carbone, Nick. "[Wcenter] Tenure Track Writing Center Directors." Received by Dawn Fels. 6 Oct. 2014.

Dean, Stacey, and Dottie Rosenbaum. "SNAP Benefits Will Be Cut For Nearly All Participants in November 2013." *Center on Budget and Policy Priorities*, 9 Jan. 2014, cbpp.org/research/snap-benefits-will-be-cut-for-nearly-all-participants-in-november-2013.

Isaacs, Emily, and Melinda Knight. "A Bird's Eye View of Writing Centers: Institutional Infrastructure, Scope and Programmatic Issues, Reported Practices." *WPA*, vol. 37, no. 2, pp. 36–67, wpacouncil.org/archives/37n2/37n2isaacs-knight.pdf.

Kahn, Seth. "The Situation at ASU." Received by Dawn Fels. 18 Dec. 2014.

Lerner, Neal. "[Wcenter] Tenure Track Writing Center Directors." Received by Dawn Fels. 6 Oct. 2014.

———. *The Idea of a Writing Laboratory*. Southern Illinois UP, 2009.

Mischler, James. "[Wcenter] Tenure Track Writing Center Directors." Received by Dawn Fels. 6 Oct. 2014.

Penrose, Ann. "Professional Identity in a Contingent-Labor Profession: Expertise, Autonomy, Community in Composition Teaching." *WPA: Writing Program Administration,* vol. 35, no. 2, 2012, pp. 108–126, wpacouncil.org/archives/35n2/35n2penrose.pdf.

U.S. Department of Labor. "Emergency Unemployment Compensation (EUC) Expired on January 1, 2014." 13 Jan. 2014, workforcesecurity.doleta.gov/unemploy/supp_act.asp.

Young, Jeffrey. "Blame States For Not Expanding Medicaid, Obama Administration Will Tell Poor Residents." *Huffington Post.* 15 July 2013, huffingtonpost.com/2013/07/15/states-expanding-medicaid_n_3599232.html.

CHAPTER 9

THE UNCERTAIN FUTURE OF PAST SUCCESS: MEMORY, NARRATIVE, AND THE DYNAMICS OF INSTITUTIONAL CHANGE

Rolf Norgaard

University of Colorado at Boulder

Threads: Organizing Within and Across Ranks; Local Changes to Workload, Pay, and Material Conditions; Protecting Gains, Telling Cautionary Tales

Even a cursory look at my institution—the University of Colorado at Boulder—might suggest that the conditions of full-time instructors have been reasonably good. We have had for some twenty years renewable multiyear appointments, full benefits, and a reasonable course load to ensure effective teaching. Our free-standing Program for Writing and Rhetoric, among other units, has benefited from this environment. To be sure, the modest salaries of instructors, most with Ph.D.s, make it a tough go in expensive Boulder, Colorado. Nevertheless, given working conditions on the larger national landscape, our campus has fared better than many.

Until now. This chapter examines a moment of institutional change when many of these gains are perceived to be at risk. A recently arrived dean in his first year leading the College of Arts and Sciences proposed a controversial new workload and pay schedule for full-time instructors. And therein lies a tale that ties together four threads—a tale about faculty governance and administrative power, about the fragile quality of institutional memory, about narratives and counter-narratives of change, all set against the backdrop of changes in key personnel. This is a tale about the uncertain future of past success.

Prior discussions of contingent labor in the academy have focused, quite understandably, on calls for improved conditions to address the worst of practices. Central to this effort are broad and now classic studies of the changing academic workforce in the context of the neoliberal university (Bousquet; Bousquet et al.; Schell). Likewise, efforts to characterize the non-tenure-track workforce have led to a number of important reports by key professional organizations (MLA, ADE, AERA, and AAUP) and special issues of disciplinary journals. And more recently, studies have turned to professional identities and fine-grained examinations of non-tenure-track faculty work (Bartholomae, Levin and Shaker, Penrose, and Lamos).

My contribution to the discussion addresses a somewhat different and often neglected issue: what happens when gains are made, and then risk being undone? Insights on this dilemma are no less important, and may reveal dynamics of institutional change bearing on institutional memory and competing narratives that may not become evident in situations where the focus lies on making important initial improvements to labor conditions.

FACULTY GOVERNANCE AND THE INSTRUCTORS' BILL OF RIGHTS

Our campus owes its generally favorable environment for full-time instructors to an administrative and faculty-governance partnership that goes back over twenty years. In 1993, an activist group of both tenured professors and non-tenure-track faculty brought a "Motion of Intent," informally known as the "Instructors' Bill of Rights," before the Boulder Faculty Assembly, our campus-wide faculty governance group. The motion addressed the inability of part-time lecturers, hired by the semester yet working on campus for many years, to enter the ranks of full-time instructors. Working in conjunction with the then dean of Arts and Sciences (the largest campus college and home to most contingent faculty), the Boulder Faculty Assembly approved this motion by a wide margin. In 1999, the "Instructors' Bill of Rights," or "IBOR," as it is known on campus, received official approval by campus administration.[1]

Although the working conditions for part-time lecturers generally surpassed those at neighboring institutions, the Boulder Faculty Assembly nevertheless recognized that a professionalized teaching faculty at a research institution was in everyone's interest. Discussion about the Instructors' Bill of Rights provided a forum for considering the changing labor landscape in higher education, and the emergence of full-time but non-tenure-track faculty as a key element in the delivery of our institution's undergraduate education. Four decades ago or so,

---

1   Although still part of our institution's historical memory, the formal document of the Instructors' Bill of Rights as approved by the Boulder Faculty Assembly in 1993 has disappeared some years ago from our institution's website. What remains is a 1999 document, approved by campus central administration and vetted by the campus legal office, which reflects many of the provisions of IBOR, but weakens the force of the original document: colorado.edu/bfa/sites /default/files/attached-files/Instructor%20Bill%20of%20Rights.pdf

the faculty workforce on our campus was predominantly tenured or tenure-track (generally teaching a 2/2 load), and undergraduate classroom teaching was an integral part of their duties. Indeed, many tenured or tenure-track faculty focused wholly or in large measure on classroom teaching. Instructor-rank faculty were far fewer in number, and the positions were seen in temporary terms, or as way stations to tenure-track appointments elsewhere. Times have changed, at CU-Boulder as they have nationally. "Part-time" lecturers were laboring semester after semester teaching the equivalent of a full-time (3/3 or 4/4) load but with minimal job security, and little prospect for advancement into more stable positions. And full-time instructors (generally teaching 3/3 load) themselves were often seen as temporary workers, despite what is often a career commitment to the institution. Not only has our campus become far more reliant on instructors and senior instructors, faculty in those positions now often make career-long contributions to the campus that have deep and ongoing relevance to its mission.

This faculty-governance discussion yielded in the early 1990s the Instructors' Bill of Rights, which provided for the following:

- Lecturers working for three years at 50 percent appointments or greater should be appointed as full-time instructors.
- Instructors should have multi-year, presumptively renewable appointments, ranging from two to four years, with three years being the default term.
- The typical workload for instructors was defined as three courses per semester (3/3 for the academic year), with a merit evaluation ratio of 75 percent teaching and 25 percent service. (Tenure-stream faculty generally teach a 2/2 load, with merit evaluations of 40 percent research, 40 percent teaching, and 20 percent service.)
- The floor for starting salaries for full-time instructors was set, at the time, at $30K (instructors are merit-pool eligible).
- After seven years in rank, instructors would be eligible for promotion to senior instructor.
- Senior instructors are eligible for a semester of reduced teaching load after every seven years of full-time teaching for purposes of pedagogical and curricular research.

The provisions were impressive at the time, and in some respects still provide a benchmark to which many peer institutions would aspire.

Although forward looking in themselves, the provisions did not come with the budgetary resources to fully enact them. For example, an individual's promotion from lecturer to instructor was by no means assured. An academic unit would need to approve of the shift, and increasingly over the years had to come up with funds on its own to offset the higher salary. Over the years, this key provision was rarely acted on. Likewise, the promotion from instructor to senior instructor was initially designed to offer a $2,000-$3,000 bump in base salary, but, again, over the years that financial commitment atrophied, and now there is no increased salary, despite increased duties and higher expectations for reappointment.

On the other hand, the prospect of multi-year, renewable appointments changed the landscape for instructors on our campus. Although technically defined as "letters of agreement" (as Colorado is an "at-will" state in terms of labor law, and until just recently was not allowed to offer multi-year contracts), these appointments were honored by our administration: to its credit, at no time has the administration broken a letter of agreement in the middle of an appointment term. The 3/3 load ensured close attention to instructional quality, and the considerable service commitment became, over time, essential to many of our campus's initiatives and the operation of many units, among them the Program for Writing and Rhetoric. Were it not for instructor service, residential academic programs in the residence halls and service-learning initiatives would not have been possible. Indeed, given that instructor appointments did not require (nor did they explicitly reward) research, service became the contractual space that permitted professional development, conference presentations, grant writing, and publishing. Thanks to this service component, instructors gained influence with administrators and began playing an active role in campus-wide faculty governance. Even the reduced teaching load every seven years was largely honored (the term "sabbatical" was eschewed). In a competitive process, some senior instructors were able to receive the opportunity to refresh their teaching and undertake curricular initiatives.

Despite the impressive public face of the Instructors' Bill of Rights, its provisions have been unevenly implemented and sometimes ignored over the last two decades. Although instructor positions themselves were improved, the integration of instructors into departmental cultures continues to be an unfinished project. Nevertheless, this Instructors' Bill of Rights has provided an ethical benchmark against which to measure the conditions of contingent faculty. Administrative power has been in some sense constrained by a shared willingness to observe—or at least give lip service to—this precedent-setting effort, accomplished through a partnership between faculty governance and campus administration.

A FRAGILE INSTITUTIONAL MEMORY

The Instructors' Bill of Rights was protected in good measure by a near constant effort to keep this document alive in our institution's cultural memory. Budget crises and occasional administrative indifference frequently set this memory at risk, but it was preserved by a cadre of activist instructors and tenured faculty who used institutions of faculty governance to promote conversation and action. Instructors themselves came to play increasingly prominent roles in the Boulder Faculty Assembly. They comprise roughly twenty percent of the assembly's membership (elected in open competition with tenure-stream faculty), and several instructors chair standing BFA committees. Instructors regularly win campus-wide BFA awards for both teaching and leadership/service.

Roughly a decade ago, the actual working conditions of contingent faculty had deteriorated through inattention to some provisions of the Instructors' Bill of Rights and a lack of willingness to address the integration of full-time instructors into the culture of the institution. In many units, instructors still had no voting rights and could not even attend department faculty meetings. Through several controversial non-reappointment decisions, issues of academic freedom for instructors became a topic of concern. Discussion among some instructors turned to possible unionization, the campus chapter of AAUP took up instructor issues, and efforts began to highlight the need for a parallel tenure track for teaching faculty. Although the campus administration had recognized the Boulder Faculty Assembly resolution to create the Instructors' Bill of Rights and its various provisions, and had responded to implement many of those provisions, the administration itself never fully enforced it as official campus policy. Over time, the Instructors' Bill of Rights even disappeared from the campus website, although it lived on deep in the archives of the Boulder Faculty Assembly. Institutional memory becomes fragile indeed when such a key document becomes, literally, invisible.

Even as concerns mounted among instructors, the place of the Instructors' Bill of Rights in institutional memory still provided not just solace but also opportunities for engaged action. At the behest of instructors and a number of concerned tenured faculty, the Boulder Faculty Assembly formed a Task Force in academic year 2007–08 to address a range of instructor issues. These issues included salary, grievance procedures, status within units, the need to maintain currency in the field, and the possibility of tenure for instructors through the creation of a tenured teaching track. The Task Force commissioned a survey of instructors and then, having to work quickly, issued a brief five-page report. The recommendations that came out of this Task Force largely endorsed the then fifteen-year-old Instructors' Bill of Rights and added recommendations to improve the working conditions of instructors. The Task Force proposed that the salary floor for instructors be raised from $30K to $40K, a welcome move that directly benefitted some instructors but also created salary compression issues among instructor ranks, generally reasserted the academic freedom of instructors, and pointed out the unequal treatment of instructors across units, with regard to participation in unit faculty governance and even such things as office space. The administration responded positively to some of the recommendations, among them raising the salary floor to $40K. And it agreed in principle with other recommendations, but not, notably, with the creation of parallel tenure track for teaching faculty. Although the Task Force brought renewed attention to the plight of instructors, and activated our institution's memory of and commitment to the Instructors' Bill of Rights, the tangible outcomes of the Task Force, apart from salary, were negligible. The integration of full-time instructors into the faculty culture of our institution remained a problem.

As a barometer of the ongoing issues facing instructors, and the limited success of the 2007–08 Task Force, the same Boulder Faculty Assembly felt the strong need to address the issue once again, and in September 2009 created a high-profile, campus-wide ad-hoc committee whose charge was to create a major report, with pragmatic recommendations that could address the status of instructors on campus. Asked to chair this committee, I was aware of a reservoir of good will toward instructors from some prominent tenured faculty and also from some in administration, but also quite cognizant of the pushback from some tenured faculty worried about the growing power and numbers of instructors and, more generally, the institutional inertia that was proving to be a very considerable impediment to change. In March 2010 our committee issued a major forty-page report, whose recommendations were approved by a wide margin in an April 2010 vote of the Boulder Faculty Assembly.[2]

Building on the Instructors' Bill of Rights and the work of the 2007–08 Task Force, our committee generated eighteen specific recommendations. Seven recommendations concerned the clarification and enforcement of current policy, ten additional recommendations addressed contractual issues in employment and career management, and a final recommendation urged the exploration of a parallel tenure track for teaching faculty (a system-level change which would involve the several campuses of our university and require the approval of the Regents). That eighteenth and final recommendation has never been acted on.

This major faculty governance initiative to improve the status of instructors has had a positive impact in many respects. Appointment and reappointment processes for instructors have been regularized, and unit by-laws are being reviewed to determine the extent of instructor participation in unit-level

---

2   The full report of the 2009–10 BFA committee can be found at: colorado.edu/bfa/sites /default/files/attached-files/bfainstr_finalreport_040210.pdf. The motion to approve the report's recommendations, which carried by a wide margin, can be found at: www.colorado.edu/bfa /sites/default/files/attached-files/bfa-x-m-022210_endorse_recommendations_of_the_ad-hoc _cmte_on_instructor_status.pdf.

faculty governance. The Boulder Faculty Assembly also realized that sporadic efforts—such as task forces and ad-hoc committees—were insufficient, and therefore created in fall 2011 a standing committee dedicated to Instructor-Track Faculty Affairs. This committee is comprised half of instructors and half of tenured professors, and includes several prominent senior faculty on campus, including a physics professor who won the 2013 national "Professor of the Year" award. Moreover, this Boulder campus report spurred the Denver and Colorado Springs campuses of the University of Colorado to undertake initiatives that would improve the lot of their own instructors. If nothing else, the report and its recommendations contributed to an institutional memory about instructors, their working conditions, and their positive contributions to the campus. But concrete progress on many other fronts still leaves much to be desired. Indeed, looking back on this report from a distance of roughly six years, I am troubled by how much has remained unchanged, and how perceived gains can quite easily be set at risk.

NARRATIVES AND COUNTER-NARRATIVES OF CHANGE

Cultivated and preserved through institutional memory, these modest gains in the professional working conditions of full-time instructors represent a narrative whose broad arc, stumbles apart, is one of positive change. Yet memory is fragile, commitment can waiver, and budget crises can loom large.

In spring 2010, just as our campus-wide Boulder Faculty Assembly committee was nearing the completion of its report and amidst budget crises brought on by the Great Recession, the dean of the College of Arts and Sciences proposed changes in instructor workload and pay. For over fifteen years, thanks to the Instructors' Bill of Rights, the default workload and salary arrangement for instructors in the College of Arts and Sciences was a 3/3 teaching load, a 75/25 percent teaching/service merit evaluation ratio, and what had become a starting salary of $40K. The dean of the College of Arts and Sciences was proposing a 4/4 teaching load, a 95/5 percent merit evaluation ratio for teaching and service, and a starting salary of $42K. This proposal for a (largely) uncompensated workload increase was addressed in the 2010 Boulder Faculty Assembly report, and a key recommendation, approved by the Assembly, argued quite strongly against uncompensated workload increases. The dean's proposal has proven to be a source of considerable contention since 2010.

With this proposed workload increase, two narratives collided. The first narrative speaks to the improving conditions of instructors and the growing awareness on campus of their contributions to undergraduate education. If this first narrative is aspirational in nature, the second narrative is grounded in fear. The second narrative speaks to grim budget cuts brought on by the Great Recession and the perceived need to make those cuts at the expense of instructors. In the perception of some tenured and tenure-track faculty, those instructors, after all, were getting a bit uppity, and didn't know their place. The proposed workload increase was an effort to wring more productivity out of instructors, while leaving tenure-stream faculty workload issues largely untouched. The sad, indeed tragic, outcome of this collision in institutional narratives is the perception, voiced by some faculty in a variety of venues, that any progress in the working conditions of instructors necessarily comes at the expense of other faculty and larger institutional well-being. Indeed, one can make quite the opposite argument: improved conditions for instructors contribute to overall institutional success, especially with regard to undergraduate education and student retention. But thanks to a budget crisis that had departments circle the wagons to protect their own interests, one narrative was met by a counter-narrative.

The proposed workload increase became the lightning rod for all discussions related to instructors, and as a consequence, a number of initiatives that would have improved instructors' working conditions and lives were left unaddressed. Most of these initiatives would involve no expense whatsoever. For example, instructors brought to the attention of the Boulder Faculty Assembly and various administrators the extent to which instructors could not participate in the intellectual and faculty lives of their departments and programs. Some instructors had no voting rights whatsoever in their units, and could not attend faculty meetings, despite being able to vote in and for the campus-wide Boulder Faculty Assembly. In one department, nine instructors had to share amongst themselves one vote in department meetings, rendering these instructors as 1/9 of a faculty member. In spring 2013, the Boulder Faculty Assembly passed, by an overwhelming margin, a resolution that established consistent minimum voting rights in departments and programs on campus. Yet the resolution met with no interest from campus administrators, who fear treading on departmental prerogatives to craft their own bylaws. Although several departments did revise their bylaws in response to this resolution, the response of nearly every department chair and dean was an apathetic shrug. (The BFA instructor committee is currently reviewing all unit bylaws on campus, in the hope of shedding the light of day on the worst practices.) But the controversial instructor workload proposal had taken all available oxygen out of the room, leaving little possibility for other initiatives, even those that had no financial expense attached to them.

For several years, there was sufficient pushback from faculty governance groups, well placed tenured faculty, and some department chairs that this proposed uncompensated workload increase was tabled and never fully implemented. Many regarded it as ill-conceived. The cost savings were modest at best, but the loss of service commitments from instructors meant that many key campus initiatives would become unviable. These initiatives included residential academic programs in the residence halls and service-learning programs, all of which were central to the campus's very own "2030 Strategic Plan." Many faculty pointed out that key campus initiatives and many core departmental functions could not be implemented or performed were it not for the service of instructors. Moreover, the workload proposal would turn full-time instructors into a more costly equivalent of overworked part-time lecturers.

Such arguments kept the proposed workload increases at bay—for a while. Sheer fatigue in fighting such battles can set in. What's more, in a battle of contending narratives, instructors literally did not have the voice to articulate their narrative; the dean of Arts and Sciences, the largest college on campus, had by comparison a megaphone. Just months before his departure after ten years in his administrative office, the dean announced, virtually by fiat (and with the apparent acquiescence of upper administration), that the plan he had proposed several years earlier was now policy. The departing dean of Arts and Sciences had been bedeviled by budget deficits for several years, and saw this new policy as a way to improve his legacy and to provide the incoming dean with something closer to a balanced budget.

NEW LEADERSHIP AND THE CHALLENGES OF AGENCY

In summer 2012 the new dean of Arts and Sciences took office (having previously served as an associate dean at a major public research institution in the Midwest), only to find on his desk a policy on instructor workloads that many agreed didn't make sense. Even campus administrators urged him to modify it, among them vice provosts. Nevertheless, during his first year in office instructor appointments were being written in conformity with this new workload policy. Faculty on campus, and most especially instructors, awaited signs of what kind of leader the new dean would become. And on the matter of instructor teaching loads, concern was palpable.

Despite being overwhelmed, I am sure, by his new duties and the need to learn about a new institution, the dean set about addressing the controversial instructor workload policy that the prior dean had left in his lap. In putting forward a draft plan for discussion, the new dean saw himself as responding to and improving the former dean's plan. Although the new dean maintained the 4/4 course load in the plan he inherited, he did acknowledge that some "instructionally related activities" might be able to count as equivalent to a course. He likewise modified the merit evaluation ratio from 95 percent teaching/5 percent service to 85/15 percent. He raised the starting salary for the 4/4 teaching load from $42K to $48K. His initial plan also sought to eliminate teaching overloads altogether, as the new dean preferred to have the shadow economy of course overloads become part of ongoing full time appointments.

Although supported in some quarters, the plan generated considerable criticism and, most especially, confusion. Would the new plan go into effect mid-appointment? Would it apply to new hires only, or to all instructors at the point of their reappointment? Would those instructors earning above $48K be teaching more courses without being compensated, or if compensated, what would that compensation be? What, exactly, might count as an "instructionally related activity"? As instructors teach more, who would pick up the service duties, upon which tenure-stream faculty and the institution as a whole depend? And how does the policy requiring a 4/4 teaching load fit with a separate policy limiting teaching on overload to a total course load of four courses per semester? These may seem operational details that could be worked out or made clear, but communication on the draft plan was quite poor. Months went by once the plan was verbally announced without a full, public draft. The dean discussed the plan with tenured faculty, but refused for months to meet with the Boulder Faculty Assembly standing committee on instructors. It would be a "conflict of interest," said the dean, if instructors were to "negotiate on terms related to their own appointment." Instructors replied that, by that logic, shared faculty governance itself would become impossible, as tenure-stream faculty routinely interact with administrators on a range of matters dealing with the nature and structure of faculty appointments and faculty work. Rumor circulated, and suspicion was rampant.

But operational details apart, most instructors and a considerable number of tenure-stream faculty were concerned with the plan on philosophical and pedagogical grounds. For twenty years, the campus had had a commitment to the Instructors' Bill of Rights, which had at its center a 3/3 teaching load and robust service, which made it possible for instructors to contribute to unit and campus initiatives and maintain currency in the field. Although research was explicitly not part of instructor expectations, many instructors had developed serious scholarly, curricular, and pedagogical projects and had national reputations. The dean's plan overturned this twenty-year commitment. Moreover, many criticized the dean's plan as making an all too facile and traditional distinction between teaching and service, and as such did not recognize how teaching and service comingle in co-curricular activities, civic engagement and service learning efforts, and residential learning initiatives. Still others on campus saw the dean's plan as nothing less than a slap in the face to instructors. Virtually overnight, hard working instructors with sometimes decades of service, saw their 3/3 full-time appointments transformed into what would count as a 75 percent appointment. Central to the worries of many on campus was that the new dean failed to appreciate the larger institutional narrative of improved conditions for instructors, and was largely oblivious to the institutional culture regarding instructors and the institutional memory of the Instructors' Bill of Rights.

Perceiving himself as—and hired to be—a change agent, the new dean felt bound to act, given that an ill-conceived policy was left on his desk by the departing dean. The exigence requiring a response to that plan did not give the new dean the opportunity to listen to faculty sentiments and better understand institutional history. What's more, the new dean saw himself as wanting to do right by instructors, and he viewed his plan as raising salaries and bringing the shadow economy of overload teaching into regular appointments that would be eligible for merit-pool raises.

The new dean wanted to create a narrative of positive change, and by his lights that was what he was doing. But without having read or appreciated the prior chapters in our institution's story about instructors, he was writing a new chapter that would radically change the story line. What instructors heard were tales of discontinuity and broken promises, and those tales threatened to overwhelm his intended tale of improvement. The dean's agency was clear, and it was his own, but it was not grounded institutionally in ways that might have lent it broad support. Instructors, in turn, struggled to find fresh agency in reviving an institutional commitment to contingent faculty as memories dimmed and narratives were being rewritten.

During the academic year 2013–14, the dean set about to revise his plan. By December 2013, although no new official revision had circulated in print, conversations suggested that the dean had softened his outright ban on overloads, and he had broadened somewhat his understanding of what might count as "instructionally related activities," leaving much to the discretion of individual units. After roughly a year of refusing to meet with instructors serving on the Boulder Faculty Assembly Instructor-Rank Faculty Affairs Committee, he relented in October 2013. At that meeting he acknowledged the confusion around his plan (as no written update had been circulated), discussed the current state of his plan, and agreed to the instructors' suggestion that both they and the dean jointly author a "frequently asked questions" document that would accompany his policy, once released, to allay the confusions that had plagued the policy for months.

At the end of February 2014, the dean announced and began acting on a revised policy for instructor appointments. Instead of an inflexible one-size-fits-all policy that instructors had feared, the plan offers three options, with course workload ranging from 3/3 to 4/4, and merit evaluation ratios for teaching and service ranging from 75/25 to 85/15. Courses that were once taught on an overload basis and are now part of a higher full-time workload are being fully compensated. The plan leaves a good deal of discretion to department chairs and program directors, which can be either a positive or a negative development, depending on how supportive the chair or director is of instructors within the respective unit. This new plan is generally seen as workable, a benign and in some quarters positive development, given the plan left in the incoming dean's lap some two years earlier. Through intense lobbying by instructors and their tenured and tenure-track allies, the campus avoided the wholesale destruction of prior gains in instructor workplace conditions. Yet the preoccupation with workload increases has left other important aspects of instructor life unaddressed. And the very troubling and unnecessarily contentious process by which this new policy came into being has frayed relationships.

The coming chapters of this narrative have yet to be written, and it is not at all certain what the arc of that narrative will be. Can instructors find and maintain an institutional voice, even as new contracts are written and the wheels of administration churn on? Is there some modest hope that the narrative about instructors at the University of Colorado at Boulder will have some joint authorship? What is clear is that past success has an uncertain future.

LOOKING FORWARD, LESSONS ON THE DYNAMICS OF INSTITUTIONAL CHANGE

Although this tale, like many others, has as of yet no final ending, we can find relevant lessons that speak well beyond the confines of our campus—lessons about partnerships forged and broken, memories cultivated and forgotten, narratives written and rewritten, and agency enacted with both opportunity and peril.

PARTNERSHIPS

Some twenty-three years ago, the Instructors' Bill of Rights came into being precisely because of a partnership between faculty governance and campus administrators. Although that partnership has occasionally fallen into neglect and disrepair over the subsequent years, it was only directly challenged two times. The first was when the prior dean, in spring 2010, advanced the aforementioned policy on instructor workloads without any consultation with instructors or faculty governance, even as a major campus report was being written on instructor issues. The second instance occurred when the new dean arrived and developed policy proposals without consulting with faculty governance or drawing on institutional history, in ways outlined earlier. The recent willingness of the dean to work with instructors in crafting an FAQ sheet represents a potential positive signal, but any true collaboration or new partnership has not yet emerged. A shared article of faith has been broken, and it remains to be seen whether it can be mended or revived.

In order for contingent faculty to have a consistent presence in faculty governance, it has been quite helpful to have a standing committee in the Boulder Faculty Assembly devoted to this issue. Regular meetings of this committee with campus administrators, precisely when a crisis did not loom, provided an opportunity to foster trust and ongoing communication that could then be drawn upon during moments of crisis. The darkest moments in this long history occurred when communication failed, trust was questioned, and joint efforts were eschewed in favor of lone action.

Partnerships are by their nature mutual. A key lesson learned was that the new dean needed and deserved to be part of a new partnership. He was at the table and his voiced needed to be acknowledged. On his part, the new dean made a damaging and easily avoided misstep in refusing to meet with Boulder Faculty Assembly instructor representatives, and thus quite visibly expressed little interest in forging a new partnership. After roughly a year, the dean did relent and agreed to meet with instructors serving in faculty governance roles. Maintaining continuity in partnerships between faculty governance and administrators is especially challenging when changes in key personnel occur.

INSTITUTIONAL MEMORY

Partnerships occur over time, and the memory of those partnerships, and the advances those partnerships made possible, must be nurtured and kept alive. But institutional memory is fragile indeed. Witness the fate of the Instructors' Bill of Rights, the motivating document in this twenty-three-year history. It is no longer on the institution's website, nor even easily found on the website of the Boulder Faculty Assembly. Some instructors and tenured faculty who were instrumental in its passage may have copies in their desk drawers. But they themselves are nearing retirement.

To maintain institutional memory, it is vital that documents detailing initiatives and successes be seen as living documents. Those documents need to serve, as did the Instructors' Bill of Rights, as a kind of ethical benchmark, one that could initiate new action. This was the case when the Boulder Faculty Assembly convened its Task Force in 2007–08 and its high-profile, campus-wide ad hoc committee in 2009–2010. New efforts and timely reviews can breathe wind into the sails of a prior commitment. Institutional memory is also best kept alive when efforts are shared among all ranks of faculty. At no time during this twenty-three-year history were instructor issues seen merely as the pleadings of one narrow interest group. Many tenured faculty have consistently advocated for instructors, and have voiced the argument that better conditions for professionalized instructors at a research university advance the undergraduate institutional mission for everyone.

Yet keeping institutional memory alive is no easy task. If one insists on the purity of the memory, it can easily become dated and ossified, and voices for its support can readily seem shrill and out of touch. On the other hand, if memory becomes all too malleable, and all too willing to accommodate new views, it ceases to serve as memory at all. Should instructors at CU-Boulder insist on the "purity" of their workload arrangements, as articulated in the Instructors' Bill of Rights, and in so doing do they run the risk of being ignored altogether? Or should instructors be willing to accommodate new arrangements that reflect new realities and new players, and in so doing run the risk of surrendering hard fought gains? Institutional memory may seem, quite literally, to be a thing of the past, but its presence invariably guides, in one way or another, future action.

NARRATIVES AND COUNTER-NARRATIVES

Institutional memory has an arc, and in that arc lies a narrative—or more properly, a range of possible narratives—that can be voiced with varying degrees of success. The narrative of improved professional conditions for instructors on our campus was widely shared for fifteen years. And many actors on the stage that is our campus voiced that narrative, and thus kept it alive and made additional chapters to that story possible. Competing narratives can arise, however, at moments of institutional crisis or doubt when commitments and values can lend themselves to counter-narratives. A major budget crisis and the perception that the self-interests of tenured faculty were somehow at odds with those of instructors made it possible in 2010 for the then dean to announce a break with what had become a shared article of faith on campus—the Instructors' Bill of Rights. This new narrative had for several years little traction on campus, as many faculty across all ranks found it ill advised. However, if one tells a new story often enough, it can become a reality. That 2010 proposal, although tabled at the time, was never withdrawn, and it acquired the force of policy when that dean left and the new dean entered his position in summer 2012. For this new dean, perhaps unaware of the prior narrative, this new policy was part of the now institutional narrative of instructors, not a moment of aberration. And so a new tale begins, largely untethered from its origins, with its own force and logic.

It is too facile to suggest that the answer to this dilemma lies in "controlling the narrative." Institutional narratives are far too complex and multifaceted for any one person, or group of persons, to control and articulate. Nevertheless, narratives, if they are to exist, must be told. By virtue of their contingent and at-will status, instructors are not the ideal group to tell and thus enact a narrative of progress. Such a narrative requires the voices of tenure-stream faculty and administrators. It matters who tells the story. When just enough of them turn silent, and just enough new faculty enter the institution without being schooled themselves in this institutional narrative, the story can turn. Narrative requires, and is itself a product of agency.

AGENCY AND CHANGE

The power to tell an institution's narrative is not equally shared. The voices raised by deans and administrators can well outweigh those of tenure-stream faculty, what to say of instructors and contingent faculty. Yet instructors are not without agency. The Instructors' Bill of Rights and its subsequent history are themselves a testament to the agency instructors have found, and to their ability to invite other, more powerful voices, to speak on their behalf, and on behalf of the interests of the institution at large. The most powerful agency occurs when voices are raised in a chorus.

But full-throated support voiced at one moment, or even over several years, does not guarantee that the same song will always be sung, or that the singers themselves don't come and go. Issues of agency are intertwined with those of continuity and change. Transition in the office of dean was central in the crisis that has unfolded on our campus over these last four years. When leaving his position, the prior dean was unconstrained by institutional consequences and had the agency to simply enact a proposal that was heretofore tabled. And when entering his new position, the current dean was surely accorded some deference to see things his way and to enact change. Thus, transitions in a key position of power amplified individual agency at a crucial moment in a narrative that had otherwise been about improved professional conditions for instructors. A new narrative was being voiced even as instructors tried to find a renewed voice of protest. And leadership among the ranks of instructors will itself change over the coming years, as those who themselves advocated for the original Instructors' Bill of Rights retire and the cause is taken up by others, who will inevitably inflect the desired narrative in new ways.

PRACTICAL LESSONS

This tale about the uncertain future of past success holds many lessons. But perhaps the foremost lesson is that gains are always at risk. The dynamics of institutional change described in this history could not let it be otherwise. Among the practical lessons that emerge from this tale:

- Leverage the power of faculty governance, and ensure that instructors can play a role in faculty governance.
- Forge alliances with tenure-stream faculty, who can advocate for instructors in ways that instructors themselves can't.
- Keep regular lines of communication open with administrators, especially when a crisis does not loom.
- Favor backchannel communication over more overt confrontation, unless absolutely necessary.
- Revisit and review prior moments of accomplishment or progress in order to build a widely shared narrative.

As new actors enter onto the institutional stage, work to educate them about the institutional narrative regarding non-tenure-track faculty and invite them to help write new, productive chapters of that narrative. For each institution there remain opportune moments for positive change—moments to forge partnerships, sustain memory, voice a narrative, and in such moments to find agency. We cannot afford to let such moments pass by unrecognized.

WORKS CITED

American Association of University Professors (AAUP). "Trends in Faculty Employment Status, 1975–2011." *AAUP*, 2013.

American Educational Research Association (AERA). "Non-Tenure-Track Faculty in U.S. Universities: AERA Statement and Background Report." American Educational Research Association, 2013.

Bartholomae, David. "Teaching On and Off the Tenure Track." *Pedagogy*, vol. 11, no. 1, 2011, pp. 7–32.

Bousquet, Marc. *How the University Works: Higher Education and the Low-Wage Nation*. New York UP, 2008.

Bousquet, Marc, et al., editors. *Tenured Bosses and Disposable Teachers: Writing Instruction in the Managed University*. Southern Illinois UP, 2004.

Lamos, Steve. "Credentialing College Writing Teachers: WPAs and Labor Reform." *WPA: Writing Program Administration*, vol. 35, no. 1, 2011, pp. 45–72.

Levin, John S., and Genevieve G. Shaker. "The Hybrid and Dualistic Identity of Full-Time Non-Tenure-Track Faculty." *American Behavioral Scientist*, vol. 55, 2011, p. 1461.

Modern Language Association. "The Academic Workforce." *MLA Issue Brief*, 2009/2014. www.mla.org/pdf/awak_issuebrief14.pdf.

———. "Education in the Balance: A Report on the Academic Workforce in English." Report of the 2007 ADE Ad Hoc Committee on Staffing, 10 Dec. 2008, mla.org/content/download/3255/81374/workforce_rpt03.pdf.

Penrose, Ann. "Professional Identity in a Contingent-Labor Profession: Expertise, Autonomy, Community in Composition Teaching." *WPA Writing Program Administration,* vol. 35, no. 2, 2012, pp. 108–126, wpacouncil.org/archives/35n2/35n2 penrose.pdf.

Schell, E. E., et al. *Moving a Mountain: Transforming the Role of Contingent Faculty in Composition Studies and Higher Education.* National Council of Teachers of English, 2001.

CHAPTER 10

NON-TENURE-TRACK ACTIVISM: GENRE APPROPRIATION IN PROGRAM REPORTING

Chris Blankenship and Justin M. Jory
Salt Lake Community College

Threads: Self advocacy; Organizing Within and Across Ranks; Professionalizing and Developing in Complex Contexts; Protecting Gains, Telling Cautionary Tales

INTRODUCTION

Composition scholars have called attention to the dismal working conditions of contingent English faculty and identified best practices for improving these conditions (see *Forum: Issues about Part-time and Contingent Faculty*[1]; Palmquist and Doe; Schell and Stock). Such practices often assume lines of communication and working relations between tenure-track (TT) and NTT faculty that too often do not exist within our home departments—and more generally, across our discipline. In fact, NTTF members have made little progress even within their home departments, and the deep professional conflicts of interest that exist between TT and NTT lines—conflicts tied to the very livelihood of the faculty members inhabiting positions in both lines—promise no immediate relief for NTTF. The problem that NTTF face in their home departments is that they struggle to organize a collective of TTF that are willing to work *with* and *for* them in meaningful and sustained ways. TTF would need to labor in new and more complex ways to sustain interest in NTTF working conditions and undertake the transformative work necessary to improve their conditions. This imagines a new component of TT work: engaged, sustained NTTF advocacy. It is for this reason NTTF struggle to gain recognition of their professional expertise

---

1   *FORUM: Issues about Part-time and Contingent Faculty* is an academic journal published twice annually, alternately in *College Composition and Communication* and *Teaching English in the Two-year College*. Since 1999, NCTE has used the venue to present and discuss institutional, programmatic, and departmental issues related to NTTF.

from their TT colleagues that is necessary to reform their now well-documented and unsustainable conditions.

To overcome this obstacle, we argue that NTTF must think particularly about ways of acting that are persuasive, timely, and aim to establish the disciplinary authority and local contributions of NTTF in order to initiate conversations within the department that are dedicated to addressing the socio-cultural tensions among TT and NTT faculty. As the narrative we will share suggests, writing—specifically, engaging in genre appropriation—can be one such approach. Genre appropriation challenges institutional expectations concerning who can participate in the production, distribution, and circulation of genres, especially those genres typically produced by individuals with institutional authority. We argue that by challenging such expectations through appropriation, NTTF can engender and re-form departmental politics.

In this chapter, we will share our experiences participating in rhetorically informed non-tenure-track activism at the University of Colorado at Colorado Springs, a mid-sized public university with a strong teaching focus. In the spring 2011 semester, the UCCS English department underwent its seven-year external program review. TTF created the required report, which was intended to speak for the department as a whole, without soliciting feedback or participation from NTTF. The report did not speak to NTTF issues articulated in the previous accreditation report and did not recognize the NTTF as an integral part of the English department. Compounding the problem, the report contained errors such as misnaming an NTTF and misrepresenting the work of another. In response to these glaring errors and omissions as well as departmental policies and culture that continuously reinforced a clear class divide between TTF and NTTF, NTT writing faculty drafted and circulated their own report alongside the TTF's report.

We argue that the creation of a countervailing report is an example of rhetorically informed activism because NTTF appropriated an institutionally-sanctioned genre to focus the attention of TTF and administrative individuals on NTT issues. This action then set off a chain of events that maintained focus on NTT issues for several semesters after the program review occurred. Importantly, as we will show in the following narrative, appropriating the genre of the program report enabled NTTF to document our struggles and manifest our concerns, effectively writing them into the department's history. As the department finds itself in the process of program reporting in the future, its faculty members will be compelled to address this history. This is why we believe institutional genres, those documents and policies and procedures sanctioned by our institutions, can be such powerful resources for NTT activism.

Our narrative offers varying perspectives on these activist efforts. First, Justin will provide information about the history of the NTTF's professionalization at

UCCS, a history that in many ways spurred and enabled the faculty's decision to engage in activism during the spring 2011 semester. Then, he will share his experience leading the genre appropriation as a NTTF member during the reporting process in spring 2011. Following Justin's story, Chris will share his experience as a NTTF member who joined the department in the aftermath of the activist efforts led by Justin and his colleagues. Chris joined the English department the semester following the appropriation, and he occupied governing positions the appropriation created for NTTF members. His story reveals the departmental tensions that arose in response to the appropriation. We conclude the essay by drawing on our narrative to consider what it reveals about genre appropriation as a strategy for rhetorically informed non-tenure-track activism.

JUSTIN'S STORY: LOCAL CONTEXT AND RHETORICALLY INFORMED ACTIVISM

LOCAL CONTEXT: A HISTORY OF NTT PROFESSIONALIZATION IN THE UCCS RHETORIC AND WRITING PROGRAM

In fall 2008, I joined the English department at UCCS as a full-time instructor of rhetoric and writing. At the time of my appointment, the program was in its eighth year of curricular reform, which began with the WPA's appointment in 2000 and included a decade-long transformation of the program's first-year writing curriculum from a modes-based curriculum to a writing-about-writing curriculum (Dew 2003). The curricular reform proved a fundamental component of the WPA's vision to transform NTT working conditions in the writing program. Drawing on the benefits of a NTTF with low turnover rates, the WPA used the long-term curricular reform initiative to compel the professionalization of the writing faculty.

During the eight years leading up to 2008 when I joined the program's faculty, she used the intellectual demands of the curricular reform initiatives to cultivate an ethos of productivity for writing program faculty and leveraged this ethos as she collaborated with the college's deans and the university's provost and chancellor to convert all adjunct lines in the program to instructorships that carried with them a minimum of a half-time teaching appointment—two courses per semester. With the creation of each new instructor line, she established an expectation among faculty within the program for ongoing and immersive professional development. Development opportunities in the program were numerous and included stipends to participate in disciplinary conferences and workshops as well as required monthly meetings in which faculty were immersed in theoretical concepts and collaborated to assume agency in the development of the first-year curriculum. In the four years I worked in the program, our NTT writing faculty members regularly assumed leadership positions during our monthly development meetings to teach each other about pedagogical issues; they continuously researched new issues and designed new assignments to introduce into the first-year curriculum; they collaboratively designed and implemented program assessment tools for the first-year curriculum; and they began drafting new outcomes for the first-year curriculum that explicitly addressed the relations between technology, rhetoric, and writing.

The instructorships ushered in a sense of improved working conditions for NTTF, and this led to a collective sense that the demands of our professionalization initiatives were well worth our labor. Most of us appreciated the opportunity for curricular involvement and the monetary support for development initiatives of our choosing. We were all grateful when the adjunct lines no longer existed, as our new positions carried rolling appointments that were renewed based on the annual merit reviews each faculty member submitted at the end of the calendar year. The reviews largely detailed the professional development work we collectively undertook while appointed in the program. And, no doubt, the newly granted health and retirement benefits, and a steadily increasing salary that grew from approximately $17,000 per year in 2000 to $32,000 in 2008 provided a sense of improved working conditions. For the large number of NTTF members who had taught in the program for a decade or longer, there was a real sense of transformation.

In addition to improved working conditions for NTTF, our professionalization had several significant impacts that, I believe, facilitated the activist efforts I share in the next section. Built into our curricular development were assessment initiatives that consistently suggested students enjoyed the curriculum we had worked so hard to develop, and for us this was the ultimate outcome of our work. Reports of student satisfaction and generally high levels of faculty engagement and productivity within our program enhanced our visibility across the campus, particularly with our deans, provost, and chancellor. Our professionalization also generated a collective consciousness among faculty in our writing program. We were organized. Unlike other programs I have worked in, our NTTF members knew each other well. Over the years, our curricular initiatives provided us ample opportunities to cultivate rich professional and personal relationships with each other and this led to a connected community among writing faculty, and between us and our WPA.

Despite a strong sense of community among faculty in the writing program, we worked in isolation from our TT colleagues—busily undertaking the work of the writing program while remaining disconnected from initiatives across the greater English department. Despite our proven ability and desire to engage in program initiatives, we were not invited to department meetings or aware of department initiatives. Despite sharing offices in the same hallways, we rarely spoke to our TT colleagues. For this reason, there was a collective sense among NTT writing faculty, a sense that we openly expressed in conversations with each other over the years, that we were mostly invisible in our home department.

It is out of this historical trajectory of professionalization and departmental alienation that our narrative about NTT activism emerges. In the next section, I discuss an activist-oriented effort led by our NTT writing faculty during the spring 2011 semester, a semester that included our English department's seven-year external program review as part of its reporting protocol. Our efforts created an uncomfortable tension that brought us into working relations with our TT colleagues, and they have generated sustained focus on our positions in ways previously unparalleled in our department's history.

RHETORICALLY INFORMED ACTIVISM: GENRE APPROPRIATION DURING PROGRAM REPORTING AT UCCS

Activist efforts hinge on momentum. They depend on staging, implementing, and forging connections across efforts that occur over time. This is why I begin the narrative of our faculty's efforts during our department's program reporting in spring 2011 with an occurrence that preceded the efforts. Several months prior, at the beginning of the 2010–2011 academic year, NTTF members in the College of Letters, Arts, and Sciences at UCCS logged into their email accounts to find a message from the then dean of LAS. In the message, the dean notified faculty that he was spearheading an initiative to overhaul the annual review process for NTTF across the college and its departments. The initiative aimed to transform the review process, which was currently conducted by department chairs, by implementing a standardized, peer-review process by which all NTTF members would be reviewed by a committee comprised of NTTF members from across the college. Seeking to form the committee that would overhaul the NTTF review process, the dean solicited participation from NTTF, revealed that participation would not be compensated, and suggested the committee's work would be completed by the end of the academic year and the new review process implemented at the start of the next.

The sense of urgency and finality that the dean's email conveyed—that this initiative *was* going to happen no matter what and that it was beginning imme-diately—brought writing faculty together within a matter of hours. The halls were abuzz with concern: What motivated this initiative? Why did we need to reform our current review process? Why didn't anyone consult with us to determine our needs for such a high-stakes initiative? The concern expressed by our faculty led several of us to draft an electronic survey seeking feedback and responses from NTTF across the college that we then distributed via a NTT listserve. After distributing the survey to approximately 150 faculty members, I, along with several of my colleagues, visited as many NTTF offices as we could to encourage participation. By the next morning, we had received nearly one hundred responses that unanimously expressed deep concern for the dean's initiative. We submitted these results to the dean for his review and asked that he halt the initiative. Facing a large number of concerned faculty, the dean immediately suspended the initiative and set up a series of open forums in which he met with NTTF to discuss their concerns and determine a best course of action for proceeding with the initiative. The forums were relatively well-attended by NTTF from departments across the college, and by the time they concluded, the dean agreed that NTTF needed to be included in high-stakes initiatives affecting their working conditions in the future, and he was persuaded to offer modest stipends to NTTF for their participation in the review committee. By the end of the 2010 fall semester, the review committee formed with full support from NTTF across the college.

I draw on this narrative because it set the stage for our activist efforts in our home department during our program review and reporting process in spring 2011. Still reeling from what we considered a small but important "victory" with the institution's administrative body, we met at the start of the spring semester only to learn from our WPA about our department's upcoming review, scheduled to take place in March. To prepare, we reflected on the 2003 external reviewers' report, looking for mention of NTTF issues that might determine a direction for our meeting with external reviewers in the upcoming reporting process. The reviewers' report from 2003 articulated poor working conditions that had greatly improved by 2011 due to our professionalization and our WPA's tireless advocacy. We still identified several unresolved issues from the reviewers' recommendations (e.g., salary compression for senior instructors, salaries that were still below the national average), but one issue in particular that demanded extended attention during our meeting was the rift between NTT and TT faculty in the department. The 2003 report noted that NTTF felt "isolated" from colleagues in the English department, and reviewers recommended the department mend this rift by incorporating NTTF into departmental initiatives in more meaningful ways. Because we had gained so many rich opportunities to participate in writing program initiatives, we simply could not overlook that we remained virtual strangers to our TT colleagues in the greater department.

Several weeks after our start-up meeting, well into February, the English department released its "official" program report for check-out in preparation for our department's external review.[2] After reading the report drafted by TTF, my NTT colleagues felt the report's structure and content confirmed our marginalized positions in the department. When referenced throughout the report, the NTTF were repeatedly othered from "the English department faculty" (read: TTF) and, adding insult to injury, several faculty members were even called by the wrong names or had their work misrepresented in a section of the report drafted by the department chair. Furthermore, just as with the dean's review committee the semester prior, we had been shut out of the process of planning and drafting the report, which we viewed as one of the only official avenues to document the status of our working conditions. For this reason, we believed the report had potentially profound impacts on our professional lives and thus warranted our participation in its development, participation that had been denied to us. This, of course, motivated us to respond.

Acting on our own accord and with the support of our WPA, at our February development meeting, we decided to write a NTTF report for the review. Each faculty member identified the top five issues he or she faced as a member of the department and institution and sent them to me via email in the days following our meeting. Using the newly distributed NCTE "Position Statement on the Status and Working Conditions of Contingent Faculty" as a frame, I worked with three colleagues to synthesize and organize our issues around three major themes: "Salary and Compensation," "Security of Employment," and "Professional Identity" (see "Appendix: UCCS Writing Faculty's Program Review for 2011"). As we collaboratively revised the report via email and in our offices, it gradually took shape as a manifesto directed at an audience of external reviewers, administrative members, and TT colleagues in our department. We completed and individually signed the report the week before our program review, distributed it to the external reviewers via the dean's office, and announced to our colleagues via email that it was available for check-out alongside our department's "official" report. Needless to say, our actions drew immediate attention to NTTF issues from all faculty in the department, causing the tension we desired in the production of our competing report, a tension we hoped would become the exigence for productive conversations leading to department reform.

---

2   An important point about the process of drafting the report: TTF from each academic unit (e.g., literature, professional and technical writing, and rhetoric and writing) drafted a report detailing the work the unit undertook since the previous program review in 2003. As NTT writing faculty, we entrusted our WPA, given our history with her, to write on our behalf, representing our program and its work. We were troubled more by sections drafted by other academic units that cross-referenced our writing program and our work as NTTF in the program and greater department. In light of the previous semester's initiative with the dean, we identified a need and time to respond.

When the external review occurred the following week, our collective of eighteen NTTF met with reviewers for one hour. Each of us arrived ready to speak to a particular issue in the report to ensure our concerns were understood. Weeks later when the reviewers' report arrived with recommendations, we were pleased to find that nearly 50 percent of its content addressed issues we raised in our NTT report. Because our document was integral to the external review process and warranted a large part of the reviewers' recommendations, we argued with TTF and administrative members to secure a role in developing our department's follow-up response. Against the desires of many TT faculty, we used this role to ensure that our department prioritized NTT issues by explicitly writing them into the department's response and, by extension, the department's history. And, again, against many of our TT colleagues' desires, we then pushed to immediately begin redressing the reviewers' recommendations, instead of waiting for the following academic year when the new chair was scheduled to begin her appointment. It was about maintaining momentum.

So began a series of bi-weekly meetings for the remainder of the semester where TT and NTT met for the first time as a collective to discuss the department's response to the reviewers' report and other departmental issues. As one might expect, our decision to release a NTT report without warning or soliciting participation from the TTF was thick in the air, and so the forums were initially disastrous attempts to communicate across NTT and TT lines. Therefore, at the recommendation of faculty from both lines, we enlisted the participation of our assistant dean to manage the forums through the implementation of Robert's Rules of Order. The structure that the dean's presence offered compelled faculty members, both NTT and TT, to listen and respond to each other's ideas and concerns. In retrospect, his implementation of Robert's Rules was a defining moment in departmental practice, as it enabled TT *and* NTT faculty to initiate high-stakes discussions, make motions in relation to discussions, and vote alongside one another on the motions. As NTTF, we used this emergent practice to our advantage. Given our organization, we strategically prepared for and controlled discussion, kairotically presented motions, and used our numbers to vote on and pass these motions. This practice enabled us to foreground the department's governing structure as the most exigent issue to address in the reviewers' report. Our collective thinking was that inclusion in the department's governing structures would plug us into departmental initiatives in meaningful ways and could potentially impact our working conditions the most substantially in the long term. It was again about maintaining momentum.

The force with which we proposed and maintained focus on larger structural issues in the department demonstrated that at any moment, during any meeting, as a department we could find ourselves engaging high-stakes initiatives that hinged on votes. For instance, TTF initiated a discussion in one of the later meetings to move first-year writing and all NTT writing faculty outside the department and under the purview of the dean's supervision. During that meeting, we suddenly found ourselves debating with our TT colleagues about the scope of the first-year curriculum—was it a skills-based course, a content course, both, or neither?—and to what degree this scope made it an integral part of the department's undergraduate program. In what was a memorable and tense moment in the discussion, we asked our TT colleagues for a strong rationale that would justify booting first-year writing from the department, effectively undoing over a decade's worth of curricular work that had led to a growing rhetoric and writing track in the department's B.A. English program. The request was quickly thrown back at us when we were asked to justify why we should be allowed to *stay* in the department. The discussion was short-lived but highly emotional for NTTF as it challenged the very foundation of the professionalization work we had undertaken for over a decade and confirmed what we felt about our positions and our work in the department: We were not *really* an integral part of the English department or its work, at least in many of our TT colleagues' eyes.

Despite this intense political pushback from TTF, by the end of the semester we secured our position within the department and were voting alongside TTF to set the department's agenda for the following academic year. Most importantly, in one of the last meetings of the semester, we were promised governance rights for the first time in our department's history. By the start of the next academic year, in consultation with our deans, we implemented a new governance structure that carried relatively strong representation by NTTF.

CHRIS' STORY: TENSION AND CHANGE

I came to UCCS as a NTT faculty member in the fall of 2011 to teach first-year writing as well as an advanced grammar course required by all English Education majors. At the time, I was also a Ph.D. candidate at Northern Illinois University. My dissertation was half finished, but I had used up all five years of my assistantship. I had applied for the position at UCCS because I had won a university award that provided me with a tuition waiver but not with any money to live on. So, I dutifully signed up for dissertation hours while listening to warnings from my committee and other professors about the dangers of working a full-time job while also trying to write a dissertation; nevertheless, I jumped into my new job with both feet. I knew that the poor job market, especially for someone without a finished dissertation, would probably not yield a tenure-track job that year, and if trends continued, maybe not at all. The NTT position at UCCS provided a stable salary, health insurance, retirement benefits, and a reasonable 4/4 load with the potential for summer teaching. I knew I could be happy in such a position for the long run, so I began work in August resolved to be an active and engaged citizen of the department by attending meetings, volunteering for committee work, and participating in professional development.

It was at the opening meeting of the year that I first learned about "the troubles." In the chatter before the meeting began, I heard occasional comments about the position of the writing program relative to the rest of the department, but not knowing the context, I just assumed that this English program was similar to others I had worked in, with first-year writing playing a somewhat subordinate role to the primarily literature-based English B.A. program. This meeting was only for writing program instructors, after all, and such grousing is to be expected. I certainly did my share as one of the few rhet/comp graduate students in my Ph.D. program.

Over the course of that meeting, however, I began to see that the problems ran deeper than what I considered to be the typical divide between writing and literature. Aside from the WPA, the only tenure-track faculty member at the meeting was the department chair. She announced that due to the "issues" from the previous year, the department governance structure would be revised and that we should have details from the dean in a few weeks. The mood in the room was . . . uncomfortable. People shifted in their seats, glanced at one another, or glared at the chair. I caught myself sharing a confused and worried look with another of the new hires. Why was this news, which seemed positive at first glance, being taken this way? Why was a new department governance structure coming down from the dean rather than through the faculty of the department? After this announcement, the chair left the meeting, and the situation became more clear as the WPA took over the meeting and began to talk about the implications of the restructure in terms of a "victory" for NTT faculty. She explained, for the sake of the new hires, that during the previous year, there had been some heated discussion about the place of the writing faculty in the English department. Most NTT faculty didn't teach courses specifically in the major, and some TT faculty believed that they then should not have a say in how the department was governed. Because this issue had gotten so heated and so personal, the dean had intervened and would be imposing a new governance structure to better integrate NTT faculty. At the time, I felt like this new governance structure would ensure that these "issues" would be on the mend. Looking back on this moment, I realize that my lack of familiarity with contingent faculty issues limited my understanding of just how difficult such changes can be.

Over the next month, however, I learned more about "the troubles" and realized that the fight was in no way finished. While many of the instructors didn't want to talk about it, Justin and a few others were willing to give me a better understanding of the situation. When I learned about the details of the program review and report that Justin discussed in the previous section, I knew that such a rift wouldn't be easily healed. During this month, though, I only heard one side of the story, which everyone I spoke to was quick to admit. Aside from the WPA, instructors and professors, from what I could see, simply didn't interact much in this department. The initial writing program meeting was the only one I attended in this first month. I later found that NTT faculty simply weren't invited to the actual department meetings. A full month into the semester, the only TT faculty members that I had met at all were the WPA and the chair, and the chair only due to her presence at our first meeting.

At our second writing program meeting, in September, the WPA announced that the new department governance structure was ready to be implemented. Because the dean had mandated that every committee have at least one TT and one NTT member, the WPA encouraged everyone to volunteer for at least one committee. I signed up to sit on the Curriculum and Requirements Committee and the Assessment Committee. The WPA also approached me separately and asked if I would sit on a committee that she was chairing. This committee would be comprised of individuals who taught writing courses within the major, and by virtue of my teaching the 300-level grammar course, I fit into this category. This committee was not an official part of the new governance structure, but as she explained to me, the Rhetoric and Writing concentration in the major needed to work on new courses and assessment, and both literature and professional writing had similar committees, also outside of the new governance structure, for such purposes already. This reasoning made sense to me, and I agreed to help.

It was during the meetings of these three committees that I truly learned about the repercussions of the NTT writing faculty's program report. The Rhetoric and Writing Committee was the first that I experienced and certainly the most contentious. It originally included the WPA, Justin, the department chair, another NTTF member who taught the grammar course, an alumnus of the program, and the other two TTF who taught rhetoric and writing courses. The business of the first meeting was to talk about curriculum reform. The WPA believed that the courses offered were top-heavy (too many 400-level courses, too few 200- and 300-level), and one of the existing NTTF members (who was not present at the meeting) had proposed a 200-level visual rhetoric course that the WPA was enthusiastic about. The ensuing discussion became quite heated, with disagreements over the necessary qualifications for teaching courses beyond the 100-level, how such a new course would fit into the curriculum, and what opportunities for new teaching *should* be available to NTTF. The meeting ended with little resolution. A few days later when the WPA called for a second meeting to continue the discussion, the two TTF sent an email stating that they would "not participate in this ad hoc committee," because they were "concerned that an ad hoc committee works against the goal of integrating the various emphases (and faculty members) within the department." While several people were skeptical of these motives given the membership of our committee and the analogous committees in the other degree concentrations that were still meeting under the new governance structure, the WPA asked us to respect their decision to not attend the meetings. The rest of the committee continued to meet over the course of the year, and at the WPA's request, we continued to include these two faculty in our email discussions; however, without the two faculty who taught the majority of the upper-division rhetoric courses in the department, little progress could be made on curriculum redesign.

During the spring semester, tensions once again rose when these two TTF came forward with a completely redesigned curriculum for the Rhetoric and Writing track. They had designed this curriculum themselves and without any input from the WPA or the NTTF who taught in the program and had already sent it through the established governance structure. By the end of the year, this new curriculum had not yet been adopted, but many who had been meeting during the year saw this as a convenient way to circumvent NTTF feedback in favor of committees with fewer NTTF voices. As the WPA pointed out, they had exchanged one "ad hoc" committee for another with purely TTF membership.

My second appointment was the Curriculum and Requirements Committee. The department chair also chaired this committee, and the members included the two TTF mentioned above as well as one other TTF in literature. I was the only NTTF on this committee, and with my status as a new hire, these three TTF seemed to feel more at liberty to speak freely in front of me. According to these three TTF, many of the TTF felt "blindsided" by the report put out by the NTTF. They felt hurt and "betrayed," particularly by the WPA, for not approaching the other TTF with these grievances before airing the problems in front of the external review committee. They were angry about things that had been said in meetings the previous year, and angry about the new governance structure that, due to its complexity, placed a larger service burden on many of them. Additionally, they were reluctant to approach the WPA about anything. They said that they felt "steamrolled" during important discussions and were thus reluctant to approach her. To her credit, the chair actually stayed out of the majority of these discussions, only occasionally making comments of general frustration that weren't directed at any person or group.

During this time, however, I continued to learn more about the NTTF side of the story. The WPA had been fighting for NTTF rights for years, and, as Justin points out, had been quite successful. According to the WPA, part of this struggle involved the education of TTF about NTTF rights and communication about the plight of the department's own NTTF. The TTF were, apparently, quite supportive of her work when it came to full-time positions and benefits, salary, and course sizes for the NTTF; however, when the discussion turned to including NTTF in department governance, that support turned into resistance, which eventually led to the genre appropriation described by Justin. I certainly understood the frustration of the NTTF and WPA with this perceived "one culture equals their culture" TTF attitude. I even experienced it myself in my interactions with some TTF. Aside from those I worked with on committees, I never spoke to any TTF, even though I saw many of them around the department office spaces on campus. However, close to the end of the spring semester, two TTF in one week stopped me in the hall to say hello and to chat briefly. When I mentioned this unprecedented event to one of my colleagues, she informed me that the WPA had announced during a meeting of most of the TTF that I had accepted a TT position myself and would be leaving the program. It suddenly made sense. While not a member of their specific club, I had still become a member of THE club.

Perhaps the most frustrating part of experiencing these events was seeing that, in some ways, a few individuals on each side were trying to improve the situation but never, it seemed, at the same time. I was involved in several conversations where, it appeared to me at least, individuals or groups were sincerely attempting to make some small step towards reconciliation; however, it always seemed like those moments were also the times when the other side would absolutely refuse to bend. The anger and frustration on each side seemed to be preventing any compromise, and as more of these failed reconciliations piled up over time, each side became less and less willing to be the first to approach the other. As someone who hadn't experienced the events that caused these negative feelings nor had been with the department long enough to have any type of influence, I could do little but continue to occupy my uncomfortably liminal space.

The continued degradation of the situation came to a head in the middle of the spring semester. After a failed mediation attempt from an outside arbitrator, the administration, in consultation with a select few TTF, began to consider officially separating the first-year writing program from the English department. The proposed plan would have the WPA holding a dual appointment as English faculty and reporting directly to the provost under the broad umbrella of "general education." NTTF would then no longer be a part of the English department except those few who taught courses other than first-year writing, who would hold similar dual appointments. The plan had advocates and opponents on each side, with the strongest advocates being several of the TTF and the strongest opponent being the WPA. In the end, the proposal failed primarily because of money and autonomy. The TTF didn't want to lose the funding that came from first-year writing students being enrolled in English classes, and the NTTF found that, due to some language in university policy, the English department chair would still be partially responsible for their annual evaluations. Though this "divorce" failed, that some TTF and the administration would consider such action at all speaks volumes to the rift in the department.

Coming in as an outsider, my year in this department and my service with TTF gave me a different perspective from Justin, who was in the thick of it from the beginning. I was able to hear the frustrations of both sides, to experience the vast cultural divide, and to see the positive changes as well as the fallout from the radical advocacy of genre appropriation. From this combination of perspectives, Justin and I have been able to learn a great deal about advocating for contingent faculty in productive ways. We'd like to end this chapter with some reflections on this unique situation.

REFLECTIONS ON THE POTENTIAL OF GENRE APPROPRIATION

As we argued in our introduction, one of the preeminent challenges that NTTF face in their home departments is that of engendering a focus on their working conditions and sustaining a network of support from their TT colleagues, whose status as resident faculty in the academy is a key component of improving such conditions; however, as we also stated, the lines of communication necessary for such support simply don't exist in many departments. In light of this challenge, our writing faculty's decision to appropriate—or participate in a way that challenges institutional expectations—the genre of the program report was rhetorically informed and significant to our NTT efforts in several ways. As rhetorical genre scholars suggest, one way to transform institutional relationships and practices is by participating in the genres that shape them; however, because genre participation is regulated by institutional policy and procedure that often excludes NTTF participation, activists must imagine creative strategies to make themselves participants in the genres and, we argue, appropriation is one such strategy. By appropriating the genre of our department's report—a report historically drafted by and circulated among TTF in our department—we subverted institutional, departmental, and external expectations for genre participation in the reporting process. As it stood alongside our department's "official" report, our NTT report enabled us to draw attention to NTT issues both within and outside of the department. It also exposed the rift between NTT and TT faculty that was such an integral component to the reviewers' report during our department's previous review in 2003 but that was omitted from the TTF's 2011 report.

As a genre and rhetorical tool for NTT activism, the program report is most interesting when thinking about how it sustains—through the subsequent responses, participation, and genres it compels—attention to, and continues to organize publics around, the departmental issues it reveals. This chain-like process of responding to genres through participation in other genres is what rhetoric scholars call *uptake* (Freadman 2003). In our case at UCCS, what we hoped would at least happen but could not know for sure, was that the program reviewers would take up our report, and by extension take up the NTTF and its concerns. The challenge for NTTF advocates using genre appropriation as an activist strategy, then, is to identify those institutional genres that more compellingly condition uptake within their particular institutional contexts.

As with any activist strategy, there are potential problems and risks associated with genre appropriation. At its most radical, genre appropriation can aggressively confront TTF and administrators alike with their complicity in creating and perpetuating unethical work conditions of NTTF. Such confrontations can put NTTF at risk unless they have allies and advocates in secure positions.

While this tactic may be perceived as antagonistic rather than constructive, particularly if used on high stakes documents like program reports, tension is necessary for change. The level of tension created by more radical forms of genre appropriation can be very difficult to control; however, it can also be worth the risk. In the situation at UCCS, the NTTF felt the long-term departmental alienation and class divide so strongly that the rhetorical intent of the genre appropriation was to produce such a degree of tension that it could no longer be ignored by the TTF. The NTTF recognized that the support that they sought from TTF would only come about once lines of communication existed, even if these lines were created through a forced response to a high-stakes situation like a program review.

While all activism entails some risk, not all genre appropriation needs to be as radical as a program report. The extreme effects of our efforts have led us to believe that the same technique applied to less risky genres, such as committee meeting minutes, department guidelines, and even course descriptions can help to bring NTT issues to the forefront and encourage discussion without such high stakes. For example, at the institution Chris moved to from UCCS, it is common for the term "faculty" to be used only for TTF in university documents. By continuing to refer to NTTF as "faculty" in the minutes of department and Senate meetings, which are uploaded to the university website, he encourages others to uptake this practice without the high stakes associated with more widely distributed documents.

Another potential problem is how to best bring new faculty, particularly NTTF, into existing discussions about advocacy. Chris' story shows just how quickly a new faculty member can become enmeshed in ongoing department politics, despite having very little context for these issues and little experience in NTTF advocacy. It is important for all new hires, again, particularly NTTF, to sit down and have frank and open discussions about the ongoing issues in the department. These conversations can be uncomfortable, but bringing new NTTF into these discussions from the start gives them a greater context for their new working environment as well as potentially marshalling another voice in support of NTTF rights. Tension and frustration can only increase if new faculty are left to learn about these issues through decontextualized conversations and department lore.

NTTF and their advocates should also be prepared to have frank discussions with TTF about the issues that surround contingent faculty rights. The forces that keep NTTF in subordinate positions are often institutional and unconscious, not personal and intentional. Certainly some TT faculty will adopt an elitist attitude and actively work against the rights of contingent faculty, but many are simply unaware of how vast the gap between ranks can be or why they should participate in such advocacy. For example, one of the Rhetoric and Writing TTF in our department once said that she didn't understand how NTTF advocacy was "part of her job." This instance speaks back to our belief that NTT efforts must aim on some level to help TTF imagine a new component of their work: engaged, sustained NTT advocacy. Start with educating the TTF and having internal discussions on why contingent faculty rights can impact an entire department. While this struggle can easily become a battle, the potential consequences can be nearly as serious as the problems that are fixed. Policies change slowly, but anger and resentment can persist for much longer and can hinder future work. Activism is a process that is much easier when everyone is informed and understands what is at stake.

And perhaps most importantly, no matter the circumstances, never stop communicating. Activist tactics are more successful if those involved commit to always continuing the discussion. Most of the anger and tension that made the NTT advocacy in the English department at UCCS less successful was due to a breakdown in the hard-fought lines of communication initially established by the NTTF genre appropriation. It may not be comfortable, and it may not be easy, but the necessary changes in culture that accompany a fair and complete integration of NTTF into the life of any department will always be predicated on sustained communication. The long-term social and political repercussions that come from the negative feelings engendered through silence and assumption can ultimately do just as much harm to the NTTF cause as eschewing activist strategies in the first place.

Our story shows the potential of genre appropriation. For NTTF at UCCS, this type of radical activism accomplished the rhetorical goal of opening virtually nonexistent lines of communication with TTF, however fraught those lines may have been. For this reason, we believe scholars must identify, theorize, and circulate narratives about rhetorically-informed activism that aims to create discourse among English faculty and encourage and sustain shared focus on NTT issues within English departments. We hope that the successes and failures of our effort can shed some light on options that NTTF have to advance their cause.

WORKS CITED

Dew, Debra Frank. "Language Matters: Rhetoric and Writing I as Content Course." *WPA: Writing Program Administration,* vol. 26, no. 3, 2003, pp. 87–104.

Freadman, Anne. "Uptake." *The Rhetoric and Ideology of Genre: Strategies for Stability and Change,* edited by Richard Coe et al. Hampton Press, 2002, pp. 39–53.

Naatonal Countil of Teachers of English. "Position Statement on the Status and Working Conditions of Contingent Faculty." *National Council of Teachers of English,* 16 Nov. 2010, ncte.org/positions/statements/contingent_faculty.

Palmquist, Mike, and Sue Doe, editors. *Contingent Faculty*, special issue of *College English,* vol. 73, no. 4, 2011, pp. 353–472.

Schell, Eileen, and Patricia Stock, editors. *Moving a Mountain: Transforming the Role of Contingent Faculty in Composition Studies and Higher Education.* National Council of Teacher of English, 2001.

CHAPTER 11

TRAVELING ON THE ASSESSMENT LOOP: THE ROLE OF CONTINGENT LABOR IN CURRICULUM DEVELOPMENT

Jacob Babb

Indiana University Southeast

Courtney Adams Wooten

Stephen F. Austin State University

Threads: Professionalizing and Developing in Complex Contexts

Despite contentious debates over the role of tenure-stream faculty and contingent faculty working in writing programs,[1] we assert the need to establish a middle ground that centers on the benefits to contingent faculty when their voices are included in curricular development. Such benefits include not only monetary compensation, even if nominal, but more importantly a curriculum that is built around the merged expertise of WPAs and contingent faculty, allowing for contingent faculty to participate in a writing program attuned to their needs. Although we both serve as WPAs now, we have worked as contingent faculty—most recently as graduate teaching assistants (GTAs) during our doctoral studies—in the past, and it is around an assessment experience we shared while in this position that this chapter revolves. The most beneficial way to build the kinds of relationships between tenure-stream and contingent faculty needed to work toward resolving the labor issues that haunt our profession is to collaborate with one another in as many ways as possible. If our suggestion sounds

---

[1] See James Sledd, Donna Strickland, and Marc Bousquet. It is also worth noting that, while we are focusing here on the relationship between tenure-stream WPAs and contingent faculty, not all WPAs actually are tenure-stream faculty, a separate issue that we acknowledge but do not address here. Deborah Coxwell-Teague and Ronald F. Lunsford's First-Year Composition: From Theory to Practice includes course designs, syllabi, and reflection on teaching first-year writing from several tenured faculty members who have served as WPAs, such as Chris M. Anson, Kathleen Blake Yancey, Victor Villanueva, and Douglas Hesse. We see this collection as an encouraging move away from the narrative of the "boss compositionist."

simple, that's because it is, even though such collaboration often does not occur. Common wisdom asks us to recognize non-tenure-track instructors as cheap, exploited laborers in a technocratic, management-driven university structure that depends on their labor to support an administration-heavy hierarchy focused on the bottom line. University administrators, whose ideologies impinge upon the work that tenure-stream faculty are enabled to do, often engage in a pattern of thinking about contingent labor that depends on two related strands: First, contingent faculty are not invested with institutional power—they are not protected by tenure and are not held to the same research and service standards as tenure-stream faculty.[2] Second, because contingent faculty do not have the same service obligations and because they are already underpaid for their labor, they either cannot or should not be expected to engage in additional professional and curricular development. Unfortunately, this pattern of thinking among administrators often restrains actions WPAs can take to professionalize contingent faculty and to seek ways of mediating material problems.

We agree that contingent faculty members are underpaid for their work, often abhorrently so, and this is a condition that continues to worsen as colleges and universities nationwide attempt to operate on shrinking budgets. Furthermore, apart from monetary compensation which we address later in this chapter, contingent faculty often are not evaluated for service, resulting in the possibility that they receive no credit for their service work. We also acknowledge the connection between the quality of writing instruction and compensation. As Eileen E. Schell astutely notes, "we cannot pretend that instructional quality is not affected by working conditions" (108). But, while the issue of financial exploitation should be a continuing concern—and this edited collection indicates that it is—contingent faculty should not be excluded from programmatic and curricular assessment and development to protect them from overextending themselves. Such a stance strikes us as an infantilizing maneuver that deprives contingent faculty of the chance to engage in professional and curricular development. Although contingent faculty occupy variably tenuous positions, their agency in curricular and programmatic decisions is—and should be—an important factor in the success of writing programs.

Our answer to this dilemma is to develop instructor agency through collaborative involvement in programmatic decisions, especially when those decisions have direct bearing on the curricula that instructors will be expected to

---

2   The 2012 confrontation between English faculty and college administration at Queensborough Community College in the CUNY system, as well as the 2013 dismissal of a veteran adjunct instructor in music and president of the adjunct union at the University of Massachusetts at Lowell (a story that continues to develop during the writing of this chapter), illustrates just how tenuous contingent positions can be.

teach in their writing courses.[3] Leaving contingent faculty out of these decisions divorces them from the content and administration of these courses, negatively impacting their relation to the writing program and their investment in instruction. The lack of collaborative engagement with contingent faculty also deprives WPAs of the invaluable practical experience that informs the perspectives of those faculty. If tenure-stream faculty who administer programs are distanced from undergraduate writing instruction because of other obligations, such as scholarship and graduate teaching and mentoring, then they should necessarily rely on the experience of the faculty who teach those courses to supplement their scholarly engagement with the field. WPAs and contingent faculty bring equally important kinds of knowledge with them into assessment and development situations. Tenure-stream faculty are obligated to remain current on scholarship in the field, meaning they should be aware of the latest best practices and innovations in writing assessment and pedagogy. And while many contingent faculty also remain attuned to those scholarly discourses, they bring practical experiences and concerns into the process. As Jacob's dean at the institution where he currently serves as WPA recently put it at an adjunct orientation session, NTT faculty (adjuncts in this case) are the "frontline instructors." While such a metaphor, reminiscent of "boots on the ground," has troubling implications regarding the expendability of adjuncts, the point ultimately is that contingent faculty teach most of the nation's writing courses, so their experience and perspectives are crucial to the ongoing development of writing programs.

From a disciplinary perspective, composition theory emerges from praxis, built around the classroom experiences of writing teachers—or "Practitioners' lore," as Stephen M. North put it (24)—and for that reason, compositionists remain invested in praxis as a heuristic to develop writing programs and scholarship.[4] Louise Wetherbee Phelps characterizes the relationship between praxis and theory as the praxis-theory-praxis (PTP) arc: "crisis [in teaching] generates methodology . . ." (37). For instance, when the Conference on College Composition and Communication was first established in 1949, it was meant to provide college writing teachers with space to converse with one another about new practices and new programmatic approaches (a role it still fulfills); CCCC was envisioned as a site for national collaboration between writing teachers seeking solutions to practical concerns. The relatively recent phenomenon of tenure-track lines

3   Editors' note: This recommendation is consistent with the CCCC Statement on Working Conditions for Non-Tenure-Track Writing Faculty, issued April 2016

4   In "The Challenge of Textbooks and Theory," William B. Lalicker emphasizes the need to encourage multiple forms of interactions among faculty teaching writing, regardless of rank, including establishing reading and writing groups, program newsletters, in-house listservs, and a lending library. All of these interactions indicate an ongoing need to consider the connection between theory and practice in the teaching of writing.

in composition points toward the scholarly focus of the field that developed in response to the emerging disciplinarity of composition, but composition's theory often connects back to praxis in real, practical ways. The assessments that we describe illustrate the importance of the theory/praxis loop, another way of characterizing the PTP arc, as much as the assessment loop itself. Involving NTT faculty in programmatic decisions, particularly curricular decisions, calls on their expertise to inform both the theory/praxis loop and the assessment loop. Without their involvement, WPAs would not have nearly as much needed insight into the classroom experiences of instructors and students in their writing programs, and contingent faculty would not benefit from exposure to the valuable theoretical frameworks that help them to talk knowledgeably about their courses and their pedagogical practices. All parties benefit from collaborating with one another: WPAs stay closely in touch with the everyday occurrences in writing classrooms and contingent faculty connect with current trends in research via the WPA, who brings theory-focused perspectives to bear on curricular issues.

Our argument on the importance of collaboration in writing programs emerges from two portfolio workshops at the University of North Carolina at Greensboro, where we both worked as GTAs and earned our Ph.D.s. Our narrative illustrates one way that this middle ground can be productively found while also reinforcing the importance of both theoretical and practical knowledge in the assessment loop. Chris M. Anson in "Assessment in Action: A Möbius Tale" describes assessment as a two-sided möbius strip that unites programmatic decisions and individual teachers' implementation of these decisions. Here, we use this idea of the assessment loop and re-frame it as involving both writing theory often located in the WPA and practical teaching knowledge often located in contingent faculty. These two sides of the moebius strip, as Anson claims, "divid[e] and conjoi[n] at different points; but both are crucial to success" (4). We do not intend this narrative as a prescription of the ways schools should undertake the moves we recommend since every institution and every writing program will be uniquely situated. However, we offer this narrative through the eyes of two formerly contingent faculty as one example of the ways that tenure-stream and contingent faculty can engage in the assessment loop and negotiate the lines between exploitation and expectations, standardization and standards—lines we think critical for writing programs to straddle if contingent faculty are the primary teachers for first-year composition courses.

PORTFOLIO ASSESSMENT WORKSHOPS, 2011–2013

In May 2011, a group of eleven lecturers and GTAs, including ourselves, and the university's tenured WPA participated in a three-day portfolio assessment workshop that resulted in an extensive collaborative revision of our first-year writing course's learning objectives, portfolio guidelines, and portfolio rubric.[5] Although UNCG offers two college writing courses, English 101 and English 102, we focused on English 101 because it is the only required writing course and English 102 was at that time in a transitional stage in response to a previous round of collaborative assessment. All of the English 101 documents we revised are vital to the direction of our writing program, and contingent instructors were integral to the process of generating these documents. Therefore, the assessment produced curricular changes that benefited contingent faculty by making the course more legible to instructors and altering course requirements to make them more responsive to instructor observations about students' needs. The broad purpose of this assessment was similar to Joseph Eng's at Eastern Washington University: finding "a needed balance between program uniformity and teacher autonomy" (para. 3). Involving a larger number of contingent faculty in this process allowed their teaching experiences and expertise to take a formative role in decision-making while this assessment also brought in theoretical knowledge from the WPA. In other words, this assessment marked a specific point where these two types of knowledge, sometimes separated as Anson points out, joined for specific reasons and to specific ends. Without the involvement of contingent faculty, furthermore, such an initiative would have been impossible because tenure-track faculty very rarely teach first-year composition and generally lack the practical knowledge of the course needed to inform this assessment. The involvement of contingent faculty thus included needed voices and led to curricular changes that impacted their working lives in positive ways, including changes to student portfolios that made the grading burden less onerous by focusing on the quality of student work included over the quantity provided.

The workshop began as a means of assessing the portfolio grading rubric then in use. The WPA and Jacob, then assistant director of the writing program and himself a GTA, convened this assessment workshop because of the sense that the rubric was not working. Because of her knowledge about assessment and assessment practices as well as input from two CWPA consultant-evaluators, the WPA questioned how well the rubric, a primary traits rubric using a points system, helped instructors accurately and fairly evaluate portfolios. Our measures to standardize a portfolio rubric were intended to measure the learning outcomes common to all sections of English 101. Additionally, contingent faculty, including both Jacob and Courtney, had complained about how difficult the rubric was to use, primarily because the language in the rubric was slippery. Therefore, both theoretically and practically the rubric did not work. As a group,

---

5   This assessment was recommended in our 2010 program review conducted by the CWPA Consultant-Evaluator Service and was supported financially by our Dean of Arts and Sciences.

we sought to create a portfolio rubric that would measure the course goals and create consistency between sections of the course.[6]

To this end, we double-read 110 randomly chosen portfolios from English 101 courses taught in fall 2010. The rubric assessed seven categories (analysis, use of source material/textual evidence, rhetorical knowledge, organization, style, rationale essay, and overall portfolio presentation), with five points available for each category and a grade assigned based on the total number of points a portfolio was given. The grades this group assigned to portfolios were typically in the C, D, or F range. We then scored the same set of portfolios with a rubric from a comparably-sized Midwest institution. This rubric was also a primary traits rubric; however, it looked at six categories (purpose/audience, topic/thesis, organization, prose, final analytic essay, and process) and, rather than points, it provided explicit language for the work representative of each letter grade in each category. Using this rubric, our sample portfolios typically scored in the C range on an exaggerated bell curve with fewer essays receiving grades in the A and B or D and F range than with our own rubric.

As a result of using these rubrics to grade the sample portfolios, we determined that we needed a rubric that would ensure more accurate and reliable grades across sections of English 101 because overall course grades, which were generally reliant on the portfolio for over 30 percent of the final grade, were typically B- and above. The disparity between portfolio grades in the assessment and course grades indicated an unwillingness of instructors to completely buy into the rubric's use value because if portfolio grades were as low for individual students and classes as the grades assigned during the assessment, course grades would be lower than they were. From a theoretical standpoint, the WPA was concerned that our rubric did not align with writing assessment scholarship supporting holistic grading. From a practical perspective, the contingent faculty did not think that the grades given by using the rubric accurately reflected the work students did or that the rubric helped them grade portfolios accurately and quickly. These were particularly problems because portfolios from different sections of the course were found to include very different writing assignments that did not help students develop the writing skills that we felt as a group they needed. To address these concerns, the new rubric would need to include more specific language than our initial rubric, along with more specific portfolio guidelines to ensure that portfolios in different sections demonstrated comparable writing skills. We would also need to revise the course goals because, in refin-

---

6   Our workshop was in keeping with the CCCC Committee on Assessment's recommendation that "Assessments of written literacy should be designed and evaluated by well-informed current or future teachers of the students being assessed, for purposes clearly understood by all the participants . . ."

ing portfolio grading standards, we were also revising what we expected students to accomplish in the course. This resulted in new course objectives, now titled Student Learning Outcomes (SLOs), and guidelines to match the university's assessment language; portfolio guidelines; a portfolio assessment rubric; and a detailed instruction sheet for using the new rubric.[7]

Upon reviewing the sample English 101 portfolios, we found that students exhibited several common issues in their writing: little critical self-reflection on writing processes and rhetorical knowledge, vague thesis statements, poor transitions between paragraphs and ideas, improper use of sources, and shortsighted conclusions. In general, the issues we found were problems with uses of rhetoric and a reader-based approach to writing.[8] The new portfolio rubric speaks to each of these issues specifically. Additionally, we determined that a holistic rubric rather than a primary traits rubric would result in more accurate and reliable assessment of the portfolios as well as better fit with current writing assessment practices. The WPA provided input about how our decisions related to current writing scholarship and contingent faculty discussed how the rubric could represent standards we felt would be clear to both instructors and students and would accurately and fairly assess the writing our students did. Furthermore, at the suggestion of the WPA, we used the university's overall grading rubric to guide our creation of this rubric so that our programmatic assessment aligned with the institution's assessment practices. Our institution defines a C grade as one that exhibits minimum competencies, which led to our definitions of what we wanted students to minimally be able to demonstrate in their final portfolios. Because a holistic rubric would be new to some English 101 instructors, we devised a rubric instruction sheet to help explain how instructors should use this rubric to determine portfolio grades.

Aside from the rubric, further curricular changes were needed to address the content of the portfolios. Because the 2011 group determined that better guidelines were needed to help students write and choose work that represented how their writing addressed the newly revised SLOs for the course, we also generated more specific course and portfolio guidelines. In addition to ensuring similar workloads in amounts of writing and reading done as well as common policies in relation to attendance and individual conferences, the course and portfolio guidelines reinforce the focus of the course on students' engagement

---

7   Libby Barlow, Steven P. Liparulo, and Dudley W. Reynolds argue that "*Design must emerge from the process*" (52), an important lesson we learned as our work shifted from simply changing the portfolio rubric to changing SLOs as well since, ultimately, the rubric is designed to measure the SLOs.

8   These issues also resulted in our revision of English 101 guidelines for instructors to encourage fewer but more sustained and complex essays, a trend that Erin Herberg notes in her discussion of portfolio assessment at Rowan University.

with outside sources and argumentative and analytical discourses. The guidelines are meant to ensure that English 101 instructors assign similar materials across course sections while also allowing them as much flexibility as possible in designing their courses. The portfolio guidelines the 2011 assessment group composed are meant to reinforce common standards in the course without forcing standardization of the course on English 101 instructors. Allowing these instructors room to create their own courses within set parameters meets the institution, department, and program's needs for consistency in instruction across course sections while allowing instructors ownership over the creation and pedagogical methods of their own courses.

After the first assessment workshop was finished, we sent a detailed message to all contingent faculty teaching in our program, explaining our assessment procedures and findings and including the revised documents as attachments. We facilitated three sessions during the summer to help instructors design new assignments and adapt old ones to fit the new SLOs. These sessions not only provided space for all contingent faculty to become involved in programmatic changes but also provided opportunities for them to participate in workshops that directly influenced their teaching, furthering our program's balancing of common purpose and individual autonomy.

Contingent faculty were also able to voice concerns about the documents before their implementation, an important aspect to consider since curricular development often elides the inclusion of contingent faculty's voices in decision-making processes. The WPA explained the theoretical underpinnings of the revised documents and how contingent faculty expressed their own concerns in the revision of the documents. This made explicit how theory and practice had been united in the construction of these changes, making the workshops part of our praxis/theory loop. In general, these documents were well received and the contingent faculty had no major concerns about them. We believe that making contingent faculty such a presence in the assessment workshop eased the concerns of the other instructors, who did not feel that the course revisions were being foisted upon them. Therefore, these documents were implemented in fall 2011.[9]

In May 2013, we held another portfolio assessment workshop, this time to determine if our portfolio rubric and corresponding documents were working

---

9   Additional opportunities have arisen since then to discuss the changes to English 101 both formally and informally as Chris Burnham and Rebecca Jackson argue are important ways of promoting "program-ness" that help contingent faculty achieve "the worldview of the professional" (160). One of these opportunities was a discussion of the changes, particularly to the portfolio rubric, at a GTA meeting in fall 2011 as GTAs began implementing the rubric in their courses.

to create consistency across sections of English 101 and had helped instructors more accurately and easily grade portfolios. The group assembled to assess portfolios was similar to the previous group in its makeup, comprised of ten GTAs, two lecturers, and the WPA. We double-read 99 portfolios from spring 2013 using our revised holistic rubric. Additionally, Jacob and Courtney, GTAs themselves at that time, circulated a survey among all faculty members who teach English 101 to gain a broader perspective about how instructors felt the rubric was working.

Rather than providing clear answers to our questions about consistency and improvement, this portfolio assessment created more questions about what instructors see happening in English 101. We found that grades we assigned for portfolios generally occurred in a bell curve, but this did not align with final grades for the course even though the portfolios are worth 40–50 percent of students' grades. In our discussion, we found that many instructors assumed that portfolio grades, if containing evidence of revision, necessarily should receive better grades than individual essay grades. Therefore, the grades we assigned for students' essays were not reflected in students' portfolios. As became clear during the portfolio assessment, this meant that portfolio and, subsequently, final grades did not reflect the quality of writing that students were producing. The survey results also indicated a dissonance between how instructors felt the rubric worked and how it corresponded to the goals of the course. Out of twenty respondents, thirteen characterized the rubric as very or extremely useful in grading portfolios, but the same respondents were strongly divided about the accuracy of portfolio grades based on rubrics in relation to course grades. Optional comments provided in the survey and comments made in the workshop suggested that the portfolio process as currently implemented led to significant grade inflation, which had been a serious concern for our writing program for several years. After two days, the workshop participants had generated numerous ideas for future directions for the course and possible assessment strategies, but the group decided that more assessment and discussion was necessary to make any changes. The second workshop produced no revisions, but instead it demonstrated the importance of engaging in continued assessment. The group's chief conclusion was to call on the incoming WPA to continue assessment activities and to lead workshops with instructors to consider new approaches to English 101.

This discussion was an important step in closing the assessment loop begun with our first portfolio assessment. Or rather, in continuing to travel along the assessment loop, since the group recognized that more information and input was necessary to make changes. The workshop participants found that the questions we began the second assessment with were not the primary questions that needed to be answered and we discovered more tension in the course's outcomes and assessment than we thought existed. The WPA alone or even a small group would likely not have arrived at similar conclusions; as Anson suggests, it took the involvement of a WPA with theoretical knowledge about assessment and writing instruction and a larger group intimately familiar with teaching first-year composition to bring up these valuable points. Positive changes based on such conversations ultimately benefit contingent faculty since their labor is in large part determined by the curricular structures in place at any given institution. Further, contingent faculty's involvement in these conversations helps create buy-in to a program's mission through the inclusion of their voices in the changes that will shape their labor.

TOWARD A RHETORIC OF EXPECTATIONS AND STANDARDS

In "Building a Program with the WPA Outcomes," Kimberly Harrison articulates the importance of revising a program to achieve "internal coherence," a move that provides a logic and stability to the writing curriculum at Florida International University and, through her use of the WPA Outcomes, a connection to the professional ethos of the field that strengthens the local, personal ethos of the WPA. She also notes that the faculty within the program benefited from the curricular revision because of their collaboration with one another: "Discussions about teaching increased; TAs and faculty got to know each other better and shared ideas, participation in frequent workshops and roundtables increased, and assignments were shared, adapted, and discussed" (36). Through curricular revision, all parties who participated built stronger collaborative relationships with one another, and continued discussions that could not have begun without the initial collaboration. Our assessment example is another demonstration that collaboration in curricular revision is necessary to maintain a strong praxis/theory connection between WPAs and contingent instructors.

Discussion about contingent faculty development frequently centers around whether asking GTAs and other contingent faculty to do "extra" work in addition to teaching their courses is exploitation.[10] For example, Anthony Edgington and Stacy Hartlage Taylor's survey of compensation for GSAs revealed various compensations for GSA work, but one writing program direc-

---

10   Exploitation is not the only argument against contingent participation in curricular development. For instance, see Ann M. Penrose, who suggests that "the tenuous status of NTT faculty" and "in some cases their limited exposure to the field's knowledge base" limits their ability to participate productively. Additionally, some schools or teaching unions prohibit the involvement of contingent faculty in activities not explicitly related to teaching.

tor tellingly argued, "'the compensation is experience . . . it's the chance to put administrative work on one's resume/vitae'" (154). Failure to provide actual compensation, such as course releases, for involvement in writing program decision-making rather than envisioned compensation, such as lines on a CV, can indeed be a form of exploitation, even though the professional experience is assumed to be valuable for job candidates. The contingent faculty partici-pants in our assessments were monetarily compensated with a stipend for their labor. Our experience as contingent faculty in this assessment was enhanced because we felt our labor was valued. In other words, not only were we helping to make positive curricular changes, but our *time and expertise* were viewed as valuable commodities deemed worthy of compensation by the institution and the writing program. We argue that no labor should go uncompensated as in some of the examples from Edgington and Taylor's survey. Despite best inten-tions, this work would then result in the exploitation of already underpaid and overworked contingent faculty.

Ed Nagelhout's "Faculty Development as Working Condition" realigns the discussion about the involvement of contingent faculty in programmatic deci-sions away from exploitation. He contends "that faculty development should be both professionalization *and* a working condition" (A14), arguing that although many claim that faculty development must be compensated through money or food, this is a result of seeing "working conditions affect[ing] faculty develop-ment rather than vice versa" (A15). In describing his own solutions to avoiding exploitation of contingent faculty, Nagelhout asserts that "Faculty development must address the problems of workload and time commitment," building fac-ulty development "into the expected workload" or designing it "to save teachers time" (A15). These are important factors to consider. We see Nagelhout as actu-ally describing faculty development in terms of *expectations* for the professional development of faculty that will benefit their teaching lives even though we argue that some compensation should still be provided to contingent faculty involved in programmatic decisions. It is to a rhetoric of expectations that we wish to align contingent faculty involvement in programmatic decisions, seeing this involvement as beneficial to contingent faculty agency, students who must learn in their courses, and writing programs that administer this instruction.

Two attempts to resolve the problem of exploitation have been either the standardization of program curricula or complete refusal to standardize. Suellynn Duffey et al. relate these two poles in their attempt to strike a balance between GTA powerlessness and agency by creating "a collaboratively structured program [that] would invite new graduate student instructors—*and* new writ-ing program administrators—to develop, proactively, their own professional identities, philosophies, and practices" (80) through collaborative peer teaching groups. What they found, however, was a double bind: "Either we all made the same assignments and conducted the same discussions in our groups, or we all went our separate ways down the slippery slope of permissive pedagogical relativism" (81). In the first instance, WPAs think they are helping contingent faculty because they are preventing them from having to develop courses, an admittedly time-consuming task. In the second instance, WPAs think they are helping contingent faculty because they are allowing contingent faculty to create courses that they enjoy teaching.

We argue that both of these responses are inherently flawed. On one hand, there is not enough evidence to indicate that a standardized syllabus actually reduces the necessary time for teaching writing courses, especially since much of that time is dedicated to assessing student writing. Furthermore, standardization has negative effects on contingent faculty ownership over their courses that have yet to be acknowledged. The standardization of curriculum also implies that instructors can easily be switched out without great impact on the course, program, or students, further lending credence to the terrible working conditions many contingent faculty labor under. On the other hand, a completely autonomous writing program cannot guarantee similarity between course sections, a distinct problem when WPAs try to tell administrators and other faculty what the course does or when students take the same course with drastically different results or try to transfer the course to another institution. Since no two sections are necessarily the same, teachers of autonomous courses lack instructional support for the teaching and assessment of their courses. This model allows for outdated or naive ideas of writing instruction to persist, particularly when no efforts are made to familiarize instructors with recent scholarship concerning writing pedagogies.

We found, as Harrison similarly did, that providing some standardization that allows instructors room to personalize courses creates the best teaching environment for both WPAs and contingent faculty. By focusing on collaboratively designing and implementing course standards (goals, guidelines, rubrics), writing programs can ensure continuity across course sections while allowing individual instructors flexibility to design their courses in line with their personal teaching practices. These standards can continue to be revised by WPAs and contingent faculty to ensure they reflect the research in the field and practices of the writing program and its teachers, supporting the instructors who, as we know, often stay in our programs for a limited amount of time. This is not a solution to the problem of contingent faculty working conditions but a way to reconceive the role of contingent faculty, particularly within the programs they work in, as they operate under less-than-ideal working conditions that the field continues to work on improving.

The integration of contingent faculty into the programmatic decision-making process can become a rationale that writing programs then use within their institutions to make an argument for sustained employment and less exploitative conditions. Although local conditions may limit the extent to which contingent faculty can be expected to do this work (due to departments and programs being unable to compensate such work, limitations owing to unionization, etc.), we propose that this involvement is one way that most writing programs can address the limited agency of contingent faculty while continuing their efforts to reduce the exploitative practices that often accompany contingent faculty lines. Our ultimate goal is still better working conditions for contingent faculty; this essay, however, argues that our field's collective focus on this larger goal, while necessary, has allowed us to ignore ways to improve the working conditions of the contingent faculty who continue to teach within our programs under potentially exploitative conditions. A rhetoric of expectations and standards rather than a rhetoric of exploitation and standardization is one way that WPAs can improve contingent faculty ownership of their courses with the goal that these efforts will further our mission of providing better working conditions for contingent faculty.

WORKS CITED

Anson, Chris M. "Assessment in Action: A Möbius Tale." *Assessment in Technical and Professional Communication,* edited by Margaret Hundleby and Jo Allen, Baywood, 2010, pp. 3–15.

Barlow, Libby et al. "Keeping Assessment Local: The Case for Accountability through Formative Assessment." *Assessing Writing,* vol. 12, 2007, pp. 44–59.

Bousquet, Marc, et al., editors. *Tenured Bosses and Disposable Teachers: Writing Instruction in the Managed University.* Southern Illinois UP, 2004.

Burnham, Chris, and Rebecca Jackson. "Experience and Reflection in Multiple Contexts: Preparing TAs for the Artistry of Professional Practice." *Preparing College Teachers of Writing: Histories, Theories, Programs, Practices,* edited by Betty P. Pytlik and Sarah Liggett, Oxford UP, 2002, pp. 159–70.

CCCC Committee on Assessment. "Writing Assessment: A Position Statement." *NCTE,* Mar. 2009, ncte.org/cccc/resources/positions/writingassessment.

Coxwell-Teague, Deborah, and Ronald F. Lunsford, editors. *First-Year Composition: From Theory to Practice.* Parlor Press, 2014.

Duffey, Suellynn, et al. "Conflict, Collaboration, and Authority: Graduate Students and Writing Program Administration." *Rhetoric Review,* vol. 21, no. 2, 2002, pp. 79–87.

Edgington, Anthony, and Stacy Hartlage Taylor. "Invisible Administrators: The Possibilities and Perils of Graduate Student Administration." *WPA: Writing Program Administration,* vol. 31, no. 1–2, 2007, pp. 150–70.

Eng, Joseph. "Embracing the Exit: Assessment, Trust, and the Teaching of Writing." *Composition Forum,* vol. 16, 2006, files.eric.ed.gov/fulltext/EJ1081658.pdf.

Harrison, Kimberly. "Building a Writing Program with the WPA Outcomes: Authority, Ethos, and Professional Identity." *The WPA Outcomes Statement: A Decade Later,* edited by Nicholas N. Behm et al., Parlor Press, 2013, pp. 32–44.

Herberg, Erin. "Can a Metamorphosis Be Quantified?: Reflecting on Portfolio Assessment." *Composition Studies,* vol. 33, no. 2, 2005, pp. 69–87.

Lalicker, William. "The Writing Program Administrator and the Challenge of Textbooks and Theory." *The Writing Program Administrator as Theorist,* edited by Shirley K. Rose and Irwin Weiser, Boynton/Cook-Heinemann, 2002, pp. 54–66.

Nagelhout, Ed. "Faculty Development as Working Condition." *Forum: Newsletter for Issues about Part-Time and Contingent Faculty,* vol. 11, no. 1, 2007, pp. A14–A16.

North, Stephen M. *The Making of Knowledge: Portrait of an Emerging Field.* Boynton/Cook, 1987.

Penrose, Ann M. "Professional Identity in a Contingent-Labor Profession: Expertise, Autonomy, Community in Composition Teaching." *WPA: Writing Program Administration,* vol. 35, no. 2, 2012, pp. 108–26.

Phelps, Louise Wetherbee. "Images of Student Writing: The Deep Structure of Teacher Response." *Writing and Response: Theory, Practice, and Research,* edited by Chris Anson, NCTE, 1989, pp. 37–67.

Schell, Eileen E. "Toward a New Labor Movement in Higher Education: Contingent Labor and Organizing for Change." *Tenured Bosses and Disposable Teachers: Writing Instruction in the Managed University,* edited by Marc Bousquet et al., Southern Illinois UP, 2004, pp. 100–10.

Sledd, James. *Eloquent Dissent: The Writings of James Sledd,* edited by Richard D. Freed, Boynton/Cook, 1996.

Strickland, Donna. *The Managerial Unconscious in the History of Composition Studies.* Southern Illinois UP, 2011.

CHAPTER 12

ADJUNCTS FOSTER CHANGE: IMPROVING ADJUNCT WORKING CONDITIONS BY FORMING AN ASSOCIATE FACULTY COALITION (AFC)

Tracy Donhardt and Sarah Layden

Indiana University-Purdue University Indianapolis

Thread: Self-Advocacy

It's no secret that adjunct faculty are poorly paid, lack resources for professional development, and rarely have adequate office space on campus. And it's no secret that universities are exploiting these contingent and part-time faculty by underpaying them and excluding most from benefits. Universities are also restricting access to resources and professional development for contingent faculty, providing none in many cases to part-time faculty. On top of all that, universities are generally devaluing these teachers by silencing their voices when it comes to university governance, grievance policies, and curriculum development decisions.

At Indiana University-Purdue University Indianapolis (IUPUI), the Associate Faculty Coalition was created to gain visibility and respect for part-time faculty, and to improve working conditions for adjuncts (which we will also use to mean part-time faculty). The group, which began in 2009 with a handful of English part-time faculty, has lobbied for—and received—university funding for conference presentations, improved office space, and modest raises. The AFC has held several annual teach-ins highlighting adjunct working conditions, and has gained local and national media coverage. Advocacy events have also helped raise the profile of adjunct faculty as members of the academic community.

But the race is far from over. Bureaucratic red tape can trip up even the most dedicated activists, so we invite contingent faculty to imagine the tape as stretching across a finish line: the point is to break through to the other side. There will be lots of such "races" for which part-time faculty must train: to receive better pay, benefits, work space/conditions, and more. This training—individually and as a collective team—will strengthen the movement, and ideally allow a better working situation for the hundreds of thousands of part-time faculty across the nation. And unlike an actual race, this one allows for many, many winners.

BACKGROUND/CONTEXT OF THE PROBLEM

The numbers are not in dispute. According to the U.S. Department of Education, more than 75 percent of all faculty at two- and four-year colleges and universities in this country are contingent, or off the tenure track. About 70 percent of contingent faculty, or half of all faculty, are part-time, meaning they are paid by the course and hired semester-to-semester, more like day-hire workers than anything else (USDOL).

This exploitation is possible because most part-time faculty want to teach full-time. Thus, they participate in department meetings without pay, sit on committees even if their vote does not count, and publish. They do these things, and more, because they strive to be the most effective teachers they can be, to be part of their department, and to provide the highest quality education to their students. The hope of full-time employment is the carrot on the stick.

All this is happening as universities use contingent faculty to teach the most vulnerable students, those in their first and second years of college where persistence, retention, and engagement are crucial to student success, despite clear evidence that this overuse of contingent and part-time faculty is detrimental to student learning. During a forum on associate faculty issues, one IUPUI student talked about the impact limited office space for part-time faculty has on students: "A big point that affects us is access. For office hours, I like to communicate in person, and some of my instructors either don't have office hours or have to hold them at Starbucks" (Schneirov).

And all this is happening despite calls for more equity and inclusion by groups like AAUP, Modern Language Association, New Faculty Majority, The Coalition on the Academic Workforce, and others. AAUP says all contingent faculty, including part-time faculty, should have a voice in faculty governance, and "be compensated in a way that takes into consideration the full range of their appointment responsibilities."

The MLA states that "the practice of hiring numerous adjunct faculty members year after year to teach courses required of large numbers of undergraduates undermines professional and educational standards and academic freedom." The group says that a pro-rated compensation formula should be used to pay part-time faculty after comparing their duties to those of full-time faculty. As a benchmark, MLA recommends that part-time faculty be paid $7,350 for a three-credit-hour semester course or $4,900 for a three-credit-hour quarter course.

The Coalition on the Academic Workforce in its monumental 2010 survey of more than 30,000 faculty (20,000 identified themselves as contingent) found that the median pay per course for part-time faculty was $2,700. These faculty said their education credentials were not taken into consideration for purposes of setting their salary, and support needed to teach as effectively as possible was "minimal." And the Campaign for the Future of Higher Education found in its study, *Who is Professor "Staff" and How Can This Person Teach so Many Classes?*, that just-in-time hiring, or the common practice of hiring part-time faculty just prior to the start of a new semester, is detrimental to student learning and "amounts to an underinvestment in and lack of commitment to the quality of students' education" (Street et al.).

Both the Campaign for the Future of Higher Education's report and CAW's survey, and reports from the Delphi Project, provide clear evidence that faculty working conditions equal student learning conditions and that change must happen.

So rather than accept the circumstances as they stand and continue to exist within a culture of disrespect, exclusion, and fear, a group of part-time faculty at IUPUI decided to be agents for their own change.

THE PART-TIME SITUATION AT IUPUI

Part-time faculty make up about 30 percent of the teaching faculty at IUPUI. This percentage continues to go against what the university's accrediting body deems an appropriate number. Three of the four previous reports by the North Central Association Commission on Accreditation and School Improvement cited IUPUI's overreliance on part-time faculty to some degree. In 1982, the university's first reaccreditation report included the recommendation, "As funds become available, attention should be given to adding more full-time faculty to reduce the dependence on part-time faculty." Ten years later, the accreditors said "IUPUI had not addressed adequately and systematically the concern expressed in the 1982 NCA report about over-reliance on part-time faculty. The percentage of instruction delivered by part-time faculty appears to have increased during the past decade as enrollment growth out-paced budget increases" ("Report" 5). Then, just prior to the 2002 site visit, IUPUI said it would hire one hundred full-time faculty over three years. Still, the accreditors said it was "not impressed by the prospect of lower division courses being taught primarily by lecturers and part-time faculty, and upper division courses taught primarily by faculty" (15).

As with most colleges and universities, the campus climate for adjuncts varies widely in terms of pay, facilities, and professional development. Generally speaking, a culture of fear permeates most efforts to collaborate, advocate, and improve the working situation and professional life for adjuncts. Part-timers often feel that their teaching appointments are tenuous, and do not want to jeopardize their jobs. Even as adjuncts may privately complain about dispari-ties in pay, most are unwilling to voice those concerns, in fear of losing even a meager salary. Many also hold out hope of becoming full-time employees, and therefore affect the stressful comportment of being on a semester-long job inter-view. In some cases, those "interviews" can last years, or indeed never end until the adjunct finds another line of work entirely.

The labyrinth of academic bureaucracy ensures that any progress on these issues occurs incrementally, as slowly as maple syrup tapped from a tree. Within the School of Liberal Arts at IUPUI, requests to negotiate with the dean over increasing salary, issuing contracts, and improving office space were delayed for months due to busy schedules; meetings and email follow-ups resulted in no progress almost a year after issuing a negotiation plan.

This is the life of adjunct faculty: trying to improve a working situation that has grown worse over time, and hitting roadblocks and dead-ends while trying to maneuver toward securing consistent employment. This culture has become so prevalent that we now see it reflected in television shows like *Community*, and novels like *Fight for Your Long Day*, by Alex Kudera. We see a national advocacy organization called New Faculty Majority. We see more and more part-time faculty in higher education coming to the realization that there is strength in numbers.

The Associate Faculty Coalition wants to use those numbers to bring adjunct faculty issues to the forefront and lobby for change. The group decided that one way to raise awareness would be to hold a teach-in as an opportunity for fac-ulty members of any status to integrate the issue of contingent labor into their pre-existing lessons. Over the winter of 2009–2010, the AFC planned the event and created a packet of materials with local and national facts and statistics, and sample lesson plans across a variety of fields that could be used if a faculty mem-ber decided to participate. The teach-in was entirely voluntary, and explicitly designed not only as an advocacy opportunity, but to provide students with a teaching moment about campus issues, social justice, and disparities in pay and professionalization among faculty members.

Administrators reacted immediately to announcements and publicity for the first annual event, describing it as a "sit-in," as if the thirty percent of part-time faculty members were planning to protest in front of the administration building. The following year, in the weeks leading up to the teach-in, deans requested a meeting with Coalition leaders to point out a section in the faculty handbook that prohibits using class time for non-course-related content. The leaders explained—again—that the teach-in could be adapted to any course material: sociology classes could explore how union efforts worked or didn't work; literature classes could feature work by or about part-time faculty, a widely published group in its own right; math classes could calculate how much tuition students bring in and compare that to the average amount an adjunct is paid per class, and so on.

Also worth noting: the faculty handbook excludes part-time faculty from holding any part in university governance, and does not recognize those members as faculty. Even though the adjuncts were following the rules, the rules don't, in fact, apply to them. Adjuncts in any institution should keep that in mind while planning advocacy work.

The teach-in garnered attention from both *The Indianapolis Star* and local news radio. Participants on campus noted that many students reacted with surprise that the majority of adjunct faculty at IUPUI receive low pay, no benefits, and are employed without contracts. The event was successful in engaging conversation across campus about the situation of those who teach at the university level. It is fair to say that the nation's universities see students not just as learners but as consumers. Shouldn't students be educated about the resources they are consuming? Shouldn't they be taught to think critically and ask questions about where their tuition money goes? Critical thinking is so valued at IUPUI that it is listed as one of the six Principles of Undergraduate Learning. Apparently, turning the critical lens on the university itself can be perceived as threatening, not part of a conversation.

The teach-in hoped to start that conversation in the classroom, imagining its migration to print and digital formats not only through the media but via the expressions of the participating instructors themselves, who might count the activity among their service to the university. The stance of administrators gave the impression that this wasn't a conversation they were willing to engage in—nor did they want to afford the opportunity to others. What could have been a professional development activity for adjuncts starved for such things (including a natural progression from the event to discussion, feedback, and eventual publication) instead became a bureaucratic struggle. At one point, fellow adjuncts approached Coalition members to express uncertainty over participating: they'd heard the teach-in was an opportunity to bash the university, and, in essence, bite the hand that feeds them. Trying to de-mythologize this event's clearly stated purpose distracted from the matter at hand: bringing attention to the issues of low pay and lack of professionalization in the ranks of adjunct faculty. And it's true that the message reached part of its intended audience. But it could have had a more meaningful impact had the administration viewed the event as a worthwhile teaching moment.

At issue for any part-time faculty lobbying for change is the lack of stability within the profession. Of the nine members who bolstered the AFC in its first year, six have moved on or become full-time faculty members and are still involved in AFC efforts. The occasional creation of more positions for part-time faculty to move into is clearly a win, but competition is fierce and as of fall 2014, no new positions were being created for the next academic year.

Additionally, the transitory nature of adjuncts could be considered something that departments and schools count on in terms of avoiding a strike or unionization. Institutional fatigue plays a role, too, as people shuffle into a system where their hands are tied, and they give up rather than continuing to fight through the bureaucratic red tape that winds around all universities. This can keep numbers of those participating in advocacy low when people see that those who have been fighting have made little progress. What incentive do they have to join the fight? It makes more sense to focus instead on the other teaching jobs they've cobbled together; to doggedly try to earn a living, hoping that a part-time appointment eventually will lead to full-time work. That dispersion of energy keeps many from mustering the strength to retaliate by raising awareness, forming a union, or going on strike: all recommended courses of action from long-time adjuncts as a means to change. In the midst of the most recent external review for reaccreditation at IUPUI, one reviewer asked why adjuncts weren't unionizing. It was, she said, the only way she'd seen change happen for adjuncts. It's an oft-heard message that too few have heeded: adjuncts must advocate for themselves and each other.

It's clear that a university isn't going to make changes based on the simple fact that it's the right thing to do. Businesses operate on capital, not kindness. One adjunct who teaches at two universities in Indianapolis overheard a business office conversation not meant for her ears: officials were comparing adjunct pay rates at different institutions in the metropolitan area and using that information to set their own rate. The prevailing "wisdom" seems to be this: if pay remains low across the board, adjuncts have fewer options for upward mobility, and little incentive for lateral movement. However, there's strength in numbers, too: if adjuncts coordinate across multiple campuses and arm themselves with this information, they can—and should—use the numbers for their own leverage. Otherwise, adjuncts are just so much human capital, shuffled annually to an institution's bottom line.

It seems as if adjuncts want the protection of a union. The AFC has fielded requests from those who want the group to advocate on their behalf. Unfortunately, those individuals often are unwilling to be named or to stand up alongside Coalition members to join the fight, something a union organization requires, which we learned when we met with a local chapter of AFSCME. One adjunct faculty member outside of the School of Liberal Arts emailed to say that the adjuncts' contracts had been voided and replaced with new ones, changing the minimum enrollment for a course from ten to fifteen. Numerous under-enrolled courses were canceled, and adjuncts who had turned down other course assignments now were left with no work. The AFC responded that it would like to support adjunct faculty across campus, but that the group needed those people to be part of the advocacy, and that the group couldn't lobby for those who weren't willing to participate in the lobbying. This faculty member who'd emailed was invited to join a meeting that week with the Executive Vice Chancellor, the second-in-command at IUPUI. We never heard back.

That was also the trend as the group tried to set a meeting with then-Chancellor Charles Bantz about the pay inequities within the Indiana University system. We were told that this was not a campus issue but an IU system issue, so we looked to get the attention of Indiana University President Michael McRobbie through an open letter that we also sent to local media. Both *The Indianapolis Star* and the *Indianapolis Business Journal* ran the letter on their editorial pages. We wrote:

> Associate faculty on the IU Bloomington campus earn substantially more than their counterparts at IUPUI—in some cases, nearly twice as much. This situation sets a double standard. We have been asking for a higher wage since the inception of the Coalition, yet few have seen any substantial gains. Associate faculty are exploited everywhere, but our question is why we are *more* exploited in Indianapolis than in Bloomington. No reasonable explanations have been offered for this glaring inequity. If an associate faculty member is qualified to teach introductory courses on either campus, location should not be the determining factor in compensation rates. (Schubert)

Soon after, the dean of the School of Liberal Arts contacted us for a meeting, even though we had not addressed the letter to him. The downward chain of command dictated that we stay in place: at the school level, where we learned once again that budgets were set at the university level. Or perhaps at the system level, depending on who was being asked and on what day.

THE ASSOCIATE FACULTY COALITION AS A RESPONSE TO THE ISSUES

We began with a small, but hugely significant goal: to get part-time faculty in the Writing Program included in the online faculty directory. This task sounded not only easy to accomplish—just ask someone, right?—but also something that surely no one would object to. We were faculty, after all, and students had trouble finding us because our bios and contact information weren't where they looked.

Including us in the faculty directory would go a long way to making part-time faculty in the university's Writing Program feel included, respected, and wholly integrated with the Program. This was only right, not only because all employees deserve these things, but because the forty-five part-time faculty, at that time, represented 67 percent of all faculty in the department. We also taught just over 51 percent of all first-year writing courses where student engagement is crucial for student retention and success. The task proved not only difficult for all its red tape and obstacles, but working through this endeavor showed us that upper administration saw this as a problem of numbers, not people.

We were ultimately successful in getting the Writing Program's part-time faculty included in the online faculty directory. This came after being told initially that it was too difficult because there were "too many of us" and so the task of maintaining the list from semester-to-semester for faculty who come and go would be too time intensive for any of the full-time staff members. Of course, it was the administration who hired "too many of us" over the years; it was and still is their decision to participate in just-in-time hiring without contracts, and so part-time faculty are often forced to come and go from semester to semester.

But we persevered and refused to accept that as the answer. We offered to maintain the directory, which required nothing more than checking or unchecking a box in a directory bio that was automatically created for us by the system upon our hire. Until our request, that box had simply remained unchecked for anyone with part-time status. And thus, the harsh reality of our plight was evident from the start: a faculty record was automatically created for us but intentionally shut off by the administration. We won the right to check that box.

We felt empowered. We also felt lucky to be encouraged and wholly supported by the Writing Program's director, Steve Fox. He was the first to suggest we get part-time faculty included in the directory and still advises us today, adding his tenured voice to our contingent voices as we seek more tangible benefits than being included in the faculty directory.

But the couple of us working on getting part-time faculty included in the faculty directory knew we needed a larger voice. So we emailed all writing program faculty asking who wanted to serve on the board of our newly formed group. Eight answered the call and the Associate Faculty Advisory Board was formed. We quickly decided to expand and "represent" part-time faculty within the School of Liberal Arts, partly because much of what went on in the Writing Program was decided at the school level.

Our First Year: Collecting Information and Getting Noticed

We held our first Associate Faculty Advisory Board meeting November 3, 2009. At that meeting, we began to form a strategy that would prove challenging for a number of reasons. The hardest challenge would be getting other part-time faculty to speak up for their rights. That challenge exists to this day. Over that first year, we did a number of things to raise awareness of part-time faculty working conditions within the school. We collected data on our numbers and teaching loads to show the impact we have on student learning. We surveyed part-time faculty on their accomplishments and service to show not only their effectiveness as teachers, but to dispute the notion that part-time faculty contribute less to their university than do full-time faculty. We found that despite clear and sometimes almost insurmountable obstacles, contingent faculty were performing service and publishing.

Our first major initiative was hosting a "Dinner with the Deans" where we found space off campus and provided dinner to a number of deans and other administrators we invited. The Chancellor and the Vice Chancellor of the campus both declined our invitation but others attended. After a lively and sometimes contentious discussion of our issues, we showed the documentary, "Degrees of Shame, Part-time Faculty: Migrant Workers of the Information Economy" to the group. The intent was to show our issues were part of a national conversation.

By the end of the meeting, while we could tell we had some support, it was equally clear we would face powerful opposition to our efforts. But our point was made: we recognized and accepted the challenge because improved working conditions for part-time faculty was not only a fundamental right but crucial to improving student learning conditions.

We then decided to focus on health insurance as benefits, something part-time faculty are excluded from at IUPUI and a common gap for adjuncts at universities across the country. This proved to be a pivotal point for our group, not only in terms of gaining local and national media attention, but once again showing the harsh realities of being part-time faculty with no voice.

In a nutshell, we were able to find group health insurance at reasonable rates by working on our own with a broker and an insurance company. Once we were ready to initiate enrollment, we sought help from Human Resources at Indiana University, which handles benefits and certain other aspects of employee life at IUPUI. The health insurance we found required neither any employer share of the premiums nor any cost to IU or IUPUI. All we needed was access to part-time faculty contact information to distribute the information. In fact, all part-time employees would be eligible for this coverage but we lacked the means to communicate with this huge population.

At this point, IU told us we were violating university policy by getting our own health insurance and we were told to cease our efforts in this area or face punishment. Our story was picked up by the local media and then the national media (Inside Higher Ed). The stories did not paint IU or IUPUI in a positive light, and while we knew this would further rankle the upper administration, it also prompted a number of full-time and tenured faculty to speak up on our behalf.

And so we continued. We gained our first board member outside of the English department when a part-time faculty member from World Languages joined the group. Communication, even with part-time and full-time faculty within a single school (let alone an entire campus) was challenging, so we asked for volunteers to serve as "liaisons," full- and part-time faculty who would help disseminate information to the others via meetings and emails.

Other initiatives included creating a Facebook page and a Twitter account. We submitted board meeting notices in the university's bi-weekly e-newsletter to all students, faculty, and staff. We got on the agenda and presented our group and mission at a department chairs meeting. We created fact sheets and flyers and distributed them around campus and at faculty and department meetings. We set up a booth at the university's annual part-time faculty orientation and resource fair. We collected reports on previous reaccreditation visits which pointed to an overreliance on part-time faculty. We reached out to the local AAUP chapter in addition to the teach-in. We launched a student letter-writing campaign to upper administration. We met with experts in labor relations, both inside and outside our university, to help us understand that we didn't have to be a union to act like one, despite being discouraged by upper administration to form a union or look like a union. And we created our own mini-documentary, *Part-time Faculty. Full-time Impact.* and uploaded it to YouTube (www.youtube .com/watch?v=NHb0PnpgWIw).

In short, we bombarded the school and the media with our presence.

And we researched our situation, which we knew mirrored what was happening on university and college campuses across the country. We learned the university had halted its practice of inputting education credentials into the permanent records of part-time faculty. Like the issue with including us in the online faculty directory, we were told there were simply "too many of us" and we were "too transient" to manage this task. Thus, there was no way to document the number of part-time faculty with advanced degrees.

We learned part-time faculty are paid using a "contract" employment status, which results in too little federal income being withheld. When we asked that this be changed so already underpaid part-time faculty are not also hit with a hefty federal tax bill at the end of the year, we were told this would be too difficult to do. We learned no single mechanism existed to communicate with all part-time faculty on campus (in 2015, we finally gained this mechanism). Worse, we learned many schools and departments across campus failed to communicate with their part-time faculty at all and even excluded them from communications sent to full-time faculty. We learned that because part-time faculty are excluded from benefits, they also lack the ability to access IUPUI's counseling services, which are free or at a reduced rate for students and full-time faculty and staff. When asked if this could be corrected given the degree of stress and health issues many part-time faculty experience due to working multiple jobs and lacking health insurance, we were simply told this was not possible.

But we also made some gains. Where previously we'd had no private space to meet with students (the 107 part-time faculty in the School of Liberal Arts shared twenty-three cubicles), some space was converted to a private conference room for us. Where no part-time faculty served on any committees, the Writing Program Coordinating Committee expanded its eligibility to include this group and welcomed one to the committee and granted her all the rights of the full-time and tenured faculty on the committee.

And so, by the start of our second year we had adopted the maxim to be "patient, persistent, and professional," recognizing we needed to consistently exhibit all three qualities if we were to effect change, however slowly. In small steps, that change happened.

By 2010, we were ready to expand again and represent all part-time faculty across campus, despite being advised against expanding by upper administration. Of course we ignored this advice as well and announced our expansion and our name change to the Associate Faculty Coalition at IUPUI via the university's e-newsletter.

Our Second Year: Mobilizing, Organizing, and Learning

And we continued our efforts into our second year. We initiated a membership drive, creating an online portal to join on the Coalition's website. Membership was free, of course, and mainly served as a way for others to show their support. We knew membership numbers would be one way to prove the dissatisfaction and frustration many part-time faculty felt about their working conditions. Within the first three weeks, we had one hundred members.

We created a listserv for members and began communicating what the Coalition was doing. We held two "quiet" demonstrations on campus: the first when the President of IU gave his State of the University address and the second when IUPUI's Chancellor gave his State of the Campus address. We formed a student delegation, recognizing that student voices were more powerful than ours. We gained a spot on one of the Reaccreditation Self-Study committees although we were told we could not speak; our role could only be as note taker. We continued posting to our Facebook page and calling for new members in the campus e-news blasts. We continued meeting with the Dean of the School of Liberal Arts on our efforts for change within that School. Importantly, we gained a board member from outside Liberal Arts to show we were a campus-wide group and not mostly just a group of disgruntled English teachers. We expanded the collection of data on our numbers and teaching assignments outside of Liberal Arts to include campus-wide data. We held a contingent faculty forum with the local AAUP chapter where we invited panel members to present their view of the issues and hear from attendees who shared stories about how their contingent status impacted their ability to teach and their students' ability to learn. At the teach-in described earlier, we collected narratives from faculty and students who participated. We chalked about our efforts on campus sidewalks and sent press releases announcing our initiatives. We partnered with students wanting to write papers and conduct research about our issues.

And we fought battles. We fought an attempt to censor us with prior restraint and argued for our right to issue our own press releases, rather than give the information to the university's media relations group and have them write the release, since there are no rules on the books against our writing our own.

We presented the Coalition and its mission to the university's faculty governance committee where we were met with skepticism about the true nature of part-time faculty working conditions (was it really as bad as we were saying?) and how part-timers view those conditions (most are fine because they teach to give back and don't need the money). The committee told us they don't control how much part-time faculty are paid; salaries are determined by the "market" and they are simply following the market. Besides, there isn't enough money to increase part-time faculty salaries. One faculty member said the committee was already "too busy" to deal with this issue. Again, this is the committee tasked with addressing faculty issues across campus, but once again, the perception that part-time faculty were not really "faculty" was sharply evident in the harsh comments. We were told we needed to survey faculty on our campus because it wasn't necessarily true that our situation mirrored what was happening and being reported on nationally. The committee said it would need to approve our survey questions.

Still, we continued to make gains. We were invited to serve on the committee to plan the campus-wide orientation for part-time faculty for fall 2011, the first such offer ever made. We increased membership in the Coalition to nearly 250 part-time faculty, full-time faculty, staff, and students. We gained additional media coverage. We met with upper administration at the campus level who agreed to hear our concerns. We created a list of conditions and practices that schools should strive for to ensure part-time faculty are treated fairly and equitably, and presented it to upper administration, deans across campus, and the campus faculty governance committee.

Where no raises for part-time faculty had been approved in years, the Coalition lobbied for and won raises for those working in the School of Liberal Arts. While extremely modest, the salary gain was a milestone in more ways than one. Whether it was the Coalition's doing or not, several other schools across campus followed the School of Liberal Arts move and raised salaries for their part-time faculty as well.

We held a "Coffee with the Coalition" event to promote our existence and remind students, faculty, and staff of our mission and the need to get involved. We held a third-annual teach-in. We gained professional development funds for all part-time faculty across campus who presented at conferences. While limited in scope, this was another huge gain as nothing of the kind had been awarded to part-time faculty in the past. This benefit has since been improved to cover registration to an annual conference for contingent and part-time faculty held in Indianapolis each year.

We continue to face the challenge of gaining more tenured faculty support. We realize this is due to several reasons. Some tenured faculty see part-time faculty as a threat, although many tenured faculty have less time for research because they are continually bombarded with the need to perform duties and service that many contingent faculty cannot be asked to do. Regardless of how much service many full-time contingent faculty are able and willing to perform, pure part-time faculty, a group that makes up 30 percent of all faculty at IUPUI, cannot be asked to perform any service given their tenuous status and extremely low pay. Thus, the more tenured faculty, the more faculty there would be to share the work needed to ensure quality learning conditions for students.

But despite the challenges, the Associate Faculty Coalition continues to exist and strive for improved working conditions for part-time faculty at IUPUI. Our initial maxim of "patient, persistent, and professional" continues to drive our efforts. Change is happening and will continue to happen, however slowly and in small steps.

PRACTICAL MATTERS FOR ADVOCACY

Perhaps the best thing part-time faculty can remember: we are hardly alone in our efforts. Joining advocacy groups can offer a sense of camaraderie for many Freeway Flyers. Part-time faculty can use social media to communicate, share ideas, and gain momentum through collective action. *The Chronicle of Higher Education* and *Inside Higher Ed* have devoted more time and space to adjunct issues, and the body of literature on the subject is growing. Joe Berry's activist book, *Reclaiming the Ivory Tower: Organizing Adjuncts to Change Higher Education*, provides his years of experience along with practical advice and support. (Berry also met with the AFC for a mini-workshop on expanding the movement to enact more sweeping change.) Berry cites isolation of part-time faculty as a contributing factor to stasis. "Contingent faculty themselves, however, almost never focused on structural barriers. Almost without exception, they saw fear, and fatalism, as the main obstacle to overcome" (89). Berry asserts that even if a group has yet to form a union, individuals can benefit from collective action. Twenty-five or thirty people with the same complaints are harder to ignore. Still harder: a hundred.

Those looking to enact change should find sympathetic full-time faculty to help advocate and advance the cause. This is a problem that has far-reaching effects; all should be concerned about the direction of faculty hiring practices. Ask for meetings with the higher-ups. Lay out the issues as they stand, and remind administrators that action is needed. When the adjunct issue seems to have fallen to the bottom of a mountain-sized "to-do" pile, the only way to remind universities that part-timers have a voice is to use it. And the only way to get past red tape is to push through.

WORKS CITED

AAUP. "New Report on Contingent Faculty and Governance." *American Association of University Professors*, 26 June 2012, aaup.org/report/inclusion-governance-faculty-members-holding-contingent-appointments.

Associate Faculty Advisory Board at IUPUI in Indianapolis, Indiana. "Part-Time Faculty. Full Time Impact." *YouTube*, 21 Mar. 2010, youtube.com/watch?v=NHb0Pnpg Wlw. 30 Mar., 2013.

Berry, Joe. *Reclaiming the Ivory Tower: Organizing Adjuncts to Change Higher Education*. Monthly Review Press, 2005.

Coalition on the Academic Workforce. "A Portrait of Part-Time Faculty Members: A Summary of Findings on Part-Time Faculty Respondents to the Coalition on the Academic Workforce Survey of Contingent Faculty Members and Instructors." June 2012.

Modern Language Association. "MLA Statement on the Use of Part-Time and Full-Time Adjunct Faculty Members." *MLA*, 1994, mla.org/Resources/Research/Surveys-Reports-and-Other-Documents/Staffing-Salaries-and-Other-Professional-Issues/MLA-Statement-on-the-Use-of-Part-Time-and-Full-Time-Adjunct-Faculty-Members.

Modern Language Association. "MLA Recommendation on Minimum Per-Course Compensation for Part-Time Faculty Members." *MLA*, 2012, mla.org/Resources/Research/Surveys-Reports-and-Other-Documents/Staffing-Salaries-and-Other

-Professional-Issues/MLA-Recommendation-on-Minimum-Per-Course-Compensa tion-for-Part-Time-Faculty-Members.

North Central Association Commission on Accreditation and School Improvement. "Report of a Comprehensive Evaluation Visit." 1992.

Schneirov, Rich. "Associate Faculty Forum." *Indiana University-Purdue University Indianapolis, Indianapolis*, 11 Feb. 2011. Speech.

Schubert, Steve, et al. "Up Adjunct Pay, Mr. McRobbie." *Indianapolis Business Journal*, 5–11 Dec. 2011, p. 12. Letter.

Street, Steve, et al. "Who Is Professor 'Staff' and How Can This Person Teach so Many Classes?" *Center for the Future of Higher Education*, Aug. 2012, futureofhighered.org /policy-report-2/.

United States Department of Education. "2009 Fall Staff Survey." nces.ed.gov/pubs 2011/2011150.pdf.

CHAPTER 13

BUILDING OUR OWN BRIDGES: A CASE STUDY IN CONTINGENT FACULTY SELF-ADVOCACY

Lacey Wootton and Glenn Moomau

American University

Threads: Self-Advocacy; Organizing Within and Across Ranks

Discussions of working conditions for non-tenure-track faculty often take one of two forms: Either they feature faculty members analyzing the problems of their condition, or they highlight tenured faculty or administrators who have helped improve contingent-faculty working conditions. Organizations such as AAUP address contingent-faculty problems and successes, but the voices heard frequently belong to non-contingent faculty, and the perspectives of the contingent faculty are often minimally present, at best, possibly creating the impression that the work towards shared governance and contingent-faculty participation is the responsibility of tenured faculty, with contingent faculty the grateful recipients of their efforts. In this chapter, we want to feature the perspective of contingent faculty in advocacy efforts.

Our own institution, American University, has been justifiably lauded for its progress in shared governance and treatment of contingent faculty over the last few years; a total of three sessions at the AAUP's conferences on governance dealt with the changes, and an article in *The Chronicle of Higher Education* reported on the increased participation in governance on the part of our contingent faculty (Schmidt, "Faculty"). These changes have resulted from collaboration between tenure-track and contingent faculty—but that collaboration itself resulted from the efforts of American's contingent faculty,[1] particularly the writing program faculty, to participate in university service and governance.

---

1   For the purpose of this chapter, "contingent faculty" will refer to full-time, non-tenure-track faculty; we use the term "adjunct" for our part-time faculty, who are outside the scope of this discussion, particularly because they recently unionized and ratified a separate contract with the university.

We argue, in fact, that contingent faculty in writing programs are among the best situated to advocate for contingent-faculty issues. Before the boom in contingent faculty lines created a majority of non-tenured faculty at the nation's colleges and universities, non-tenure-line writing faculty were already there, along with language and mathematics instructors, staffing freshman courses. Writing faculty have been operating for years in what has historically been a low-status job, and in our case, that position led to a clear vision of our circumstances and the solidarity to do something about our situation. In this chapter, we will describe our own self-advocacy process, emphasizing three main components: faculty reputation, alliances with tenure-line faculty, and participation in teaching unit and university governance. We will also discuss our current successes and remaining challenges, and offer suggestions to other faculty. We believe that contingent faculty can advocate for themselves—if they take advantage of and create the conditions in which they can do so.

INSTITUTIONAL CONTEXT

Located in Washington, DC, American is a private, liberal arts, doctoral-granting (AAUP-I) institution with a combined undergraduate and graduate student body of 12,000. The university comprises four professional schools, a law school, a school of extended studies, and a college of arts and sciences. Within that college, the College Writing Program is housed in the Department of Literature. All College Writing faculty are contingent or adjunct, with most classes taught by full-time faculty. Almost all the faculty who teach "literature" courses (as distinct from composition) are tenure-line, with a handful of contingent and adjunct faculty.

Over the past two decades, like most colleges and universities, AU has seen a steady growth in full-time contingent faculty in teaching-only appointments. Before the year 2000, there were few full-time contingent faculty, and those faculty were limited by a five-year cap on their employment. Once multi-year appointments after five years became available in 2000 through faculty-senate legislation, our numbers grew significantly, and as of 2009 we had long-serving faculty who had earned reputations as excellent teachers, with a high concentration of such faculty in our writing program. As Maria Maisto notes, "stabilization" leads to contingent faculty "establishing institutional roots deep enough to build the kind of knowledge and relationships that facilitate both commitment and reform" (192), as well as building "relationship[s] between contingent faculty members and the institutions and communities in which they work" (193). Indeed, Maisto says, case studies indicate that "contingent faculty leaders who have been able to plant strong roots in their institutions and communities are usually the most successful change agents" (193). While the very fact of contingency works against such roots, Maisto makes clear that they are at the same time essential.[2]

Over the past decade, non-tenure-track faculty—especially in the full-time ranks—grew significantly. As of academic year 2013–2014 American University employed 495 tenure-line, 353 full-time non-tenurable, and 796 adjunct faculty, which means AU's non-tenure-track faculty make up 48 percent of all full-time faculty appointments. In 2007, a new provost took the helm at our institution and immediately sought to raise the research profile of the institution. In order to accomplish this goal, tenure-line faculty went from a 3-2 to a 2-2 teaching load—which produced a need for more full-time contingent faculty.[3] The provost recognized the implications of this changed faculty make-up for the university, and soon after arriving, he began to refer to "career term faculty." As Adrienne Kezar and Cecile Sam note, such recognition matters: For positive change for contingent faculty to occur, "institutions would have to acknowledge two ideas. The first idea is that a change in the faculty composition has occurred, making the current policies and practices for faculty inapplicable to the majority of faculty. The second idea is that change needs to occur for institutional policies and practices to align with the new faculty majority, because ignoring the issue is unsustainable; long-term inaction would lead to negative impacts on the professoriate, the institution, and the students" (30). We thus found ourselves in an institutional context that was in many ways typical but that had the perhaps atypical advantage of some awareness of and support for contingent faculty at the highest administrative level. And in 2009, with a major revision of our faculty manual in the works, we had our first opportunity to weigh in on the "policies and practices" that most affected us.

ADVOCACY AND CHANGE

In 2009, we had an increasingly stable population of contingent faculty, an administration that was at least beginning to acknowledge us as more than just "temporary" faculty, and an opportunity in the form of the faculty manual revision. At the same time, we had a recent history, even within our department, of marginalization in department decisions and a commonly held view that we were, in the words of a former department chair, the "cheap labor" supporting the "real" work of the department. As is the case in many institutions, we faced implicit and explicit barriers to full participation as faculty in the department

---

2   Degrees of contingent-faculty participation in governance vary widely across institutions; we acknowledge that the favorable climate at AU resulted in part from factors that were not under our control but that nevertheless benefited us.

3   Concurrently, AU was striving to reduce the number of adjunct faculty.

and university. But one of our biggest barriers was our own timidity, our sense that we were neither qualified nor welcome to engage in the larger work of the university. So in order to exploit the changing conditions of the university, we had to overcome that timidity, educate ourselves in the workings of the university, and make inroads at every available opportunity. The three main components of this work were faculty reputation, alliances with tenure-line faculty, and participation in unit and university governance. These components matter because they all pertain to visibility; contingent faculty are often overlooked or ignored. We had to establish ourselves as active, expert faculty members deserving of personal, professional, and policy recognition.

Faculty Reputation

While Maisto rightly points to faculty stability as leading to alliances and the power to enact change, longevity alone isn't enough; we still had to prove ourselves—not through a tenure process, but through a process that lacked codified procedures or clear rules and expectations. In our College Writing Program, we took advantage of the inattention on the part of the tenure-line literature faculty (who saw the literature courses as the real work of the department) to fashion a strong curriculum that served a large number of undergraduates, and we could point to our success as teachers in terms that the university administration valued: while we gave some of the lowest grades in the university, we had, on average, among the highest student evaluations. But we were also able to develop a set of professional standards that reflected the values of our field to use in the reappointment and promotion of writing faculty. For contingent faculty university wide, as the university's undergraduate retention rate increased and NSSE ratings of freshman satisfaction rose, by 2012 it became clear that the large percentage of the full-time faculty who were non-tenured were making an impact on the university's increasing reputation for excellence. One lesson we learned was that with faculty retention and teaching excellence comes a modicum of respect, not just from tenure-line faculty, but from deans and administrators; in other words, the "relationships" that Maisto describes arose because our capable teaching allowed us to be seen as something akin to "faculty."[4]

---

4   Some have argued that the increased reliance on contingent faculty has hurt student learning and engagement and that this harm can be used in persuading administrators to improve contingent-faculty conditions. At AU, however, contingent faculty's success with students was a persuasive point in our arguments to administrators and tenure-track colleagues.

ALLIANCES

Over time, as many contingent faculty became long-term faculty who had strong reputations as committed teachers (and sometimes as productive scholars, too), we found and created opportunities to work with tenure-track faculty across the university. Because our writing program operates within the Department of Literature, the tenure-line "literature" faculty saw us at department meetings and were familiar with our work. Also, our position as composition instructors, teaching academic writing applicable to a number of disciplines, gave us ways to reach out to colleagues across the university. For example, for the university's annual in-house teaching conference, we created multidisciplinary panels to give presentations about teaching writing in different disciplines; on one of these panels, we developed a relationship with a math professor who would go on to chair the senate subcommittee that revised the faculty manual and later become the Vice Provost for Undergraduate Studies. Such initially innocuous connections over time became valuable—even indispensable—partnerships, and many of us began to be seen as individual faculty members, with our own expertise and commitment to the institution, not just as part of the virtually invisible mass of non-tenure-track faculty. And just as importantly, we became acquainted with tenure-track faculty as individuals, not just as part of a privileged group.

GOVERNANCE

As we've noted, College Writing faculty faced the kinds of implicit and explicit barriers to participation in governance that many contingent faculty must confront. As our program's faculty grew and became more stable, we began regularly attending department meetings, and from there, we offered to participate in departmental committees. AU, like many institutions, has some difficulty finding faculty to take on service obligations, so our participation was often welcome—and over time, became expected. As we worked with more people across the university, we expanded our participation, serving on university committees that formed policy and hired administrators. For example, when a search committee for a dean was formed, we made sure that one of our faculty was on the ballot—and then we lobbied our contingent colleagues to vote for that person. These efforts helped us form even more alliances, gain credibility, demonstrate our commitment to the university, and develop political insights and knowledge.

However, opportunities to participate in governance have been mixed at AU, with some departments welcoming contingent-faculty participation and others forbidding it. At the same time, the focus on research productivity for tenure-line faculty has put contingent faculty in administrative positions, such as directing programs, managing labs, and directing artistic productions, and has created opportunities for university service, such as committee work, senate service, and independent work with students. And contingent faculty across the university are taking notice of those departments, such as ours, where their colleagues have full participation in unit governance. Increasingly, contingent-faculty participation in the work of the university is becoming normalized.

THE PROCESS OF CHANGE

As the writing faculty and other contingent faculty across the university were becoming increasingly active and visible, the moment for action came in 2009 when the faculty senate began a comprehensive and long-overdue revision of the faculty manual. The old version of the faculty manual essentially codified the invisibility of contingent faculty—indeed, contingent faculty policies took up one paragraph of a lengthy document. While the faculty themselves were active, engaged, and successful members of the institution, the institutional policies had not yet caught up to the realities of the composition of the faculty as a whole. AU was not unusual in this discrepancy, though; John G. Cross and Edie N. Goldenberg, in their study of non-tenure-track faculty, found that even as those faculty became the "new faculty majority," many tenure-track faculty, administrators, and human-resources personnel paid little attention to them: "Who are the faculty who teach undergraduates on these select campuses, and what are their employment arrangements? One of the major surprises of our study is that nobody seems to know" (3).

The faculty-manual revision process would prove informative in this regard. A draft of the revised manual was distributed to the campus community. The writing program's faculty were taken aback that the proposed extensive changes to the manual did not address AU's contingent faculty. In fact, the one paragraph that had previously described us remained with no additions or revisions. It was as if the university still couldn't see that at that time over one-third of its full-time faculty labored right alongside its tenure-line professors and deserved equitable attention.

Thus, everyone involved was surprised when a large group of contingent faculty and their tenure-line supporters attended the faculty-manual town hall meeting reserved for contingent faculty —what would be the largest turnout of any of the faculty manual committee's town halls. It was a lively and at times contentious gathering, but at the meeting's close, the committee urged us to propose specific changes to the manual's contingent faculty language. It was a first for non-tenured full-time faculty at American: not only had we been invited, as a class, to attend a meeting about university policies governing our positions, we were also being asked to define our concerns and propose solutions. In one day, a previously invisible group suddenly made itself known.

Over the next six months, a small group of writing faculty, who had all worked at the university for some time and had earned the respect of their tenure-line colleagues, proposed changes to the faculty manual sections concerning full-time contingent faculty that included a promotion track, contract lengths, specific criteria for reappointment, and equal access to benefits and policies enjoyed by the tenure-line faculty.[5] We also pushed for language guaranteeing academic freedom for those without tenure.[6] Our experiences over the previous few years helped us in this project: we'd earned respect and credibility by demonstrating our commitment to the university and the students, we'd forged alliances with tenure-track faculty members working on the manual revision (particularly the chair of that committee), and we had some knowledge of the workings of the university so we knew what to ask for. The committee not only adopted all of our proposals, they expanded some of them to accommodate the wide variety of contingent-faculty positions across the university. After faculty senate ratification, faculty vote, and board of trustees ratification, the revised faculty manual, with a long section on contingent faculty, was finalized. In the biggest sense, this document recognized, for the first time, that the university possessed a dedicated teaching faculty that was interested in pursuing these teaching-only positions as academic careers.

CURRENT STATUS AND CHALLENGES THAT REMAIN

The revision and ratification of the faculty manual, which at long last recognized the presence of the majority of faculty, was the largest and most significant change that we've seen in our years at AU. But those of us involved in advocacy didn't view these new policies as the last step in our work; instead, we saw them as the groundwork for changes not just in the language used to describe us and our work but in our actual working conditions and roles in the university.

For example, the new faculty-manual policies inspired a number of questions about how to implement them; a senate committee was formed to create implementation recommendations—which was another opportunity for con-

---

5   The lack of awareness and knowledge of contingent faculty can sometimes work to their advantage: A policy vacuum can also be seen as an opportunity to craft new policy, which is often easier than trying to change entrenched policies and attitudes.

6   Of course, as the AAUP has noted, there is no true academic freedom without tenure, so this language offered just a thin layer of protection and served perhaps more of a symbolic purpose. At the same time, while we're under no illusions that contingent faculty have academic freedom equivalent to that of tenured faculty, the new language at least provides the grounds for contesting violations of academic freedom.

tingent faculty to push for positive change (multiple contingent faculty were on this committee). We proposed—and got—a dedicated seat on the faculty senate for a contingent-faculty member—an opportunity for contingent faculty to have a voice in university policy.[7] And we have earned some tangible rewards: contingent faculty can now earn promotions, more money is available to them for professional development, they have greater protection in cases of financial exigency, and, in the case of College Writing faculty, we successfully argued for a market adjustment in our salaries.

Our work is ongoing, of course. Another iteration of the senate's committee on contingent faculty continues to advocate for better and more consistent working conditions across the university. And a college-level taskforce recently produced a lengthy report detailing the lengths we must go before contingent faculty are treated equitably—as faculty.

So while we've seen positive and heartening changes at AU, and it's been exciting to have been so much a part of those changes, we also see many areas in which we still must work for improvement. For example, even though our status is officially better within the university, hierarchical attitudes persist, to our detriment. Contingent faculty in most institutions face prejudices, as Kezar points out: "non tenure-track faculty are considered to have lesser qualifications, to be less competitive for faculty jobs, to be inferior teachers, to not understand the research process, and to lack the knowledge necessary to contribute toward governance" (Kezar, "Needed" 18). While there is a variety of reasons for such prejudices (for example, at AU, contingent faculty are hired without the intense vetting process used for tenure-track hires), we suspect that these attitudes arise out of tenure-line faculty's unfamiliarity with our contributions to our students and the institution as a whole and out of the tenure-track fear of contingency— that we are some dreadful, growing force just waiting to take over all the jobs. Even those tenure-track faculty who might not fear contingent faculty and might genuinely care about us as faculty members often inadvertently reveal their view of us as "lesser." In the *Chronicle of Higher Education* article on governance changes at AU, a tenured professor praised the changes by saying, "We are treating [contingent] faculty like real people. They may be second-class people, but at least they are real people" (Schmidt, "Faculty" np). The language here is telling; this faculty member both reinforces the class distinctions and the sense that contingent faculty are somehow not quite as legitimate as their tenured colleagues. And of course, these attitudes are widespread. Even those texts that are,

---

7   While contingent faculty have served on the senate fairly regularly as representatives of academic units or committees, it has historically been difficult to get elected as an at-large senator if one is a contingent-faculty member. As a sign of the great changes over the past few years, the current chair of the faculty senate is a contingent-faculty member.

overall, sympathetic to contingent faculty often reveal the authors' prejudices. For example, Cross and Goldenberg have an entire book about the plight of "off-track profs"—with a section detailing the risks they pose to governance: "With full voting rights comes the possibility that untenured specialists will sway votes on issues that are judged likely to affect their own conditions of employment" (133–34). The assumptions here are disturbing: that contingent faculty's interests somehow run counter to the interests of tenure-track faculty (whose interests, presumably, are somehow "better") and the good of the university.

Such comments sting, of course; as faculty members who are fully committed to our careers teaching students and to the university, and who conduct ourselves professionally, we don't want to be characterized as second class or suspect. But emotional reactions aside, such attitudes should matter both to contingent faculty and to the university faculty as a whole because these hierarchical divisions work against our shared goals and against our ability to stand strong when faced with changes to our working conditions. In her article in *Academe*, Anne Cassebaum discusses this loss of collegiality using the terms of organized labor, saying, "When no one uses either *union* or *solidarity*, the administration more easily controls faculty" (n.p.). And in the same issue, Monica Jacobe talks about the necessity of all faculty speaking "collectively" to "align the public sense of the university with reality" (n.p.). As Steve Street asks in his *Chronicle of Higher Education* article, "So why can't faculty members hang together on equity issues? What can stop this trend that has already divided and is about to conquer us?" (n.p.). At a time when higher education is increasingly under attack on a variety of fronts, we need to recognize our common goals, needs, and strengths instead of focusing on historical status distinctions.

We still face more concrete challenges, too, such as the bane of contingent faculty everywhere: numerical student evaluations of teaching. Despite faculty manual language that insists that personnel decisions cannot be based solely on evaluation numbers, contingent faculty get the message, both implicitly and explicitly, that when it comes to reappointment, numbers matter more than anything else. While we were able to use this emphasis on numerical evaluations to our advantage, we have also strived, within our program, to develop more substantive and meaningful evaluation measures. But these measures have not been consistently replicated among administrators evaluating us. We've also learned that other teaching units—in direct contradiction to faculty manual policy—only use student evaluations for reappointment decisions.

Moreover, this emphasis on evaluations, combined with our contingent status, in effect puts our supposed academic freedom out of reach. While the university might insist that yes, we have academic freedom, if students object to what we say, they'll voice their displeasure numerically—and we will lose our jobs because of our ideas and opinions, or perhaps because we have criticized a student's "voice." This problem is creating a large population of faculty members who still want to teach students but who must entertain, please, and not disturb them when doing so—hardly the rigorous and dynamic intellectual environment one would hope for.[8]

But the greatest remaining problem for most contingent faculty, in which all these other issues converge, is inadequate pay. In her *Academe* article, Jacobe describes professors who can't afford to send their children to college themselves. In our own program, we have experienced, full-time faculty who also work as bartenders or nannies in order to make ends meet. And the starting salary for full-time writing faculty puts them in the category of "working poor" in the DC area. These problems extend beyond the less-experienced contingent faculty, and more senior faculty find it difficult to envision a career at our institution when, after ten or fifteen years of employment, they still struggle to maintain a middle-class life. Thus far, our administration has resisted making these across-the-board inequities a priority, and if we are all meant to be university faculty, engaged in the shared endeavors of teaching students and fostering the creation of knowledge, there is an ethical problem: one group earns a comfortable living and the other struggles. There is also the problem of how contingent faculty, under such economic duress, can be expected to be excellent teachers who juggle planning dynamic lessons, responding to student writing, conferencing with students, and keeping abreast of developments in our field—much less participating in the new governance opportunities presented to them.

And the opportunity to participate in governance is, perhaps, a mixed blessing in terms of these ongoing problems. On the one hand, increased participation in governance can lead to the sort of self-congratulation and complacency that work against further progress: Why, you get to vote in department meetings, and you even have a seat on the faculty senate. Look how far you've come—why are you still complaining? Advice to managers often includes the idea that it's better to offer intangible rewards—better titles, for example—so they don't have to actually increase salaries. A seat on the faculty senate doesn't lead to enough pay so a colleague can quit her second job.

Except that it might. As we have noted, our increased credibility, alliances with other faculty, and participation in governance have led to tangible changes in policies and working conditions. Kezar and Sam quote a contingent-faculty member: "You will always be a side order of fries unless you participate in gov-

---

8   College writing faculty are fortunate in that we evaluate each other for reappointment and promotion, just as tenure-track faculty do; we found that once we won the right to review our colleagues, we were evaluated much more substantively, using extensive portfolios.

ernance. Some contingent faculty think governance is a luxury and we should just focus on rights like benefits. But, if you are going to be a real member of the community, treated as a professional, and included, you must participate in governance" (40). And as Peter Schmidt has reported in the *Chronicle of Higher Education*, a recent study indicates that non-tenure-track faculty "had made the most progress at colleges where they tried to transform the campus climate to be more inclusive of them, rather than simply fighting to change one employer practice at a time" ("When Adjuncts" n.p.). This type of transformation can only result when contingent faculty participate in the institution *as* faculty—faculty who are long-serving, collegial, and respected, who demand, implicitly and explicitly, to be seen as full-fledged members of the university faculty.

LESSONS LEARNED

Clearly, AU's contingent faculty used their earned reputations, alliances with tenured faculty and administrators, and participation in unit and university governance to achieve recognition and most importantly, improvement in their working conditions. A benefit of concentrated, long-term advocacy has been that we can see much more clearly where we stand and what still needs to be done. We have also realized the necessity of paying attention to what is transpiring at other institutions, both nationally and regionally, and we've been encouraged by recent white papers published by committees tasked with reforming contingent-faculty working conditions at institutions such as University of Maryland, College Park and Virginia Polytechnic Institute. Three key lessons have become apparent from our work.

START SMALL

We've been realistic in focusing first on uncontroversial goals, such as governance, professional development, and promotion criteria. As Kezar rightly points out, "sometimes getting a change in place quickly builds momentum, so determining the 'low-hanging fruit' can be a helpful strategy" ("Needed" 21).

CREATE A DATA-DRIVEN ENVIRONMENT

Perhaps our biggest realization has been the importance of data collection. As Patricia Hyer points out, a "data-driven environment can help facilitate change by seeing problems and inequities within data collected and through interest in looking at models and benchmarks and comparing to other campuses" (129). But one has to ask the right questions. Two committees—one sponsored by the university senate and the other by the College of Arts and Sciences—issued data-intensive reports on AU's contingent faculty. The senate report, chaired by a tenured faculty member, offered extensive and enlightening institutional data. However, the other report, based on institutional data and self-reported data from approximately one hundred contingent faculty, uncovered two issues not recognized by the senate report: the majority of contingent faculty were serving more than five years on single-year contracts that offered little job security; and their salaries were not only far lower than their tenure-line colleagues, but also could not sustain them. The issues of multi-year contracts and salary equity are budget issues—issues that are likely more controversial than the advances we'd already achieved—and were a sober reminder that perhaps much more difficult advocacy work lay ahead. The awareness of these crucial issues for our contingent colleagues also has made us realize that we need to create an action plan if any progress is to be made on these fronts.

Realize that the Process is Fundamentally Political

Perhaps the most important lesson we can take from the decade of preparation and advocacy is the realization that change is a finely tuned political process. In our early years of advocating inside our teaching unit, we experienced the same learning process as faculty did at Villanova when advocating for change: "When they relied solely on logic, empathy, morality, or rationale, their proposed changes were often met with resistance. . . . One cannot underestimate the importance of maximizing existing relationships, advocating for needed changes, and actually gathering votes" (Kezar, "Building" 186). We built such relationships—by improving our reputation, creating alliances within our teaching unit and beyond, and participating wherever allowed in unit and university governance. But such a process takes time, and that time necessarily makes change a sometimes painfully slow process.

CONCLUSION

When we look back over the changes that have happened at AU over the past fifteen years, we are heartened that an academic institution such as ours, which is by nature tradition-bound, hierarchical, and risk averse, can adapt positively to a changed workplace environment that mirrors the national situation. But while a number of tenure-line colleagues worked willingly and hard to effect those adaptations, contingent faculty, such as those of us in the writing program, fought for years in our department for equal political rights, and the literature department, no more or less conservative than any other department, adapted, sometimes with some heat, to the reality that half of its full-time faculty were working off the tenure track. Those changes only came about because we were all colleagues who saw one another every day and who were part of a department that values democratic discourse and analytical thought. Proximity, however, wasn't sufficient; our reputations as excellent teachers, our building of alliances with friendly tenure-track colleagues, and our strong participation in service and governance gave us leverage. And winning over our tenure-track departmental colleagues had two great outcomes: it taught us how to persuade an insular, conservative professoriate of the necessity of recognizing that the academic world had changed, and it gave us the confidence and ability to take the fight on behalf of all of our contingent faculty colleagues to the entire university.

WORKS CITED

Cassebaum, Anne. "Memory Loss." *Academe*, Sept./Oct. 2011, aaup.org/article/memory-loss#.WDidi30XvkY.

Cross, John G., and Edie N. Goldenberg. *Off-Track Profs: Nontenured Teachers in Higher Education*. MIT P, 2009.

Hyer, Patricia. "The Instructor Career Ladder and Addressing the Needs of Research Faculty: Evolving Policies at Virginia Tech." *Embracing Non-Tenure Track Faculty: Changing Campuses for the New Faculty Majority*, edited by Adrianna Kezar, Routledge, 2012, pp. 190–204.

Jacobe, Monica. "Making It." *Academe*, Sept./Oct. 2011, aaup.org/article/making-it#.WDiewH0XvkY. Aug. 2013.

Kezar, Adrianna. "Building a Multi-prong, Context-Based Strategy for Change at a Private Catholic College." *Embracing Non-Tenure Track Faculty: Changing Campuses for the New Faculty Majority*, edited by Adrianna Kezar, Routledge, 2012, pp. 190–204.

———. "Needed Policies, Practices, and Values: Creating a Culture to Support and Professionalize Non-tenure Track Faculty." *Embracing Non-Tenure Track Faculty: Changing Campuses for the New Faculty Majority*, edited by Adrianna Kezar, Routledge, 2012, pp. 2–27.

Kezar, Adrianna, and Cecile Sam. "Strategies for Implementing and Institutionalizing New Policies and Practices: Understanding the Change Process." *Embracing Non-Tenure Track Faculty: Changing Campuses for the New Faculty Majority*, edited by Adrianna Kezar, Routledge, 2012, pp. 190–204.

Maisto, Maria. "Taking Heart, Taking Part: New Faculty Majority and the Praxis of Contingent Faculty Activism." *Embracing Non-Tenure Track Faculty: Changing Campuses for the New Faculty Majority*, edited by Adrianna Kezar, Routledge, 2012, pp. 190–204.

Schmidt, Peter. "Faculty Leaders at American U. Seek Old-School Rights for a New Work Force." *Chronicle of Higher Education*, 12 June 2011, chronicle.com/article/Faculty-Leaders-at-American-U/127883/.

———. "When Adjuncts Push for Better Status, Better Pay Follows, Study Suggests." *Chronicle of Higher Education*, 1 Nov. 2009, chronicle.com/article/When-Adjuncts -Push-for-Better/48988/.

Street, Steve. "Why Don't We Insist on Equity?" *Chronicle of Higher Education*, 2 Dec. 2010, chronicle.com/article/Why-Dont-We-Insist-on-Equity-/125557/.

CHAPTER 14

WHAT WORKS AND WHAT COUNTS: VALUING THE AFFECTIVE IN NON-TENURE-TRACK ADVOCACY

Sue Doe

Colorado State University

Maria Maisto

New Faculty Majority and the NFM Foundation

Janelle Adsit

Humboldt State University

Threads: Self-Advocacy; Organizing Within and Cross Ranks

It is not uncommon in 2017, even among those seeking social justice, to uncritically accept and use the economic language *du jour* with its allegiance to notions of productivity. We submit that this emphasis on output and efficiency is increasingly characteristic of advocacy discussions around contingency in the academic labor force and that such an emphasis can be deleterious to the people (students in one context and contingent faculty in the other) that it seeks to support. Having now reached a degree of maturity, the academic labor movement is certainly at a moment when material change must be demanded and achieved. Indeed, it is appropriate that at this point we expect to see action and outcomes. Yet it is also important to recognize that social change is not linear but proceeds as a series of starts and stops. Movements go through stages, including one that activist and author Bill Moyer (not to be confused with the journalist) has called the stage of "identity crisis and powerlessness." At this stage, which often takes place at precisely the moment when a movement has begun to "take off," it is common for activists, paradoxically, to feel despair. Moyer notes that it is not unusual for activists at this stage to decry the lack of "'real' victories." As Moyer puts it:

> This view is unable to accept the progress that the movement
> has made along the road of success, such as creating a mas-
> sive grassroots-based social movement, putting the issue on
> society's agenda, or winning a majority of public opinion.
> Ironically, involvement in the movement tends to reduce
> activists' ability to identify short-term successes. Through the
> movement, activists learn about the enormity of the problem,
> the agonizing suffering of the victims, and the complicity of
> powerholders. The intensity of this experience tends to in-
> crease despair and the unwillingness to accept any short-term
> success short of achieving ultimate goals.

In such contexts and impatient to achieve these ultimate goals, activists may fixate on the outcomes of the movement, ignoring subtle but important shifts that have occurred and the emotional reorientations that have followed, both of which may be more difficult to identify and quantify than idealized outcomes. We are particularly interested in emotion both as a catalyst and as a reorienta-tion. As Moyer's observations suggest, the tendency to focus on outcomes and to exclude emotion may, ironically, be coming out of a deeply emotional response to the evolution of the movement—one of doubt, despair, or even a kind of existential agony around lost causes.

A movement's trajectory is not necessarily linear, and it is not necessarily programmable into a set of fixed outcomes. Measuring success by a limited set of predetermined outcomes can cause activists to overlook important work that is not readily measurable and to be dismissive of unexpected variations on suc-cess. Wary of the pervasive, market-driven language of productivity, we therefore argue that effective advocacy is not necessarily contained in large-scale attain-ments but in the small changes that are characteristic of the slow and plodding work of culture change. The ideology of productivity, rooted as it is in the mar-ket economy, can risk sanitizing advocacy of the very humanity that underlies its conviction, displacing the circulating emotions that called for a response in the first place. It can be dismissive of hard-wrought incremental victories and unseen important steps and realizations that occur along the way. It can glide over the affective economies associated with the commitment and effort entailed in sustained advocacy. Perhaps most ironically for the academic labor move-ment, it can trivialize the labor associated with advocacy and as a result demor-alize those who undertake it.

The relentless push for productive practices and quantifiable outcomes in advocacy can thus reinforce and appropriate the same managerial approaches that contribute to the exploitation of academics. In calling for a "move beyond emotion," we risk falling into a managerial imperative that works to "change the attitude" of the workers it marshals for programmatic ends, without changing the structures that condition these emotions and attitudes. To focus on the programmatic outcomes of activist work to the exclusion of the affective and material realities of its workers is to fall into this kind of managerial discourse wherein disparaging the affective realities of faculty members slides swiftly into an "increasingly negative view of teachers as chaotic, disordered bodies in need of professional [outcomes-based] discipline" (Strickland 64). Calls to "transition from affect to action" implicitly locate the reason for slow change within the contingent faculty members themselves—in pathologizing affect as stymying real change and in privatizing emotion as an internal state, rather than taking seriously the ways that emotion is culturally conditioned and circulating (Ahmed, *Cultural Politics*). This suggests a paternalism that adds troubling layers of complexity to the interplay of affect and advocacy.

It is in this highly contested context, querying the role of emotion and affect in adjunct advocacy, that we situate our work. If, as we believe, emotion and outcry foment dissent, then policies, such as professional association position statements, codify the changes demanded by outcry. Emotion and action thus exist in relation to each other and are even, perhaps, commensal. Shortchanging emotion in favor of action risks dismissing the corporeal realities of those who experience the phenomenon of contingency. We therefore argue that the relationship between emotion and action might be explored more fully by considering alternative forms of advocacy, such as listening and storying, which are genres of understanding that connect to the affective. To demonstrate how such affective advocacy can work, we offer a pair of cases where emotion has been connected to real, if incremental, change. Following our affective analyses of these cases, we present our own experiences with affective advocacy, suggesting that these, too, constitute cases while also suggesting usable techniques for moving forward. To begin, though, we justify our varied research approaches as reflective of our feminisms.

A FEMINIST REVISIONING OF ADVOCACY

The conviction to do something about the academic labor situation is fueled by understandable impatience, but *doing* is accompanied by *feeling*. Emotion causes us to act, and it saturates our action, but this key part of the advocacy process tends to get lost in academic contexts, where faculty members are educated to distrust the pathos of the individual story and to favor the scientific standard of generalizability, to move quickly, one might say, from affect to effect. To signal our resistance to the dominant paradigm of generalizability and emotional detachment, which we view as part of a masculinist and hegemonic economic metaphor, we discuss documented cases of emotion's role in academic labor advocacy as well as provide personal stories about situations that have motivated us to action. We participate in activities consistent with the ethical, methodological, and epistemological features of feminist research, including self-disclosure, empowerment of participants, the equalization of the status of the researcher and the research subject, considerations of our own positionality and our own critical self-reflexivity—all of which we see as obligatory functions of inquiry and action. With Shalumit Reinharz and Lynn Davidman, we hold ourselves constrained to no single set of approaches but assert instead the right and the necessity of activist rhetoricians to utilize a range of methods as an explicit counterargument to traditional inquiry and reporting practices (12). As such, our approach includes analysis of both texts and experience.

Furthermore, in asserting the validity of emotion as a component of effective advocacy, we argue along with Sandra Harding for "alternative origins of problematics" (preface) and assert that "there is no such thing as a problem without a person: a problem is always a problem *for* someone or other" (6). Moreover, with Rebecca Campbell and Sharon Wasco, we take the feminist epistemological stance which accepts "women's stories of their lives as legitimate sources of knowledge" and a feminist methodological approach by undertaking the "ethic of caring through the process of sharing those stories" (778). We further argue along with Campbell and Wasco that there should be an acknowledgement of the emotionality of research, a recognition that feelings shape research and form "a natural part of inquiry" (786). With Mary Margaret Fonow and Judith Cook we offer a "refusal to ignore the emotional dimension of the conduct of inquiry," arguing instead for the central role of the affective in the production of knowledge (9). Moreover, with feminist methodologists, we elevate the "situation at hand," or the everyday lived experience of marginalization as an otherwise "hidden process" that we are compelled to uncover (11).

With these theoretical tools, we reexamine examples of both documented and personal activism in light of their affective dimensions and contexts; in doing so, we hope to bring to light the role of affect in effectiveness. We divide this discussion into two major parts. First, we examine two texts as "cases," starting with the landmark artifact of emotion in academic labor advocacy—the Wyoming Resolution—which arguably launched mainstream discussions of adjunct labor within professional associations. As a second case and textual artifact, we examine Catherine Stukel's letter to the editor of the *Chronicle of Higher Education*, "Is that Whining Adjunct Someone We Want Teaching Our Young?" which came thirty years after Wyoming and shows how slow attitudes can be to change even when advocacy has been robust. We then turn to examine our own stories, our non-generalizable selves, asserting that it was emotion that got each of us going, and emotion that keeps us going even today as academic laborers and activists. We show how our varying contexts led to techniques that might be described as advocacy fueled by emotion, or affective advocacy—Maria through leadership of a national advocacy nonprofit; Sue through arts-based institutional critique; and Janelle through her own charting of an academic career. Our purpose is to examine the emotions that accompany advocacy and activism, to show how social change is spurred by and maintained through emotion. We put this examination forward in genres of understanding—reading each artifact and testimony as unique windows onto the problem of academic labor.

CASE 1: HOW EMOTION CAN CATALYZE ACTION: REVISITING THE WYOMING RESOLUTION

The Wyoming Resolution was an exercise in emotion and an example of both independent argument and preparation for other arguments (CCCC Committee; CCCC Executive Committee; Robertson et al.). Some might say that the Wyoming Resolution was a single intensely felt moment, followed by years of machinations, intrigue, and inertia, but the importance of Wyoming can hardly be denied as a catalyst, a game-changer that assured it would no longer be possible to glide over the costs of unjust academic labor policies. While some might argue that Wyoming was a failure, justice delayed and hence denied, others would argue that Wyoming was among the first in a series of revelatory moments in the academic labor movement, the end of which is nowhere in sight. Here we describe how the Wyoming Conference and the Resolution that resulted were steeped in emotion, and how emotion did not undermine the argument but instead caused the stage to change, the conversation to reset. The Wyoming Resolution marked a moment wherein the re-alignment of academic labor could no longer be denied or ignored but instead demanded to be noted.

In their 2011 article in *College English*, James McDonald and Eileen Schell describe the role of affect in the event of the Wyoming Conference which eventually led to the Resolution. From McDonald and Schell's description we can envision the intimate context of that Conference wherein friendships and professional relationships were cemented, forged, and catapulted forward. Indeed there seems to have been a kind of hiatus on academic rank hierarchies and untouchable topics that was unofficially called in that space. They describe graduate students conducting "inkshedding" at the end of each day; their versions of the day's events, like the conversation in "the ladies room," offering a different view on events than the official responses and receptions (McDonald and Schell). A context of candor seems to have provided space for growing murmurs of discontent and the growth of feeling that eventually bubbled to the surface. James Sledd, in his talk at a regular session, lamented the conditions under which composition instructors and programs labored, to which he received great applause. But then his talk was ignored during the discussion period, leading Susan Wyche, according to Schell and McDonald, to stand up at the urging of others and demand that the conversation follow Sledd's lead. She asked, "What is happening here?" (365). She then spoke of her own oppression and that of her students. Schell and McDonald report this moment in the language of emotion—Wyche describing herself as having "choked out each word" before she "sat down and *burst into tears*" [italics ours] (365). She was subsequently shuttled off to her hotel room and left alone for about an hour, as presumably she needed this time to recover. Senior faculty meanwhile reconvened at a local bar and began discussing strategy and drafting a resolution for the professional association, presumably in the rational, if shaken, tones of senior faculty called to action. McDonald and Schell describe this entire event as "the turning point of the conference" (364).

We repeat this story at some length because we see the affect-reason binary at work in its details. A formal talk's difficult topic (Sledd's talk) was initially sidestepped by attendees, arguably due to its proximity to a felt tear in the fabric of the profession. It was then recovered by Wyche, who had personal experience with that tear. Yet given her positionality as an adjunct, to call out the issue after a sidestepping of it by others of more senior status required confrontation with her own emotions—among them, we imagine, fear and courage—as well as that of others, which likely included shame, embarrassment and anger. Wyche had to summon great strength to speak to her experience and status, thus illustrating the emotional labor demanded of the activist. In turn, the tenured leadership then gathered to strategize, a highly rational approach more readily available to those functioning from a position of power and authority. Yet that rationality appears also to have been tempered by a new-found sense of forceful and resolute conviction that something had to be done. This initial conversation took place in a bar, perhaps connoting that a stiff drink was needed as these leaders took on what they knew to be the difficult task at hand. In any case, a resolution of lasting importance resulted. That this resolution was followed by as yet unfinished decades of discussion and revision does not detract from the importance of Wyoming as a demonstration of emotion's importance and gravity. Rather, this moment, infused as it was with emotion and commitment, sparked efforts to formalize positions and policy statements by the Conference on College Composition and Communication and its parent organization the National Council of Teachers of English as well as the MLA. Arguably, the move toward formalizing and regulating had the effect of diluting and cooling the Wyoming

Resolution's call for change, but it did not squelch it. It might be said that emotion launched the ship of labor advocacy among professional organizations.

The Wyoming Resolution stands as an essential moment in the affective history of the non-tenure-track faculty movement. It was a moment characterized by a panoply of emotions ranging from incredulity to shame to outrage and then capitulating toward reasoned accommodation and compromise. While the initial moment of galvanization has been followed by years of struggle and eroded expectations, the Wyoming Conference and its associated Resolution nonetheless launched passionate conversations that are still going on. Those conversations have led to some changes, however glacial, which have been fueled by the understandings that were first confronted there. The Wyoming Resolution should thus be read as an important and legitimate advocacy effort, even though it may not fit with certain definitions of "outcomes" or "products." The example provided by the Wyoming Resolution demonstrates that affective work may not produce linear or predictable results yet may still be a driver for long-term change. The Wyoming Resolution stands in the archives as a clear example of the power of emotion to incite a group toward change and to begin processes that move toward progress.

CASE 2: HOW EMOTIONS CAN BE RE-READ: THE WHINING ADJUNCT

A second artifact suggesting the role of "feeling" in the history and development of effective advocacy efforts is Catherine Stukel's recent letter to the editor in the *Chronicle of Higher Education* "Is That Whining Adjunct Someone We Want Teaching Our Young?" This artifact suggests that making unhappiness known can be a powerful act of advocacy, but in an environment where happiness is the "expected 'default position' for those who are oppressed" (Ahmed, *Promise* 66), there is great risk in expressing unhappiness. Nearly thirty years after Wyoming, Stukel states, "I cannot comprehend why any adjunct professor complains with such entitlement about their inability to get a full-time teaching position." She characterizes the adjunct professor as an adolescent with a sense of entitlement, "in a new world where every child is special." Becoming infantilized in this way is one of the risks of making unhappiness known. Stukel's letter thus represents the ideology that happiness is something that one can achieve or fail to achieve. Happiness is constructed to be a personal endeavor that is divorced from context. "Sometimes we fail to achieve happiness no matter what our line of work or income is," Stukel writes. The adjunct professor can achieve happiness and "inner peace" despite circumstances, in Stukel's view, so all the "whining" is unjustified and is a sign of poor personal character—the kind of character that we don't want in front of the classroom. Stukel's letter ends with the injunction to "be happy," affirming the hegemonic meritocratic belief that those who are not happy have only themselves to blame.

Because of such conceptions of emotion, those who demonstrate unhappiness can become further marginalized. "You might refuse proximity to somebody out of fear that you will be infected by unhappiness," Ahmed notes, and, in this moving away from the unhappy other, "certain bodies are pushed to the margins, in order that the unhappiness that is assumed to reside within these bodies does not threaten the happiness that has been given" (*Promise* 97–98). The "disgruntled adjunct"—like the "feminist killjoy" or the "unhappy queer"— is further marginalized because of her unhappiness.

Yet "[w]e must stay unhappy with this world" (*Promise* 105), Ahmed claims, if there is cause for changing it. Occluding, pathologizing, or minimizing the emotional constellations that come under the rubric of "unhappiness" is thus a quietist gesture that affirms the status quo. Here Ahmed does not mean to affirm a model of the heroic, unhappy revolutionary "whose suffering is a gift to the world" (169), but she does find a necessity for unhappiness in activist efforts. Happiness signals an acceptance of the status quo. Unhappiness stirs things up. Ahmed sees the "political will to be affected by unhappiness . . . as a political freedom" (195). Unhappy emotions are, in this sense, active. They are "creative responses" to conditions (217), and they are ripe for instigating change.

Making unhappiness known is one step, but effective advocacy may also require conversations about what counts as valid emotion, about emotional normativity and how unhappiness comes up against emotional expectations that affirm the status quo. Stukel's editorial was prompted by an adjunct union's use of the Margaret Mary Vojtko story as an emotional appeal to galvanize support. In order for such emotional appeals to be received, open dialogue about the workings and expectations of emotion may be a necessary part of affective advocacy work. Publicly raised questions about how emotions are interpreted and evaluated can prompt critical thought and dialogue about how an adjunct professor comes to be dismissively designated as "whiny."

This example suggests that to affirm the emotion/rationality and affect/action binaries is not only conceptually problematic, it also may have damaging and marginalizing effects. It can reaffirm the "[p]sychologically reductive accounts that pathologized protest and protesters," which Deborah Gould notes, "did not die out in the nineteenth century but rather continue to circulate widely today" (19). As Gould explains, those "with a vested interest in maintaining the status quo frequently describe social justice activists as driven by emotion (which they pit against reason) and protest activities as irrational and childish, rather than a legitimate mode" of advocacy (19). Ahmed echoes this point in *The Promise of Happiness,* describing the common conception of the "angry activist" as one who commits "acts of senseless violence, which stops any hearing of ways in which revolution makes sense. . . . [T]he revolutionaries expose violence, but the violence they expose is not recognized as violence: structural violence is violence that is veiled" (170). These preconceptions surrounding activism help to explain how a sit-in can be construed as a violent act that warrants the use of pepper spray and batons by police counterforces. These preconceptions promote fear as they figure the activist as irrational and violent, the assumed results of an overly emotive positionality. Yet we can think of academic labor activism as exposing the *unhappy effects* of policies and hiring practices that characterize higher education. Identifying the "sadness" of the "sad women in the basement" (Miller) remains a powerful means of recognizing the problems of academic labor conditions. While "sadness equals injustice" is a false equivalence (as we should also not equate the "happy" with the "good"), unhappy emotions—like physical pain—make us acutely aware of the conditions pressed upon us.

Taken together, the Wyoming Resolution and the Whining Adjunct letter shed light on the false emotion-action binary. Emotions may be a primary means of collective action as they are always already shaping our allegiances and ways of being. Sara Ahmed convincingly makes this case, arguing that "emotions align some bodies with others . . . by the way they move us" (*Cultural Politics* 195). These bodies are part of what Ahmed calls "affective economies," which are "social and material, as well as psychic" (46). While affect is to some degree beyond our control or decision, as Denise Riley and John Protevi have reminded, we can also make use of emotional resources, knowing that expressions of anger and despair have material effects and can work to bring people together to move toward collectivized action. For Protevi, "Affect is inherently political." Because "bodies are part of an ecosocial matrix of other bodies, affecting them and being affected by them: affect is part of the basic constitution of bodies politic" (50).

The process of accounting for emotion is not a preliminary or nascent stage of political activism that we need to move beyond. Too often, emotional accounts are dismissed as a type of adolescent need for expression of personal anger and frustration. In these common conceptualizations, emotional expressions of anger and frustration are separated from the "real work" of rational argument and action. Similarly, accounts that emphasize "softer" emotions, such as compassion, are often dismissed as naiveté or cowardice that require replacement with shrewdness and savvy. The logical/affective division implied in such claims is untenable (not least because of the sexism that is embedded within it) as emotions "involve a stance on the world, or a way of apprehending the world" (Ahmed, *Cultural Politics* 7) that is deeply embedded in the so-called "rational" ways of knowing. Moreover, "cool rationality" is an emotional style, as Lauren

Berlant notes (27). She argues that "The seeming detachment of rationality . . . is not detachment at all, but an emotional style associated normatively with a rhetorical practice" (27). Real work, it turns out, is always invested and is always emotional. The emotional styles we perform matter, and they should be continually put up for examination.

To claim a need to move beyond emotion is to obscure the role of emotion in social change and erase the material processes that give rise to—and are shaped by—emotional realities. Emphasizing the role of emotion in protest and social change, we can reread social history, as Mihnea Moldoveanu and Nitin Nohria do, "as a set of emotional dynamics, of struggles, games and dialectics played out by embodied feelings" (230).

ENTER NOW OUR NON-GENERALIZABLE SELVES, OR HOW MASTER PASSIONS AND AFFECTIVE ATTACHMENTS HAVE GUIDED OUR ACTIONS

As individuals, we three—Sue, Maria, and Janelle—have experienced moments that catapulted us into action. We explain some of those moments in the paragraphs that follow, situating our stories within the notion of "master passions"—i.e., emotions and emotion-narratives that "cut across people" and both "generate and are generated by social phenomena" (Moldoveanu and Nohria 3)—and inviting others to consider the moments that have moved them toward action. We might all ask: To what extent have affective responses, such as the felt anguish of ourselves or another, moved us to action? We then move toward a discussion of the forms of affective activism these circumstances have led us to undertake.

Maria has told the various stories that comprise her personal journey to activism in several venues (in *Inside Higher Education* and *Working Class Studies* and at the Campaign for the Future of Higher Education Columbus Conference). These stories all have in common the theme of a sudden realization—not the warm illumination of insight and inspiration, but rather the jolting or chilling fear that accompanies the perception of danger and precipitates a fight-or-flight response. In Maria's case, that response was to fight, and to fuel the determination to fight with the anger that could otherwise be self-destructive.

The first story, which she related in a 2009 *Inside Higher Ed* essay modeled on a 1971 feminist manifesto and titled "The Adjunct's Moment of Truth," described how in late 2008, Maria had joined forces with activists across the country who were determined to start a national nonprofit organization—New Faculty Majority—to focus exclusively on the contingent faculty crisis. However, in the spring of 2009 Maria's husband lost his job, having fallen prey in part to vicious workplace politics. Maria was faced with the terrifying prospect of singlehandedly supporting, as an adjunct, a very young family, which included a toddler and a child with special needs. At the same time, her fury at the injustice that had been perpetrated on her husband by his employer, a Catholic school, concretized her experience of the institutional hypocrisy that afflicts higher education as deeply as it afflicts the Catholic Church. Maria gratefully accepted the financial support of extended family and the moral support of her newfound colleagues—both critical to her ability and desire to fight rather than to fly.

In later public accounts, one at a conference of the Campaign for the Future of Higher Education and another for the journal *Working Class Studies*, Maria described more complex emotional experiences that sustain her activism but also have roots in fear and anger. At the conference, during a session designed to address the power imbalances between tenure-track and non-tenure-track faculty, she described how a tenured male colleague responded to her request for feedback on a teaching demonstration that might have led to a full-time job. Rather than say anything about her teaching, he complimented her on the physical beauty of her hands. Startled and dismayed, even as she was conscious of her need to support her family, she suppressed the desire to confront him and soon found herself mired in the self-doubt and anger that is all too familiar to too many women whose economic vulnerability is deepened by experiences of personal and institutional sexism in both micro and macro forms. Meanwhile, in the *Working Class Studies* piece, she reflected on how her experience of her own family's working class roots helped her understand the class-based fear that stands in the way of many adjunct faculty members' efforts to self-advocate.

In each of these experiences, activism—both in the organizing work and in the public engagement these essays embodied—was not just action for a greater cause but was both consciously and unconsciously, personally and professionally, therapeutic. Not only did the activism mitigate the destructive power of the fear that these experiences engendered, it also revitalized Maria's teaching, as she felt reconnected to pedagogical purpose and process. Maria's example suggests that while particular constellations of local and individual variables will always shape lived experiences, certain "master passions"—often, frustration and anger—emerge from accounts of working conditions. While an equation of "bad feeling equals injustice" is always too simple (Ahmed, *Cultural Politics* 193), frustration and anger can readily become externalized and channeled into speech and action. Furthermore, by tapping into master passions, it is possible for the iconic slogan "the personal is political" to be deftly flipped, allowing social consciousness to double as self-care, both personal and professional, to the benefit of teacher and students alike.

For Sue, the master passion of empathy and the recognition of its complements—anger and care of self—led to advocacy and activism. In the fall of 2004—twenty years into her adjunct career, three years before she obtained that rarest of commodities, a tenure-track position, and ten years since the most recent pay raise to the base salary of contingent faculty in her local setting—a short experiment came to a close. In this experiment, a few instructors had been hired under improved circumstances that were associated with higher pay and the assurance of two years of employment. In the summer of that year, prior to the start of classes and under the leadership of a new dean, it was disclosed that these somewhat secure appointments were in violation of Colorado law which held that all non-tenure-track faculty were employees at-will and that the university had no legal right to enter into contract (for one day, much less two years) with an at-will employee, a law that wasn't rescinded until 2012. When Sue's officemate, who held one of these positions, returned from her second day of teaching having just found out that her "better job" was no longer in place and that she had neither modest job security nor the pay she had been promised nor even the courtesy of notification before the start of the semester, Sue was incensed. Although activated by the sight of her colleague's marginalization, Sue was not yet at the place where she could recognize her own. Rather, at this moment, when Sue's friend and colleague returned from class betrayed and hurt, she saw only that her friend was being badly treated. Sue undertook a series of what were risky acts such as calling the Provost's office and demanding a personal appointment. Within weeks, Sue had organized a press conference and invited state elected officials to hear about the adjunct's plight. A few weeks later, and bolstered by the support of a key tenure-track faculty member, Sue authored a letter to the provost that argued for an immediate salary increase and implicitly threatened a walk-out.

These initial moments, conducted largely in a kind of blinding rage, led to other more measured but arguably less effective approaches. For instance, when asked by her Dean's office (and subsequent to these initial efforts) to lead a newly formed college committee for adjuncts—which was to be exclusively focused on non-tenure-track faculty working conditions and status—Sue started learning about participation in shared governance. She initially imagined there being inherent value in having a seat at the table and saw participation in governance as the coin of the realm. But eventually she saw that her advocacy was being coopted and redirected toward sanctioned efforts led by administrators. Soon she was asked to be part of a task force that eventually led to the creation of a standing committee reporting to the faculty senate, even as contingent faculty had no representation on that senate. Through such flatteries of inclusion was her energy diverted. However, she and colleagues began to chip away at the soft edges of institutional vulnerability, asserting, for instance, that if the faculty manual said faculty had certain rights, then unless it stipulated otherwise, those rights belonged to all faculty, not just those on the tenure track. These events became an education in the machinations of institutional authority and power, even as they also introduced Sue to the opportunities and limits of non-emotive advocacy. Sue came to understand how a "governance" approach to activism can use existing, rational mechanisms to argue for change, but such efforts also involve the management and control of faculty (of all ranks) and seek to domesticate the emotions of disgruntled workers. Piecemeal participation in shared governance, she began to see, functions less as an opportunity for change agency than as the institutional regulation of faculty emotion, a taming of an unruly body politic.

For Janelle, the master passions of grief and anxiety thread through her experiences of higher education. Janelle lost her sister in a tragic accident in 2007, a week before Janelle graduated from college; consequently, the start of Janelle's professional life was shaped by the consciousness of the imminent proximity of loss and an acute awareness of the shortness of life. A few short years later, as she reached the end of her Ph.D. program, she realized that when strategizing a career in the anxious context of current academic hiring practices, one cannot assume that things will fall into place—or that they will remain in place. She was again made acutely aware of life's fragility and her own vulnerability. Learning steadily about the nature of contingency, she found that the scarcity of available positions converted to a sense of urgency, which translated into a felt need—responsibility even—to take the first position that was offered. It was this context—overlaid with the grievable recognition that life can be cut too short— that led Janelle to accept and hold a full-time non-tenure-track teaching position as a writing center director and unofficial WPA before she finished her Ph.D. This position required thirty-five hours a week on campus but did not include office space. Janelle says that new scholars like herself, even if they have not had an experience of great and sudden loss/vulnerability, are receiving the message, intentionally sent or not, that they are working in a market where they must take whatever they can get, whenever they can get it.

Before defending her Ph.D., Janelle had taught at a small Catholic college, a smaller private art school and at a large state research university. The one commonality among the radically different contexts was that they all shared bleak labor conditions—lack of office space, low wages, uncertainty surrounding continued funding, and recurring layoffs. These conditions, Janelle has since concluded, are for new scholars the "air they breathe" since many have known no other reality. This fact conditions their approach to the job market and leads to further disenfranchisement as applicants feel that they are in no position to negotiate for better conditions. To choose to negotiate or to not accept the first position offered, is a great risk—one that Janelle was not initially able to take. Rather, given today's academic climate and her own personal loss, she was hyper-conscious of the potential truncation of life's opportunities, and strategizing a career meant taking the first position that was offered, even when there were clear indications of problems with the work environment. Ultimately, the same survival reflex that prompted Janelle to take the writing center administrative position also motivated her to leave it. Although it took some courage to leave, her professional survival, it became clear, depended upon her doing so. She resigned from this position after less than a year, choosing instead a dedicated research postdoctoral fellowship that would allow her to better position herself on the job market and build toward a better future in higher education.

Acknowledging the master passions and master narratives that maintain and work upon individual careers and institutional policies is an important part of the academic activist project. Master passions motivate us and stick with us as we shape our careers and our institutions. Knowing these master passions and the ways they work can help us to do our work more effectively. Also, the case study, the testimony, the personal story—these genres of understanding—can provide us with intimate knowledge of the master passions as they operate in academic contexts and advocacy efforts. These genres can prompt empathy, but such channeling of emotion actually amounts to more than a mere "change of attitude" or privatizing of emotion. Emotions can enact change. Harnessing this potential is the work of affective advocacy, as we now discuss.

OUR ADVOCACY AND ACTIVISM: HOW EMOTION INFORMS OUR WORK

Our initial contexts led to varying forms of advocacy. As Moyer explains in the passage referenced earlier, the experience of disillusionment and despair that comes through intense confrontation with the emotional realities of movement building can best be understood as success rather than failure when the big picture, the "long term strategic framework," is kept in mind. In light of this, we extend our personal cases to identify some of the techniques of emotion that we have witnessed and used in our activist work.

For Maria, the challenges of establishing and helping to lead a national advocacy organization exclusively focused on transforming academic contingency have, for more than five years, intersected with her efforts to advocate for her son, who is on the autism spectrum. Having discovered that special education students and their teachers are often treated as "adjunct" to the general education population consisting of neurotypical students, she has had to employ many of the same skills and much of the same effort to advocate for his right to what is called in federal legislation a Free and Appropriate Public Education (FAPE) and to being educated in a Least Restrictive Environment. As she has tried to negotiate for her son a complex, but legally required, balance between unmarked inclusion and individualized support, the parallels with advocacy for contingent faculty have become apparent. Her son became unable to attend school due in no small part to the school's inability to provide him with appropriate support because it could not (or would not) provide his teachers, especially the ones most committed to supporting him, with the professional support that they need. The slogan "faculty working conditions are student learning conditions" became as real to her and her son as it is for millions of college students and faculty.

Faced then with the prospect of an unwarranted truancy charge, she came to understand what is known as "the school to prison pipeline" which indiscriminately channels "difficult" disadvantaged students—overwhelmingly those who are poor, minorities and/or students with disabilities—into segregated, often disciplinary and punitive programs. This is the school system's preferred method of "bringing to scale" practices which are supposed to address—but more often are meant to control—student need. Maria knows that the school had been expecting her simply to extricate her son from the pipeline that usually hums along without disruption, particularly since she fits the profile of the type of parent who can choose this option. However, aside from the fact that economic reality prevented her from making this choice, she also knew that if she did this, the school would have no incentive to change its coercive and regressive treatment of children on the spectrum. So her personal decision to advocate for her son's rights was also a conscious decision to connect those rights to the rights of all students with disabilities and indeed, by extension, of all students. Indeed, as her advocacy for her son has taken shape, she has realized the degree to which her son's fate, along with those of her other children, are intertwined with the fates of their classmates and their teachers. As a result of this highly personal experience, Maria has found it easier to argue, in the arena of contingent faculty advocacy, for the importance of solidarity in all its forms, highlighting the interconnectedness of members of the educational system. The challenges of forging solidarity between part-timers and full-timers; contingent faculty with M.A.s and those with Ph.D.s; tenure-track faculty and non-tenure-track faculty; faculty and administrators; activists of different gender identities; academic laborers and so-called "unskilled" laborers; college professors and K-12 teachers—all become more real, but also more able to be overcome.

In Sue's case, the period since becoming tenure-track has been as much about learning the ropes as about attempting to use or change them. Her experience has involved a kind of transmogrification, a self-conscious adoption of the language of the master in order to challenge it. With her research agenda focused on the rhetorics of academic labor, she aims to use her tenure to talk back to its privilege, but her sense of vulnerability remains central to the core of her being, sometimes stifling her voice and her ability to address large concerns. So she was perhaps especially attuned to emerging opportunities when a graduate student introduced her to the work of Jim Walsh and the Romero Theater Troupe of Denver.

The Romero Troupe does advocacy work built on the model of Boal's Theater of the Oppressed; Romero focuses on contingency of all types, challenging immigration law and bringing untold stories of Colorado's minority populations' histories to contemporary Colorado audiences. The troupe confronts audiences with various forms of subjugation and marginalization that exist in the culture using a notion called organic theater wherein the group depicts scenes from the (marginalized) participants' everyday lives. For Sue, this work was liberating. Along with a group of graduate students and non-tenure-track faculty, she began working on a play about faculty contingency and the costs borne by contingent faculty. The campus performance at her home institution led to a linked performance with contingent faculty from the community college just down the road. In turn, both productions featured the voices of public school teachers whose stories of workplace vulnerability, especially in light of education reform, were also integrated into the performance.

In time, these performances, featuring educators from all levels, were linked to the Romero Troupe's concerns, which offer a sprawling depiction of the marginalization and exploitation running throughout mainstream American society. The contingent faculty play that had been done on the university and community college campuses was folded into a larger production of the Romero Troupe. Called *An Adjunct at Ludlow* the production depicted, among other things, scenes of racial profiling by police, deportation proceedings, scenes of homeless veterans, and monologues by young DACA (Deferred Action for Childhood Arrivals)—so-called DREAMers—who spoke to their hopes for obtaining a college education in the United States. In this space and connecting faculty contingency to broader economic trends, Sue was able to see anew the opportunities for advocacy that were presented by her conversion to tenure; her research focus on academic labor could link higher education's academic labor movement to broader discussions of political and economic violence and marginalization in American society. Furthering this, she saw how those acting in the Romero troupe had, as their greatest hope, the idea of a college education.

Janelle's experience while still a graduate student at SUNY Albany established the context for her internalized vulnerability. Due to a $640 million budget cut in 2010, the then president of the University at Albany, George Philip, suspended five programs in the humanities. This resulted in outcry from both the campus community and the public—discourses that were saturated in emotion. Professor of French and eminent Derrida translator David Wills expressed "shock" and "anger" over the decision in an interview with NPR (Adler). Hélène Cixous wrote in an open letter to President George Philip, "You cannot imagine how stupefied and indignant I was to learn that that institution was about to mutilate itself." This rhetoric made use of emotion, recognizing affect as a technique for advocacy.

Further utilizing techniques of emotion, at a campus protest of the decision, Jil Hanifan, Director of the Writing Center at SUNY Albany, read before a silent crowd the names of the contingent faculty members whose jobs were to be cut. Hanifan's gesture overtly adopted a mode of memorializing—reciting the names of the "lost." Hanifan made rhetorical use of the master passion of grief and its performances in genres of memorial. Hanifan's gesture powerfully revealed how the discourse surrounding the closing of the humanities programs at SUNY Albany tended to focus on the humanities as an important conceptual, intellectual territory, without sufficiently attending to the role of contingency and the lives that would be materially affected by the decision.

Despite these public statements of grief over the ramifications of the SUNY "closing of the humanities," the decision was at times remembered as a relatively minor occurrence since the tenured faculty members were relocated and didn't lose their jobs. The effects on the contingent faculty members were less often remembered. The lesson was not lost on Janelle, however, who felt contingency's sting acutely and set about to find a stable position for herself. However, she ironically situated herself in exactly the kind of position (the writing center administrative job) that would destine her to experience marginalization firsthand. Today Janelle contends that keeping present the grief over the closing of positions and departments would help all in the SUNY local setting remain mindful of the ways that the bottom-line-driven value systems of the academy ignore the professional concerns of the faculty. Indeed, in an illustration of the kind of long-term trajectory that affective advocacy takes, several years later in the fall of 2015, contingent and non-contingent faculty at SUNY Albany came together in solidarity to secure a commitment from the administration to a groundbreaking plan to transform conditions for contingent faculty at the university.

Janelle contends that continuing to express grief can provide a means of recognition of the affective and material realities of faculty employment. Keeping a collective grief present, and addressing it outright, might reduce the felt vulnerability of graduate students who may be too quick to take the first job that comes their way, as Janelle did. This "keeping present" of emotion is an important advocacy strategy because it refuses the privatization of emotion and understands job cuts, under-compensation, and poor working conditions to be issues of collective concern. Shared affect can actualize the idea that contingency affects us all. It can prompt and continue action as it works to sustain concern. At the same time, the minority affective position (e.g., unhappiness in a context where happiness is assumed to be the "default" position) can be instigating, a type of counter-force. Such emotions can be productive, in that they produce effects that may not always be documentable but are nonetheless material.

CONCLUSION

Precarious employment traumatizes the people who bear it, disrupting their foundational narratives. Such trauma can utterly dismantle the narratives of academic success and achievement that are often central to the self-image of persons prepared for and dedicated to careers in higher education. Such affronts to personal and professional agency can prompt both emotion and action, and these manifestations require that the story be re-told, the emotions articulated, the effects registered, as acknowledgement itself becomes an exercise in emotion and empathy. As Howard Zehr points out, the twin acts of listening and testifying bring victim and victimizer together so that the capacity for understanding is increased in both. Zehr's restorative testimony shares much in common with Wendy Hesford's notion of layered testimony, through which identities are inscribed and alternative versions of history talk back to dominant culture and to one another. Restorative testimony also allows a confrontation of what Sidonie Smith calls "the limits of the autobiographical" (227) in which extreme identity categories, such as persons in witness protection, or persons with Alzheimer's may seem unable to "situate themselves in various locations through their personal storytelling" (232). Marginalized academics, functioning without access to traditional modes of shared governance and due process might find themselves similarly silenced by identity category. There is, therefore, an important role to be played by the re-storying of adjunct trauma for both testifier and the witness, wherein emotions, including those of disappointment, loss, hurt, grief, anger, and shame can be told and legitimized, then subsequently integrated and transformed. Such efforts ought not be pushed aside or dismissed by an advocacy agenda bent on outcomes, no matter how essential those outcomes might be.

As the unhappy effects of contingency are brought to the fore, we must also recognize the attachments that keep professionals in exploitive labor conditions. As Sara Ahmed and Lauren Berlant, among others, have theorized "emotion can attach us to the very conditions of our subordination" (Ahmed, *Cultural*

Politics 12). While we must continue to heed Eileen Schell's warning against the stereotypes of the "dabbling" academic "who is motivated to teach for a 'psychic income'" (Schell 50), we should also recognize the ways that a psychic income represents a very real force in the labor economy of higher education. Material, structural forces keep contingent laborers in the classroom, but the "emotional rewards" of the academic life also motivate people to take teaching positions over (potentially better compensated) jobs at places like Starbucks. Many, if not most, faculty members are motivated affectively by their concern for their students and by hope for a model of a non-corporatized university that values the independent, free life of the mind for the sake of the public good.

A priority for academic labor activist efforts is to reevaluate and transform the "cruel optimism" (to use Berlant's term) that clings to nostalgia for an ideal of the university, trusting that traditional approaches to academic hiring will one day be restored. Rather than preserving this hope for the restoration of previous academic hiring practices, we should instead use as an exigency for action the lasting nature of the shifts in faculty hiring that have occurred. Contingency has become a generalized condition, and it should prompt all of us to act. Even tenured positions may be lost as the university, increasingly driven by the "bottom line," finds cause to close academic departments. The fantasy of academic job security is quickly fraying, in the midst of other, more widespread "fraying fantasies" including "upward mobility, job security, political and social equality . . . meritocracy, the sense that liberal-capitalist society will reliably provide opportunities for individuals to carve out relations of reciprocity that seem fair and that foster life as a project of adding up to something" (Berlant 3). Anger and frustration at such fraying fantasies can prompt activist efforts that seek to improve working conditions. Within the context of the university, we can make use of the eidolon of secure academic employment to underscore that the "adjunct activist" agenda has the best interests of all faculty in mind. While we know that contingency is not evenly distributed in academe, it is nonetheless the case that contingency affects us all. The idea that tenure means security is rapidly being exposed as anachronistic, if not mythical. This reality should translate into a united cause—contingency as an issue that involves the faculty at large.

We believe that the idiom of affect theory can prompt academic labor theorists to ask questions that may be essential to any possibility for change: What affective bargains do contingent faculty (and arguably tenure-line faculty as well) make to maintain their careers in academe? What emotional habitus maintains the status quo? And what modifications to that habitus are needed for activist work to take hold in a local setting? Effective activism finds resources for reshaping the material-affective structures that condition the lived experiences of the academic worker.

Finally, we argue for reflective rather than reactive approaches and for the validity of emotions. We should read the emotional output of academic labor activists as also effective alongside traditional argumentation and action. We argue for any and all approaches, including emotional and affective efforts, that define meaningful work in as capacious a way as possible, rather than singularly in service of market values. Moreover, we recommend reflective approaches for evaluating effectiveness in light of contingency's emotional dimensions. Such reexamination stands to reveal that ongoing results are rooted in an understanding that is accessed in affect.

As we reflect on the affective and emotional dimensions of the advocacy work we do in the academy, we need to reconsider what counts as advocacy. What we deploy in our local, regional and national contexts—whether a data-driven rational argument, testimony on Capitol Hill, a piece of theater that generates discomfort, or advice given to new academics—can be valid advocacy work that changes hearts and minds. Taking this stance opens up what we might value as advocacy, honoring the work that people have done and continue to do on behalf of the cause yet oftentimes without a direct connection between effort and outcome. This reorientation sheds new light on the history of academic labor activism, highlighting events that might otherwise be all too casually dismissed. It also places value on the emotional labor tied up in advocacy work, putting it alongside and equal to results that might follow. Would we argue, for instance, that Susan Wyche's stand-and-deliver moment in Wyoming in 1987 was inconsequential because it led to year after year of endless policy machinations? Or was Wyche's statement unimportant because it was steeped in emotion? No to both questions. Her emotion was an essential catalyst and was emotional because it was steeped in importance.

WORKS CITED

Adler, Margot. "Cuts to University's Humanities Program Draw Outcry." *NPR.org*, 16 Nov. 2010, npr.org/2010/11/15/131336270/cuts-to-university-s-humanities -program-draw-outcry.

Ahmed, Sara. *The Cultural Politics of Emotion*. Edinburgh UP, 2004.

———. *The Promise of Happiness*. Duke UP, 2010.

Berlant, Lauren. *Cruel Optimism*. Duke UP, 2011.

Campbell, Rebecca, and Sharon M. Wasco. "Feminist Approaches to Social Science: Epistemological and Methodological Tenets." *American Journal of Community Psychology*, vol. 28, no. 6, 2000, pp. 773–91, *Springer Link*, doi:10.1023/A:10051597 16099. 28 May 2014.

Cixous, Hélène. "Open Letter to George Philip, President University at Albany-SUNY." 29 Nov. 2010, static1.squarespace.com/static/56f092c327d4bd8d4214

93a4/t/5720ea7722482e2e25b34333/1461774967344/Letter+from+H%C3%A9l
%C3%A8ne+Cixous.pdf.

CCCC Committee on Professional Standards. "CCCC Initiatives on the Wyoming Conference Resolution: A Draft Report." *College Composition and Communication,* vol. 40, no. 1, 1989, pp. 61–72.

CCCC Executive Committee. "Statement of Principles and Standards for the Postsecondary Teaching of Writing." *College Composition and Communication,* vol. 40, no. 3, 1989, pp. 329–36.

Fonow, Mary Margaret, and Judith A. Cook. *Beyond Methodology: Feminist Scholarship As Lived Research.* Indiana UP, 1991.

Gould, Deborah. "On Affect and Protest." *Political Emotions,* edited by Janet Staiger and Ann Cvetkovich, Routledge, 2010, pp. 18–45.

Harding, Sandra G. *Feminism and Methodology: Social Science Issues.* Indiana UP, 1987. EBSCO eBook Collection.

Hesford, Wendy. "'Ye Are Witnesses': Autobiography and Commemorative Practices." *Framing Identities: Autobiography and Pedagogy.* U of Minnesota P, 1999.

Maisto, Maria. "Adjuncts, Class, and Fear." *Working-Class Perspectives.,* 23 Sept. 2013, workingclassstudies.wordpress.com/2013/09/23/adjuncts-class-and-fear/.

———. "The Adjunct's Moment of Truth." *InsideHigherEd.com,* 10 Sept. 2009 insidehighered.com/views/2009/09/10/adjuncts-moment-truth. Accessed 28 May 2014.

———. Untitled conference paper. *Campaign for the Future of Higher Education Columbus Conference,* Columbus, Ohio, 18 May 2013.

McDonald, James C., and Eileen E. Schell. "The Spirit and Influence of the Wyoming Resolution: Looking Back to Look Forward." *Contingent Faculty,* special issue of *College English,* vol. 73, no. 4, 2011, pp. 360–78.

Miller, Susan. *Textual Carnivals: The Politics of Composition.* Southern Illinois UP, 1991.

Moldoveanu, Mihnea, and Nitin Nohria, editors. *Master Passions: Emotion, Narrative, and the Development of Culture.* MIT P, 2002.

Moyer, Bill. *The Practical Strategist: Movement Action Plan (MAP) Strategic Theories for Evaluating, Planning, and Conducting Social Movements.* Social Movement Empowerment Project, 1990.

Protevi, John. *Political Affect: Connecting the Social and the Somatic.* U of Minnesota P, 2009.

Reinharz, Shulamit, and Lynn Davidman. *Feminist Methods in Social Research.* Oxford UP, 1992.

Riley, Denise. *Impersonal Passion: Language as Affect.* Duke UP, 2005.

Robertson, Linda R., et al. "The Wyoming Conference Resolution Opposing Unfair Salaries and Working Conditions for Post-Secondary Teachers of Writing." *College English,* vol. 49, no. 3, 1987, pp. 274–80.

Schell, Eileen. *Gypsy Academics and Mother-Teachers: Gender, Contingent Labor, and Writing Instruction.* Heinemann, 1998.

Smith, Sidonie. "Taking It to the Limit One More Time: Autobiography and Autism." *Getting a Life: Everyday Uses of Autobiography*, edited by Sidonie Smith and Julia Watson, U of Minnesota P, 1996, pp. 226–48.

Strickland, Donna. *The Managerial Unconscious in the History of Composition Studies.* Southern Illinois UP, 2011.

Stukel, Catherine. "Is That Whining Adjunct Someone We Want Teaching Our Young?" *The Chronicle of Higher Education,* 2014, chronicle.com/blogs/letters/is -that-whining-adjunct-someone-we-want-teaching-our-young/.

Waggoner, Jeff. "UAlbany Panel Asks Raises for Adjuncts, UUP Ups the Ante." *Times Union, Capitol Confidential,* 11 Dec. 2015, blog.timesunion.com/capitol/archives /244270/suny-albany-panel-asks-raises-for-adjuncts-uup-ups-the-ante/.

Zehr, Howard. "Doing Justice, Healing Trauma: The Role of Restorative Justice in Peace Building." Peace Prints. *South Asian Journal of Peace Building,* vol. 1, no. 1, 2008, rjbc.ca/wp-content/uploads/2010/08/Howard_Zehr_Paper.pdf.

CHAPTER 15

HITTING THE WALL: IDENTITY AND ENGAGEMENT AT A TWO-YEAR COLLEGE

Desirée Holter
Whatcom Community College and South Puget Sound
Community College

Amanda Martin and Jeffrey Klausman
Whatcom Community College

Threads: Organizing Within and Across Ranks; Professionalizing and Developing in Complex Contexts; Protecting Gains, Telling Cautionary Tales

Whatcom Community College (WCC) was among a handful of two-year colleges in the state of Washington that offered a three-course composition sequence, English 100, 101, and 102. At one point, WCC offered more sections of English 100 than English 101 even though the Intercollegiate Relations Council (ICRC), which brokers the transfer agreement between two-year and four-year colleges in the state, had deemed that English 101 would be the statewide first-year course, and no course numbered 100 or above could be a prerequisite for it. Faculty in English, well aware of the "politics of remediation" (see Shor and Wiener), had fought for years to maintain English 100 as a credit-bearing course, an unlisted elective that students could apply to their transfer degrees though not transfer directly. Designed as a stretch-model 101 and responsive to the work of Shaughnessy as well as Bartholomae and Petrosky among others, English 100 provided students with a rich curriculum not very different from the English 101 curriculum, but offering greater depth and time for reflection. English 100 also provided "protection" from what faculty viewed as an overly prescriptive developmental education curriculum, housed in a different academic division.

However, research coming out of the Community College Research Center (CCRC) at Teachers College of Columbia University beginning in 2011–12 raised serious questions about the efficacy of a three-course sequence built on top of a two-course developmental sequence (see Cho et al.; Jenkins et al.). At the same time, common course numbering proliferated across the state, whereby courses with a "common number" (e.g., English 101, Sociology 101) were considered equivalent no matter at which campus they were taught; the result of this development was to highlight WCC's difference: since over half of all incoming students were placed into English 100—not the more common "first-year writing course," English 101—English 101 at Whatcom was arguably not the same. Thus, when in 2014, the ICRC enforced their ruling that English 100 be eliminated or numbered below 100, English faculty had no choice but to comply.

Nonetheless, everyone involved, especially department and program leadership, recognized that this would place undue hardship on the adjunct faculty who taught and continue to teach approximately 75 percent of all English classes and outnumber tenure-track faculty two to one. Moreover, the vast majority of adjunct faculty have taught at Whatcom for many years, some for over twenty. They comprise among the most experienced and dedicated teachers on campus. Department leadership recognized the potential loss to the college as well as the personal debt owed these faculty and sought innovative ways to meet the needs of students to gain access to college-level courses and the needs of faculty for continued employment.

In this chapter we focus on how a small, tight-knit community college English department dealt with a drastic change to its day-to-day operations, how that change affected the identities of two adjuncts within that department, and how, despite prior and continuing efforts made within the college and department to mitigate the professional gap between adjunct and full-time TT faculty, the realities of this two-tiered system cannot be eradicated. We reflect upon the events through a lens of "underemployment" as a means of accounting for and better understanding the impact of the announcement on the adjunct faculty's sense of personal and professional identities, especially as the realities of class cancellations and staffing decisions were realized.

Part of our aim is to recognize the inherent disparity between one college's efforts to ameliorate unjust working conditions for adjunct faculty and the unintended consequences of those efforts, not as a recommendation to end those efforts but rather to suggest that those efforts be placed in the larger context of personal and professional identity issues that continue to plague higher education, especially at two-year colleges, which rely even more heavily than other sectors of higher education on overqualified, underpaid, and underemployed faculty (see AFT "Survey"). What we argue below is that more aggressive efforts made by the college and English department—equality in proposing and teaching professional development workshops, equality in staffing of non-sequence courses, for example—in the absence of explicit acknowledgement of the reality of adjunct professional status actually *accentuate* the divide between "professional identity" of the college faculty member and the identity of the disposable laborer in the new corporate institution.

As a clarification to the discussion to follow, we are choosing to use the terms *adjunct* and *part-time faculty*. While many have already done work to complicate these terms and suggest new ones, such as *contingent faculty* (see Bilia et al.), *adjunct* and *part-time faculty* are the terms commonly used at our own college. Since WCC does not have full-time contingent positions, all adjunct faculty at WCC are "part-time," a status rigorously enforced by WCC administrators and the faculty union, only allowing adjuncts to work a maximum of 80 percent of a full-time credit load.[1] This means, in our context, the terms *full-time* and *tenure track* or *tenured* are conflated, as are the terms *part-time* and *adjunct*, the latter carrying the connotations associated with the aforementioned older conceptions of contingent labor.

DESIRÉE'S STORY

When I learned that English 100 would be removed from the composition sequence, I was worried about how this would affect me, my students, and the English program. However, I thought my employment would not be impacted because I had taught at Whatcom for six years and was significantly involved in department and campus work. In fact, I thought that my considerable contributions and apparent desire to obtain a full-time instructor position would secure stable employment; unfortunately, this was not the case, as other adjunct faculty members and I lost at least one class for the upcoming year and have continued to lose even more due to fewer course offerings, low enrollments, and the priority of full-time faculty staffing. The loss of these classes has illuminated the reality that I, as an adjunct faculty member, am in a precarious and contingent position which undervalues and disregards my professional contributions to the college in the sense that I am "disposable" labor.

When I started teaching at Whatcom and other community colleges, I did not realize the significant impact that working as an adjunct would have on my

---

1   As of this writing, the college administration and faculty union have negotiated an agreement whereby adjunct faculty can teach full loads of classes, equivalent to that of tenure-track faculty. At WCC, that means forty-five credit-hours of classes. While this development is lauded by some, responding to requests by many adjunct faculty for opportunities to teach more, others consider this simply a furthering of current exploitative practices as the full-time-equivalent teaching loads do not come with any raise in salary or improvement of employment security. Future union negotiations will likely seek to address these issues, possibly pursuing full-time lecturer positions similar to those available at other institutions which offer longer contracts and increased salaries.

personal and professional identities and on my well-being, self-esteem, and over-all job satisfaction. I started my career as a hopeful recent college graduate with the intent to be hired into a full-time English position; I envisioned a future in academia where I would be hired as a tenure-track faculty member, recognized for my skills, qualifications, and expertise, and valued by my fellow colleagues. When I first started as an adjunct, I imagined that I would continue to work as part-time, contingent labor for two or three years at the most, so as I reflect on my current employment status, I can see now that working as an adjunct has deteriorated my confidence in my career plan and my goals for a future in this profession. My vision of a future that had once seemed limitless now seems uncertain, ambiguous, and especially restricting to my full potential. I once had a clear path in front of me, a specific plan to achieve my goals with obvious outcomes attached to my efforts, but since I have been unable to secure a full-time position, I am uncertain what the future will bring.

In an effort to develop professionally and to become a valuable candidate for a full-time position, I have made significant contributions to the English department and eLearning program at Whatcom. I have worked as the English 100 co-coordinator, helping with the administration of the English 100 Reading Panel process, a quarterly campus-wide assessment activity; I worked with English curriculum development and program assessment groups on various projects; and I served as a volunteer reader for the Whatcom *Noisy Water Review*, a journal which publishes student writing and art, and the Anna Rosemary Harris Scholarship Foundation, which awards funding for students to attend the Chuckanut Writers Conference, a local creative writing conference sponsored and run by Whatcom Community College. I have also developed my eLearning expertise by serving as a volunteer member of the eLearning Advisory Committee, which supports a successful eLearning program at Whatcom; I was a member of the eLearning Advisory Subgroup, which drafted an evaluation rubric to assess online instructors; I presented at the 2014 Assessment, Teaching, and Learning Conference, an annual statewide conference held by the Washington State Board of Community and Technical Colleges about evaluating online instructors; I participated in a one-year Faculty eLearning Community in which we studied and developed our online courses based on Quality Matters standards; I completed Quality Matters courses and other online certification programs; and I contributed to a professional development course at Pierce College about using Canvas for teaching. These are just a few of the professional and scholarly development opportunities I have accomplished while teaching as an adjunct and while seeking full-time employment.

Although I have often gone far beyond what is required of me as an adjunct, the precarious nature of contingent employment has become a discouraging reality for me. I have realized that my aspirations for full-time employment, as well as my perceived job security and stability, have merely been a façade, inherent in the structure of the labor system at two-year colleges and elsewhere, which dangles incentives before adjuncts in order to keep them "on the hook." I have come to realize that I have little hope of becoming a full-time faculty member at my college and that I am not protected from the unpredictable and unstable nature of working as a contingent faculty member. Unfortunately, regardless of the significant achievements and efforts I have made, I have yet to break free from an oppressive system which dismisses my value and expertise as I remain underemployed and working for what on average equates to less than minimum wage when the hours I *actually* work are factored into my salary. My "involuntary employment in part-time, temporary, or intermittent work" and the "low pay, relative to a previous job or others with similar educational backgrounds" that I receive places me in a saturated market which is overwhelmed with overqualified and underemployed adjunct labor (Maynard and Joseph 141). In an effort to combat the precarious and unpredictable nature of working in this position, and in order to remain financially stable, I often have to teach at multiple community colleges during the school year (sometimes teaching up to five composition courses a quarter—more than most full-time instructors teach) and frequently have to take on additional summer jobs as well, just to make ends meet. I do all of this in addition to spending time (often unpaid) developing professionally and contributing to other department and campus programs.

Unfortunately, my efforts to advance in my career have not succeeded yet (if they ever will). Although I have made substantial attempts to develop professionally and to secure full-time employment, my personal and professional identities have been compromised as I am left wondering: Will I escape this oppressive and underemployed position? And, will I achieve my personal and professional goals?

AMANDA'S STORY

Like Desirée, I too am active in departmental projects and professional development opportunities. To increase my level of current disciplinary knowledge, I attend regional and statewide conferences about once a year and the CCCC when it is close by and hence more affordable. I served on the committee that edited the second edition of our custom English 101 textbook, published through the independent Fountainhead Press; advise an animation club; present at professional development days on campus; and attend various workshops concerning diversity, student-centered teaching, and new reading pedagogy. All of these activities are enthusiastically supported by my department and the college as a whole.

When the end of English 100 loomed I knew immediately I would not have the fairly stable expectation of six courses a year that would keep me financially solvent and allow me to keep the basic health and retirement benefits that Whatcom provides its adjuncts who work over 50 percent of a full-time credit load. I was an adjunct, and a relatively new one with only five years of teaching at the college. My father is blue collar; I know firsthand the unintentional but no less cold realities visited upon workers viewed as "the amorphous mass," to quote Angela Bilia (Bilia et al. 387). Worst case scenario, I would lose classes starting in the fall of 2015, so I had to make contingency plans.

To provide a bit of context, MIT professor Dr. Amy Glasmeier's Living Wage Calculator project, which calculates the average hourly and annual incomes an individual would need to earn to pay for basic yearly expenses in a particular area, reports that the annual salary for one person in Whatcom County in 2016 would need to be $20,617 before taxes. For one person with a dependent child, that total would need to be $45,644 (Glasmeier and the Massachusetts Institute of Technology). From 2012 to 2014, I averaged $26,000 a year, teaching the same or nearly the same amount of credits as a full-time tenured faculty member annually. This means, at best, I manage to live just above poverty level, in the same bracket as restaurant servers and custodians in my area. If I had a child, I would almost certainly need a second household income from a spouse, partner, or family member. And I am not alone. Many of our college's other "full-time" adjuncts, those teaching at or near the maximum credit load allowed in our contract and relying on WCC as their main or only source of income, make about the same amount ("Washington State Salaries"). At this level, a threat to employment produces a lot of anxiety, as it could affect an individual's ability to meet basic expenses and to keep basic benefits like medical insurance. In displaying these facts I do not intend to dwell on the dismal state of funding for higher education, but to illustrate the precariousness of an adjunct's economic status and ability to meet basic needs.

To make matters worse, enrollments already had dropped for the 2015 academic year. In the spring of 2015, I was "bumped" from a humanities course I was scheduled to teach by a full-time tenure-track faculty member whose class was canceled. I was already adjusting to a shortfall, from having two courses in the spring of 2015 to one, but then I learned my section of English 102, which had run with low enrollment the prior year, had also been cancelled. This left me with no classes for the spring. Despite extensive efforts by my department chair to substitute my cancelled class for an unstaffed English 100, low enrollments struck again, and this class, too, was cancelled. For the first time in five years, I was left with no courses at all when I refused to "bump" a less senior adjunct faculty from an already prorated course, as I would not want this to happen to me if the roles were reversed.

While I was able to financially survive the spring by cobbling together an income from three different part-time jobs, the effects on my own identity are worth noting. For the five years I worked primarily at Whatcom, I identified myself as a "college instructor" to those who asked "What do you do?" But what do you say when that identity has been compromised, and not by your choice or abilities? While I appreciated all the efforts of my department chair, and did not blame her, the department, nor the college for my employment troubles, I was still faced with the sad fact that my ability to support myself and do a job I loved was not, in the end, solely dependent on my abilities or effort. Despite taking advantage of every avenue to be a "good" faculty member, I faced spring quarter beaten down and discouraged. Who was I? What did I want? Was all this effort for the "love of teaching"—a problematic term that makes poor working conditions somehow acceptable—even worth it?

UNDEREMPLOYMENT IN THE COLLEGE SETTING

The over-reliance on part-time, contingent labor, at two-year colleges creates an environment in which many qualified professionals are chronically and permanently underemployed. Douglas C. Maynard and Todd Allen Joseph, in "Are All Part-Time Faculty Underemployed? The Influence of Faculty Status Preference on Satisfaction and Commitment," offer a cogent overview of the nature of underemployment. They say that someone is "underemployed when he or she holds a job that is somehow inferior to, or of lower quality than, a particular standard" (141). This underemployment creates psychological stress due to an incongruence in either the fit of "job demands–worker abilities," which is the "match between the requirements of the job and the knowledge, skills, and abilities of the employee," or the fit of "worker needs–job supplies," which is the "match between the employee's desires or preferences for certain work conditions and the actual work conditions on that job" (142).

Put another way, underemployment is caused in the first model by the job demanding less than an employee can provide in terms of knowledge and abilities and, we would hazard to add, the mental and emotional demands of that particular job and/or its environment. In the second model, underemployment is caused by the employee demanding more in terms of mental challenge and/ or physiological needs (i.e., food, shelter, and safety) than the job can provide. If there is no incongruence, then there is no underemployment, which led Maynard and Joseph to divide part-time faculty into two categories: voluntary and involuntary (142). Voluntary part-time faculty are satisfied with the job's demands and conditions. Involuntary part-time faculty are not satisfied with the job's demands or conditions, which, in the case of educated, experienced, and motivated faculty, leads to underemployment. Currently, adjunct faculty across the United States are split, 50 percent preferring part-time, and 47 percent preferring full-time (AFT "Survey" 8), which allows us to suggest that at least 47 percent of current part-time faculty are underemployed.

Maynard and Joseph offer "five dimensions" of underemployment, citing Feldman:

> (a) more education than required by the job, (b) involuntary employment in a field outside of area of education, (c) more skills or experience than required by the job, (d) involuntary employment in part-time, temporary, or intermittent work, and (e) low pay, relative to a previous job or others with similar educational backgrounds. (141)

At Whatcom, many adjunct faculty members experience multiple dimensions of underemployment. For example, we have several faculty members with Ph.D.s from R1 or similar institutions with long careers of teaching in various institutions. They have more education and broader experience than required by the college to teach first-year writing,[2] experience and education underutilized in the first-year writing classroom. This is not to say that first-year writing as a specialty does not warrant the same highly educated and experienced instructors that other English specialties demand, merely that these adjunct instructors, whose specialties and experiences often encompass scholarship in areas outside first-year-writing, are not given opportunities to fully utilize all aspects of their knowledge and skills or encouraged to continue developing professionally in those directions. Moreover, these faculty are seeking full-time positions, and they are being paid less than other adjunct faculty at most other colleges in the state and certainly only a percentage of what a full-time faculty member makes. They are thus underemployed in four of the five dimensions simultaneously (a, c, d, e) and in the case of faculty trained in literature studies, five of the five (a, b, c, d, e). Other faculty, such as Amanda, with years of experience at multiple colleges, supplement their income with work outside of academia, in Amanda's case as a PATH (Professional Association of Therapeutic Horsemanship) certified equine specialist in mental health and learning at Animals as Natural Therapy, as a freelance editor, and as a front-counter and marketing supervisor at a local deli. Amanda and others can be said to experience potentially three to four dimensions of underemployment simultaneously at the college (b, d, e) *and* at their other jobs (a, b, c, e).

---

2   The minimum requirements for adjunct faculty to teach English 101 is a master's degree in English. Preferred qualifications include graduate coursework in composition/rhetoric and teaching experience in a post-secondary institution.

Perhaps what is so intriguing about this model of underemployment is that it makes conscious a mostly unconscious network of relationships that adjunct faculty work to resist and yet which, simultaneously, shapes their identity. In Desirée's and Amanda's stories, we see this compelling need to "prove" themselves capable and qualified for a full-time position. Certainly they knew, at some level, that they were underemployed—or else, why the desire to prove themselves? They knew they had more skills than the adjunct position gave them opportunity to use and that they were involuntarily limited to part-time work. What they did not quite know, perhaps, is the degree to which this underemployment played upon their identities as professionals, nor how much their professional identities impacted their personal identities.

To understand why, we have to look at the local situation, which allows and encourages underemployment in a particular way. Whatcom is one of only two two-year colleges in the area and is located only four miles from Western Washington University. Western graduates a dozen or so people each year with a master's degree in English, nearly all of whom have completed coursework in composition and have taught in a writing program with a well-known mentor. Thus, there is an endless stream of hopeful post-graduates who are optimistic and excited to begin teaching college courses at Whatcom. This pool of ready labor allows or even encourages a cycle of consumption (see Hammer). This in turn privileges underemployment at the expense of the well-being of adjunct faculty members.

Because adjuncts are essentially disposable labor, they are often marginalized from the institution in which they serve. As Jeff has said in "Not Just a Matter of Fairness: Adjunct Faculty and Writing Programs in Two-Year Colleges," adjunct faculty are "often invited to join full-time faculty in program work but have very little incentive to do so" (363). The main incentive for Desirée's and Amanda's involvement has not been the tiny stipend WCC's English department offers for meeting and project hours out of its own small WPA and department budgets, but the idea of long-term recognition and rewards.

But while such work and service to the college and department is dutifully recorded on annual evaluations for tenure-track faculty as evidence for promotion, this is not the case for adjunct faculty, whose only incentive is an often unstated and implicit "love of teaching" (see AFT "Survey"). But "love" or doing the job because adjuncts "enjoy teaching" may be slowly starting to lose its romanticism: 64 percent of adjuncts over 50 claim they teach not for the compensation but for the enjoyment, but only 49 percent of adjuncts under 50 make this claim (AFT "Survey" 9–10). While these statistics are more suggestive than conclusive, they may reflect an increasing disillusionment of adjuncts, like Amanda and Desirée, who have recently entered the adjunct pool or a situation where disillusioned adjuncts leave the profession.

As Desirée and Amanda have both discovered in those short six years, no amount of program work or administrative responsibilities can change a person's employment status, which in turn defines them more rigidly than any intrinsic desire. This long-term marginalization leads to resentment and creates a poor work environment (see Eagan et al.; Harris; Maynard and Joseph). Jeff recognized that many experienced or long-term adjunct faculty "feel marginalized in their own campuses and are somewhat to very resentful at teaching so much of a program's courses while receiving so little in terms of pay and benefits" (Klausman 363). As Maynard and Joseph note, this marginalization is the inevitable consequence of underemployment and is a key cause of dissatisfaction in the workplace (141).

Interestingly, while some articles written by academics point towards being respected and sharing governance as the largest issues affecting faculty satisfaction and thus underemployment (see Bilia et al.), the 2010 AFT "Survey of Part-Time and Adjunct Higher Education Faculty" indicates that the largest issues for adjuncts are, in order of importance, salaries, access to full-time positions, access to healthcare benefits, and job security (12). In the context of the survey report, one could deduce that "full-time positions" might be more closely linked in the minds of adjuncts to job security and its corresponding reliable income and benefits, rather than the political status such positions may carry. Maynard and Joseph conclude that the desire to have a full-time position and a livable wage connects closely to feelings of underemployment. They recommend that institutions might benefit from focusing on initiatives that attempt to increase the proportion of part-time faculty who prefer not to teach full-time, such as the targeted recruitment of professionals with full-time positions elsewhere who might find value in applying their expertise to the classroom, and for whom the typically meager compensation is less problematic (150).

As a recommendation, Maynard and Joseph do not take into account that *teaching* is also a professional skill, and those that know how to work in their profession may not be the best at teaching that profession. This would also skew toward part-time STEM faculty, a majority of whom already prefer to teach part-time (AFT "Survey" 9), and not those teaching in the social sciences or humanities, where there are limited lucrative opportunities to work in those fields outside academia.

Perhaps in tacit acknowledgement of the realities sketched above, we discuss below how WCC attempts to make part-time status feel like enough of a fit, to give it the voluntary status that leads adjuncts to be more satisfied with their jobs and institution, and hence to end underemployment. For example, adjunct faculty members are often encouraged to contribute to or participate in professional development in their department or on their campus (Bilia et al.; Klausman), and many do so eagerly and enthusiastically. Yet in Desirée's and Amanda's cases, there has been very little recognition of their contribution and participation in real terms, in the terms that make up underemployment, as their stories show.

Angela Bilia sums this phenomenon up well: "I have never viewed myself as contingent to the production and delivery of academic knowledge; yet, the power to construct my own identity has been in the hands of others. I have become 'other'" (390). Bilia expresses what Barbara Ehrenreich helps us understand as a paradox at the heart of the identity conflict inherent in the adjunct position. Ehrenreich has identified the professional middle class as "all those people whose economic and social status is based on education, rather than on the ownership of capital or property" (qtd. in Harris 47). As Joseph Harris notes, adjunct faculty are trained to believe they are, and invited to behave as, members of a professional middle class; yet as we and others have found, adjunct faculty are in a disposable labor situation that too often becomes permanent. The effects of this disjuncture between the promoted and the real identity are the basis of what we believe is a progression of disengagement that reflects the dissatisfaction inherent in underemployment.

THE PROGRESSION OF EMPLOYMENT DISSATISFACTION AMONG ADJUNCT FACULTY

This frame of underemployment helps explain a progression of professional disengagement that many adjunct faculty members seem to experience. Years of working in a system which both marginalizes and encourages, both offers opportunities for professionalism and withholds them, plays out in a person's professional identity and wears on the resilience of the person's personal identity. While scholarship on resilience has mostly fallen under the purview of child development, mental health, and K-12 education (see Boss; Doll et al.; Masten), it is worth defining briefly and in its simplest form for our context. The American Psychological Association defines *resilience* as "the process of adapting well in the face of adversity, trauma, tragedy, threats, or significant sources of stress." Many factors contribute to a person's level of resiliency, including having caring relationships in which the individual feels supported, encouraged, reassured, and trusted. Several additional factors are (1) the capacity to make realistic plans and take steps to carry them out, (2) a positive view of yourself and confidence in your strengths and abilities, (3) skills in communication and problem solving, and (4) the capacity to manage strong feelings and impulses (APA). According to the APA, ways to build resiliency pertinent to this discussion include the following: making connections with people and groups that support and listen to the individual, moving toward the completion of realistic goals, taking decisive action in challenging situations, looking for opportunities of self-discovery and self-actualization through managing challenging situations and ideas, nurturing a positive and confident view of one-self, keeping situations within a long-term ("big picture") perspective, maintaining a hopeful outlook focused on what one wants not what one fears, and taking care of oneself physically, mentally, and emotionally (see APA).

Adjunct faculty who have not already been scared away or discouraged from pursuing an academic career may start out hopeful of building a professional identity around a personal identity that already proved resilient by surviving the emotional, mental, and physical burdens of the education system and initial hiring processes. As in Desirée and Amanda's cases, however, as these identities repeatedly encounter a wall that was not supposed to be there, at least according to the encouraging words of graduate school professors and the overt statements and practices of progressive colleges and writing programs, these identities get compromised, and a capacity for resiliency may decline.

Consequently, we can sketch out the progression of faculty identity, with its related effects on faculty engagement and resiliency, in this way: Adjunct faculty members who seek full-time teaching positions tend to:

1. begin their professional careers with enthusiasm, hope, and some naïveté;
2. become professionally engaged, developing their professional identities while anxious about the realities of the position;
3. experience setbacks that arouse disillusionment, bitterness, or suspicion;
4. become resolved to the reality of permanent adjunct status; often become resentful; disengage from the profession and refocus personal and some-times professional identity elsewhere while continuing to teach classes.

There may be an interesting correlation between this progression and the amount of time an adjunct has been in her position. While 59 percent of adjuncts with five years or less of teaching experience preferred full-time, this number shrinks to 49 percent at six to ten years, and shrinks further to 39 percent at eleven or more years of teaching (AFT "Survey" 8). This correlation suggests the above identity progression may be especially stark for those 60 percent of younger faculty members with about five years of teaching who hope to garner a full-time position (AFT "Survey" 8) from an ever-shrinking tenure-track pool. This last demographic is the one to which Desirée and Amanda belong, both on the cusp of that first decrease in desire for a full-time position at six to ten years.

We have seen in Desirée's story how she moved through the first two stages and is, perhaps, in the third. She is suspicious and becoming disillusioned; she may not yet be bitter, yet there is evidence of disappointment and a sense of betrayal. Desirée knows that she is at a crossroads. The elimination of English 100 not only cost her at least one class per year, a financial hardship, but excluded her from teaching online classes, where she has developed her expertise as part of her professional identity. That expertise, when it came to staffing, was not acknowledged, and the online classes were offered to a full-time faculty member to better accommodate her needs. It's clear that her identity as a professional based on her professional accomplishments is not acknowledged because of her employment status.

Desirée knows she has a choice to make. She can rededicate herself to finding a full-time position most likely elsewhere, which might include leaving the state, as a colleague of hers has recently done. She can seek employment outside academia, as did another of her adjunct colleagues with a Ph.D. Or she can resign herself to permanent adjunct status, as many do, and accept the relative stability and relatively good benefits as sufficient and give up her potential power as a decision-maker and leader. This is not to say that adjuncts cannot be leaders, and some institutions allow adjuncts to contribute to decisions about curriculum, as WCC does, but the reality is that no major policy change or curriculum decision can be made *only* by adjuncts. A tenured faculty member and/or administrator will always have the last word.

Amanda's story reveals that she, perhaps in light of her prior and current work experiences, falls farther along the scale, somewhere between the third and fourth stage of the progression. Her desire for a full-time position is perhaps diminishing as she redirects her energies into other career paths outside academia, specifically her professional role as a PATH-certified instructor and equine specialist in mental health and learning, and her work as a freelance editor, both of which provide a good person–job and demand–ability fit (see Maynard and Stephen). Increasing her relationships and professional options with WCC, with local organizations, and with local businesses speaks to the history of "flexible identities" Mendenhall claims have sustained composition faculty since the birth of the "specialty" in the 1970s, both in terms of an interdisciplinary and pedagogical asset, and in terms of perpetuating "unfair or exploitative practices," as "flexible" employees are shuffled to the less-desired general education classes (27). In some ways, diversifying herself has made Amanda less marketable for specialized tenure-track positions, identifying her instead as just another "flexible" adjunct, capable only of "fill[ing] the holes," a "[mechanic] in the assembly line, plugging in little parts" that keep the day-to-day "service" courses operating at maximum capacity (Bilia et al. 387).

WCC EFFORTS TO LIMIT THE IMPACT OF UNDEREMPLOYMENT

WCC has made many of the more obvious efforts toward creating a more inviting, supportive, and inclusive work environment for adjunct faculty members. At WCC, our faculty union welcomes and represents all faculty, adjunct and tenure-track, in an effort to encourage faculty equality and job satisfaction. Many of our tenured faculty in the English department have taken leadership roles in the faculty union and support efforts to ameliorate unfair labor practices. The same can be said generally for all faculty at our institution. In fact, during the last faculty contract negotiations in 2014–2015, increasing adjunct pay with the college's own resources, in response to six years of stagnant state funding for community and technical colleges, became one of the main priorities of the joint faculty union. Moreover, the Adjunct Affairs Advisory Committee, made up almost exclusively of adjunct faculty across the college, seeks to bring adjunct-specific issues and concerns to the attention of top college administrators.

At WCC, adjunct faculty are always invited to participate in various committees and programs across campus, encouraging them to have a campus voice and allowing them to take part in important projects and decision-making processes. Adjunct faculty members serve on textbook selection committees, serve as faculty mentors for the creative writing and literature clubs, and edit the annual journal of student writing. Adjuncts also receive support from the college or specific departments to complete professional development opportunities through applying for professional development funds or stipends. For example, adjunct faculty can receive funding to attend or present at academic conferences; they can receive funding to attend professional development courses; they are invited and paid a small stipend to attend opening-week activities or other campus events; and so on. Adjuncts are also provided with designated office spaces and personal computers (albeit shared whereas nearly all tenure-track faculty have private offices). Adjunct faculty names are listed on a plaque at each of their office doors as well, which confirms that they have a designated space in which they "belong" on campus. Additionally, adjunct faculty names appear in the list of faculty in all departmental and college web pages and catalogs, further enhancing the professional recognition of adjuncts on our campus. Adjuncts also have access to campus email, our learning management system, and so on, so they have access to official forms of campus communication. These are obvious and essential first steps toward inclusion that WCC has implemented (see Heller et al.).

What WCC and our English department has done that is, perhaps, a bit more than the obvious is to offer adjunct faculty the opportunity to lead professional development workshops for the entire campus, sending the invitation to propose a course to all faculty, regardless of employment status. Similarly, when the English department needs work done that adjunct faculty are best qualified for, there's no hesitation to call upon them. Currently, several "master courses" are being developed for our Canvas learning management system to support the curricular development of new courses. Two of those master courses are being developed, for a stipend, by adjunct faculty who have the expertise in those areas. Also, adjunct faculty have been asked and paid to coordinate our English 100 Reading Panel, a quarterly campus-wide assessment process. There are currently efforts within our department to replace this effective assessment tool with an English 101 Reading Panel, and adjunct faculty are heavily involved with that.

The English department also seeks to provide adjunct faculty equal access to teaching a variety of courses. Since we're a two-year college, our course offerings are nearly all composition. We have a small number of what we call "non-sequence courses," including various literature offerings as well as creative writing. These courses are highly sought after by all faculty, since most of our faculty are trained in literary studies or creative writing. However, we made a decision several years ago to distribute equitably the assignment of these courses, with all faculty submitting an application to teach a course and no faculty member getting more than one non-sequence class per year, unless there are exceptional circumstances (e.g., no faculty members applying for the course, limited expertise, etc.). This policy is changing as the department diversifies its offerings to fill the educational gap for students that the elimination of English 100 left behind. Without English 100 and the "soft landing" it provided for first-year and at-risk college students, and in light of recent scholarship reviving the idea of reading as a process and essential skill across disciplines (see Carillo), our department is also experimenting with offering more diverse first-year literature courses that do not have prerequisites. This triply benefits, as students get more opportunities for college-level reading and writing with faculty experienced in both literature and composition studies, more English courses get offered per year, and faculty with literature experience have more chances to utilize their skills.

Similarly, adjunct faculty have the same opportunity to propose and teach courses in our honors program, and many do, which allows some to teach within their specific area of expertise, which is unique at the two-year college level where the primary focus is on offering general education courses. For example, one of our adjunct faculty members has a Ph.D. in medieval literature. She has few opportunities to teach in her field except through honors courses and the occasional 200-level literature course that has been made available to her in a process that treats her the same as tenured faculty.

Although significant efforts have been made to provide a more inclusive and equal work environment, adjuncts are still frequently faced with divisions in labor equality, value, and recognition. For example, when Amanda submitted a proposal to teach a professional development course for a campus-wide workshop, she was asked by an incredulous adjunct faculty member, "Why would you do that?" intimating that as an adjunct, she really shouldn't be putting herself forward as an expert in the field. When Desirée volunteered to serve on the eLearning Committee, she found that her qualifications and expertise were overlooked in favor of what full-time faculty members preferred, even though her expertise in that particular area far exceeded that of her full-time colleagues. In this case, her analysis of an issue related to online teaching was ignored, even though she had taught numerous online classes and studied online teaching extensively. The administrator-faculty member who ignored her insights had never taught an online class.

In some ways, part-time friendly practices, which have been populating the recommendation sections of articles on contingent labor since at least the 1980s (see Eagan et al.; Harris; Heller; Maynard and Joseph; Torgovnick), made the situation for these two adjuncts worse in terms of demands on their resiliency. They know logically that a small community college does not have the budget to support many TT faculty, and that it does not make good business sense to run a low-enrolled class. But they felt cared about and supported by their fellow full-time and part-time faculty members, by the clerical staff, and to a limited extent by other administrators. They believed that surely those who helped them build their resiliency would not also be the ones to test it, to put up an insurmountable wall? And yet that is exactly what happened.

This "bait and switch," promoting a professional middle-class identity while simultaneously relegating to a disposable labor class, threatens an adjunct's constructed professional identity and spurs an adjunct's progression toward disillusionment and disengagement. Other scholars (see Bilia et al.) also allude to the bitterness and resentment that arises when the reality of their extrinsically enforced identities as contingent, part-time, non-tenure-track, *adjuncts*—all just another term for "outsider," "other," or worse, "appendage"—become apparent, as it must in an institutional structure built upon a two-tier system of labor made essential by a near constant threat of financial shortfalls (see Harris; Mendenhall; Hammer).

This is *not* to say that colleges should abandon practices that are friendly and supportive of adjunct identities. In fact, adjuncts such as Amanda and Desirée may feel more confident about critiquing the system that threatens them, as we do in this chapter, *because* they have been supported in the past by full-time faculty and the college, making their resiliency stronger relative to adjuncts without such support. Therefore, they may be more likely to confront issues rather than run from them (see APA).

Still, though adjunct faculty members at WCC and in the English department often receive the message that they may be separate by employment status only but in all other ways are equal, this does not necessarily mitigate the deep-seated inequities that permeate the contingent labor system that has been so widely documented (see Flaherty; Gavaskar; Mendenhall). This explicit message of inclusivity, as we've seen, masks the implicit inequality of the contingent situation and further encourages the substantial divide between adjuncts and full-time faculty members.

PROFESSIONAL COLLEGE ADJUNCT FACULTY MEMBERS ARE ENTICED BY THE "BAIT AND SWITCH" PROMISE OF PROFESSIONAL IDENTITY: DESIRÉE'S ANALYSIS

I recently completed a required Faculty Professional Plan and Report, which serves as a part of the five-year cyclical evaluation process at Whatcom. In the report, I was asked a series of self-evaluation questions, which focused on my current teaching and professional development effectiveness as well as my future goals. What was especially challenging to me about this self-evaluation process was that I was asked to identify what my goals were for the following academic year, and yet I am not sure if I will have work for next quarter let alone next year.

I found this self-evaluation process to be disingenuous and misleading. Although I am expected to have plans to develop the quality of my teaching and professional experiences now and in the future, the college is still not committed to me in any professional or legal way. When asked on the evaluation what the college could do to support my "professional growth needs," I wrote

> The lack of pay, recognition, and appreciation for what adjuncts do to promote the success of the college and our students is significantly overlooked, which is disheartening. From my own experience, I find it becomes disappointing to contribute so significantly to a program or college that does not seem to value or appreciate my contributions or my expertise. If the department and administrators made more effort to acknowledge the significant work that adjunct faculty members do to contribute to the college and to develop professionally, it would provide incentive for these faculty to engage more thoroughly and actively.

As I suggested in my self-evaluation report, the paradox of this situation seems to exemplify and even exaggerate the underlying issues of the under-employed professional labor forces. Although the college expects adjuncts to develop professionally and advance as more effective instructors, this expectation contradicts the very nature of the contingent position in which the college is not legally bound to adjunct instructors beyond the limitations of the quarterly contracts. This self-evaluation process then places the full responsibility of developing professionally on an instructor who is systematically barred from full participation in the system. By placing the expectation for development on faculty who are already undervalued and underemployed, adjuncts are further burdened by the pressures of committing to a system which is not committed to them.

Although there are efforts made at Whatcom and other community colleges to deflect the inequities or instabilities that adjuncts encounter, these efforts do little to change the effects of a contingent workplace that is saturated with overqualified and underemployed faculty members (see Bilia et al.; Maynard and Joseph). So while these opportunities to contribute professionally might seem inclusive, they also encourage the kind of "bait and switch" mentioned above, in which adjuncts who want to develop their résumés will agree to take on additional responsibilities in hopes that this will establish credibility with and recognition by their tenured colleagues. This rarely happens. Instead, the message I have received from the three colleges where I have worked is "build up your résumé here and apply elsewhere." As Bilia et al. note:

> We can begin to see that the isolation and exile of contingent faculty common across the disciplines and across institution types create a body of faculty who are likely to see themselves as outsiders and outcasts, taking on and expressing all of the psychological traits thereof. The ultimate result of this movement toward increasing contingency, then, is in every sense a "disbanded professoriate." (381)

Unfortunately, this "disbanded professoriate" is the result of adjunct faculty members experiencing the Progression of Employment Dissatisfaction among Adjunct Faculty we outlined above. The saturated and endlessly consumptive work environment is a system that will ultimately fail adjunct faculty members because this career path is not sustainable for those who desire to achieve more than contingent labor.

During an informal discussion about the nature of adjuncting, Jeff posed an intriguing question to Amanda and me. He asked, if we had known what we know now about the lack of full-time position opportunities and the lack of recognition or incentives for development when we first were hired as adjuncts, would we have still choosen to accept the adjunct job offer? I had a hard time answering this question. While part of me feels completely discouraged and hopeless about my professional future, I cannot help but feel that maybe my passion, expertise, and commitment will eventually be valued and recognized by my full-time colleagues somewhere, some time.

I think that my refusal to settle into the idea of working indefinitely as an adjunct and my refusal to move on to another career are the result of many factors. First, I think that this contingent labor system is one that encourages adjuncts to remain hopeful or optimistic for the future, regardless of the lack of real opportunities available to them, by providing incentives and implicit promises. Second, I and many other adjuncts have resiliency, which has already motivated me to achieve what I have. I do not give up easily, I do not like to accept "no" for an answer when something is important to me, and a part of me knows I deserve to be hired for a full-time position, even if I am competing with other equally qualified and well-deserving candidates.

Perhaps these are the characteristics of the adjuncts who stick around until they burn out. These are the hard working, committed, persevering, and motivated instructors who form the core and foundation of the two-year colleges. These are the professional adjunct faculty members who will likely endure a discouraging and relentless cycle of disappointment as they become "homeless, silenced, and abandoned to the margins of academic life" (Bilia et al. 380). These "silenced" and "homeless academics" who are unable to break away from the cycle of underemployment and adjunct labor consumption "are in a utopia—literally a no-place; what [they] do does not have a legitimate place to exist" (Bilia et al. 388). As I have progressed through the stages of developing my own faculty identity, I cannot help but wonder: Will anyone hear my voice? Where do I belong? And, will my efforts ever find a permanent home?

THE NEXT QUESTION: AMANDA'S ANALYSIS

It is job security, an oft-cited factor in job satisfaction (see Bilia et al.; Eagan et al.; Maynard and Joseph) and therefore underemployment, that has the biggest impact on my own relation to my job as a part-time instructor. But while I desire job security, I also must forward a caution to the proposal made by fellow scholars that more full-time *non*-tenured positions are part of the answer to underemployment (see Murphy). While they will provide another stepping stone to advancement, they may be no more than more bait to adjuncts desiring recognition and respect. The end of that path may still be the same: your position is still not secure (see Bilia et al.). To paraphrase another adjunct in WCC's English department, introducing a three-tier system might just increase the hierarchical relationships among faculty, placing a "middle class" of full-time contingent faculty as a buffer between the "rabble" of the part-time contingent faculty and the elite full-time tenured faculty (Spaich). Such a system may simply keep part-time faculty competing for full-time non-tenured positions while ignoring the disparity between those at the bottom and those at the top.

I still enjoy working for Whatcom and its English department, mainly because they have done all they can, within the limiting factors of policy, budgets, and enrollment, to handle creatively and compassionately the precarious position of contingent labor through personal communication, summer courses (for those of us who lost our spring classes), and opportunities to be involved in curriculum building and restructuring that will potentially help mitigate the loss of English 100 and enrollments.

But these efforts still carry no guarantee, and cannot change the overall precariousness of the adjunct position. Having to rely on other jobs, to put more effort into other professional identities that can meet my needs and build my resilience, has in some respects weakened my ties to WCC. For instance, I had been co-advising a student animation club for the past two years, unpaid, with another adjunct. With no classes in the spring, it was not economically feasible to make the trip to campus one time a week for two hours when I could leave that time open for paying jobs, every hour of which I needed. Reluctantly, I told the students that I could not advise them in the spring. And, admittedly, I felt a smidgen of that bitterness from stage three of the Progression of Dissatisfaction directed toward a service that had been offered to two adjuncts, who did not have governance included in their salaries, because there was no full-time faculty member interested or able to advise the new club, according to the students in the club. What was unpaid service then fell to one adjunct during a time when the club was going to have its biggest and most complex event, a city-wide comic-con. I could not even get the day off work to attend the conference.

For an institution that professes to be student-centered, this example stands in direct opposition to its mission. And it resulted at least in part due to my position as an adjunct. Adjunct labor *does* affect student performance, but it is not because of lack of knowledge or professional identity. Job security for adjuncts equals learning security for students. I cannot support students when I am not at the college or when I need to squeeze in extra hours at another job to meet my basic needs. An instructor for PATH once told me that PATH instructors "come for the horses but stay for the people." To adapt this phrase, I think adjuncts come for the disciplinary knowledge but stay for the students. As Desirée noted, we adjuncts are resilient; we can take a fair amount of abuse and still come back for more. But when the precariousness of our position and the conditions under which we work affects our *students'* resiliency—that is a larger problem.

When survival and lower order needs are made paramount, when an adjunct's sense of self and carefully cultivated professional identity are threatened, boundaries are drawn, and contingent faculty start making contingencies of their own. Hitting the wall in the college setting, unavoidable for part-time and non-tenure-track faculty, takes power away from the individual, partly by denying her the ability to construct her own positive identity (see Bilia et al.). Whatcom may try to hide its wall behind inclusive practices and efforts to give growth opportunities to its 75 percent part-time labor force, but disparities persist in terms of resources, pay, benefits, and advancement, and an adjunct's voice is still relatively small and undeniably vulnerable in the larger college context. As much as WCC tries to grow its part-time faculty into something "bigger" and more professional, the reality is that systematic marginalization will always counteract these efforts (see Bilia et al.; Klausman) and make adjuncts feel like the inconsequential, easily-replaceable accessory the term *adjunct* implies, and may eventually encourage them to take their energies and skills elsewhere. And as much as large professional organizations like the NCTE and MLA might wish it, and have been wishing it for the past fifteen odd years (see Bilia et al.), the demand for cheap and easily disposable adjunct labor shows every sign of increasing (AFT "Tenure by Rank"). If this is the case, as many have already argued (see Bilia et al.; Hammer; Harris), we will need to rethink the terms "adjunct" and "contingent labor."

I was asked by a representative for the Washington State Board of Community and Technical Colleges at its 2015 annual Assessment, Teaching, and Learning Conference what colleges could do to increase the engagement of adjuncts in their schools' service and governance. I told her she was asking the wrong question. The question that might help us unravel why a myriad of good recommendations made over the past thirty years have gone largely ignored is, "What are the historical and political conditions that have led adjuncts to be systemically marginalized, economically exploited, and treated like second-class citizens?" In *Forum: Issues about Part-time and Contingent Faculty,* the editor, Vandana Gavaskar, asks, "Can the [adjunct] subaltern speak?" (A1). The next question should be, "Will anyone listen?"

CONCLUSIONS

Underemployment provides a valuable lens to understand Desirée's and Amanda's situations and that of many adjunct faculty. They have sought to develop themselves professionally while working in a system of labor that precludes recognition of their professionalism. This disjuncture between a personal identity—identification with the perceived professionalism within a system— and the realities of that system leads to a sense of betrayal, anger, and resentment, which affects the personal identity: "Unfortunately, regardless of the significant achievements and efforts I have made, I have yet to break free from an oppressive system which dismisses my value and expertise," as Desirée says. This movement, from hope to disillusionment, seems to follow a progression, leading to resignation of professional identity and disengagement from the profession. A permanent "subaltern" class is created, as Gavaskar has noted.

At a two-year college, where "equality" and "open access" are key terms and where all faculty are qualified to teach nearly all classes, the disjuncture between what is offered, what is promised, and what is delivered is even more egregious and difficult to accept. After all, neither Desirée nor Amanda, both with an M.A. in English and postgraduate experience, would expect a tenure-track position at a university. However, they might expect a full-time teaching position. But no such opportunities exists at Whatcom and the tenure-track positions, like the carrot on the stick, are only dangled, never achieved. The English department ostensibly works under an egalitarian mindset and yet the realities of the divide in labor is absolute, as made evident when classes had to be cut, other classes assigned. It's not too much to say that the promises implicit in these egalitarian efforts at inclusion have actually exacerbated Desirée's and Amanda's disillusionment.

We do not want to argue that WCC nor any other college stop offering opportunities for adjunct faculty. To the contrary, all colleges in our state and across the country must recognize the need for and put into practice better employment standards (see Heller et al.). In fact, we join Joseph Harris in calling for a greater awareness of class consciousness in hiring and promoting all faculty. And with Michael Murphy, we call for full-time teaching positions, ones commensurate with faculty experience and expertise, and compensated appropriately, though we remain cautious about its effects.

But just as importantly, especially to the personal identity of the people involved, we call for explicit acknowledgement of, and communication about, the working conditions a person is hired into as adjunct faculty. Adjunct faculty must be made aware from the moment they begin their employment and even in graduate school that teaching is a service, that it is labor in a tiered system, and while it can be intrinsically rewarding, it is not likely to be a stepping-stone to a tenure-track position without making significant personal sacrifices and without some luck. It is time for all faculty to acknowledge what bell hooks calls the "dominator culture" (75) that maintains this system of inequality and to stop pretending that laborers are of the professional middle class. Then, the perils of underemployment can at least be mitigated and the cycle of consumption and the progression of disengagement can begin to be undone.

WORKS CITED

American Federation of Teachers (AFT). "Survey of Part-Time and Adjunct Higher Education Faculty." *American Academic. American Federation of Teachers*, vol. 2, Mar. 2010, pp. 1–15, aft.org/sites/default/files/news/aa_partimefaculty0310.pdf.

American Federation of Teachers (AFT). "Tenure by Rank." Higher Education Data Center. *American Federation of Teachers*, 2013, highereddata.aft.org/instit/national/tenure_wmn.cfm.

American Psychological Association. "Road to Resilience." *American Psychological Association*, 2015, www.apa.org/helpcenter/road-resilience.aspx.

Bilia, Angela, et al. "Forum on Identity." *Contingent Faculty*, special issue of *College English*, vol. 73, no. 4, 2011, pp. 379–95.

Boss, Pauline. *Loss, Trauma and Resilience: Therapeutic Work with Ambiguous Loss.* WW Norton & Co., 2006.

Carillo, Ellen. *Securing a Place for Reading in Composition: The Importance of Teaching for Transfer.* Utah State UP, 2015.

Cho, Sung-Woo Cho, et al. "New Evidence of Success for Community College Remedial English Students: Tracking the Outcomes of Students in the Accelerated Learning Program (ALP)." *CCRC Working Paper No. 53*, Dec. 2012.

Doll, Beth, et al. "The Promise and the Caution of Resilience Models for Schools." *Psychology In The Schools*, vol. 48, no. 7, 2011, pp. 652–59.

Eagan, M. Kevin, et al. "Supporting the Academic Majority: Policies and Practices Related to Part-Time Faculty's Job Satisfaction." *The Journal of Higher Education*, vol. 86, no. 3, 2015, pp. 448–80.

Gavaskar, Vandana. "Can the Subaltern Speak? Contingent Faculty and Institutional Narratives." *Forum, College Composition and Communication*, vol. 64, no. 1, 2012, pp. A1–A3.

Glasmeier, Amy. "Living Wage Calculator for Whatcom County, Washington." *Livingwage.mit.edu*, 2016, livingwage.mit.edu/counties/53073.

Hammer, Brad. "The 'Service' of Contingency: Outsiderness and the Commodification of Teaching." *Forum, College Composition and Communication*, vol. 64, no. 1, 2012, pp. A3–A7.

Harris, Joseph. "Meet the New Boss, Same as the Old Boss: Class Consciousness in Composition." *College Composition and Communication*, vol. 52, no. 1, 2000, pp. 43–68.

Heller, Janet Ruth. "Contingent Faculty and the Evaluation Process." *Forum, College Composition and Communication*, vol. 64, no. 1, 2012, pp. A8–A12.

Heller, Janet Ruth, et al. "Forum on Organizing." *Contingent Faculty*, special issue of *College English*, vol. 73, no. 4, pp. 450–65.

hooks, bell. *Teaching Community: A Pedagogy of Hope.* Routledge, 2003.

Jenkins, Davis, et al. "Progress in the First Five Years: An Evaluation of Achieving the Dream Colleges in Washington State." *Community College Research Center, Teachers College, Columbia University*, Dec. 2012.

Klausman, Jeffrey. "Not Just a Matter of Fairness: Adjunct Faculty and Writing Programs in Two-Year Colleges." *Teaching English at the Two-Year College*, vol. 37, no. 4, 2010, pp. 363–71.

Masten, Ann S. Ordinary *Magic: Resilience in Development.* Guilford Press, 2014.

Maynard, Douglas C., and Todd Allen Joseph. "Are All Part-Time Faculty Underemployed? The Influence of Faculty Status Preference on Satisfaction and Commitment."

Higher Education: The International Journal of Higher Education Research, vol. 55, no. 2, 2008, pp. 139–54.

Mendenhall, Annie S. "The Composition Specialist as Flexible Expert: Identity and Labor in the History of Composition." *College English*, vol. 77, no. 1, 2014, pp. 11–31.

Murphy, Michael. "New Faculty for a New University: Toward a Full-Time Teaching-Intensive Faculty Track in Composition." *College Composition and Communication*, vol. 52, no. 1, 2000, pp. 14–42.

Shor, Ira. "Our Apartheid: Writing Instruction & Inequality." *Journal of Basic Writing*, vol. 16, no. 1, 1997, pp. 91–104.

Spaich, Jim. Adjunct meetings concerning contract negotiations. July–Aug. 2014. Meeting.

Torgovnick, Marianna. "How to Handle an Adjunct." *College Composition and Communication*, vol. 33, no. 4, 1982, pp. 454–56, *Jstor*, ncte.org/journals/ce/.

"Washington State Salaries." *Washington State Fiscal Information*. Legislative and Accountability Program (LEAP) Committee and the Office of Financial Management. 12 Apr. 2016, fiscal.wa.gov/salaries.aspx.

Wiener, Harvey S. "The Attack on Basic Writing—And After." *Journal of Basic Writing*, vol. 17, no. 1, 1998, pp. 96–103.

CHAPTER 16

THE PROBLEM OF SPEAKING FOR ADJUNCTS

Seth Kahn
West Chester University

Thread: Organizing Within and Across Ranks

As a tenured professor who came to adjunct-equity activism a few years ago after training for many years as an activist, ethnographer, and action researcher, I wish I could say that my approach has been as thorough as the term *action research* evokes. Unlike most activists for adjunct equity, I've never been or supervised adjunct faculty. I have no direct experience of contingency (except as a graduate student, which for me was nowhere near as viscerally precarious as adjunct positions). I have just about every possible form of academic and cultural privilege on my side. Yet I'm still compelled to do work with and for adjunct faculty in pursuit of equity and labor justice, even though I'm the *other* from their community.[1]

Linda Alcoff's "The Problem of Speaking for Others," the obvious source of my title, explicates the tension between *speaking for others* as an act of collectivity and as an act of colonial aggression. Privileged speakers always speak our own subject-positions and should do so self-reflexively, but can often subvert even the best motives if we aren't extremely cautious. Activists must be well aware of the dangers in appointing ourselves *spokespeople* for groups we don't represent.

She closes her analysis with a set of four "interrogatory practices" (24) designed to help those of us speaking from privilege to maximize our ethical engagement with communities whose interests we share and wish to advance:

> 1. The impetus to speak must be carefully analyzed and, in many cases (certainly for academics!), fought against. . . .
>
> 2. We must also interrogate the bearing of our location and context on what it is we are saying, and this should be an explicit part of every serious discursive practice we engage in. . . .

---

1 I have become a member of the community to some extent, including election (in April 2015) to the Board of the New Faculty Majority Foundation. However, I'm well-known as "one of the tenured allies" and, as such, always marked in that way.

3. Speaking should always carry with it an accountability and responsibility for what one says. . . .

4. Here is my central point. In order to evaluate attempts to speak for others in particular instances, we need to analyze the probable or actual effects of the words on the discursive and material context. One cannot simply look at the location of the speaker or her credentials to speak, nor can one look merely at the propositional content of the speech; one must also look at where the speech goes and what it does there. (24–26)

Loosely invoking Alcoff's practices, in this chapter I present a series of recommendations, elaborated through a mix of textual and narrative evidence, along with a mix of my own experiences and the work of allies, for tenured faculty who feel the urge to advocate for (ideally *with*) contingent faculty. To be clear, I don't mean to offer my experience as models, and neither do any critiques I make of my own or other people's efforts aim to minimize the importance of their work. I should also say that very little of what I'm arguing for touches on the kind of program/department-level actions that most other chapters in this book are focused on. My interest is in larger-scale advocacy and organizing at what we might call a *movement* level.

DON'T OVER-IDENTIFY WITH THE COMMUNITY

If you're tenure-track, you don't face the same struggles; don't say that you do. Tenured faculty face struggles, yes, but "struggles" doesn't mean "the same struggles." Martin Kich, Professor of English Education at Wright State University and regular contributor to AAUP's *Academe* blog, put it well in early 2014 when he wrote about the tragic death of Margaret Mary Votjko of Duquesne University and coverage of it using the slogan/hashtag #IAmMargaretMary:

So it has struck me very pointedly and poignantly that I am not Margaret Mary Vojtko, the adjunct professor who taught for decades and died in destitution. Indeed, whatever sympathy and outrage that I felt when I first became aware of her story has been much intensified by my now more immediate and visceral recognition of what it must be like to deal with a major medical crisis while worrying about how you will pay for your treatment and how you will possibly pay all of your other bills while trying to convalesce. (Kich)

Sympathy and empathy? Yes. Declarations of solidarity? Of course. But the truth is that Kich, like me and many of you, simply doesn't face the stress and fear of contingency and the dangers—physical, financial, social, emotional—that come with it. To an audience that has good reason to be suspicious of tenured faculty's motives for engaging contingent faculty, such declarations sound disingenuous.

A healthier move is for tenured faculty to acknowledge both the advantages we have—in terms of security and compensation—and to acknowledge the extent to which what we do as tenured faculty isn't necessarily or obviously worth all that extra money. Biologist Terry McGlynn, blogging at Small Pond Science, makes both points in "On Being a Tenure-Track Parasite of Adjunct Faculty":

> While I do have some additional responsibilities that are not expected of our adjuncts, this disparity between job expectations is tiny compared to the massive disparity between our relative pay, benefits and job security. . . . I also am conscious that many tenure-line faculty in my university do little to nothing more than some of the adjuncts. . . . I have particularly benefited from the contributions of adjunct labor. . . . I actually have never taught the full base teaching load, as I've always had some fraction of my time reassigned to additional research, administration, outreach or professional development activities. . . . The only way that I have been able to carve out time. . . is because others have stepped in to get the work done. (McGlynn)

Along similar lines, Amy Lynch-Biniek makes a very strong case that the very conditions tenured faculty often complain about (metonymized as "writers neck") —arise directly from the very privilege of our status and, more important, from a system of labor exploitation on which that privilege rests:

> On this "day off" that is really a day of catching up on work for so many U.S. academics, remember that, **if you're tenure-track or tenured, the work you do is made possible by a labor system that piles work onto contingent faculty** [emphasis in original]. You can research and attend conferences and write articles because the academic labor system exploits faculty in a system of cheap teaching that privileges a very, very few. (Lynch-Biniek)

Along with the importance of recognizing our privilege, we can articulate some advantages we have working with and for adjunct equity; not to say that adjuncts can't win their own fights, but that our privilege can be helpful if we invoke it wisely. In November 2013, I was on a panel at the Coalition of Academic Labor conference hosted by SEIU in Washington, DC as part of their Adjunct Action campaign. Two adjunct activists—Lee Kottner, a former New Jersey/New York-area adjunct well-known in various parts of the network, and TL Mack, who left adjuncting to organize for Adjunct Action—invited me to do a session with them, my part of which was to talk about collaborating with tenured faculty.

From the beginning, I anticipated being seen—by at least some—as an interloper. I already knew from listservs and social networks about an often-expressed animus towards tenured faculty. We're sometimes seen as competitors if not opponents, and because I knew some people who thought so would be in the audience, I wrote with them in mind. The talk focused on tactical concerns—articulating common enemies faculty face across statuses, identifying venues for mutual organizing, and so on. An example of the complex stance I was trying to take:

> But tenured faculty are still a set of allies to cultivate. As
> directly as I can say it, the group on campus that has the
> most ethos with other faculty and management are the senior
> tenured folks. I'm not arguing that the ethos is deserved,
> and more important I'm not arguing that tenured faculty
> should be making decisions about the movement for you. The
> grounds for common cause between tenure track and adjunct
> faculty are complicated to navigate for members of both
> groups, but there nonetheless. (Kahn, "Organizing")

Note not only the "But" that opens the passage, which is responding to a charge nobody actually made, but more substantively the quick move away from the heart of the argument—that administrations willing to treat contingent faculty poorly aren't likely to listen to contingent faculty arguments for equity. As Lee Artz argues in "Speaking Truth to Power: Observations from Experience," the powerful already know the truth; if they're not convinced yet, repeating it isn't going to change anything. Instead, Artz argues, the response to power is power; at this moment, the power (job security, cultural capital, ethos, access to administrators, and so on) is generally among the tenured. I had to make the point that I understand the risk of colonizing contingent faculty in the name of trying to support the effort, though, and I had to make it loud and clear.

A similar moment occurred later in the talk in a section about the *shared* part of *shared governance*:

> To the extent that tenured faculty resist including adjuncts in shared governance, it's often because many of us feel like our governing power is already too defused—and diffused. More people fighting against neoliberal hegemony are likely to be more successful than fewer people, but that hasn't quite registered yet. But the riff that tenured faculty are over-privileged fat cats who willingly exploit adjunct faculty so we can be all elite just isn't right. The very large majority of tenured faculty understand well that we're threatened, but don't understand that responding to the threat requires allies, one group of whom we *already work with* and *who already understand the issues a lot better than we think they do*. (Kahn, "Organizing")

As an exercise in Burkean identification, the passage leaves something to be desired, but as an attempt to convince a skeptical audience that I understand we can and must acknowledge their academic and professional expertise, it works somewhat better.

What I didn't anticipate in advance was the odd sensation of being the only identified tenured faculty member in the room. It helped that I was vetted by TL and Lee, and that I already knew a few other people electronically. Still, there was a palpable sense of, not animus or anger, but not entirely friendly curiosity, about what I had to say. There was applause from the floor when I talked about some of the good things our union has done for adjunct faculty; there were nodding heads most of the time, which suggested I'd gotten the stance right.

Response to the content aside, two points are important. First, I was able to hear conversations, to participate, and to strike a conciliatory and collaborative tone that has helped me connect with more people doing more activism. Second is what I felt like I couldn't say, i.e., the limit-situation (to borrow Freire's phrase) of conciliatory rhetoric, or recognizing the moment at which I'd have been over-identifying. I rarely feel like I'm on eggshells in a group of academics, but I did that day. I wanted to channel friends who have often correctly bucked against mischaracterizations of the tenure track. I also wanted to make clear that I recognize how myopic some of the positions defending the tenured are. Since then, I've spent a lot of time on social networks, blog/news comment threads and listservs contending that overgeneralizations about both "tenured fat cats" (a riff that pops up on listervs and social networks now and again) and "the adjunct narrative" (as if there were such a thing), accomplish nothing except pissing off people with whom we actually agree substantively.

A healthy balance between conciliation and candor can be hard to find, but the important principle is to make sure that claims of solidarity are grounded in actual issues on which solidarity is reasonable. Over-claiming solidarity risks the solidarity you're claiming, and as a result can undercut possibilities for meaningful work.

BE CLEAR ABOUT YOUR MOTIVES AND
PURPOSE FOR THE WORK YOU DO

The first principle of Action Research is that your work benefits the community first, and you second—if ever.

There's a wide array of possible actions for tenured faculty to conduct with and for contingent faculty. Jennifer Ruth of Portland State University lays out a case for tenured faculty involvement in adjunct equity in a post called "When Tenure-Track Faculty Take on the Problem of Adjunctification" on the blog *Social Science Space*:

> When we went on the market, getting a tenure-track job already meant you were the one person standing in the rubble-strewn city of your profession. There was no denying the corpses. At the very least, we understood that luck played a bigger role in our fate than merit had. We hadn't earned something so much as been spared something else—namely, the miserable life of the freeway flyer. And we drew the obvious conclusion from this, the survivor's-guilt conclusion: we would prove worthy of these tenure-track jobs only if we dedicated ourselves to creating more of them for others. We would fight the neoliberal adjunctifcation of the professoriate in the name of our no less talented but less fortunate friends. (Ruth)

I find the rationale she describes to be a little problematic—not because of what she and her colleagues did, much of which is perfectly sensible, but because of its motive ("survivor's-guilt") and purpose. When I first read the piece, it occurred to me that there wasn't any reference to what the contingent faculty in her department wanted. I eventually registered this:

> For months, every other week, three of us would invite a new handful of people we considered influential on campus to have drinks—tenured faculty and chairs, people who were positioned to do something about the problem. It's not that we were excluding non-tenure-track faculty—far from being our untouchables, they were our friends with whom we had

coffees, lunches, dinners; with whose kids our kids shared playdates—but rather we took seriously what some of them were saying, which was You guys have the power, and thus the responsibility, to reverse this trend. We don't. (Ruth)

She may well be right that the contingent faculty in her department and across the university were prepared to hand off their own agency, or to acknowledge the absence of it. But the post, writ large, suggests a potential disjuncture between the motives of Ruth and her tenure-track colleagues, on the one hand, and their adjunct colleagues on the other. When Ruth says at the end that the group's motivations had shifted such that their fight was to protect a certain notion of academic culture against the incursion of corporatism, that seems to match the specifics of their actions quite closely, but it's unclear—at least within this post— that the adjunct faculty wanted them to "fight neoliberal adjunctification" by "creating more [tenure-track jobs] for others." Possible? Of course; I wasn't there and wouldn't argue that she's colonized the adjunct faculty on her campus for her own purposes. Her declaration of "survivor's-guilt" raises that concern to some degree. At the same time, as long as the adjunct faculty she worked with under-stood what motivated the collaboration, that's all we can ask for.

When our individual motives are challenged explicitly, such challenges call for substantive answers. Many of us tenured faculty who identify as adjunct-equity activists are quick to say our work is obviously about social/labor justice, and that we can't imagine not being committed to it. Along with my commitment to labor justice, I would extend Terry McGlynn's point about recognizing the priv-ileges of tenure to say that such recognition *requires active response*. Mea culpas aren't wrong, but they don't fix anything.

Twice I've made statements (letters on behalf of contingent faculty who were unjustly dismissed from their positions) that I shared among activist networks as templates—or provocations—for other supporters to use as they found help-ful. In spring 2012, an adjunct criminology instructor named Sissy Bradford was let go from her position at Texas A&M-San Antonio after a battle with the university had become contentious and public, during which the university seemed not be taking seriously explicit threats on Bradford's life. When the story first broke in *Inside Higher Ed* (Jaschik, "Crosses") in May, I wrote an open letter to the Texas A&M administration that I posted on Facebook, Google+, and various listservs.

When Josh Boldt from the Adjunct Project posted it on the Adjunct Project blog (Boldt) under the headline "A Tenured Professor Responds to Texas A&M," the story was that a tenured faculty member was publicly speaking out for an adjunct—which was gratifying but distressing. While I already knew I wasn't the only tenured faculty member who would (and did) speak out, I understand that it doesn't happen often. At the same time, I already felt awkward *speaking for* Bradford, although (obviously) not awkward enough not to do it. I didn't go out of my way to consult adjunct faculty before I wrote; I wrote *as an activist* and *as a labor advocate* calling on university management to reverse a reckless and deplorable decision. Although I announced my membership in and position working for my faculty union, I was clear about not representing the union or my university. The goal was to be an individual, ideally with some professional ethos, arguing for Texas A&M management to do the obvious right thing.

The letter didn't work (and for the record, the second on behalf of James Kilgore, dismissed from the University of Illinois in 2014, didn't either). The university didn't give Bradford her job back. I never got even a form letter in response from A&M. Somebody who seems to have been involved in harassing Bradford sent an anonymous letter to my department chair accusing me of consorting with terrorists (because Bradford had given an interview to Al Jazeera), which happened to show up while my promotion application to full professor was in progress—slightly nerve-racking, but otherwise harmless.

As it turns out, the Bradford letter did serve a purpose I couldn't have anticipated, earning me an entry into the community of adjunct activists that was forming around the New Faculty Majority and around the Adjunct Project, not necessarily connected to CCCC or even to English Studies. Since then, those networks have expanded and intertwined, and the national movement for adjunct equity has begun to coalesce and see some success, at least at finding space in mainstream media (as we note in the Introduction) and on social media. Because of my brief "fame" as Sissy Bradford's advocate, and because I've since been vetted by some outspoken movement leaders, I'm able to work with a certain degree of comfort with the community. So the letter didn't accomplish its explicit purpose, but it has been instrumental in helping me establish my motives: not to become another "Tenured Radical" who blogs and exhorts and does little else, but to be someone who at least tries to work on the ground with as many activists as possible in whatever roles I can play helpfully.

LISTEN

By "listen," I mean more than just nod, smile, and wring your hands in empathetic frustration when contingent faculty bring problems to your attention.

All too commonly I hear, "Thank you for listening to us. We feel like nobody is paying attention." I've heard it in response to major efforts and simple questions, e.g., a recent vote taken in my department about whether to move our offices to a new building. In the discussion, which ensued after a week-long email conversation among tenured/tenure-track faculty (with adjunct faculty included but none having participated) on our department faculty email list, I wrote to all the adjuncts offlist and told them if they had a near-consensus opinion about the move, I'd vote with them. Among the respondents, only one didn't sound disproportionately happy about the offer (his reply, roughly paraphrased, was "Who cares, given the real problems we should be talking about?"). In the end, I didn't get a clear directive, but I got lots of thanks that felt much too avid. In many ways this vignette is symptomatic of what pro-adjunct faculty seem to think is sufficiently "activist."

Too often, tenured faculty—even those of us motivated to work for labor justice—seem to think we understand "the adjunct problem" without really hearing what adjunct faculty are telling us. And sometimes we react defensively when critiqued, as blogger Elizabeth Keenan points out (somewhat aggressively, but that's part of the point) in a post called "How Not to Be a Tenured Ally":

> So, when we are critiquing "the tenured" for their lack of
> action and failure to support our efforts, we are critiquing the
> position of power that those with tenure have in relation to
> our own lack of power. We are critiquing a group with a voice
> that could well be used to assist in improving our situation,
> but that often fails to acknowledge that any of our problems
> exist. We are critiquing a group that has, over the past forty
> years, ignored the growing "adjunct problem" as long as their
> own jobs remained secure.**
>
> We are not critiquing *you in particular.*
>
> Though, you know, maybe we are. Reading critiques of "the
> tenured" as a personal slight makes you part of the problem.
> It means that you have, despite any protestations, absorbed
> the idea that you are meant to be in your position of power,
> via a route within the meritocracy. And it means that you are
> in denial of the very real stratification of the university that
> affects some people to a much greater extent than it affects
> you. (Keenan)

It's hard not to feel defensive every time I read this. The last line is the one that I need to amplify, that we all need to *hear.* The simple fact of the matter is that attacks on academic freedom (for example) simply don't affect the tenured the same as they affect the contingent. MOOCs don't threaten our jobs to the same extent they threaten contingent faculty positions. When I call on us to listen, I'm calling on us to get arguments like this through our heads, more than well-intentioned but paternalistic exhortations to "treat our adjuncts like colleagues!"

Another way of putting this lesson, I realize, is to recognize that almost anything we say is likely an overgeneralization, or a misrepresentation of at least some of the contingent faculty population. Their reasons for taking and keeping contingent positions, their goals for workplace reform, their personal priorities—there's nothing approaching a consensus, even a plurality, in survey after survey. As a result, to assert a position, even one that seems ostensibly to be just and equitable, without knowing that it has the support of your target population is exactly the kind of mistake Alcoff is cautioning against.

A worse mistake, of course, is to hear contingent faculty critiques of structures designed to maintain the status quo and simultaneously not hear them—to *not listen*. As "Post-Academic in NYC" puts it:

> What is stoking the rage of adjuncts and graduate students is not the ability to lob 140 character rage bombs into the ether. Rather, it's that people like Tenured Radical still get to frame the operative questions, even thought [sic] they don't know much about the reality on the ground because they don't have to know. (Post-Academic)

This post was in response to a flap between adjunct-activist-blogger-human-lightning-rod Rebecca Schumann and the blogger Tenured Radical regarding travel to MLA for job interviews. Karen Kelsky, blogger and director of The Professor Is In, picked up the thread in the post, "How the Tenured Are to the Job Market as White People Are to Racism," in which she argues that even tenured faculty "believe their gains are the result of their own effort and merit, not systematic structural advantage." It may be late in this chapter for me to be saying this, but if you still believe that, I'm probably not talking to you.

DON'T (EXPECT TO) BE A SAVIOR

One of the hardest lessons I've learned over years as an activist is not to lose hope and faith when efforts don't pan out quickly, and I've had to relearn that lesson in my recent work for adjunct equity. In my own department (which Amy Lynch-Biniek and William B. Lalicker describe in Chapter 6), my vocal—sometimes evangelical—support for adjunct equity has alienated at least some of my colleagues, so much so that if I even say the word "adjunct," some of them stop listening. At the same time, the department has made strides towards equity in the last three years: converting eight adjunct faculty members into tenure-lines (via the union contract provision Bill and Amy discuss in their chapter); inviting adjunct faculty into department governance via committee service for people who want it. Notably, in November 2014, our department offered reassigned time for department service (supervising our student-produced literary magazine) to an adjunct faculty member for the first time in a non-emergency situation via a transparent process. *Something* has changed, and in the spirit of action research, it doesn't make a bit of difference to me how credit for that change is allocated; in the spirit of Linda Alcoff's argument, I must continue to reflect on how my argumentativeness, bordering on self-righteousness, about equity may have set back our efforts as much as helped them.

TRUST, EARNED AND GIVEN

As a tenured faculty member working with adjunct activists, understand that adjuncts are always vulnerable, often angry and frustrated, often suspicious of outsiders, and coalescing right now into a movement with real potential that could be threatened by careless but well-meaning tourists. We have to earn *trust* (maybe the most important concept in my entire argument, and so deeply embedded in my thinking that I didn't realize I needed to say it until now) from the members of communities in which we organize/advocate; it's not reasonable for us simply to expect it because we're tenured and interested. Part of that trust is, as I hope I've shown, a demonstrated willingness to be involved and public about equity issues. But trust takes more than that. We risk trust when we make arguments in public about what *we think* is best for *the adjuncts*, referring them as a class rather than actual people; when we overgeneralize about what a huge and diverse group of people wants or needs. We have to trust that when they voice anger or make demands that it's not our place—from on high—to tell them they shouldn't sound that way (tone-policing) or shouldn't want those things (tenuresplainin'). That's not to say that we can never act without permission from or consensus among our adjunct activist comrades, but to say that we are neither free agents nor leaders in efforts for equity simply because we're interested and sympathetic. Alcoff is exactly right that we are responsible for what we say, to which I would add, we're responsible *to* adjunct faculty for what we say *about* them and *with* them, and given the contingency and vulnerability (material and otherwise) of their conditions, that responsibility comes first.

As simply as I can put it: if we find ourselves wondering whether something we're about to say/do will antagonize people we think we're helping, try asking instead of simply plunging ahead. If we feel impelled to join the chorus of people speaking out for adjunct equity but don't know what to say, just listen for a while. They'll let us know when they need us.

WORKS CITED

Alcoff, Linda. "The Problem of Speaking for Others." *Cultural Critique*, no. 20, 1991–1992, pp. 5–32.

Artz, Lee. "Speaking Truth to Power: Observations from Experience." *Activism and Rhetoric: Theories and Contexts for Political Engagement*, edited by Seth Kahn and JongHwa Lee, Routledge, 2011, pp. 47–55.

Barlow, Aaron. "To My Tenured Colleagues." *Academe Blog*, 14 Oct. 2013, academeblog.org/2013/10/14/to-my-tenured-colleagues/.

Boldt, Josh. "A Tenured Professor Responds to Texas A&M." *Adjunct Project Blog*, accessed 29 May 2012.

Fulwiler, Megan, and Jennifer Marlow. *Con Job: Stories of Adjunct and Contingent Labor*. Computers and Composition Digital Press/Utah State UP, 2014, ccdigital press.org/conjob/.

Jaschik, Scott. "Crosses, Threats, and an Adjunct." *Inside Higher Ed*, 29 May 2012, insidehighered.com/news/2012/05/29/adjunct-loses-courses-after-going-public -about-threats-she-received.

Kahn, Seth. "'Never Take More Than You Need': Tenured/Tenure-Track Faculty and Contingent Labor Exploitation." *Forum: Issues about Part-Time and Contingent Faculty*, vol. 16, no. 2, Spring 2013, pp. A12–A16, www.ncte.org/library/NCTEFiles /Resources/Journals/TETYC/0403-mar2013/TETYC0403Forum.pdf.

———. "Organizing Tenured/Tenure-Track Allies for Adjunct Equity." Coalition of Academic Labor Conference, Washington, DC, 17 Nov. 2013. Presentation.

Keenan, Elizabeth. "How Not to Be a Tenured Ally." *Bad Cover Version*, 28 Oct. 2013, badcoverversion.wordpress.com/2013/10/28/how-not-to-be-a-tenured-ally/.

Kelsky, Karen. "How the Tenured Are to the Job Market as White People Are to Racism." *The Professor Is In*, 1 Jan. 2014, theprofessorisin.com/2014/01/01/how-the -tenured-are-to-the-job-market-as-white-people-are-to-racism/.

Kich, Martin. "I Am Not Margaret Mary Votjko." *Academe Blog*, 22 Jan. 2014, academeblog.org/2014/01/22/i-am-not-margaret-mary-vojtko/.

Lynch-Biniek, Amy. "Writer's Neck: A Privilege." *Compositionist*, 13 Oct. 2014, compositionist.net/blog/writers-neck-a-privilege.

McGlynn, Terry. "On Being a Tenure-Track Parasite of Adjunct Faculty." *Small Pond Science [updated]* 27 Sept. 2013, smallpondscience.com/2013/09/24/on-being-a -tenure-track-parasite-of-adjunct-faculty/.

A Post-Academic in NYC. "There Is No Academic 'Profession.'" *A Post-Academic in NYC*, 27 Dec. 2013, postacademicinnyc.wordpress.com/2013/12/27/there-is-no -academic-profession/.

Ruth, Jennifer. "When Tenure-Track Faculty Take on the Problem of Adjunctification." *Social Science Spaces*, 16 July 2013, socialsciencespace.com/2013/07/when-tenure -track-faculty-take-on-the-problem-of-adjunctification/.

Schumann, Rebecca. "The End of the College Essay." *Slate*, 13 Dec. 2013, slate.com /articles/life/education/2013/12/college_papers_students_hate_writing_them _professors_hate_grading_them_let.html.

CHAPTER 17

THE RHETORIC OF EXCELLENCE AND THE ERASURE OF GRADUATE LABOR

Allison Laubach Wright
Lone Star College-North Harris

Threads: Professionalizing and Developing in Complex Contexts; Protecting Gains, Telling Cautionary Tales

In 2011, the University of Houston (UH) was ranked by the Carnegie Foundation as a "Very High Research Activity" university. Billboards went up across the city, banners were hung from every lamp post on campus, and every letterhead and email was changed to announce to the world that UH was "Houston's Tier One University." Becoming a "Tier One" university had been a key part of UH's long term goal since the current president was hired in 2008, and UH is not the only large public university in Texas that has been concerned with such a push. Thanks to a push from the Texas Higher Education Coordinating Board, Tier One status means greater funding potential from the state in addition to a higher caliber undergraduate student body and increased recognition both within and outside of Texas. UH, which had previously functioned more as a community-based university, could become known as on par with the University of Texas at Austin and Texas A&M, the only other two research universities designated "Very High Research Activity" in the state. To be known as "Tier One," in other words, was both a *marker* of excellence and a *means* to achieving further excellence as an academic institution. Tier One status here functions as a brand which the university has claimed, monetized, and profited from. Since 2011, tuition has gone up along with the average high school GPAs and SAT scores of undergraduate students, and a new student center and stadium have been constructed to improve life on campus for undergraduate students.

The designation of "Very High Research University," in other words, has been used to market the university as an undergraduate institution despite the fact that the Carnegie designation is based primarily on graduate degrees conferred and the research of professors who teach few (if any) undergraduate courses. It is also a designation that is not meant to be a measure of quality, but rather only a way to group universities with similar student bodies. In this chapter, I'm primarily concerned with the way that the construction of the University of Houston as "excellent"—through the branding of Tier One based on this measure—functions to erase the work of graduate student workers, marking them as disposable in pursuit of a larger capitalist goal. This move happens within a system that already devalues the work of graduate students by falsely constructing them as apprentices who are the primary beneficiaries of their work in the academy. I'll begin by looking more closely at the rhetoric of excellence, especially as it has been adopted by the University of Houston, because the institutional narratives that define excellence are closely tied to labor conditions. In this case, graduate labor provides a huge part of the material conditions on which a public research university can build its image in order to claim excellence; however, the very presence of graduate student teachers as the face of lower division education undermines that narrative of excellence, especially where a university is concerned with "World Class Faculty" as a marketing strategy.

The language of excellence is one of the more insidious ways that neoliberal discourse circulates in the university, in part because it *appears* to be so ideologically neutral. In *The University in Ruins*, Bill Readings shows that part of the reason for this is that excellence generally functions without a direct referent, such that "parking services and research grants can each be excellent, and their excellence is not dependent on any specific qualities or effects that they share" (Readings 22). Readings sees excellence as an "entirely meaningless" and "non-referential" descriptive term, which

> effectively brackets all questions of reference or function, thus
> creating an internal market. Henceforth, the question of the
> University is only the question of relative value-for-money,
> the question posed to a student who is situated entirely as a
> *consumer.* (22; 27, emphasis in original)

When excellence works as a key way of valuing the university, it makes a university education—and college degrees—function more like any other commodity. Although Readings believes that excellence is an empty term and therefore non-ideological, he does acknowledge the way that its emptiness functions to draw people in, bringing members of the academic community at all levels—even those who would normally eschew capitalist language and goals—to use a discourse that connects the university to a consumption model. He writes that the "need for excellence is what we all agree on. And we all agree upon it because it is not an ideology, in the sense that it has no external referent or internal content" (23). Excellence is therefore a marker that is hard to turn away from because there is no direct content to critique, and it becomes one of the ways that academic capitalism spreads not just in the corporate world or in the university administration, but in the behaviors of faculty and students.

While Readings suggests that excellence is an easy idea for both the academy and the corporate world to agree on in part because of its ideological emptiness, Christopher Carter asserts in *The Rhetoric of Resistance* that this analysis ignores a key part of the way that excellence works. Although Carter does agree that excellence operates without solid referents—it is applied across many different fields and used to judge disparate ideas—he adds that even when it seems empty of content, it operates "within the boundaries of market rationality; and what's more, it helps to preserve those boundaries while feigning no relation to them" (31). Because of this emptiness and the almost universally positive understanding of the term, excellence actually works to hide the connections to practices that are concerned only with competition, allowing academic programs that have embraced market logic to paint themselves as student-centered. This erasure is part of how excellence functions as what Carter calls "a seedbed of ideology," working like Weaver's God terms to rhetorically "constitute and reconstitute an ideology that binds higher education to global capital" (31). Carter thus begins to move towards defining the rhetorical work of excellence as working to establish and spread ideology.

Bill Readings points to the use of rankings such as that done by *Maclean's* in Canada and the *US News & World Report* in the US as one of the problematic ways that universities try to demonstrate excellence. Such reports offer evaluations that function like *Consumer Reports*, offering data to compare schools as one might compare any similar product for consumption. There has even been an increase in the past few years of language suggesting that one should find the best *value* in an educational institution. The problem, though, comes when universities use these ideas in order to develop and change their programs. They take an external evaluation—one which is already steeped in the language of consumption, such that a student is choosing which university to attend in the same way she might choose to buy a car—and use it as an internal measure of excellence. As university administrators, professors, staff, and students cater to these rankings, they are buying into the idea of excellence as it is linked to a profit-oriented model of consumption.

Certainly part of the overall "Tier One push" at the University of Houston, and in the state of Texas as a whole, has been a process of wanting more national recognition on such lists, but the use of the Carnegie Foundation listing as a measure of excellence works somewhat differently. The Carnegie Foundation designation is, for the purposes of measuring real quality, an empty designation outside of grouping institutions for further comparison, but it is because of this emptiness that it can stand in so easily for the branding that the UH administration wants to do. Here, as Carter and Readings suggest, excellence has no referent; the measure to which administrators point is a meaningless one. But the way that the university has used the Carnegie designation as a measure of excellence is nonetheless instructive in looking at the way that certain kinds of labor—in this analysis, specifically graduate labor—are erased in constructing these institutional narratives.

Since branding itself as a Tier One University, the University of Houston, has marketed itself to bring in first-time-in-college undergraduate students with higher GPAs and SAT scores, and pushing those with more mediocre numbers into the undergraduate programs in other campuses across the university system—ones that are not identified as Tier One—or to the many community college campuses nearby. From 2007 to 2013—the period immediately before the Tier One Push until the most recently collected institutional data available—the number of first-time-in-college freshman applicants to the University of Houston increased from 10,978 (with a 77 percent acceptance rate) to 17,407 (with a 58 percent acceptance rate). In addition, for those same years, freshmen in the top ten percent of their high school classes increased from 20 to 34 percent, while the students scoring above a 600 on the verbal portion of the SAT increased from 16 to 29 percent (University of Houston IR). The increase in applicants and selectivity coincides with UH's Tier One marketing campaign, which functions both as a signifier of the University's excellence *and* a means by which the university is making itself more excellent. In these same years, we've seen massive construction projects focused primarily on a new student union center and a new stadium, with both locations functioning much more like mini-malls. These changes speak to the consumerist lifestyles of undergraduate student populations and speak towards the way "Very High Research Activity" slips towards "Tier One Research" slips towards "Tier One undergraduate" institution.

But the university, in promotional materials highlighting the importance of being a Tier One Research University, is also sure to declare that the "Tier One Push" isn't over, and that UH is still concerned with "broadening our overall excellence" (University of Houston, "Tier One"). The "overall excellence" in need of broadening refers to the fact that although the Tier One brand has been used as a recruiting tool for undergraduates, the university is still lacking in many metrics that would typically define an "excellent" undergraduate institution, particularly because UH has a six year graduation rate of below 50 percent. The relative success of UH's marketing campaign —which ignores low graduation rates in emphasizing a "Tier One education"—demonstrates the slipperiness of the language of excellence. Even when it has nothing to do with undergraduate programs, a brand that is associated with excellence comes to stand for the kind of undergraduate experience that draws larger numbers of applicants with higher high school GPAs and standardized test scores. The changes at the University of Houston are operating like a self-fulfilling prophecy, improving metrics usually associated with undergraduate educational quality—average high school GPA, test scores, students living on campus, and selectivity in admissions—by changing the student body instead of the programs. The university can expect improvements in retention and graduation rates because they are able to select students who are more likely to persist, more likely to graduate in three years, and come from family backgrounds that enable them to pay for on-campus housing.

The fact that the discourse of excellence functions to erase connections to market logic, as Christopher Carter suggests, is important for the analysis of the University of Houston's use of Tier One as a brand. Part of the way that the Tier One discourse operates is to forward the parts of a "Very High Research Institution" that might be good for students—for example, the presence of world renowned research faculty, which has been heavily advertised on UH promotional material. However, we all know that when research is emphasized as the primary goal for faculty, teaching is treated with reduced importance, particularly in the case of introductory and freshman classes, which are more likely to be taught by graduate and contingent faculty. It is only logical that increasing the research output of the faculty implies not only the research of professors, but the teaching labor of graduate students who subsidize such research while also earning the advanced degrees that are measured to determine the Carnegie Foundation designation. "World Class Faculty" becomes one of the selling points implied by "Very High Research Activity" status, but it ignores the material reality that such faculty members rarely have anything to do with undergraduate education, especially lower division courses, at large public universities. Instead, the labor of teaching undergraduates falls to graduate students, whose teaching labor is erased within this narrative.

Such labor is generally justified as being part of the education of graduate students, as part of an apprenticeship in the academy, which already serves to devalue much of the labor of graduate students within the institutional narrative. Kevin Mattson clarifies the progress of an apprenticeship historically in his essay "How I Became a Worker," which describes the ideal system in which one "proceeded from apprentice (graduate student) to journeyman (teaching assistant) to master artisan (professor)" (90). The system, in this ideal form, works to train and then place individuals into top jobs, serving the best interests of all parties. We know, though, that the system in the academy is not operating in its ideal form. My concern is that clinging to the language of apprenticeship is harmful when the system no longer works as described, and certainly not in the best interest of all parties. When it prevents new thinking about a broken system and silences dissent for exploitative labor situations, maintaining the language of the apprenticeship model is directly implicated in the larger problems of the labor system.

As an example, Mattson points to the historical situation in nineteenth century New York, where the labor system become more and more exploitative. Journeymen were closed out of master artisan jobs, instead finding that their "'training' became longer and longer stints of employment and hourly wages," leaving them with little option but to "sell their labor to master craftsmen who looked increasingly like small factory owners" (90). In this situation, clinging to the language of the apprenticeship model served the best interests of the shrinking class of master artisans, who could fight against unionization and workers' rights under the guise of the value of an increasingly non-existent system. This is strikingly similar to the current situation of contingent faculty, to whom Mattson refers as permanent journeymen. Such a classification is important because it ties the more recognized labor problem in the academy—that of the growing number of contingent faculty and shrinking number of tenure-track jobs—back to the system that produces labor. In other words, the labor problem begins with the production of graduate degrees, which form the base of what Marc Bousquet refers to as the primary operation of the academic system: the "extraction of teaching labor from non-degreed persons, primarily graduate employees and former graduate employees now working as adjunct labor—as part-timers, full-time lecturers, postdocs, and so on" (86).

The point that I want to make here is that the labor of graduate students —in roles as students/scholars and as workers in the university—is *vital* to the ability of the university to brand and market itself as Tier One. But the material reality of graduate students in these positions is hidden under the branding of the "Tier One University" and the narrative of apprenticeship. The story of building the university brand of excellence that I see is very different from the common institutional narratives of graduate education, in which graduate students are *students* first and teaching fellowships are support offered by a generous university. But when we know that graduate students are a vital part of the university machine and a fairly steady 20 percent of the academic labor force since at least 2003 (Curtis and Thornton 7), we have to acknowledge that the narrative is wrong. And the narrative we hold to—that of the graduate student as an apprentice who is learning a trade—helps create the conditions which erase the work of graduate students and make it that much harder to change the system. Nowhere is this tension more obvious than in English departments, where four year universities have graduate students teaching the labor-intensive first year writing (FYW) course while minimizing both the presence of the course and the work of the graduate students. We see this particularly in James Slevin's observation that even though FYW courses make up around 70 percent of undergraduate courses offered, those courses appear as two or three entries in the course catalogue, where they are taught by "STAFF" rather than a named individual (Slevin 5). At large research universities, FYW courses are generally taught by graduate students, whose names are absent from the course history of the university.

When the Wyoming Resolution was taken up in the 1989 CCCCs "Statement on Principles and Standards," graduate teaching assistants (GTAs) were clearly defined as "primarily students" within the document. Although I take this to be an attempt at protecting graduate students, it unfortunately functions more as a means of sweeping aside the labor of graduate students, as though declaring that the 1/1 or 2/2 courseload suggested for GTAs *should not be* the primary source of labor for the teaching of FYW somehow makes it so. In a department like that at UH, though, with around seventy GTAs, each teaching one or two classes per semester (depending on semester progress of her program), graduate labor *is* the labor foundation of the department. Only three or four tenured faculty per semester volunteer to teach a section of FYW, and any other leftover sections are taught by contingent instructors. Most tenured faculty at large research universities, meanwhile, teach primarily graduate and upper division courses in their field areas, while rarely (most likely never) teaching any introductory freshman course.

Because we know that only about 7 percent of introductory undergraduate courses in English were taught by tenure-track faculty as of the 1999 CAW-CCCC study of contingent faculty (Scott 153), claiming the work of teaching FYW as part of an apprenticeship is problematic because it is clearly *not* an education in doing the work of a tenured faculty member. Instead, an education that includes teaching a 2/2 load of FYW with minimal training, no private office space to consult with students, a low salary, little chance of shared governance, little representation on department committees, and few benefits sounds like an apprenticeship towards a contingent faculty position. Or, more to the point, like a contingent faculty position. In this case, the label of "apprenticeship" ignores the reality: GTAs being treated like contingent faculty in a system where tenure-track lines are decreasing while contingent jobs become more common. The use of the apprenticeship model of graduate education is therefore operating as part of the system while erasing the material realities of graduate student labor in order to cover over that reality.

The "Tier One push" at the University of Houston offers a specific example of the way that the rhetoric of excellence and the rhetoric of apprenticeship work together to erase both the immediate work of graduate students *and* the reality of the larger labor system. It's only by examining these rhetorics that we have a chance to name the system in which we find ourselves and thereby to create the possibility for unified collective action.

WORKS CITED

Bousquet, Marc, et al., editors. *Tenured Bosses and Disposable Teachers: Writing Instruction in the Managed University.* Southern Illinois UP, 2004.

Bousquet, Marc. "The Waste Product of Graduate Education: Toward a Dictatorship of the Flexible." *Social Text,* vol. 20, no. 1, 2002, pp. 81–104, marcbousquet.net /pubs/Waste.pdf.

Bullock, Richard, et al., editors. *The Politics of Writing Instruction:Postsecondary.* Boynton/Cook, 1991.

Carter, Christopher. *Rhetoric and Resistance in the Corporate Academy.* Hampton Press, Inc, 2008.

CCCC Executive Committee. "Statement of Principles and Standards for the Postsecondary Teaching of Writing." *College Composition and Communication,* vol. 40, no. 3, 1989, pp. 329–36, jstor.org/stable/357777?seq=1#page_scan_tab_contents.

Curtis, John W., and Saranna Thornton. "The Annual Report on the Economic Status of the Profession 2012–13." *Academe,* vol. 99, no. 2, 2013, pp. 4–19, aaup.org /report/heres-news-annual-report-economic-status-profession-2012-13.

Mattson, Kevin. "How I Became a Worker." *Steal This University: The Rise of the Corporate University and the Academic Labor Movement,* edited by Benjamin Johnson et al. Routledge, 2003, pp. 87–96.

Scott, Tony. "Managing Labor and Literacy in the Future of Composition Studies." *Tenured Bosses and Disposable Teachers: Writing Instruction in the Managed University,* edited by MarcBousquet et al., Southern Illinois UP, 2004, pp. 153–64.

Slaughter, Sheila, and Gary Rhoades. *Academic Capitalism and the New Economy: Markets, State, and Higher Education.* Johns Hopkins UP, 2004.

Slaughter, Sheila, and Larry Leslie. *Academic Capitalism: Politics, Policies, and the Entrepreneurial University.* Johns Hopkins UP, 1997.

Sledd, James. "Why the Wyoming Resolution Had to be Emasculated: A History and a Quixotism." *JAC,* vol. 11, no. 2, 1991, pp. 269–81, jstor.org/stable/20865795? seq=1#page_scan_tab_contents.

Slevin, James F. "Depoliticizing and Politicizing Composition Studies." *The Politics of Writing Instruction: Postsecondary,* edited by Richard Bullock et al., Boynton/Cook, 1991, pp. 1–22.

Readings, Bill. *The University in Ruins.* Harvard UP, 1996.

University of Houston. "Houston's Public Tier One University." *University of Houston,* uh.edu/about/tier-one/.

University of Houston. "UH Common Data Set (2007–2008)." *University of Houston,* uh.edu/ir/reports/common-data-sets/.

University of Houston. "UH Common Data Set (2013–2014)." *University of Houston,* uh.edu/ir/reports/common-data-sets/.

CHAPTER 18

BRUTAL(IST) MEDITATIONS: SPACE AND LABOR-MOVEMENT IN A WRITING PROGRAM

Michelle LaFrance
George Mason University

Anicca Cox
University of Massachusetts, Dartmouth

Threads: Local Changes to Workload, Pay, and Material Conditions; Professionalizing and Developing in Complex Contexts

> Stories about places are makeshift things. They are comprised of the world's debris. . . . Things extra and other (details and excesses coming from elsewhere) insert themselves into the accepted framework, the imposed order. One thus has the very relationship between spatial practices and the constructed order. The surface of this order is everywhere punched and torn open by ellipses, drifts, and leaks of meaning: it is sieve-order.
>
> —Michel de Certeau, *Walking in the City*

The first time we heard an adjunct at UMass Dartmouth (UMD) refer to "the third floor," we knew that she was speaking to power. Full-time tenure-track offices occupy the third floor. The department's main office, all faculty mailboxes, the support staff offices—the people and resources "central" to the function of the English department—are on the third floor. The space designated for the twenty to thirty adjuncts (dependent upon program needs)—a single office with five working computers and two banks of desks—is located on the second floor, tucked down a hallway. The office for Part Time Lecturers (PTLs), numbered and named 201B, metonymically stands in for the First Year English teaching pool in the same way "the third floor" metonymically speaks to tenure line faculty. "What is the third floor thinking?" we would overhear in the hallways. "We'll want to share that with 201B," we sometimes found ourselves saying. And so, like the title of the British television show *Upstairs/Downstairs*, a metonym of our relationship was enacted.

Space and resources, this personal, ethnographic, and photo essay will show, are the material manifestations of our institutional discourses. A complex story of space and place requires a complex framework: and so, we will break the generic form of the academic narrative as necessary, weaving anecdote, image, personal reflection, theory, history, and observation into this chapter. Our work here will be composite—like the concrete that is the primary medium of the UMD campus, a compilation of mortar and stones. Anicca, a photographer and creative nonfiction writer, and Michelle, an academic ethnographer, will mix voices and visions to tell this story. To further represent the divisions we are discussing, we will present Michelle's narrative in the traditional left-justified form of an academic essay. Michelle's academic argument will ground and scaffold the whole as it narrates history and theorizes the politics of space. Anicca's photos and personal exposition will punctuate and expand the places we might open out; appearing in italics and aligned to the right. This organization reflects our professional positions. Michelle served as the tenure-track director of the First Year English program at UMD for three years, the "Boss Compositionist" of the site evoked here. The position Anicca holds is named Full-Time Lecturer (FTL), a model of slightly more secure staffing that many writing programs have turned to, that is a unique space "in between" the usual dichotomies of higher ed labor—neither tenure line nor "adjunct," but still contingent upon annual renewal.

We do not intend for the different texts presented here to read seamlessly, or even as easy poetic compliments to one another. Rather, the juxtaposition of narratives, experiences, and photos visually reinforce the ways that space reflects, shapes, and even reifies our working relationships. The shape of our text, then, demonstrates the parallel existence of tenure-track (third floor) and adjunct (second floor) faculty at UMD, enacting the separate and unequal structures of status, employment, and economic system to which this collection responds. In an essay about space and labor, an essay that will also be about the ways we move, the ways movement shapes our work and our work shapes our movement, you as reader may move between textual passages in ways that resemble how we have moved, making connections between textual cues, spanning juxtapositions, bridging the disjunctions we offer. Just as this collaboration brings us together, allowing us, through language, to create a dynamic space that refuses easy understandings and simple reproductions of power, so we will argue the possibilities of space and practice for the contingent faculty-instructor.

I

The interview/site visit for my position was scheduled in mid-February, a time when New England is reduced to a grey slate sky and biting cold. Campus seemed to mirror the weather. I would describe the buildings of our college as bunker-like—bunker-chic, if you will. Oppressive. Heavy concrete rises in stacked geometric patterns above a featureless quad. A beehive of colorless concrete ringed in by parking lots. During my first visit, I wasn't sure how I would or could survive the concrete forms that gave shape to the institution. I couldn't imagine a life here. Maneuvering the concrete hallways seemed a gargantuan task. A few steadfast spruce trees between the building and the parking lot offer me a tiny but important reminder of light, air, and life, outside the imposing grey walls.

Highly coercive and symbolically laden, a space—a campus, an office, a desk—dramatically shapes labor practice and reinforces a sense of institutional values. On the one hand, the story to be told is about the character of the campus-space itself, especially as this character seems to support the entrenchment of power differentials and labor inequality in higher education. The architectural style of UMD offers a metonymic backdrop for a deeper understanding of the adjunct-negotiation of space today. Aptly named, "Brutalism," a highly cost-effective and efficient-to-erect architecture that was favored in the 1960s for industrial, government and institutional structures, the style renders UMD structures into pictures of austerity and discipline—bare concrete, sharp angles, and built-in furnishings. The discourses of efficiency and cost-effectiveness that characterize the unique features of the UMD design-aesthetic resonate eerily with today's ongoing discussions of the adjunct position—the UMD campus is a space where professional marginalization is built quite literally into the concrete. In fact, Henry Giroux names the current neoliberal restructuring of higher education, the "New Brutalism" —a comprehensive right-wing attack on the ideals that supported the open university of the 1960s resulting in the degradation of faculty governance, a focus on what makes for effective pedagogy, and the increasing marginalization of faculty labor.

II

My job here became a means to a full-time position, professional growth, and job stability. Before the start of that semester, I contacted a few members of our contingent or part-time faculty and met with some of them to get acquainted with the program and institutional culture. One of these women looked at me sadly and said, "I don't envy you at all." This was striking because here I was the outsider, younger than most instructors, with a full-time position, an opportunity many other contingent faculty members might want. My conversations with them made it clear to me that my work was going to be, in large part, about navigating division.

On the other hand, this story is also about the fight for contingent faculty rights. In 2003, "PTLs" (part-time lecturers/the official name for adjuncts at UMD) went on strike, successfully organizing for more job security, stepped pay increases, and benefits. The stories they tell—about picketing campus, visiting the offices of deans, the provost, the chancellor, posting fliers, and speaking out—demonstrate that resistance takes place in the choices, large and small, that individuals make every day. In turn, the purposeful use of space, sharing of resources, and impromptu collaboration are a means of talking back to those institutional discourses that would devalue adjunct-labor and diminish the professional standing of writing program instructors.

The interweaving of these two stories about the campus architecture and the PTL strike, punctuating points with a bit of the French critical theory of de Certeau and Lefebvre, structuring our narrative visually and layering in photos, brings to light a story about how space and place speak explicitly to the inequities of adjunct labor. Space is too often conceptualized as an unmovable face of the status quo. "The subject experiences space as an obstacle, as a resistant 'objectality,'" Lefebvre notes (74). We often experience space as foreboding and totalizing, de Certeau reminds us. The structures of our everyday lives are often symbols of an unyielding technocratic or social order (de Certeau 93). The buildings of any campus may trick our eyes into exactly this place of misrecognition; the concrete forms, the dark hallways that impose a particular type of passage and order our spaces of belonging, the realities of a small office shared by many instructors, may close down our view—at least for a moment—of the ongoing dynamic activities and active processes of repurposing that constitute daily life.

III

Few of these divisions are explicit or easily anticipated; they are most often learned through experience. Or accidents. An example: To recognize the many accomplishments of UMD's "PTLs," my director and I started to construct a bulletin board in the hallway leading to 201B—many of these instructors attend local and national conferences, write books, or publish their creative and scholarly work. We asked for submissions for this bulletin board, but only two instructors in the pool offered to share publications or accomplishments. When we made inquiries about the project, we were met with silence and avoidance. It was a little baffling. Why wouldn't our instructors want us to celebrate their accomplishments? Why wouldn't they want us to post these examples of their intellectual and creative lives where students and colleagues could see them? Later, a friend who works in 201B explained to me that people were angry because they felt that their achievements should be posted alongside those of the senior and full-time faculty at the entrance to the department on the third floor. And so, without realizing it, our efforts became another symbol of the lack of recognition afforded the "second floor."

But hierarchies, too, are collaborative (Mack and Zebroski), and in this recognition, we begin to imagine a different critical space to occupy. A space of activism and movement. While institutions are physical locations, and while the allocation, arrangement, and furnishing of space create a physical reality that cannot be easily ignored, the movements of laborers within a site are always dynamic, fluid, and uncontained. Fixed notions of the institution as a monolith, as a site of static power, or as the endpoint of our practice, fail to capture the potential of individuals to recreate the institution on an every-day basis. How a space like 201B is used can teach us much about the ways spatial narratives and narratives of work refuse, resist, and complicate one another. A story of possibility, if temporal.

We tell this story because we have been moved to think critically about how individuals occupy and put space to use. If institutions are both rhetorical in nature and a unique location in time and space (as claimed by Canadian sociologist Dorothy Smith), then individuals must negotiate the sense of order and purpose that circumscribe the spaces they occupy, choosing how they respond to material conditions as they take up practice (LaFrance and Nicolas). Even as we recognize their limitations and the ways these spatial allocations do and do not serve individuals within a hierarchical system of labor, storytellers do no one any favors if we misrecognize the complexity and possibility, the liminality, these spaces afford.

CONCRETE CAMPUS: HOW DO WE UNDERSTAND SPACE?

> Let's talk for a moment about Brutalism. It was a style that arose in France and Britain in the 1950s and '60s, led by the legendary French modernist Le Corbusier. The name comes from the French "béton brut," meaning raw concrete. It's just by chance that in English "brut" sounds like "brutal," but the name has stuck for good reason. Brutalist buildings tend to be, well, a little brutal. They're usually made of industrial materials, especially concrete, a substance most people associate with highway ramps or gun emplacements rather than great architecture.
>
> —Robert Campbell, *Paul Rudolph's Brutalism, Reworked, at UMass Dartmouth*

The titles of articles that deal with architectural designs like UMD's campus are telling: "In Praise of Ugly Buildings" one *Boston Globe* piece is named. "Celebrated and Reviled" is the title of another. As the quotation above relates, the architectural style of UMD is not just unusual and not just largely unappealing to the eye, it is—with little exaggeration—*brutal*. The entire inner space, from floor to ceiling, is shaped from concrete. The hallways, the stairs and walkways, the classrooms, the meeting rooms, the offices are all concrete. Architecturally, the campus buildings are utilitarian value on display. Floors. Walls. Ceilings. Benches. Stairs. Window Wells. Made of durable, unmovable, inexpensive, industrial concrete.

One wonders why anyone would think that was a good idea.

But, this utilitarian aesthetic was actually the point, according to *Boston Globe* columnist, David Hay. The UMD campus (designed by Paul Rudolph), as most architecture designed in the Brutalist aesthetic, is a political statement cast in concrete—an attempt to demonstrate the contradictions of over-valuing economy and utility. The Brutalist form seeks to make real the aesthetics of frugality and institutional power that inform the construction of public sector buildings. Metonyms of power. "Many of Brutalism's earliest champions were English," writes Hay.

In the 1950s, architects Peter and Alison Smithson famously promoted a philosophy dubbed the New Brutalism. It promised a raw and rough materiality that had a social and artistic purpose. "Brutalism tries to face up to a mass-production society, and drag a rough poetry out of the confused and powerful forces which are at work," [the Smithsons] wrote in *Architectural Design*. "Up to now Brutalism has been discussed stylistically, whereas its essence is ethical." (n. pag.)

Rudolph designed many buildings on these same principles; making visible what state power would be pleased to have us forget.

On campus, lore tells that busloads of architectural tourists come to admire the buildings Rudolf designed. On the flip side, campus lore also notes that student tour guides have been known to tell visitors that Rudolph was a Satanist. Those of us who have lived and worked in buildings designed under Brutalism cannot help but feel dismay . . . much like state power, anyone who works in one of these buildings must take on an uneasy relationship with it. The hardness. The darkness. The cold lack of comfort. The space will act upon you whether you like it or not. Concrete buildings are marked by a number of issues—because bare concrete is porous, it dirties readily and literally cannot be cleaned or polished. Because concrete cannot easily be patched, concrete structures are prone to leaks and cracks.

"Dirty D" our students call campus.

IV

The divisions are physical as well as symbolic. The people I met that first summer and spent time with, all members of the adjunct faculty pool, became elusive in these hallways, existing a floor down, teaching heavy course loads and commuting between multiple institutions. Though some receive benefits and have union representation, their work is "contingent" on the demands of the program and remains unstable. Performing unrecognized advising work, attending meetings for which they do not get any compensation, they are allowed to remain invisible. Over time, I came to realize how important it was for me to be diligent in my interactions; I needed to reach out repeatedly. I needed to offer myself in service and collaboration. These efforts and the tenuous relationships built from them over time certainly still remain imperfect. My unique subject position as a person who isn't exactly part of the third floor, but who is also separate from the second floor, a person who is interstitial or "between," has worked for and against me in various ways. I am never sure of my next steps.

On the best days, campus feels inhospitable. On the worst days it is an unmovable reminder of our place in a system of inequality and disenfranchisement.

Appreciation of the aesthetic message these buildings project is one way to surf this spatial *dis*-ease. And there is much to appreciate. According to the UMD history website, the campus began with the state recognition of the promises of education. A rising tide lifts all boats, so to speak. At the tail end of the Gilded Age (1895), the Massachusetts legislature chartered the New Bedford Textile School and the Bradford Durfee Textile School in Fall River, a move to educate the children of textile workers and to increase the economic strength of the region. Both colleges continued to expand through the last century, fed by G.I. bill enrollment waves and the increasing economic diversification of the region. In 1962, the legislature merged the two institutions to create the Southeastern Massachusetts Technological Institute (SMTI) and in 1964, 710 acres outside of North Dartmouth were dedicated to a formal site for the institution. And so, Paul Rudolph designed the first buildings on campus, using this style embraced by state governments for its cost effectiveness and by others for its edgy-alignment with working class sympathies and cultural critique. In 1969, the campus became Southeastern Massachusetts University and in 1991 the University of Massachusetts Dartmouth.

V

In winter, in particular,
there is one hallway I avoid.
From the doorway, I must turn,
left and left and left,
up and up the spiraling concrete
across many steps worn through the center.
Pieces of aging concrete crumbling
under my feet.
I pray no student falls here.
I hope that I, too, remain moving.
Sometimes workers come and make attempts
at repair.
But the steps mostly remain broken.

And so campus history tells us that the ligaments of industry and economy are always beneath the veneer of twenty-first century higher education.

Institutions so often perpetuate the issues they were created to address.

VI

201B—the PTL Office:
Six long desks.
One round table.
Five computers in various states of function and dysfunction.
Difficulty connecting to Wifi.
A dingy carpet.
five to ten instructors sharing space, grateful not all of the pool
is vying for the space on any given day.
Freshman writers trying to find their teachers.
Copy codes,
punched with an awareness of paper limits imposed by administration.
Work being done quietly;

jokes being told;
secrets being shared.
Whispers,
resignation, and resistance.

How do we read such a space? How do we read the 201B/third floor divide in light of this history? Lefebvre refers to the "space of social practice," which he describes as "the space occupied by sensory phenomena, including products of the imagination such as projects and projections, symbols and Utopias . . . " (12). Space for Lefebvre is regularized by the state and social forms of domination. The space of UMD, at once Rudolph's remarkable vision and the face of state power (or intentional neglect), is ordered by levels and highly personal geographies—our offices are ordered in ways that recognize the prestige granted to us by the institution. Thinking through Lefebvre, the space is both a place of "habitation" and a "tool of thought and action" (26); and so through our labor (another name for movement and action), the space is imbued with socio-political and personal significance, despite its rigidity and coldness. This is a theory that easily maps onto the descriptions I've leveled above, where space and place are so clearly layered with the contests of meaning entailed in the creation of a public institution, so clearly evocative of the other inequities of labor and value in high education.

VII

Some of the instructors in the 201B office jokingly refer to it as "the caul-
dron" and they avoid working there. They will instead meet with students in
the library or in an empty classroom. But 201B is also a place where some
instructors choose to dialogue about the challenges of their position, a place
to share teaching materials, ideas and solidarity. Some of the instructors
refer to themselves as a "cohort" (a reminder that many started their work
in the FYE as graduate students, taking their first appointments as "teach-
ing assistants" to supplement their graduate study in the professional writing
program). Many will step up for others, helping direct someone else's students
to advisement and/or office hours, creating space for each other to conference
while they are also trying to prepare to teach, respecting the boundaries of
space with personal possessions, or nominating a person to communicate with
administration around issues like a leak in the ceiling, broken equipment
or a need for office supplies. With little reward, they persist with grace. It's
always struck me, too, that these instructors know more about our campus as
a whole—they traverse it, move more freely between points, make temporary

spaces temporarily theirs to meet the needs of students. After all, they teach in the most far-flung rooms on campus, have the least access to computer labs close to the department that has employed them, they have no permanent professional space. The PTLs have found ways to work around these collective constraints. Conversely, most full-time faculty are afforded the ability to perform their work with students in the sanctity of their own, private, offices.

And so, too, the resonance.

Of the third floor and second floor divide, office space allocation, access to the tools that make work within these spaces possible—desks, chairs, computers, printers, photocopiers, and all those other essentials—the power differentials of office and resources allocation for part-time, adjunct instructors are so clearly cast within these topoi. These positions and the spaces allocated them are not accidents of history, even if they are the result of complex issues related to design and institutional status. We can read this metonym in no other way; the lack of resources faced by adjunct instructors at UMD is the product of broader efforts to shrink the power of public institutions, the result of a class war eroding middle-class institutions, and the face of a neoliberal turn in public discourse that questions the value of the liberal arts, enacting corporate models of education as job training. These forces would seemingly pull apart civil institutions to make way for the privatized, the militarized, and global capital. The position of the contingent faculty instructor exists in a landscape of scarcity, economic contraction, and political uncertainty.

VIII

People who work on the third floor become adept at sidestepping a recycling container placed directly in front of the single women's bathroom to catch a drip whenever it rains. We speculate about why the leak cannot be fixed—physical improvements and facilities maintenance inhabit a mysterious realm beyond our grasp. We all just adjust.

The container has been used to catch the rain for the full five years I have been in my position.

And yet, Lefebvre also cautions us against overdetermining our reactions to these circumstances of space and labor—space is a complex system of codes, he reminds us. A layering of historical-production, culture, and meaning. But, these codes never have a "one-to-one" relationship (36). As I noted in the introduction, Lefebvre recognizes that as individuals, we experience space in the moments where it limits and determines our efforts: "[A]t times as implacably

289

hard as a concrete wall, being not only extremely difficult to modify in any way but also hedged about by Draconian rules prohibiting any attempt at such modification" (74). But we can resist, repurpose, and recast those meanings: "The texture of space affords opportunities not only to social . . . but also to a spatial practice that it does indeed determine, namely collective and individual use: a sequence of acts which embody a signifying practice even if they cannot be reduced to such a practice" (74).

IX

I have learned in my brief years here just how shaped I am by space—my emotions, my confidence, my ability to work well are influenced by the physical forms around me. I don't think I am alone in this. A favorite topic of conversation amongst colleagues is how difficult it can be to concentrate on our work with water trickling in around the edges of windows or a layer of ice frosting the inside of an office during winter. It's often so cold that inhabitants wear gloves and hats at their desks. We stash illicit heaters by our feet. We make cynical jokes about how bleak it is. And in a way, there is a solidarity in that too.

And so we encounter 201B/the second floor as doubly encoded. Yes, it is marginal to the third floor's more recognized location for departmental activities. And this marginality has its drawbacks, including a separate copier, little actual desk space shared by many, and a lack of privacy for student meetings, personal phone calls, or conversations with colleagues. Historians of composition, such as Miller and Strickland, have reminded us that the nature of our labor in the composition classroom has been and will be fundamentally misunderstood, undervalued, and under-recognized. 201B speaks to that history, making it real, reinforcing the message that these classes and their teachers are not central to the mission of the university. Institutional status shapes a larger experience that is semiotically telling.

But in the same moment, the collective and individual use of this space cannot be circumscribed so easily.

X

My first semester teaching, I was scheduled in RM 114 or, "the room under the stairs" as I came to think of it. A former storage room now converted to a classroom, the space held about twenty elementary school type desks. The slim windows, nearly below ground, are dingy and don't open. My laptop and whiteboard markers were of little use; the room offered a chalkboard (but, no chalk) and an ancient overhead projector that didn't work. The layout of the room made it difficult for all students to see me at all times. At the end of the class—a developmental writing section with students who I view as some of the hungriest, most important learners at our institution—I made an offhanded apology about the room, offering to find us a new one. One student remarked that he just figured it was because the class was "remedial." As if he and his classmates did not expect to be treated with the same courtesies granted "regular" students.

Space is also the site of resistance: the movements of those who do and do not use 201B, these movements often unnoticed and temporal, represent a constant shifting of power and affiliation. Inner and outer worlds of these instructors always overlap and take on highly individualized meanings—201B becomes the site where PTLs meet in small groups to organize communications with the union. It becomes a site avoided when interpersonal conflicts erupt between instructors. Leaving personal items or teaching materials is discouraged, but people leave folders, handouts, textbooks, and boxes of files on tables or in drawers out of need, defiance, neglect, or forgetfulness. (Who cleans or organizes such a space? Who is responsible for its upkeep and character?) This very personal relationship to an impersonal space and its use will always escape the totalizing influences of institutional discourse. Space can never be entirely mastered. People misappropriate it. Traverse it. Reassign its use. Occupy or refuse it. Ignore it. Ultimately, space allocations are semiotic allusions to power structures. Those with institutional privilege prefer to ignore these gestures. Those without power must live in them.

For space requires movement and action. And movement and action require purpose. And so our daily routines echo with dominant notions of our status, our value, our place.

XI

Don't get me wrong, there are a lot of things I love about working here. In fact, in most ways, I love my job. Despite the physically difficult space, the darkness, the heavy brutalism of it all, unexpected beauties appear. A custodian brings a plant to my office, a dean works long hours as an ally for the betterment of all students and faculty, other instructors take me in, guide me, mentor me into a professional life that I had little to no experience with before taking this position. And yet, the beauty of the people I encounter here cannot erase the impenetrable nature of the concrete forms we inhabit.

CALLING FOR MORE MOVEMENT AND RECOGNITION

> Representational space is alive: it speaks. It has an affective kernel or
> centre: Ego, bed, bedroom, dwelling, house; or: square, church, grave-
> yard. It embraces the loci of passion, of action and of live situations. . .
> Consequently, it may be qualified in various ways: it may be directional,
> situational, or relational, because it is essentially qualitative, fluid, and
> dynamic.
>
> – Lefebrve, *The Production of Space*

The regional and architectural press may be surprisingly vocal about Rudolph, the historical need to preserve even ugly/uncomfortable buildings, and the working class history of the UMD campus, but it is notably silent about the moment of labor history when the adjunct instructors on the UMD campus went on strike. There are no titles to call up, no op-ed pieces, no news coverage at all. A troll through the *Boston Globe* archives turns up a single voice—a letter to the editor. In this letter Andrew Nixon, institutionally unaffiliated (though from the letter's tone, he is likely one of the striking workers at UMD), explains the reasons instructors at UMD have decided to stand up for better working conditions:

> Today, 35 percent of the school's faculty are classified as part-
> time. Collectively, they shoulder so much of the teaching load
> that without them, the university could not fulfill its basic
> mission. Like their full-time colleagues, they are committed,
> well educated, successful in the world outside of teaching, and
> experienced. Unlike their full-time colleagues, they receive
> low pay without benefits. Although many have taught 10
> years or more, they are classified as "visiting" and survive on
> annual or semester contracts that arrive two weeks before
> classes start. Part-timers are paid at a rate roughly half that of
> the lowest-paid full-time professor. Most make under $20,000
> a year. Many are limited to teaching one course a semester for
> as little as $3,000. Working "part time" can also mean teach-
> ing 100 percent of a full-time teaching load without full-time
> pay. Unlike their counterparts at the Amherst and Boston
> campuses, Dartmouth's part-time faculty members have no
> health or pension plan. (Nixon)

This letter stands in as one of the only public recognitions of the successful organization of PTLs on the UMD campus. The strike allowed adjunct instructors to effectively negotiate for stepped pay increases, job security, and benefits. It also taught them the power of their movement and collective action.

XII

I cannot help but reflect on how many things have changed for me as an inhabitant of this space, as a participant in our program. Though the physical form of this institution has not changed, my movement within it has become more fluid, more nuanced, less resistant in some ways, more so in others. I now see students I know in the hallways and feel a deep loyalty to them. I move more freely through the space without getting lost and I run into colleagues with whom I stop and talk about how smart, bright and dedicated our students are. I have become a faculty advisor for a sustainability initiative on campus, and we move into the outdoor spaces of campus together. We talk about change and campus community. Like many here, the work I do with students is a consistent source of joy.

And it is this movement that is key.

The instructors who work for the First Year English program determined—well before my arrival on campus—that an office could not determine them.

Working against the metonym of rigid separation and reified hierarchy, these writing instructors carry on this tradition even now, engaging in active and invigorating collaborations and moments of mindful resistance, repurposing, recoding, and reappropriating the spaces they had been "granted" by the powers that be and working to reconceptualize the most effective sites of their labor. They co-create curricula. They share handouts and activities. They discuss a collective response to institutional policies that recast the value of their labor. They become active members of campus initiatives outside of English. They develop important long term relationships with colleagues in other departments. While the spaces they occupy are often temporary, depersonalized, and sometimes unauthorized—a crowded office, hallways, open and public spaces, remote corners, parking lots and the quiet of a car; almost always borrowed and so subject to interruption, distraction, and, at times, eviction—this fluidity and dynamism is an element of their strength.

In his piece, "Walking and the City," Michel de Certeau echoes Lefebrve's concern for the overly simplistic ways we imagine space—we read the structures that order our lives as symbols of an unmoving technocratic, social order. The buildings of a city, or a campus like UMD, may trick our eyes into exactly this place of misrecognition; the concrete forms, the clear channels for our passage, and clear spaces of belonging may eclipse our view—at least for a moment—of the dynamic activities that do not fit those molds.

XIII

For better or worse, a part of me has learned to resist less. I can forget the concrete at times, the black mold that blossoms on the walls (marking the third floor entrance to the English department) in the wake of certain leaks, the wind blowing in my office window, the stains that cannot be removed, the sounds of construction drowning out my conversations with students during office hours, the constant emails welcoming another "vice provost of something" (hired at a hefty salary while our departmental budgets get cut). These are the places that feel like compromise in ways that I am not proud of. I am surprised by my anger and frustration. Emotions which also make it possible to continue forward.

But so much of our lives take shape "below the thresholds at which visibility begins" as de Certeau writes (93). The forces that demand allegiance to ideals of space cannot overwrite, erase, or eradicate the networks, the trajectories, the many decision-points, or the rich experiences that circulate through and repurpose them. Because we move, because we work, because we interact as individuals, we *cannot* be totalized. In the interplay between these stories of space, history, and daily practice, what emerges is a story of possibility. Again, de Certeau:

> Linking acts and footsteps, opening meanings and directions
> . . . become liberated spaces that can be occupied. A rich
> indetermination gives them, by means of a semantic rarefac-
> tion, the function of articulating a second, poetic geography
> on top of the geography of the literal, forbidden or permitted
> meaning. They insinuate other routes into the functionalist
> and historical order of movement. (105)

To misunderstand these spaces as only temporary, as only marginal, is to forget the power—the *poetic geography*, to draw from de Certeau—that comes of everyday movement.

There is no way to discount the problem of 201B and the lack of resources that restrict the workday and work practices of the adjunct instructor at UMD. The space is simply unacceptable. Too small. Too crowded. Too restrictive. For an administrator of an important first year program, there is no other response to the deplorable conditions granted these instructors of the first year writing classes. But to understand this situation as the only story to be told loses sight of the rich possibilities that were claimed by these workers in the 2003 strike and the possibilities that await those who embrace continuing collective action.

XIV

It is late February again and with a heavy workload, I end up in my office later into the evening than usual. I turn on my space heater and I lock my door. I am in a time capsule. Outside no one moves or walks; there is no sound and no light. The motion sensor flickers off the the weak fluorescents that line the narrow, dim hallway. My slim window looks out over more concrete . . . I am barely aware of night falling. I work until my head hurts and even past that.

When I am ready to leave, I steel myself against the isolation and venture out down the hallway. I have been working on the handbook we are developing for our First Year English program, a document whose language enacts the authority of the institution over the labor of FYE instructors. I reflect that, though this is my first full "professional" position in the academy—most of my experience has been as a contingent laborer—my experiences as the Assistant Director of the program are often incongruous to that adjunctified-identity.

Based on my title and because I have my own office on the third floor, I am generally perceived as being aligned with the third floor, with tenure-line faculty or even the university's administration. But to some of the people on the third floor—senior male literature professors in particular—I do not completely belong either. I am not tenure track, I hold an M.A. in composition, and it is often clear that they do not recognize composition as a scholarly field. The work I do reflects those subject positions. On one small window of the heavy, steel fire doors that lead to the stairwell, there has long been a sticker. It reads: "PTVL means exploited professor." This remnant of the 2003 PTL strike calls up an era that feels long gone. And, yet, it is still so present it shapes my every action.

I make my way home in the dark.

Even as the spaces granted adjunct instructors at UMD are, as we noted above, almost always temporary, depersonalized, and unauthorized, this reality and constraint upon space imposes a remarkable fluidity and dynamism upon the movements of these resilient laborers. Movement between sanctioned and unsanctioned sites of practice (the movements instructors tell me they were proud to take part in during the 2003 strike: occupations of key administrative offices, picketing, letter writing, meetings) become both a form of resistance and a way to revise the story told. In composition, we have long known that our marginalization as a field also allows us to imagine a different form of resistance—this most often takes the form of a critical consciousness shared by many members of the field. We discuss the political dimensions of our work; we imagine the transformative potentials of our pedagogical work. As Mack and Zebroski suggest: "A commitment to transformation is what draws people together and makes it necessary to write in the first place" (163).

After a number of months of working with instructors in 201B and fretting over the limitations the shared office imposed and represented, I also came to learn that the space afforded a number of things that having a private office on the third floor did not. Because there were no walls between them and no doors to close, instructors in the adjunct-office collaborated freely on assignments and classroom designs, investing deeply in the community-of-practice they had built over the years. They shared their personal lives and their teaching materials with equal openness. They built relationships with their officemates in between classes, discussing textbooks, pedagogical approaches, and lesson plans. The public nature of 201B meant that there were always witnesses to difficult student outbursts or student dilemmas, and someone else on hand to answer questions, troubleshoot, and pass the time with. Those with more experience supported and mentored those who had just joined the teaching pool. New faces enlivened and reinvigorated the familiar with questions and excitement.

XV

The stairs, once navigated,
lead in the colder, wetter months
to a pool of water that must be crossed.
Some mornings, it is a slab of ice,
inside,
blocking my way.

These activities, too, were the result of spatial politics. A culture of whole-person teaching and learning took root organically and authentically. An administrator cannot make such things blossom or thrive. These practices—infused as they were with the everyday and the personal—circulated well below the range of "official" program discourse. A hidden reservoir of strength and meaning.

CONCLUSION

My arguments for more space for the instructors of first year writing were met with stories of the other adjunct instructors for other departments and programs at UMD who had no dedicated office space at all. I argued that our students needed private spaces to discuss grades and delicate topics. I argued that our instructors could not teach effectively if they did not have full access to more and better working equipment. I argued that we were the only first year program that served the entire first year class—that alone should afford us the same sorts of resources as a full department or more prestigious program. My appeals were ineffective. And, as I heard about more and more tenure-track hires being required to share office space, I began to realize that the institution's growth had not been supported by adequate space-planning.

The student body and faculty numbers were growing.

Campus buildings were not.

So it often is with smaller branch campuses. When public institutions are under fire, economic limitations and spatial relations shape instructional moments as much as any teacher might. Within this infrastructure, we lived the material conditions that were the products of much larger historical and cultural structures.

And so, if I could not procure more space, I determined to work against the second floor/third floor metonym. Purposeful movement between the second and third floors—as well as movement to other offices on campus as I invited our instructors to travel with me to meetings, to other campuses in the region, and to national conferences—became a way of resisting the metonyms of power that were handed to us all. Over and again, we rewrote the values ascribed to our movements as instructors, as employees of a state institution, and as colleagues. Marginality be damned. We would find a way to speak together. We would find a way to create an ongoing conversation that defied proscriptive forces.

My efforts seem meager in retrospect: visiting 201B as often as possible, dropping in to say hello, to check in, to hang out. On coffee dates with instructors, we sat on the median between floors, between offices. Several instructors co-authored with me, attended national and regional conferences with me, and welcomed me to their workshops and classrooms.

There was power in meeting these colleagues in the stairwells and walkways, saying hello, and chatting with people in between classes and in borrowed corners, of course. There was a different sort of power and pride in our movements to national and regional conferences—where we all presented as experts and innovators, offering insights that extended the important ongoing conversations we had about student writers and writing instruction. When we claimed local spaces of traffic and bustle as our checkpoints, standing for as long as we could between floors, between recognized spaces for formalized interaction, we told each other stories about our teaching that might otherwise not leave our assigned locations. On other campuses and in other cities, we claimed, as well, our knowledge for ourselves and our institution.

XVI

I sometimes sign my emails: "Yours in the concrete."

These efforts to break down metonyms of power and movement were always imperfect, too often incomplete in one way or another, and did not undo the larger social orders that had led to the deeply hierarchical stratifications we were seeking to overcome and rewrite. (I was still the "Boss" and I do not intend to write us as heroes into the stories of 201B. Many of the stories of that office, will *never* be mine to tell.) But the moments of resistance and collaboration we hoped to create (meetings, shared spaces, collaborative projects, co-authored publications) had the ability to *disrupt the rote ways these stories played out between the divergent spaces that were ours.* As such, they held deep resonance for us—and were our primary means of holding the line against the spatial and institutional discourses that would diminish the status of our professional endeavors. In the struggle to reconcile the discourses of the field with the on-the-ground conditions for writing instruction, the architecture of UMD and the PTL strike of 2003 taught me that it is not enough to simply sympathize with instructors around the sorts of material constraints that our designated spaces and managerial discourses impose.

*We must actively pose our work and our movements on campus to erode
the metonymic structures that reify and prescribe value to our labor. We
must actively work to hear, to tell, to promote a different sort of story.*

These stories, we hope, cultivate a deeper understanding—and even celebration—of the adjunct use of space.

XVII

*Let the cement surfaces of this campus speak:
there are leaks in the hallways and offices.
The edifice always . . .
eventually . . .
cracks.*

AFTERWORD

A year and a half after submitting this chapter, UMD opened ten "FTL" lines, similar to the lines held by Anicca, for English to staff the FYE program. These positions would be full time teaching positions with a 4/4 load, offer benefits, longer term contracts, and more integration into the life of the department. Several PTLs applied for the positions, excited by the prospect of more security and more recognition of the service they were already providing to the English department. The hiring committee interviewed a handful of the PTL applicants, but after the first round of interviews continued the hiring conversation/process with only a select few who were ABD or held a Ph.D.

WORKS CITED

Campbell, Robert. "Paul Rudolph's Brutalism, reworked, at UMass Dartmouth." *Boston Globe*, 24 Nov. 2012, bostonglobe.com/arts/2012/11/24/paul-rudolph
-brutalism-reworked-umass-dartmouth/wso1ewaN4xxHr9Gddr0Q1K/story.html.
"Celebrated and Reviled, County Government Center to be Replaced." *Warwick Advertiser*, 19 Aug. 2010, www.warwickadvertiser.com/apps/pbcs.dll/article?AID=
/20100819/NEWS/308199869/0/SEARCH.
de Certeau, Michel. *The Practice of Everyday Life*. Translated by Steven Rendall, U of California Press, 1984.
LaFrance, Michelle, and Melissa Nicolas. "Institutional Ethnography as Materialist Framework for Writing Program Research and the Faculty-Staff Work Standpoints Project." *College Composition and Communication*, vol. 64, no. 1, 2012, pp. 130–50.

Lefebvre, Henri. *The Production of Space*. Translated by Donald Nicholson-Smith, Blackwell Publishing, 1991.

Giroux, Henry. "Higher Education and the New Brutalism." *Truthout.com*, 28 Oct. 2014, truth-out.org/news/item/27082-henry-a-giroux-higher-education-and-the -new-brutalism.

Hay, David. "Defending Brutalism: The Uncertain Future of Modernist Concrete Structures." *National Trust for Historic Preservation*, 1 Jan. 2013, savingplaces.org /stories/defending-brutalism#.WEyR2n0XvkY.

Mack, Nancy, and James Thomas Zebroski. "Transforming Composition: A Question of Privilege." *Composition and Resistance*, edited by C. Mark Hulbert and Michael Blitz, Boynton/Cook Publishers, 1991, pp. 154–66.

Miller, Susan. *Textual Carnivals: The Politics of Composition*. Southern Illinois UPress, 1991.

Schweitzer, Sarah. "In Praise of Ugly Buildings." *Boston Globe*, 24 Jan. 2010, archive .boston.com/bostonglobe/magazine/articles/2010/01/24/in_praise_of_ugly _buildings.

Strickland, Donna. *The Managerial Unconscious in the History of Composition Studies*. Southern Illinois UP, 2011.

Nixon, Andrew. "An Unfair Deal for Part-Time UMass Faculty." *Boston Globe*, 12 Nov. 2003, pp. A.15, archive.boston.com/news/education/higher/articles/2003/11/12 /an_unfair_deal_for_part_time_umass_faculty/.

UMass Dartmouth. "History of UMass Dartmouth." *UMass Dartmouth*, umassd.edu /about/historyofumassdartmouth/.

CONTRIBUTORS

Janelle Adsit is Assistant Professor of English at Humboldt State University in Arcata, California, specializing in writing practices. She has previously taught at Siena College, the University at Albany/SUNY, and the San Francisco Art Institute. She recently completed a postdoctoral fellowship in English at Simon Fraser University. She can be reached at janelle.adsit@humboldt.edu.

Jacob Babb is Assistant Professor of English and Writing Program Coordinator at Indiana University Southeast. He has published articles and book chapters on epideictic rhetoric, monuments and memorials, and writing assessment. He is co-editor of the forthcoming collection, *WPAs in Transition: A Traveler's Guide.* He is the Associate Book Review Editor of *WPA: Writing Program Administration.*

Chris Blankenship is Assistant Professor of English at Salt Lake Community College. His recent scholarship includes work on composition pedagogy, writing assessment, and labor in higher education.

Rebekah Shultz Colby teaches in the University of Denver Writing Program where she teaches courses that use games to teach rhetoric and disciplinary writing. She co-edited the collection *Rhetoric/Composition/Play through Video Games* and a special issue of the journal *Computers and Composition Online* on game-based pedagogy within composition. Also with Richard Colby, she co-authored an article about using *World of Warcraft* to teach disciplinary research writing for *Computers and Composition* and has written an article about how game-based pedagogy impacts female students for *Computers and Composition Online.*

Richard Colby teaches in and is Assistant Director of the University of Denver Writing Program. He co-edited the collection *Rhetoric/Composition/Play through Video Games* and a special issue of the journal *Computers and Composition Online* on gaming and composition. His work on using games in teaching has been published in *Computers and Composition* and *Computers and Composition Online.* He teaches courses on the rhetoric of games and disciplinary research.

Anicca Cox worked as a WPA in a first-year English program at University of Massachusetts, Dartmouth. She teaches courses in composition, basic writing and writing center practice and theory. She has published creative nonfiction essays and poetry on nature/culture/place and scholarly work in WAC/WID, FYC, and labor equality and social justice in writing studies.

Sue Doe teaches courses at Colorado State University where she serves on the Committee on Non Tenure-Track Faculty and was part of the original Provost's Task Force calling for changes in working conditions of contingent faculty. She has been a member of the Committee on Part-Time, Adjunct, or Contingent

Labor, Conference on College Composition and Communication; is past chair of the MLA Discussion Group on Part-time Faculty; represents the National Council of Teachers of English to the Coalition on the Academic Workforce; and serves on the board of the New Faculty Majority Foundation. She can be reached at sue.doe@colostate.edu.

Tracy Donhardt has taught various writing courses for the English department at IUPUI in Indianapolis since 2004. She earned her Master's degree in English with a Teaching Writing Certificate from IUPUI and dual Bachelor of Arts degrees in English and journalism. Her work advocating for part-time faculty began as part of her thesis while a graduate student and grew into a coalition of other part-time faculty, full-time faculty, students, and staff which is still active today. Tracy has published on adjunct issues in *FORUM: Issues About Part-time and Contingent Faculty*, which ran in the September 2013 issue of *College Composition and Communication*.

Dawn Fels currently teaches composition at the University of Pittsburgh. Over the course of her career, she has taught a range of writing courses, developed and/or directed both high school and university writing center programs, and served on several committees and the Executive Board for the International Writing Centers Association (IWCA). Her dissertation, which took up the effects of standardized writing instruction and assessment on students' composing processes, identities, and membership in academic and professional communities of practice, won the Honorable Mention for the Berlin Award in 2011. That same year, she published *The Successful High School Writing Center: Building the Best Program with Your Students,* a co-edited collection that showcases high school writing centers that were created for diverse, under-represented student bodies. In it, she describes how a writing center she created at an urban high school placed on corrective action brought community members together to fight the negative effects of federal literacy policies on students and teachers. Her experience at that school led Fels to develop research interests that lie at the intersection of literacy policies, writing pedagogy, assessment, ethnomethodology, and the labor conditions of those who teach writing. This fall, Fels and her team of co-researchers launched "An Investigation into the Working Conditions of Contingent Writing Center Workers," a study that currently has over one hundred participants. She and her team have already shared preliminary findings from the study; they appear in *Forum: Issues about Part-time and Contingent Faculty* and were recently the focus of the *Writing Center Journal's* new blog feature.

Barbara Heifferon, Professor of English, is currently teaching at Louisiana State University and has also done administrative work at LSU, Clemson and in New York. She has published articles and monographs on medical rhetoric, medical history, disability studies, composition and professional communication. Along with two others, Heifferon was a founder of the sub-discipline of medical rhetoric over twenty years ago. She has garnered numerous grants and fellowships along with earning four teaching and faculty excellence awards. With Anna K. Nardo, she has been a proud member of LSUnited, an independent faculty advocacy group.

Desirée M. Holter is an adjunct English Instructor at Whatcom Community College and South Puget Sound Community College, with additional teaching experience at Edmonds Community College and Western Washington University. Her research and certifications are focused on multimodal composition and developing the quality of eLearning composition courses. In particular, she is scheduled to present at the 2016 Assessment, Teaching & Learning conference about integrating multimodality in composition courses; she is a volunteer member of the WCC eLearning Advisory Committee; she participated in a Faculty eLearning Community which focused on strengthening online instruction; she completed a Quality Matters certification course which focused on aligning online courses with the QM Rubric Standards; and she presented at the 2014 Assessment, Teaching & Learning Conference about evaluating online courses and instructors. Her English department contributions at Whatcom include serving as the former English 100 Co-Coordinator; serving as an English 101 Challenge Portfolio Reviewer; volunteering for the Anna Rosemary Harris scholarship selection committee; and volunteering for the Noisy Water Review writing selection committee.

Justin Jory is Assistant Professor of English at Salt Lake Community College. He served as a non tenure-track instructor in the rhetoric and writing program at UC-Colorado Springs from 2008–2012. His teaching and research interests are in writing studies, rhetorical theory and criticism, and program development and design.

Seth Kahn is Professor of English at West Chester University, where he teaches courses primarily in rhetoric and writing. He has served as co-chair of the CCCC Committee on Part-time, Adjunct, and Contingent Labor and currently serves as co-chair of the CWPA Labor Committee. Recent publications include "What Is a Union?" in *A Rhetoric for Writing Program Administrators;* "'Never Take More Than You Need': Tenured/Tenure-Track Faculty and Contingent Labor Exploitation" in *Forum: Issues about Part-Time and Contingent Faculty*; and a co-guest-edited special issue of *Open Words* on "Contingent Labor and Educational Access."

Jeffrey Klausman is Professor of English and WPA at Whatcom Community College, where he has been on the faculty since completing a doctor of arts in 1996. He has published four articles on two-year-college writing programs, including a study of the impact of adjunct faculty on program development. Based on that research, he was a featured speaker at the 2013 CCCC in Las Vegas. As co-chair of the TYCA Research Committee, he co-authored two white papers, one on developmental education reform and another on placement reform. In addition, his book chapter examining the impact of changing missions of two-year colleges on writing programs will appear in spring 2016 through Parlor Press. He serves on the CCCC executive committee (through 2017).

Michelle LaFrance is Assistant Professor of English and Director of the Writing Across the Curriculum program at George Mason University. Michelle teaches graduate and undergraduate courses in writing course pedagogy, ethnography, cultural materialist and qualitative research methodologies. She has published on peer review, preparing students to write across the curriculum, e-portfolios, e-research, writing center/WAC-pedagogy, and Institutional Ethnography. In her free time, she gardens, hangs out with three four-legged friends, and explores wild spaces on the East Coast.

William B. Lalicker is Professor of English at West Chester University. A former co-chair of the Council on Basic Writing, and a veteran of multiple roles in writing program administration frequently over the past two decades, his publications and presentations include research on structural equity and labor justice in writing programs; basic writing; and transnational and intercultural composition pedagogies. His chapter "The Five Equities: How to Build a Progressive Writing Program in a Department of English" appears in *Minefield of Dreams: Promises and Perils of Independent Writing Programs* (Justin Everett and Cristina Hanganu-Bresch, editors), published by the WAC Clearinghouse and University Press of Colorado.

Sarah Layden is Lecturer in the English Department at Indiana University-Purdue University Indianapolis, where she was an adjunct for eight years before being hired full-time. She is the author of a novel, *Trip Through Your Wires,* and her short fiction can be found in *Boston Review, Blackbird, Booth, PANK,* and elsewhere.

Carol Lind is Instructional Assistant Professor of English at Illinois State University with a Ph.D. in English Studies, specializing in Medieval Literature. She has been awarded the Outstanding University Teaching Award and has served the last two years as the NTT representative on the University Teaching Committee. Her course assignments regularly include the three main areas of English Studies at Illinois State: Composition (English 101—Composition as Critical Inquiry), Literature (English 110—English Literature and Its Contexts) and Linguistics (English 241—Growth and Structure of the English Language). Her research interests include medieval riddle collections, the linguistic implications of the Pictish stones, and literary humor theory.

Amy Lynch-Biniek is Associate Professor of English and the Coordinator of Composition at Kutztown University, where she teaches composition, pedagogy, and research writing. She serves as the editor of the NCTE publication *Forum: Issues about Part-Time and Contingent Faculty* through January 2018. Her publications include articles in *Teaching English in the Two-Year College, CCC,* and *Reflections: Writing, Service-Learning, and Community Literacy.* Amy co-guest-edited a special issue of *Open Words* on "Contingent Labor and Educational Access." A member of the CCCC Labor Caucus since 2009, she has served on its steering committee (since 2010), as chair (2013–2015) and as secretary and archivist (since 2015).

Maria Maisto is a co-founder and president/executive director of New Faculty Majority and the NFM Foundation, national nonprofits dedicated to reforming the contingent faculty employment system. She has taught composition, literature, or film as an adjunct faculty member at the University of Maryland at College Park, the University of Akron, and Cuyahoga Community College. She also co-founded the Ohio Part-time Faculty Association. She has published and presented on academic labor issues in many academic venues as well as in the mainstream media, and serves or has served on committees in the Modern Language Association and in the Conference on College Composition and Communication that deal with academic labor and professional issues. She is a visiting scholar for 2015–16 at the New England Resource Center for Higher Education. She can be reached at maria.maisto@newfacultymajority.info.

Amanda Martin is an adjunct English and humanities Instructor at Whatcom Community College, teaching a range of courses from first-year composition to literature, and is currently researching reading for composition and capacity-based teaching models. She is an active participant in curriculum and program development projects, and recently created and piloted an online textbook through collaboration with WCC's library. She is serving a two-year term on the Adjunct Affairs Advisory Committee, and is vocal in campus conversations concerning contingent labor. Outside of academia, she is a Certified Equine Specialist in mental health and learning and riding instructor through the Professional Association of Therapeutic Horsemanship, Intl., which enables her to bring expertise in experiential learning, mental health, and disability to her campus work.

Over the past two decades, **Mark McBeth** has taught and administered at the City University of New York. From 1992 to 2001, he coordinated the composition program at City College of New York, after which he directed the college's writing center. After completing a Ph.D. at the CUNY Graduate Center, he became the Deputy Chair of Writing Programs at John Jay College of Criminal Justice from 2003 to 2008. While in this position, he designed and implemented a new writing curriculum, restructured the WAC program, and developed a variety of college-wide literacy initiatives. Beyond local administrative leadership, he has also contributed to the national conversation on writing and writing administration through his participation with the CWPA/CCCC. Beyond the walls of Academia, he and his partner live in Manhattan, enjoying the artistic and cultural overflow of New York City.

Assistant Professor **Tim McCormack** has directed the first-year writing program at John Jay College for seven years. In his career, McCormack has worked extensively at all levels of writing program administration, including in high school-to-college bridge programs, writing centers, first-year writing, WAC programs and graduate-level writing programs. He has written about writing program administration for the *Journal of the Council of Writing Program Admi nistrators* and *Composition Forum*. McCormack is currently at work on an ethnographic study of first-year writing courses at City College of New York and Bronx Community College, titled *The Dividing Line*. This research chronicles the impact of high stakes placement testing on student learning outcomes and retention rates in senior and community college writing programs.

Currently Executive Director of the University Writing Program at the University of North Carolina Charlotte, **Joan Mullin** has established and directed writing centers and WAC programs, served as consultant-evaluator for the Council of Writing Program Administrators, edited the *Writing Center Journal*. She has participated in national and international organizations and initiatives and researched and written on visual communication; writing centers and writing across the curriculum; plagiarism and knowledge claims; and, in the last fifteen years, how our paradigms about these singular areas need to shift in light of international perspectives. The common thread through her work is the necessity of developing program structures that support languaging differences as opportunities.

Assistant Professor of English **Dani Nier-Weber** lives in the Catskills and teaches writing and literature at SUNY Sullivan Community College. After teaching ESL in Germany for thirteen years, Dani earned her Ph.D. in English with a concentration rhetoric and composition from Ball State University. She has served as writing center director at three universities and taught a variety of classes, from composition and literature to technical and creative writing. A certified online instructor, Dani has also taught creative writing camp and held writing workshops at the local correctional facility. Currently, she is working on several articles examining political rhetoric in the last presidential election and the rhetoric of shame in the Greek economic meltdown.

Glenn Moomau is Senior Lecturer in the College Writing Program at American University. Currently, his teaching and research focuses on creative nonfiction, post-humanist theory, and information literacy.

Michael Murphy is Associate Professor of English at the State University of New York at Oswego, where he directs the College Writing Program and serves as the Coordinator of Writing Across the Curriculum. He has published articles on composition theory and academic labor in *Journal of Advanced Composition, College Composition and Communication, Pedagogy,* and the *Chronicle of Higher Education.*

Anna K. Nardo, Alumni Professor Emerita, taught at Louisiana State University for forty years. She has published articles and monographs on John Milton, seventeenth-century poetry, Shakespeare and film, early modern romance, George Eliot, and curriculum revision. She served as chair of the Department of English, as a member of the Executive Committee of the Association of Departments of English, and as secretary of LSUnited, an independent faculty advocacy group.

Rolf Norgaard (Ph.D. Stanford University) is a long-time faculty member at the University of Colorado at Boulder, where he serves as Associate Director of the Program for Writing and Rhetoric. He has published widely on the rhetorical dimensions of writing instruction in institutional and curricular contexts, information literacy, technical communication and design, and writing as a vehicle for civic engagement and ethical inquiry. He has received campus-wide awards for excellence in teaching and in service and leadership.

Courtney Adams Wooten is first-year writing program administrator and Assistant Professor of English at Stephen F. Austin State University in Nacogdoches, Texas. She has been published in *Composition Studies* and *Harlot: A Revealing Look at the Arts of Persuasion.* Her current research projects center on the rhetorics of childless-by-choice women as they construct their identities and the perception of student evaluations of teaching by WPAs. She is also co-editing a book collection about WPAs as they transition into and out of administrative positions. She has served on CWPA's WPA-GO Committee and Nominating Committee.

Lacey Wootton is a Hurst Senior Professorial Lecturer at American University. A faculty member in the College Writing Program, she is also a former chair of the AU faculty senate. She is currently in the Ph.D. program in Writing and Rhetoric at George Mason University; her research interests include the connections among the institutional contexts of writing programs, contingency, and students' transfer of learning.

Allison Laubach Wright is Assistant Professor of English at Lone Star College—North Harris and is completing her Ph.D. in Rhetoric, Composition, and Pedagogy from the University of Houston. Her areas of study are materialist feminist rhetorics, the rhetoric and practice of TA and contingent faculty training, and first year composition pedagogies in the two-year college.